5 Comedies

HOUGHTON BOOKS IN LITERATURE

HOUGHTON
BOOKS IN
LITERATURE

ADVISORY EDITOR
KENNETH S. LYNN

5

Comedies

DAVID SCANLAN

HOUGHTON MIFFLIN COMPANY • BOSTON

NEW YORK ATLANTA GENEVA, ILLINOIS DALLAS PALO ALTO

Printed in the U.S.A.

Hardcover Edition ISBN: 0-395-12031-4

Softcover Edition ISBN: 0-395-12049-7

Library of Congress Catalogue Card Number: 79-140998

ABOUT THE AUTHOR AND EDITOR

David Scanlan is a teacher committed to making good drama available to more students. He has directed summer theater and drama workshops at a number of colleges and served as theater consultant to the Educational Laboratory Theatre Project, an organization dedicated to bringing professional theater to the New Orleans public schools. Dr. Scanlan is now chairman of the Department of Theatre Arts at C. W. Post College in Brookville, Long Island, New York.

Kenneth S. Lynn, advisory editor for the Houghton Books in Literature, is an authority in American literature. The author of *Mark Twain and Southwestern Humor* and *The Dream of Success: A Study of the Modern American Imagination*, he is also preëminent for his editing of classic American writers. Dr. Lynn is now a professor at the Johns Hopkins University.

CONTENTS

Introductory

What do we think of when we think of comedy? Jokes and laughter, probably: a witty remark or an unsuspecting victim doused with a bucket of paint. We may also think of tragedy, which is "serious"—the opposite of comedy. Comedy is happy and funny while tragedy is sad and gloomy. Comedy has a happy ending while tragedy ends in death and calamity. We may think of the masks which symbolize the muses of the theater, Thalia (comedy) and Melpomene (tragedy). For it is the theater that gave us comedy and continues to bring it to us today, through the media of film and television as well as live performance.

But there is more to comedy than jokes and laughter and happy endings, just as there is more to tragedy than sadness and death. All theater is a celebration of our common humanity, shared and affirmed whenever people gather in a public place to enjoy a play or, by implication, when we enjoy a play through the medium of print. And since what we call our humanity is a complicated thing, this celebration takes on many different forms, qualities, moods, and attitudes. Comedy can be wild and hilarious to the point of insanity—consider the frantic, anything-goes atmosphere of television's *Laugh-In*. Or, as when Hamlet jokes with a pair of gravediggers, comedy can be wry, caustic, even bitter. Or it can be gentle and humane, as in *Our Town* when Emily Webb and George Gibbs discover they love each other. Just as each of us is capable of many different moods, so the comic artist reflects and celebrates the many variations of the human comedy we all play in our daily lives.

The five plays in this volume present a wide range of comic experiences, but they share certain characteristics common to all comedy. First, they are lively and they are funny. They generate a creative vitality which can pick up our spirits and sharpen our wits. Furthermore, by keeping the action at a distance from our feelings and appealing mainly to our intellects, the comic artist provides us with images of human folly which we can laugh at without hurting anyone. This temporary setting aside of the feelings is essential to comedy, for if we thought that the victim of the paint-dousing episode was risking lead poisoning, we probably wouldn't laugh.

Besides making us laugh, these comedies show us a picture of human society and the process of social renewal which makes it possible for people to live in harmony with each other. While tragedy shows us the struggles of the lonely human spirit against forces beyond its control—forces which the ancients called Fate—comedy depicts the reconciliation of the human spirit to its social condition. The comic viewpoint assumes that all human beings, young and old, beautiful and plain, witty and dull, and perhaps most importantly, good and evil, must finally warm themselves at the same fire and eat from the same pot. But the price of the happy ending is compromise. Those who expect to join in the final feast must show their good will by giving up selfish, willful, and anti-social behavior.

The art of comedy has one of the longest histories of any creation of human civilization. In the Western world, the writing and performing of comedies had its beginning centuries before Christian civilization. Comedies were played long before any written record of them was made and the list of comic playwrights includes some of the great artists of the world: Aristophanes and Menander in ancient Greece; the Romans Plautus and Terence; the French actor-author Molière; and in England, Shakespeare, Ben Jonson, Congreve, Sheridan, Oscar Wilde, and George Bernard Shaw. In more recent times the list of outstanding comic playwrights includes France's Jean Giraudoux and Eugene Ionesco; England's Noël Coward and Christopher Fry; the Irish playwrights Sean O'Casey and Brendan Behan; the great Russians Chekhov and Gogol; and, in America, Thornton Wilder, William Saroyan, Tennessee Williams, and the many young playwrights who are creating today the comic art of our own time and place. The list is much longer than these few names picked at random. And, of course, the theaters of Asia and

Africa have traditions of comedy which will, we can hope, become better known to us in this age of accelerated communication.

This book presents the work of five artists from this enduring tradition. Each play is the product of a different man and a different era. Richard Brinsley Sheridan lived in eighteenth-century London and wrote and produced *The Rivals* when he was twenty-three years old. George Bernard Shaw, whose life bridged two centuries, presented *Arms and the Man* to London playgoers in 1894, in the midst of a theatrical revolution which gave birth to the modern drama. Two of the plays, *The Time of Your Life* and *The Madwoman of Chaillot,* were first played directly before and directly after World War II, the first in New York and the second in Paris. Barry Pritchard's one-act, *Captain Fantastic Meets the Ectomorph,* was introduced to its first audience in Portland, Oregon, in 1965. Each of the plays has been steadily revived on the stage since its premiere performance, and *The Time of Your Life* and *The Madwoman of Chaillot* have been made into motion pictures.

According to a French proverb: "He who feels, weeps. He who thinks, laughs." In the following five comedies, there is both thought and laughter in abundance.

The Rivals

Miss Lydia Languish, the heroine of this eighteenth-century comedy of manners, wants life to be like a romantic novel. However, her lover, Captain Jack Absolute, is a shrewd and practical young man who knows you can't live on love alone. He wants money as well and his main problem is not to win Lydia but to prevent her from sacrificing her large inheritance by eloping. Love versus money is a familiar comic motif. In *The Rivals* the man who can arrange to end up with both is the true hero. Another lover, Faulkland, has a different problem: he is jealous. Faulkland must be cured, for jealousy is as much an enemy to love as romantic illusions are. Like poverty, jealousy is not practical, and impractical love affairs stand in the way of social harmony—may even, indeed, lead to tragic consequences, as in *Romeo and Juliet.*

Besides romanticism and jealousy, the characters of this play are beset by a whole medley of foibles which keep them in an endless dither. There are the preposterous affectations of Mrs. Malaprop and the presumption and social climbing of Bob Acres. There is the absurd truculence of Sir Lucius O'Trigger and the precipitate frenzies of that oldest of comic characters, the irate father, Sir Anthony Absolute. However, the people possessed by these "humors"* are oblivious to the demands of reality and must be cured of their madness and made to see the light. In comedy, absurdity and imposture, however amusing, must receive their comeuppance.

The tradition of the comedy of manners demands that anti-social behavior be laughed off the stage, but in *The Rivals* the people who indulge in such behavior remain. Sir Anthony Absolute may be a hot-tempered and bossy father but his heart is in the right place. Lydia Languish's affectations can finally be forgiven her simply because she is so young and so charming. If Bob Acres is perhaps a bit bumptious, he is also a good loser and shows real generosity of spirit in abandoning his misguided pursuit of Lydia. Even the ludicrous Mrs. Malaprop is not hopeless. She is as romantic as everyone else and we somehow feel that Sir Anthony's offer to find her a husband will meet with success. *The Rivals* is essentially a friendly and genial play in which human faults, rather than estranging us from people, endear them to us.

* **Humor:** an obsession or affection which robs its victim of good sense and good will. In eighteenth-century psychology, an excess of any of the humors, or bodily liquids (blood, phlegm, yellow bile, black bile), was thought to produce an eccentric disposition.

The Rivals

RICHARD BRINSLEY SHERIDAN

Characters

SIR ANTHONY ABSOLUTE, a wealthy country gentleman
CAPTAIN JACK ABSOLUTE, his son
LYDIA LANGUISH, JACK's beloved
MRS. MALAPROP, LYDIA's aunt and guardian
FAULKLAND, friend of JACK ABSOLUTE
JULIA MELVILLE, LYDIA's cousin, beloved of FAULKLAND
BOB ACRES, LYDIA's suitor
LUCY, LYDIA's maid
SIR LUCIUS O'TRIGGER, a belligerent Irish nobleman
FAG, JACK ABSOLUTE's valet
DAVID, servant to BOB ACRES
MAID, BOY, SERVANTS, etc.

THE SCENE: *Bath, a fashionable resort in eighteenth-century England.*

TIME: *1775. The action takes place within one day.*

ACT ONE

SCENE 1

A street in Bath. Two men, dressed in the breeches, frock coats and tricorn hats of the time, pass each other. Then FAG, *whose short pigtail of natural hair is tied with a ribbon in the latest fashion, turns as he recognizes* THOMAS, *whose wig marks him as a steadfast conservative.*

FAG. What, Thomas! Sure, 'tis he! What, Thomas, Thomas!

THOMAS. Hey! Odd's life,[1] Mr. Fag! Give us your hand, my old fellow-servant!

FAG. Excuse my glove, Thomas. I'm devilish glad to see you, my lad! Why, my prince of charioteers, you look as hearty—but who the deuce thought of seeing you in Bath?

THOMAS. Sure, Master, Madam Julia, Harry, Mrs. Kate and the postilion be all come.

FAG. Indeed!

THOMAS. Aye! Master thought another fit of the gout was coming to make him a visit, so he'd a mind to gi't the slip—and whip!—we were all off at an hour's warning.

FAG. Aye, aye, hasty in everything or it would not be Sir Anthony Absolute!

THOMAS. But tell us, Mr. Fag, how does *young* master? Odd, Sir Anthony will stare to see the captain here!

FAG. I do not serve Captain Absolute now.

THOMAS (*amazed*). Why, sure!

FAG. At present I am employed by Ensign Beverley.

THOMAS. I doubt, Mr. Fag, you ha'n't changed for the better.

FAG. I have not changed, Thomas.

THOMAS. No? Why, didn't you say you had left young master?

FAG. No. (*He looks slyly at* THOMAS.) Well, honest Thomas, I must puzzle you no further. Briefly then—Captain Absolute and Ensign Beverley are one and the same person!

THOMAS. The devil they are! But do tell us, Mr. Fag, the meaning o't. You know I ha' trusted you.

[1] **Odd's life:** "God's life," disguised to avoid profanity. Other fashionable oaths heard in the play are "Zounds" (God's wounds), "Sdeath" (God's death), and "Lud" (Lord).

FAG. You'll be secret, Thomas?

THOMAS. As a coach-horse.

FAG. Why then the cause of all this is—L. O. V. E. Love, Thomas, who, as you may get read to you, has been a masquerader ever since the days of Jupiter.[2]

THOMAS. Aye, aye, I guessed there was a lady in the case. But pray, why does your master pass only for *ensign*? Now if he had shammed *general*, indeed—

FAG. Ah, Thomas, there lies the mystery o' the matter. Hark'ee, Thomas. My master is in love with a lady of a very singular taste, a lady who likes him better as a half-pay ensign than if she knew he was son and heir to Sir Anthony Absolute, a baronet of three thousand a year.

THOMAS. That is an odd taste, indeed! But has she got the stuff, Mr. Fag? Is she rich, hey?

FAG. Rich? Why, I believe she owns half the stocks! Zounds, Thomas, she could pay the national debt as easily as I could my washerwoman! She has a lap-dog that eats out of gold! She feeds her parrot with small pearls, and all her thread-papers are made of bank-notes!

THOMAS. Bravo, faith! Odd, I warrant she has a set of thousands, at least. But does she draw kindly with the captain?

FAG. As fond as pigeons.

THOMAS. May one hear her name?

FAG. Miss Lydia Languish. But there is an old, tough aunt in the way, though by the by, she has never seen my master, for we got acquainted with Miss while on a visit in Gloucestershire.

THOMAS. Well, I wish they were once harnessed together in matrimony. But pray, Mr. Fag, what kind of a place is this Bath? I ha' heard a deal of it. Here's a mort o' merrymaking, hey?

FAG. Pretty well, Thomas, pretty well, 'tis a good lounge. In the morning we go to the pump room,[3] though neither my master nor I drink the waters. After breakfast we saunter on the parades or play a game at billiards. At night we dance.

[2] **masquerader . . . Jupiter:** probably an allusion to the disguises Jupiter (Zeus) assumed in his many love affairs.

[3] **pump-room:** meeting place where the spa's medicinal drinking water is dispensed.

But damn the place, I'm tired of it. Their regular hours stupefy me—not a fiddle nor a card after eleven! However, Mr. Faulkland's gentleman and I keep it up a little in private parties. I'll introduce you there, Thomas, you'll like him much.

THOMAS. Sure I know Mr. Du-Peigne. You know his master is to marry Madam Julia.

FAG. I had forgot. But Thomas, you must polish a little, indeed you must! Here now, this wig! What the devil do you want with a wig, Thomas? None of the London whips of any degree of *ton*[4] wear wigs now.

THOMAS. More's the pity, more's the pity, I say. Odd's life, when I heard how the lawyers and doctors had took to their own hair, I thought how 'twould go next. Odd rabbit it, when the fashion had got foot on the bar, I guessed 'twould mount to the box! But 'tis all out of character, believe me, Mr. Fag. And look'ee, I'll never gi' up mine, the lawyers and doctors may do as they will!

FAG. Well, Thomas, we'll not quarrel about that.

THOMAS. Why bless you, the gentlemen of the professions ben't all of a mind, for in our village now, though Jack Gauge the exciseman has ta'en to his carrots,[5] there's little Dick the farrier[6] swears he'll never forsake his bob,[7] though all the college should appear with their own heads!

FAG. Indeed, well said, Dick. But hold!

FAG *points excitedly at two figures who are conversing at the door of an elegant house halfway down the street.*

FAG. Mark, mark, Thomas!

THOMAS. Zooks, 'tis the captain! Is that the lady with him?

FAG. No, no, that is Madam Lucy, my master's mistress's maid. They lodge at that house. But I must after him to tell him the news.

THOMAS. Odd, he's giving her money! Well, Mr. Fag!

FAG (*laughing at* THOMAS' *innocence*). Good-by, Thomas. I

[4] **ton:** fashion.
[5] **carrots:** natural red hair.
[6] **farrier:** horse veterinarian.
[7] **bob:** a wig in which the ends turn up into short curls.

have an appointment in Gyde's Porch this evening at eight. Meet me there and we'll make a little party.

FAG *hurries off to find* CAPTAIN JACK ABSOLUTE, *leaving* THOMAS *to scratch his wig and wonder at the strange doings in Bath.*

SCENE 2

A room in the house of MRS. MALAPROP, *the "old, tough aunt" mentioned by* FAG. LYDIA LANGUISH *reclines on a sofa, reading.* LUCY *has just returned from an errand.*

LUCY. Indeed, ma'am, I traversed half the town in search of it! I don't believe there's a circulating library in Bath I ha'n't been at.

LYDIA. And could you not get *The Reward of Constancy?*

LUCY. No, indeed, ma'am.

LYDIA. Nor *The Fatal Connection?*

LUCY. No, indeed, ma'am.

LYDIA. Nor *The Mistakes of the Heart?*

LUCY. Ma'am, as ill luck would have it, Mr. Bull said Miss Sukey Saunter had just fetched it away.

LYDIA. Heigh-ho! Did you inquire for *The Delicate Distress?*

LUCY. —or *The Memoirs of Lady Woodford?* Yes, indeed, ma'am, I asked everywhere for it and I might have brought it from Mr. Frederick's, but Lady Slattern Lounger, who had just sent it home, had so soiled and dog's-eared it, it wa'n't fit for a Christian to read.

LYDIA. Heigh-ho! Yes, I always know when Lady Slattern has been before me. She has a most observing thumb and I believe cherishes her nails for the convenience of making marginal notes. Well, child, what *have* you brought me?

LUCY. Oh, here, ma'am. (*Taking books from under her cloak and from her pockets.*) This is *The Gordian Knot* and this *Peregrine Pickle*. Here are *The Tears of Sensibility* and *Humphrey Clinker*. This is *The Memoirs of a Lady of Quality, Written by Herself* and here the second volume of *The Sentimental Journey*.

LYDIA. Heigh-ho! What are those books by the glass?

LUCY. The great one is only *The Whole Duty of Man,* where I press a few blonds,[8] ma'am.

LYDIA. Very well. Give me the *sal volatile.*

LUCY. Is it in a blue cover, ma'am?

LYDIA. My smelling-bottle, you simpleton!

LUCY. Oh, the drops! Here, ma'am.

LYDIA. Hold, here's someone coming! Quick, see who it is!

LUCY *hurries out of the room.*

LYDIA. Surely I heard my cousin Julia's voice!

LUCY (*sticking her head through the door*). Lud, ma'am, here is Miss Melville!

LYDIA. Is it possible?

JULIA *enters,* LUCY *disappears.*

LYDIA. My dearest Julia, how delighted am I! (*They embrace.*) How unexpected was this happiness!

JULIA. True, Lydia, and our pleasure is the greater. But what has been the matter? You were denied to me at first.

LYDIA. Ah, Julia, I have a thousand things to tell you! (*They sit together on the sofa.*)

LYDIA. But first inform me what has conjured you to Bath? Is Sir Anthony here?

JULIA. He is. We arrived within this hour, and I suppose he will be here to wait on Mrs. Malaprop as soon as he is dressed.

LYDIA. Then before we are interrupted, let me impart to you some of my distress! I know your gentle nature will sympathize with me, though your prudence may condemn me. My letters have informed you of my whole connection with Beverley. But I have lost him, Julia! My aunt has discovered our intercourse by a note she intercepted and has confined me ever since! Yet, would you believe it? She has fallen absolutely in love with a tall Irish baronet she met one night since we have been here, at Lady Macshuffle's rout.[9]

JULIA. You jest, Lydia!

LYDIA. No, upon my word. She really carries on a kind of correspondence with him, under a feigned name, though, 'til

[8] **a few blonds:** laces made originally from blond-colored raw silk.
[9] **rout:** fashionable evening gathering.

she chooses to be known to him. But it is a "Delia" or a "Celia," I assure you.

JULIA. Then surely she is now more indulgent to her niece?

LYDIA. Quite the contrary. Since she has discovered her own frailty, she is become more suspicious of mine. Then I must inform you of another plague! That odious Acres is to be in Bath today, so that I protest I shall be teased out of all spirits.

JULIA. Come, come, Lydia, hope for the best. Sir Anthony shall use his interest with Mrs. Malaprop.

LYDIA. But you have not heard the worst. Unfortunately I have quarrelled with my poor Beverley, just before my aunt made the discovery, and I have not seen him since to make it up.

JULIA. What was his offense?

LYDIA. Nothing at all! But—I don't know how it was—as often as we had been together, we had never had a quarrel. And somehow I was afraid he would never give me an opportunity. So last Thursday I wrote a letter to myself to inform myself that Beverley was at that time paying his addresses to another woman. I signed it "Your Friend Unknown," showed it to Beverley, charged him with falsehood, put myself in a violent passion and vowed I'd never see him more.

JULIA. And you let him depart so and have not seen him since?

LYDIA. 'Twas the next day my aunt found the matter out. I intended only to have teased him three days and a half, and now I've lost him forever.

JULIA. If he is as deserving and sincere as you have represented him to me, he will never give you up so. Yet consider, Lydia, you tell me he is but an ensign and you have thirty thousand pounds!

LYDIA. But you know I lose most of my fortune if I marry without my aunt's consent, 'til of age! And that is what I have determined to do, ever since I knew the penalty! Nor could I love the man who would wish to wait a day for the alternative.

JULIA. Nay, this is caprice!

LYDIA. What, does Julia tax me with caprice? I thought her lover Faulkland had inured her to it.

JULIA. I do not love even *his* faults.

LYDIA. But apropos—you have sent to him, I suppose?

JULIA. Not yet, upon my word, nor has he the least idea of my being in Bath. Sir Anthony's resolution was so sudden, I could not inform him of it.

LYDIA. Well, Julia, you are your own mistress, though under the protection of Sir Anthony. Yet have you, for this long year, been a slave to the caprice, the whim, the jealousy of this ungrateful Faulkland, who will ever delay assuming the right of a husband, while you suffer him to be equally imperious as a lover.

JULIA. Nay, you are wrong entirely. We were contracted before my father's death. That and some consequent embarrassments have delayed what I know to be my Faulkland's most ardent wish. He is too generous to trifle on such a point. And for his character, you wrong him there, too. No, Lydia, he is too proud, too noble to be jealous. If he is captious, 'tis without dissembling, if fretful, without rudeness. Unused to the fopperies of love, he is negligent of the little duties expected from a lover, but being unhackneyed in the passion, his affection is ardent and sincere, and as it engrosses his whole soul, he expects every thought and emotion of his mistress to move in unison with his. Yet, though his pride calls for this full return, his humility makes him undervalue those qualities in him which would entitle him to it, and not feeling why he should be loved to the degree he wishes, he still suspects that he is not loved enough. This temper, I must own, has cost me many unhappy hours, but I have learned to think myself his debtor for those imperfections which arise from the ardor of his attachment.

LYDIA. Well, I cannot blame you for defending him. But tell me candidly, Julia, had he never saved your life, do you think you should have been attached to him as you are? Believe me, the rude blast that overset your boat was a prosperous gale of love to him.

JULIA. Gratitude may have strengthened my attachment to Mr. Faulkland, but I loved him before he had preserved me. Yet, surely, that alone were an obligation sufficient—

LYDIA. Obligation! Why, a water-spaniel would have done as much! Well, I should never think of giving my heart to a man because he could swim!

JULIA. Come, Lydia, you are too inconsiderate.
LYDIA. Nay, I do but jest. What's here?

LUCY *hurries into the room.*

LUCY. Oh, ma'am, here is Sir Anthony Absolute just come home with your aunt.
LYDIA. They'll not come here. Lucy, do you watch. (LUCY *departs.*)
JULIA. Yet I must go. Sir Anthony does not know I am here and if we meet he'll detain me to show me the town. I'll take another opportunity of paying my respects to Mrs. Malaprop, when she shall treat mc, as long as she chooses, with her select words so ingeniously misapplied without being mispronounced.
LUCY (*entering*). Oh, Lud, ma'am, they are both coming upstairs!
LYDIA. Well, I'll not detain you, coz. Adieu, my dear Julia, I'm sure you are in haste to send to Faulkland. There—through my room you'll find another staircase.
JULIA. Adieu.

They embrace and JULIA *slips away.* LYDIA *scurries about the room.*

LYDIA. Here, my dear Lucy, hide these books. Quick, quick! Fling *Peregrine Pickle* under the toilet, throw *Roderick Random* into the closet, put *The Innocent Adultery* into *The Whole Duty of Man,* thrust *Lord Aimworth* under the sofa, cram *Ovid* behind the bolster—there! Put *The Man of Feeling* into your pocket—so, so! Now lay *Mrs. Chapone* in sight and *Fordyce's Sermons* open on the table.
LUCY. Oh, burn it, ma'am, the hairdresser has torn away as far as *Proper Pride!*
LYDIA. Never mind, open at *Sobriety.* Fling me *Lord Chesterfield's Letters.* (*Sitting on the sofa.*) Now, for 'em!

Enter MRS. MALAPROP *and* SIR ANTHONY ABSOLUTE.

MRS. MALAPROP. There, Sir Anthony! There sits the deliberate simpleton who wants to disgrace her family and lavish herself on a fellow not worth a shilling!
LYDIA. Madam, I thought you once—

MRS. MALAPROP. You thought, miss? I don't know any business you have to think at all. Thought does not become a young woman. But the point we would request of you is that you will promise to forget this fellow, to illiterate him, I say, quite from your memory.

LYDIA. Ah, madam, our memories are independent of our wills. It is not so easy to forget.

MRS. MALAPROP. But I say it is, miss! There is nothing on earth so easy as to forget, if a person chooses to set about it. I'm sure I have as much forgot your poor dear uncle as if he had never existed. And I thought it my duty so to do. And let me tell you, Lydia, these violent memories don't become a young woman.

SIR ANTHONY. Why sure she won't pretend to remember what she's ordered not! Aye, this comes of her reading!

LYDIA. What crime, madam, have I committed to be treated thus?

MRS. MALAPROP. Now, don't attempt to extirpate yourself from the matter. You know I have proof controvertible of it. But tell me, will you promise to do as you're bid? Will you take a husband of your friend's choosing?

LYDIA. Madam, I must tell you plainly, that had I no preference for anyone else, the choice you have made would be my aversion.

MRS. MALAPROP. What business have you, miss, with "preference" and "aversion"? They don't become a young woman. And you ought to know that as both always wear off, 'tis safest in matrimony to begin with a little aversion. I am sure I hated your poor dear uncle before marriage as if he'd been a blackamoor! And yet, miss, you are sensible of what a wife I made! And when it pleased heaven to release me from him, 'tis unknown what tears I shed! But suppose we were going to give you another choice, will you promise us to give up this Beverley?

LYDIA. Could I belie my thoughts so far as to give that promise, my actions would certainly as far belie my words.

MRS. MALAPROP. Take yourself to your room! You are fit company for nothing but your own ill humors!

LYDIA. Willingly, ma'am. I cannot change for the worse. (LYDIA *sweeps out of the room.*)

MRS. MALAPROP (*settling angrily into a chair*). There's a little intricate hussy for you!

SIR ANTHONY (*looking with distaste at the books*). It is not to be wondered at, ma'am. All this is the natural consequence of teaching girls to read. Had I a thousand daughters, by heaven, I'd as soon have them taught the black art as their alphabet!

MRS. MALAPROP. Nay, nay, Sir Anthony, you are an absolute misanthropy.

SIR ANTHONY. In my way hither, Mrs. Malaprop, I observed your niece's maid coming forth from a circulating library. She had a book in each hand! They were half-bound volumes with marble covers. From that moment I guessed how full of duty I should see her mistress!

MRS. MALAPROP. Those are vile places, indeed!

SIR ANTHONY. Madam, a circulating library in a town is as an evergreen tree of diabolical knowledge. It blossoms through the year. And depend on it, Mrs. Malaprop, that they who are so fond of handling the leaves will long for the fruit at last.

MRS. MALAPROP. Fie, fie, Sir Anthony, you surely speak laconically.

SIR ANTHONY. Why, Mrs. Malaprop, in moderation now, what would you have a woman know?

MRS. MALAPROP. Observe me, Sir Anthony. I would by no means wish a daughter of mine to be a progeny of learning. I don't think so much learning becomes a young woman. For instance, I would never let her meddle with Greek, or Hebrew, or algebra, or simony, or fluxions, or paradoxes or such inflammatory branches of learning. Neither would it be necessary for her to handle any of your mathematical, astronomical, diabolical instruments. But, Sir Anthony, I would send her, at nine years old, to a boarding school, in order to learn a little ingenuity and artifice. Then, sir, she should have a supercilious knowledge in accounts, and as she grew up I would have her instructed in geometry, that she might know something of the contagious countries. But above all, Sir Anthony, she should be mistress of orthodoxy, that she might not misspell and mispronounce words so shamefully as girls usually do, and likewise that she might reprehend the true meaning of what she is saying. This, Sir Anthony, is what I would have a woman know, and I don't think there is a superstitious article in it.

SIR ANTHONY. Well, well, Mrs. Malaprop, I will dispute the point no further with you, though I must confess that you are a truly moderate and polite arguer, for almost every third word you say is on my side of the question. But, Mrs. Malaprop, to the more important point in debate. You say you have no objection to my proposal?

MRS. MALAPROP. None, I assure you. I am under no positive engagement with Mr. Acres, and as Lydia is so obstinate against him, perhaps your son may have better success.

SIR ANTHONY. Well, madam, I will write for the boy directly. He knows not a syllable of this yet, though I have for some time had the proposal in my head. He is at present with his regiment.

MRS. MALAPROP. We have seen your son, Sir Anthony, but I hope no objection on his side?

SIR ANTHONY. Objection! Let him object if he dare! No, no, Mrs. Malaprop, Jack knows that the least demur puts me in a frenzy directly. My process was always very simple. In their younger days 'twas, "Jack, do this." If he demurred, I knocked him down, and if he grumbled at that, I always sent him out of the room.

MRS. MALAPROP. Aye, and the properest way, o' my conscience! Nothing is so conciliating to young people as severity. Well, Sir Anthony, I shall give Mr. Acres his discharge and prepare Lydia to receive your son's invocations. And I hope you will represent her to the captain as an object not altogether illegible.

SIR ANTHONY. Madam, I will handle the subject prudently. Well, I must leave you. And let me beg you, Mrs. Malaprop, to enforce this matter roundly to the girl. Take my advice, keep a tight hand. If she rejects this proposal, clap her under lock and key. And if you were just to let the servants forget to bring her dinner for three or four days, you can't conceive how she'd come about! (*He bows and takes his leave.*)

MRS. MALAPROP (*alone*). Well, at any rate I shall be glad to get her from under my intuition. She has somehow discovered my partiality for Sir Lucius O'Trigger. Sure, Lucy can't have betrayed me? No, the girl is such a simpleton, I should have made her confess it. (*Calling*) Lucy! Lucy! Had she been one of your artificial ones, I should never have trusted her.

LUCY (*entering*). Did you call, ma'am?

MRS. MALAPROP. Yes, girl. Did you see Sir Lucius while you was out?

LUCY. No, indeed, ma'am, not a glimpse of him.

MRS. MALAPROP. You are sure, Lucy, that you never mentioned—

LUCY. Oh, Gemini! I'd sooner cut my tongue out.

MRS. MALAPROP. Well, don't let your simplicity be imposed on.

LUCY. No, ma'am.

MRS. MALAPROP. So, come to me presently, and I'll give you another letter to Sir Lucius. But mind, Lucy, if ever you betray what you are entrusted with—unless it be other people's secrets to me—you forfeit my malevolence forever. And your being a simpleton shall be no excuse for your locality. (*After a severe glance at* LUCY, MRS. MALAPROP *exits.*)

LUCY (*alone*). Ha, ha, ha! So, my dear *simplicity*, let me give you a little respite. (*She makes herself at home, putting her feet up on the sofa.*) Let girls in my station be as fond as they please of appearing expert and knowing in their trusts. Commend *me* to a mask of silliness and a pair of sharp eyes for my own interest under it. Let me see to what account I have turned my *simplicity* lately. (*She takes a small notebook from her pocket and reads from it.*) "For abetting Miss Lydia Languish in a design of running away with an ensign: in money, sundry times—twelve pounds twelve; gowns—five; hats, ruffles, caps, etc., etc.—numberless! From the said ensign, within this last month—six guineas and a half." About a quarter's pay! "Item. From Mrs. Malaprop, for betraying the young people to her—" when I found matters were likely to be discovered! "Two guineas and a black paduasoy.[10] Item. From Mr. Acres, for carrying divers letters—" which I never delivered! "Two guineas and a pair of buckles. Item. From Sir Lucius O'Trigger—three crowns, two gold pocket pieces and a silver snuffbox." Well done,

[10] **paduasoy:** strong rich silk fabric.

simplicity. Yet I was forced to make my Hibernian[11] believe that he was corresponding, not with the aunt, but with the niece. For though not over rich, I found he had too much pride and delicacy to sacrifice the feelings of a gentleman to the necessities of his fortune. (LUCY *hugs herself and giggles with pleasure.*)

ACT TWO

SCENE 1

The lodgings of CAPTAIN JACK ABSOLUTE (*alias Ensign Beverley*). FAG *is helping* JACK *in the completion of his morning toilet.*

FAG. Sir, while I was there, Sir Anthony came in. I told him you had sent me to inquire after his health and to know if he was at leisure to see you.

JACK. And what did he say on hearing I was at Bath?

FAG. Sir, in my life I never saw an elderly gentleman more astonished! He started back two or three paces, rapped out a dozen interjectoral oaths, and asked what the devil had brought you *here?*

JACK. Well, sir, and what did you say?

FAG. Oh, I lied, sir. I forget the precise lie, but you may depend on't, he got no truth from me. Yet, with submission, for fear of blunders in future, I should be glad to fix what *has* brought us to Bath, in order that we may lie a little consistently. Sir Anthony's servants were curious, sir, very curious indeed.

JACK. You have said nothing to them?

FAG. Oh, not a word, sir, not a word. Mr. Thomas, indeed, the coachman, whom I take to be the discreetest of whips—

JACK. 'Sdeath, you rascal, you have not trusted him!

FAG. Oh no, sir, no, no, not a syllable, upon my veracity! He was, indeed, a little inquisitive. But I was sly, sir, devilish sly. My master, said I, honest Thomas—you know, sir, one always says "honest" to one's inferiors—is come to Bath to

[11] **Hibernian:** native of Ireland.

recruit. Yes, sir, I said, to recruit, and whether for men, money or constitution, you know, sir, is nothing to him, nor anyone else.

JACK. Well, recruit will do, let it be so.

FAG. Oh, sir, recruit will do surprisingly. Indeed, to give the thing an air, I told Thomas that your honor had already enlisted five disbanded chairmen,[12] seven minority waiters[13] and thirteen billiard-markers.[14]

JACK. You blockhead, never say more than is necessary.

FAG. I beg pardon, sir, I beg pardon, but with submission, a lie is nothing unless one supports it. Sir, whenever I draw on my invention for a good current lie, I always forge endorsements as well as the bill.

JACK. Well, take care you don't hurt your credit by offering too much security. Is Mr. Faulkland returned?

FAG. He is above, sir, changing his dress.

JACK. Can you tell whether he has been informed of Sir Anthony's and Miss Melville's arrival?

FAG. I fancy not, sir. He has seen no one since he came in but his gentleman who was with him at Bristol. I think, sir, I hear Mr. Faulkland coming down.

JACK. Go, tell him I am here.

FAG. Yes, sir. (FAG *pauses in the doorway.*) I beg pardon, sir, but should Sir Anthony call, you will do me the favor to remember that we are recruiting, if you please?

JACK. Well, well.

FAG. And in tenderness to my character, if your honor could bring in the chairmen and waiters, I shall esteem it as an obligation, for though I never scruple a lie to serve my master, yet it hurts one's conscience to be found out. (*Exits.*)

JACK. Now for my whimsical friend. If he does not know that his mistress is here, I'll tease him a little before I tell him.

Enter FAULKLAND.

JACK. Faulkland, you're welcome to Bath again. You are punctual in your return.

[12] **chairmen:** those who carried sedan chairs.

[13] **minority waiters:** unemployed or not regularly employed waiters.

[14] **billiard-markers:** score keepers.

FAULKLAND. Yes, I had nothing to detain me. When I finished the business I went on. Well, what news since I left you? How stand matters between you and Lydia?

JACK. Faith, much as they were. I have not seen her since our quarrel. However, I expect to be recalled every hour.

FAULKLAND. Why don't you persuade her to go off with you at once?

JACK. What, and lose two-thirds of her fortune? You forget that, my friend. No, no, I could have brought her to that long ago.

FAULKLAND. Nay then, you trifle too long. If you are sure of her, propose to the aunt in your own character and write to Sir Anthony for his consent.

JACK. Softly, softly, for though I am convinced my little Lydia would elope with me as Ensign Beverley, yet am I by no means certain that she would take me with the impediment of our friends' consent, a regular humdrum wedding and the reversion of a good fortune on my side. No, no, I must prepare her gradually for the discovery and make myself necessary to her before I risk it. Well, but, Faulkland, you'll dine with us today at the hotel?

FAULKLAND. Indeed, I cannot. I am not in spirits to be of such a party.

JACK. By heavens, I shall forswear your company! You are the most teasing, captious, incorrigible lover! Do love like a man!

FAULKLAND. I own I am unfit for company.

JACK. Am not *I* a lover? Aye, and a romantic one, too? Yet do I carry everywhere with me such a confounded farrago of doubts, fears, hopes, wishes and all the flimsy furniture of a country miss's brain?

FAULKLAND. Ah, Jack, your heart and soul are not, like mine, fixed immutably on only one object. You throw for a large stake, but losing you could stake and throw again. But I have set my sum of happiness on this cast and not to succeed were to be stripped of all.

JACK. But, for heaven's sake, what grounds for apprehension can your whimsical brain conjure up at present?

FAULKLAND. What grounds for apprehension, did you say? Heavens, are there not a thousand? I fear for her spirits, her health, her life! My absence may fret her. Her anxiety for my return, her fears for me may oppress her gentle temper. And for her health—does not every hour bring me cause to be alarmed? If it rains, some shower may even then have chilled her delicate frame! If the wind be keen, some rude blast may have affected her! The heat of noon, the dews of the evening, may endanger the life of her, for whom only I value mine! Oh, Jack, when delicate and feeling souls are separated, there is not a feature in the sky, not a movement of the elements, nor an aspiration of the breeze but hints some cause for lover's apprehension!

JACK. Aye, but we may choose whether we will take the hint or not. So then, Faulkland, if you were convinced that Julia were well and in spirits, you would be entirely content.

FAULKLAND. I should be happy beyond measure. I am anxious only for that.

JACK. Then to cure your anxiety at once, Miss Melville is in perfect health and is at this moment in Bath!

FAULKLAND. Nay, Jack, don't trifle with me.

JACK. She is arrived here with my father within this hour.

FAULKLAND. Can you be serious?

JACK. I thought you knew Sir Anthony better than to be surprised at a sudden whim of this kind. Seriously then, it is as I tell you. Upon my honor.

FAULKLAND. My dear friend! Hollo, Du-Peigne, my hat! My dear Jack, now nothing on earth can give me a moment's uneasiness.

FAG *appears in the doorway.*

FAG. Sir, Mr. Acres, just arrived, is below.

JACK. Stay, Faulkland, this Acres lives within a mile of Sir Anthony and he shall tell you how your mistress has been ever since you left her. Fag, show the gentleman up.

Exit FAG.

FAULKLAND. What, is he much acquainted in the family?

JACK. Oh, very intimate. I insist on your not going. Besides, his character will divert you.

FAULKLAND. Well, I should like to ask him a few questions.

JACK. He is likewise a rival of mine. That is, of my other self's, for he does not think his friend Captain Absolute ever saw the lady in question, and it is ridiculous enough to hear him complain of one Beverley, a concealed, skulking rival who—

FAULKLAND. Hush, he's here!

Enter BOB ACRES, *out of breath.*

ACRES. Hah, my dear friend, noble captain and honest Jack, how do'st thou? Just arrived faith, as you see. (*To* FAULKLAND) Sir, your humble servant. Warm work on the roads, Jack! Odd's whips and wheels, I've travelled like a comet with a tail of dust all the way as long as the Mall!

JACK. Ah, Bob, you are indeed an eccentric planet. But we know your attraction hither. Give me leave to introduce Mr. Faulkland to you. Mr. Faulkland, Mr. Acres.

ACRES. I am most heartily glad to see you, sir, I solicit your connections. Hey, Jack! What, this is Mr. Faulkland who—

JACK. Aye, Bob, Miss Melville's Mr. Faulkland.

ACRES. Od'so! She and her father can be but just arrived before me. I suppose you have seen them. Ah, Mr. Faulkland, you are indeed a happy man!

FAULKLAND. I have not seen Miss Melville yet, sir. I hope she enjoyed full health and spirits in Devonshire?

ACRES. Never knew her better in my life, sir, never better. Odd's blushes and blooms, she has been as healthy as the German spa.

FAULKLAND. Indeed! I did hear that she had been a little indisposed.

ACRES. False, false, sir, only said to vex you. Quite the reverse, I assure you.

FAULKLAND. There, Jack, you see she has the advantage of me. I had almost fretted myself ill.

JACK. Now you are angry with your mistress for not having been sick?

FAULKLAND. No, no, you misunderstand me. Yet surely a little trifling indisposition is not an unnatural consequence of absence from those we love. Now confess, isn't there something unkind in this violent, robust, unfeeling health?

JACK. Oh, it was unkind of her to be well in your absence, to be sure.

ACRES (*inspecting the room*). Good apartments, Jack.

FAULKLAND. Well, sir, but you was saying that Miss Melville

has been so exceedingly well. What then, she has been merry and gay, I suppose? Always in spirits, hey?

ACRES. Merry! Odd's crickets, she has been the bell and spirit of the company wherever she has been, so lively and entertaining, so full of wit and humor!

FAULKLAND. There, Jack, there! Oh, by my soul, there is an innate levity in woman that nothing can overcome! What, happy and I away?!

JACK. Have done, how foolish this is. Just now you were only apprehensive for your mistress's spirits.

FAULKLAND. Why, Jack, have *I* been the joy and spirit of the company?

JACK. No, indeed, you have not.

FAULKLAND. Have *I* been lively and entertaining?

JACK. Oh, upon my word, I acquit you.

FAULKLAND. Have *I* been full of wit and humor?

JACK. No, faith, to do you justice, you have been confoundedly stupid indeed.

ACRES. What's the matter with the gentleman?

JACK. He is only expressing his great satisfaction at hearing that Julia has been so well and happy, that's all, hey, Faulkland?

FAULKLAND. Oh, I am rejoiced to hear it. Yes, yes, she has a happy disposition!

ACRES. That she has, indeed. Then she is so accomplished, so sweet a voice, so expert at her harpsichord, such a mistress of flat and sharp, squallante, rumblante and quiverante! There was this time month, odd's minnums and crotchets,[15] how she did chirrup at Mrs. Piano's concert!

FAULKLAND. There again, what say you to this? You see, she has been all mirth and song! Not a thought of me!

JACK. Pho, man, is not music the food of love?

FAULKLAND. Well, well, it may be so. Pray, Mr—what's his damned name? Do you remember what songs Miss Melville sung?

ACRES. Not I, indeed.

JACK. Stay now, there were some pretty, melancholy purling-stream airs, I warrant. Perhaps you may recollect. Did she sing, "When Absent From My Soul's Delight"?

[15] **minnums and crotchets:** symbols for musical notes.

ACRES. No, that wa'n't it.

JACK. Or, "Go, Gentle Gales"? (*Sings*) "Go, gentle gales—"

ACRES. Oh no, nothing like it. Odd's, now I recollect one of them! (*Sings*) "My heart's my own, my will is free—"

FAULKLAND. Fool! Fool that I am to fix all my happiness on such a trifler! 'Sdeath! To make herself the pipe and ballad-monger of a circle! To soothe her light heart with catches and glees![16] What can you say to this, sir?

JACK. Why, that I should be glad to hear my mistress had been so merry, sir.

FAULKLAND. Nay, nay, nay, I'm not sorry that she has been happy, no, no, I am glad of that. I would not have had her sad or sick. Yet surely a sympathetic heart would have shown itself even in the choice of a song. She might have been temperately healthy and, somehow, plaintively gay. But she has been dancing, too, I doubt not!

ACRES. What does the gentleman say about dancing?

JACK. He says the lady we speak of dances as well as she sings.

ACRES. Aye, truly, does she! There was at our last race ball—

FAULKLAND. Hell and the devil! There! There, I told you so! I told you so! Oh, she thrives in my absence! Dancing! But her whole feelings have been in opposition with mine. I have been anxious, silent, pensive, sedentary. My days have been hours of care, my nights of watchfulness. *She* has been all Health! Spirit! Laugh! Song! Oh, damned, damned levity!

JACK. For heaven's sake, Faulkland, don't expose yourself so. Suppose she has danced, what then? Does not the ceremony of society often oblige—

FAULKLAND. Well, well, I'll contain myself. Perhaps, as you say, for form's sake. What, Mr. Acres, you were praising Miss Melville's manner of dancing—a minuet, hey?

ACRES. Oh, I dare insure her for that. But what I was going to speak of was her country dancing. Odd's swimmings, she has such an air with her—

FAULKLAND. Now disappointment on her! Defend this, Absolute! Why don't you defend this? Country dances, jigs and reels! Am I to blame now? A minuet I could have for-

[16] **catches and glees**: rounds and unaccompanied compositions for three or more solo voices.

given. I should not have minded that. I say I should not have regarded a minuet. But country dances! Zounds! Had she made one in a cotillion, I believe I could have forgiven even that. But to be monkey-led for a night! To run the gauntlet through a string of amorous palming puppies! To show paces like a managed filly! Oh Jack, there never can be but one man in the world whom a truly modest and delicate woman ought to pair with in a country dance! And even then, the rest of the couples should be her great uncles and aunts!

JACK. Aye, to be sure, grandfathers and grandmothers!

FAULKLAND. If there be but one vicious mind in the set, 'twill spread like a contagion. The action of their pulse beats to the lascivious movements of the jig, their quivering, warm-breathed sighs impregnate the very air, the atmosphere becomes electrical to love and each amorous spark darts through every link of the chain! I must leave you. I own I am somewhat flurried. (*Looking at* ACRES, *who stands amazed and speechless.*) And that confounded looby has perceived it! (*He starts for the door.*)

JACK. Nay, but stay, Faulkland, and thank Mr. Acres for his good news.

FAULKLAND. Damn his news! (*Exits.*)

JACK. Ha, ha, ha, poor Faulkland! Five minutes since, nothing on earth could give him a moment's uneasiness!

ACRES. The gentleman wa'n't angry at my praising his mistress, was he?

JACK. A little jealous, I believe, Bob.

ACRES. You don't say so! Ha, ha, jealous of me, that's a good joke!

JACK. There's nothing strange in that, Bob, let me tell you. That sprightly grace and insinuating manner of yours will do some mischief among the girls here.

ACRES. Ah, you joke. Ha, ha! Mischief! Ha, ha! But you know I am not my own property. My dear Lydia has forstalled me. She could never abide me in the country because I used to dress so badly, but odd's frogs and tambours,[17] I shan't take matters so here! Now ancient madam has no voice in it, I'll make my old clothes know who's master! I shall straightway

[17] **frogs and tambours:** ornamental fastenings for a coat and embroideries for a vest.

cashier the hunting frock and render my leather breeches incapable. My hair has been in training some time.

JACK. Indeed!

ACRES. Aye, and though the side curls are a little restive, my hind-part takes it very kindly.

JACK. Oh, you'll polish, I doubt not.

ACRES. Absolutely, I propose. Then if I can find out this Ensign Beverley, odd's triggers and flints, I'll make him know the difference o't.

JACK. Spoke like a man. But pray, Bob, I observe you have got an odd kind of a new method of swearing.

ACRES. Ha, ha, you've taken notice of it! 'Tis genteel, isn't it? I didn't invent it myself, though. But a commander in our militia, a great scholar, I assure you, says there is no meaning in the common oaths and that nothing but their antiquity makes them respectable. Because, he says, the ancients would never stick to an oath or two but would say "By Jove!" or "By Bacchus!" or "By Mars!" or "By Venus!" or "By Pallas!" according to the sentiment. So that to swear with propriety, says my little major, "the oath should be an echo to the sense." And this we call "the oath referential" or "sentimental swearing." Ha, ha, ha, 'tis genteel, isn't it?

JACK. Very genteel, and very new indeed, and I daresay will supplant all other figures of imprecation.

ACRES. Aye, aye, the best terms will grow obsolete. Damns have had their day.

Enter FAG.

FAG. Sir, there is a gentleman below desires to see you. Shall I shew him into the parlor?

JACK. Aye, you may.

ACRES. Well, I must be gone.

JACK. Stay. Who is it, Fag?

FAG. Your father, sir.

JACK. You puppy, why didn't you show him up directly?

FAG *scurries out of the room.*

ACRES. You have business with Sir Anthony. I expect a message from Mrs. Malaprop at my lodgings. I have sent also to my dear friend Sir Lucius O'Trigger. Adieu, Jack, we must meet at night, when you shall give me a dozen bumpers to little Lydia.

JACK. That I will with all my heart.

After an elaborately awkward bow, ACRES *exits.*

JACK. Now for a parental lecture. I hope he has heard nothing of the business that has brought me here. I wish the gout had held him fast in Devonshire, with all my soul!

Enter SIR ANTHONY.

JACK. Sir, I am delighted to see you here, and looking so well! Your sudden arrival at Bath made me apprehensive for your health.

SIR ANTHONY. Very apprehensive, I dare say, Jack. What, you are recruiting here, hey?

JACK. Yes, sir, I am on duty.

SIR ANTHONY. Well, Jack, I am glad to see you, though I did not expect it, for I was going to write to you on a little matter of business. Jack, I have been considering that I grow old and infirm and shall probably not trouble you long.

JACK. Pardon me, sir, I never saw you look more strong and hearty and I pray frequently that you may continue so.

SIR ANTHONY. I hope your prayers may be heard with all my heart. Well then, Jack, I have been considering that I am so strong and hearty, I may continue to plague you a long time. Now, Jack, I am sensible that the income of your commission and what I have hitherto allowed you is but a small pittance for a lad of your spirit.

JACK. Sir, you are very good.

SIR ANTHONY. And it is my wish, while yet I live, to have my boy make some figure in the world. I have resolved, therefore, to fix you at once in a noble independence.

JACK. Sir, your kindness overpowers me. Such generosity makes the gratitude of reason more lively than the sensations even of filial affection.

SIR ANTHONY. I am glad you are so sensible of my attention, and you shall be master of a large estate in a few weeks!

JACK. Let my future life, sir, speak my gratitude! I cannot express the sense I have of your munificence. Yet, sir, I presume you would not wish me to quit the army?

SIR ANTHONY. Oh, that shall be as your wife chooses.

JACK. My wife, sir!

SIR ANTHONY. Aye, aye, settle that between you, settle that between you.

JACK. A wife did you say, sir?

SIR ANTHONY. Aye, a wife. Why, did not I mention her before?

JACK. Not a word of her, sir.

SIR ANTHONY. Odd so! I mustn't forget her, though. Yes, Jack, the independence I was talking of is by a marriage. The fortune is saddled with a wife. But I suppose that makes no difference?

JACK. Sir, sir, you amaze me!

SIR ANTHONY. Why, what the devil's the matter with the fool? Just now you were all gratitude and duty.

JACK. I was, sir. You talked to me of independence and a fortune, but not a word of a wife.

SIR ANTHONY. Why, what difference does that make? Odd's life, sir, if you have the estate, you must take it with the livestock on it as it stands.

JACK. If my happiness is to be the price, I must beg leave to decline the purchase. Pray, sir, who is the lady?

SIR ANTHONY. What's that to you, sir? Come, give me your promise to love and to marry her directly.

JACK. Sure, sir, this is not very reasonable, to summon my affections for a lady I know nothing of!

SIR ANTHONY. I am sure, sir, 'tis more unreasonable in you to object to a lady you know nothing of!

JACK. Then, sir, I must tell you plainly that my inclinations are fixed on another. Sir, my heart is engaged to an angel.

SIR ANTHONY. Then pray let it send an excuse. It is very sorry but business prevents its waiting on her.

JACK. But my vows are pledged to her.

SIR ANTHONY. Let her foreclose, Jack, let her foreclose. They are not worth redeeming. Besides, you have the angel's vows in exchange, I suppose, so there can be no loss there.

JACK. You must excuse me, sir, if I tell you, once for all, that in this point I cannot obey you.

SIR ANTHONY. Hark'ee, Jack! I have heard you for some time with patience. I have been cool, quite cool. But take care. You know I am compliance itself—when I am not thwarted.

No one more easily led—when I have my own way. But don't put me in a frenzy!

JACK. Sir, I must repeat it. In this, I cannot obey you.

SIR ANTHONY. Now damn me if ever I call you Jack again while I live!!

JACK. Nay, sir, but hear me!

SIR ANTHONY. Sir, I won't hear a word, not a word, not one word! So give me your promise by a nod. And I'll tell you what, Jack—I mean, you dog!—if you don't by—

JACK. What, sir, promise to link myself to some mass of ugliness! To—

SIR ANTHONY. Zounds, sirrah! The lady shall be as ugly as I choose. She shall have a hump on each shoulder. She shall be as crooked as the crescent. Her one eye shall roll like the bull's in Cox's museum. She shall have a skin like a mummy and the beard of a Jew. She shall be all this, sirrah, yet I'll make you ogle her all day and sit up all night to write sonnets on her beauty.

JACK. This is reason and moderation indeed!

SIR ANTHONY. None of your sneering, puppy! No grinning, jackanapes!

JACK. Indeed, sir, I never was in a worse humor for mirth in my life.

SIR ANTHONY. 'Tis false, sir, I know you are laughing in your sleeve. I know you'll grin when I am gone, sirrah!

JACK. Sir, I hope I know my duty better.

SIR ANTHONY. None of your passion, sir! None of your violence, if you please! It won't do with me, I promise you!

JACK. Indeed, sir, I was never cooler in my life.

SIR ANTHONY. 'Tis a confounded lie! I know you are in a passion in your heart, I know you are, you hypocritical young dog! But it won't do!

JACK. Nay, sir, upon my word.

SIR ANTHONY. So you will fly out! Can't you be cool, like me? What the devil good can passion do? Passion is of no service, you impudent, insolent, overbearing reprobate! There, you sneer again! Don't provoke me! But you rely upon the mildness of my temper, you do, you dog! You play upon the meekness of my disposition! You take care, the patience of a saint may be overcome at last! But mark, I give you six hours and a half to consider of this. If you then agree, without any condition, to do everything on earth that I choose, why—confound you!—I may in time forgive you. If not—zounds!—don't enter the same hemisphere with me! Don't dare to breathe the same air or use the same light with me, but get an atmosphere and a sun of your own! I'll strip you of your commission! I'll lodge a five-and-threepence in the hands of trustees and you shall live on the interest. I'll disown you, I'll disinherit you, I'll unget you! And damn me if ever I call you Jack again! (*Exit.*)

JACK. Mild, gentle, considerate father, I kiss your hands. What a tender method of giving his opinion in these matters Sir Anthony has! I dare not trust him with the truth. I wonder what old, wealthy hag it is that he wants to bestow on me? Yet he married himself for love, and was in his youth a bold intriguer and a gay companion!

Enter FAG, *in confusion.*

FAG. Assuredly, sir, our father is wrath to a degree. He comes downstairs eight or ten steps at a time, muttering, growling and thumping the bannisters all the way. I and the cook's dog stand bowing at the door. Rap! He gives me a stroke on the head with his cane, bids me carry *that* to my master. Then, kicking the poor turnspit[18] into the area, damns us all for a puppy triumvirate. Upon my credit, sir, were I in your place and found my father such very bad company I should certainly drop his acquaintance.

JACK (*moves menacingly towards* FAG). Cease your impertinence, sir, at present! Did you come in for nothing more? Stand out of the way! (*Pushes* FAG *aside, exits.*)

FAG. So! Sir Anthony trims my master; he is afraid to reply to his father, then vents his spleen on poor Fag! When one is vexed by one person, to revenge oneself on another who happens to come in the way is the vilest injustice! Ah, it shows the worst temper, the basest—

An ERRAND BOY *comes into the room and tugs at* FAG'*s sleeve.*

[18] **turnspit:** dog used in a treadmill to turn a roasting spit.

BOY. Mr. Fag! Mr. Fag! Your master calls you.

FAG. Well, you little, dirty puppy, you need not bawl so!—The meanest disposition, the—

BOY. Quick, quick, Mr. Fag.

FAG. Quick? Quick? You impudent jackanapes, am I to be commanded by you, too, you little, impertinent, insolent, kitchen-bred—(FAG *kicks and beats the* BOY *out of the room*).

SCENE 2

The North Parade, a public park. LUCY *is alone, waiting.*

LUCY. So, I shall have another rival to add to my mistress's list—Captain Absolute. However, I shall not enter his name 'til my purse has received notice in form. Poor Acres is dismissed! Well, I have done him a last, friendly office in letting him know that Beverley was here before him. (*Looking about.*) Sir Lucius is generally more punctual when he expects to hear from his dear Delia, as he calls her. I wonder he's not here! I have a little scruple of conscience from this deceit, 'though I should not be paid so well if my hero knew that "Delia" was near fifty and her own mistress.

SIR LUCIUS O'TRIGGER *approaches, unseen by* LUCY.

SIR LUCIUS. Hah, my little ambassadress! Upon my conscience, I have been looking for you. I have been on the South Parade this half-hour.

LUCY (*instantly adopting her "simple" manner*). O Gemini! And I have been waiting for your Worship here on the North!

SIR LUCIUS. Faith, maybe that was the reason we did not meet! And it is very comical, too, how you could go out and I not see you, for I was only taking a nap at the Parade Coffee House and I chose the window on purpose that I might not miss you.

LUCY. My stars! Now I'd wager a sixpence I went by while you were asleep.

SIR LUCIUS. Sure enough it must have been so, and I never dreamt it was so late, 'til I waked. Well, but my little girl, have you got nothing for me?

LUCY. Yes, but I have. I've got a letter for you in my pocket.

SIR LUCIUS. Oh, faith, I guessed you weren't come empty-handed. Well, let me see what the dear creature says.

LUCY (*gives a letter*). There, Sir Lucius.

SIR LUCIUS (*reads*). "Sir: There is often a sudden incentive impulse in love that has a greater induction than years of domestic combination. Such was the commotion I felt at the first superfluous view of Sir Lucius O'Trigger." Very pretty, upon my word. "Female punctuation forbids me to say more. Yet, let me add that it will give me joy infallible to find Sir Lucius worthy the last criterion of my affections. Delia." Upon my conscience, Lucy, your lady is a great mistress of language. Faith, she's quite the queen of the dictionary, for the devil a word dare refuse coming at her call, though one would think it was quite out of hearing.

LUCY. Aye, sir, a lady of her experience.

SIR LUCIUS. Experience! What, at seventeen?

LUCY. Oh, true, sir! But then she reads so. My stars, how she will read, off hand!

SIR LUCIUS. Faith, she must be very deep read to write this way, though she is rather an arbitrary writer, too. For here are a great many poor words pressed into service of this note that would get their *habeas corpus* from any court in Christendom.

LUCY. Ah, Sir Lucius, if you were to hear how she talks of you!

SIR LUCIUS. Oh, tell her I'll make her the best husband in the world and Lady O'Trigger into the bargain! But we must get the old gentlewoman's consent and do everything fairly.

LUCY. Nay, Sir Lucius, I thought you wa'n't rich enough to be so nice!

SIR LUCIUS. Upon my word, young woman, you have hit it. I am so poor that I can't afford to do a dirty action. If I did not want money, I'd steal your mistress and her fortune with a great deal of pleasure. However, my pretty girl, here's a little something to buy you a ribbon. (*Gives her money.*) And meet me in the evening and I'll give you an answer to this. (*Indicates letter.*) So, hussy, take a kiss beforehand, to put you in mind. (*Kisses her.*)

LUCY. Oh lud, Sir Lucius! I never seed such a gemman! My lady won't like you if you're so impudent.

SIR LUCIUS. Faith, she will, Lucy. That same—pho!—what's the name of it?—modesty—is a quality in a lover more praised by the women than liked. So, if your mistress asks you whether Sir Lucius ever gave you a kiss, tell her fifty, my dear.

LUCY. What, would you have me tell her a lie?

SIR LUCIUS. Ah then, you baggage, I'll make it a truth presently! (SIR LUCIUS *grapples with* LUCY.)

LUCY. For shame now, here is someone coming.

SIR LUCIUS *looks over his shoulder and sees* FAG *approaching.*

SIR LUCIUS. Oh, faith, I'll quiet your conscience! (SIR LUCIUS *kisses her quickly and walks away humming a tune, as* FAG *comes into view.*)

FAG (*eyeing the retreating figure of* SIR LUCIUS). So, so, ma'am, I humbly beg pardon.

LUCY. Oh, lud, now, Mr. Fag, you flurry one so.

FAG. Come, come, Lucy, here's no one by, so a little less simplicity, with a grain or two more sincerity, if you please. You play false with us, madam. I saw you give the baronet a letter. My master shall know this, and if he don't call him out, I will.

LUCY. Ha, ha, ha! You gentlemen's gentlemen are so hasty. That letter was from Mrs. Malaprop, simpleton. She is taken with Sir Lucius' address.

FAG. How! What tastes some people have! Why, I suppose I have walked by her window an hundred times. But what says our young lady? Any message to my master?

LUCY. Sad news, Mr. Fag. A worse rival than Acres! Sir Anthony Absolute has proposed his son.

FAG. What, Captain Absolute?

LUCY. Even so. I overheard it all.

FAG. Ha, ha, ha! Very good, faith. Good-by, Lucy, I must away with this news.

LUCY. Well, you may laugh, but it is true, I assure you. (*She starts to go, then stops.*) But, Mr. Fag, tell your master not to be cast down by this.

FAG. Oh, he'll be disconsolate! (*He starts to go.*)

LUCY. And charge him not to think of quarrelling with young Absolute.

FAG. Never fear! Never fear!

LUCY (*going*). Be sure. Bid him keep up his spirits.

FAG (*going*). We will, we will.

LUCY *and* FAG *disappear.*

ACT THREE

SCENE 1

The North Parade. CAPTAIN JACK ABSOLUTE *is meditating.*

JACK. 'Tis just as Fag told me, indeed. Whimsical enough, faith. My father wants to force me to marry the very girl I am plotting to run away with! He must not know of my connection with her yet a while. He has too summary a method of proceeding in these matters. However, I'll read my recantation instantly. My conversion is something sudden, indeed, but I can assure him it is very sincere. So, so, here he comes. He looks plaguy gruff. (JACK *conceals himself for a moment as* SIR ANTHONY *approaches.*)

SIR ANTHONY. No! I'll die sooner than forgive him. Die, did I say? I'll live these fifty years to plague him. At our last meeting his impudence had almost put me out of temper. An obstinate, passionate, self-willed boy. Who can he take after? This is my return for getting him before all his brothers and sisters, for putting him, at twelve years old, into a marching regiment and allowing him fifty pounds a year besides his pay ever since! But I have done with him. He's anybody's son for me. I never will see him more. Never, never, never, never!

JACK. Now for a penitential face. (*Steps into* SIR ANTHONY'*s path.*)

SIR ANTHONY. Fellow, get out of my way.

JACK. Sir, you see a penitent before you.

SIR ANTHONY. I see an impudent scoundrel before me.

JACK. A sincere penitent. I am come, sir, to acknowledge my

error and to submit entirely to your will.

SIR ANTHONY. What's that?

JACK. I have been revolving and reflecting and considering on your past goodness and kindness and condescension to me.

SIR ANTHONY. Well, sir?

JACK. I have been likewise weighing and balancing what you were pleased to mention concerning duty and obedience and authority.

SIR ANTHONY. Well, puppy?

JACK. Why then, sir, the result of my reflections is—a resolution to sacrifice every inclination of my own to your satisfaction.

SIR ANTHONY. Why now you talk sense, absolute sense! I never heard anything more sensible in my life. Confound you, you shall be Jack again!

JACK. I am happy in the appellation.

SIR ANTHONY. Why then, Jack, my dear Jack, I will now inform you who the lady really is. Nothing but your passion and violence, you silly fellow, prevented my telling you at first. Prepare, Jack, for wonder and rapture, prepare. What think you of—Miss Lydia Languish?

JACK. Languish? What, the Languishes of Worcestershire?

SIR ANTHONY. Worcestershire? No! Did you never meet Mrs. Malaprop and her niece, Miss Languish, who came into our country just before you were last ordered to your regiment?

JACK. Malaprop? Languish? I don't remember ever to have heard the names before. Yet, stay. I think I do recollect something. Languish, Languish. She squints, don't she? A little red-haired girl?

SIR ANTHONY. Squints! A red-haired girl! Zounds, no!

JACK. Then I must have forgot. It can't be the same person.

SIR ANTHONY. Jack! Jack! What think you of blooming, love-breathing seventeen?

JACK. As to that, sir, I am quite indifferent. If I can please you in the matter, 'tis all I desire.

SIR ANTHONY. Nay, but Jack, such eyes, such eyes! So innocently wild, so bashfully irresolute! Not a glance but speaks and kindles some thought of love! Then, Jack, her cheeks, her cheeks, Jack! So deeply blushing at the insinuations of her telltale eyes! Then, Jack, her lips! Oh, Jack, lips smiling at their own indiscretion and, if not smiling, more sweetly pouting, more lovely in sullenness!

JACK (*to himself*). That's she, indeed. Well done, old gentleman.

SIR ANTHONY. Then, Jack, her neck! Oh Jack, Jack!

JACK. And which is to be mine, sir, the niece or the aunt?

SIR ANTHONY. Why you unfeeling, insensible puppy, I despise you! When I was of your age such a description would have made me fly like a rocket! The aunt, indeed! Odd's life, when I ran away with your mother I would not have touched anything old or ugly to gain an empire!

JACK. Not to please your father, sir?

SIR ANTHONY. To please my father! Zounds, not to please—oh, my father! Odd so, yes, yes! If my father indeed had desired—that's quite another matter. Though he wa'n't the indulgent father that I am, Jack.

JACK. I dare say not, sir.

SIR ANTHONY. But, Jack, you are not sorry to find your mistress is so beautiful?

JACK. Sir, I repeat it. If I please you in this affair, 'tis all I desire. Not that I think a woman the worse for being handsome. But, sir, if you please to recollect, you before hinted something about a hump or two, one eye, and a few more graces of that kind. Now, without being very nice, I own I should rather choose a wife of mine to have the usual number of limbs and a limited quantity of back, and though one eye may be very agreeable, yet as the prejudice has always run in favor of two, I would not wish to affect a singularity in that article.

SIR ANTHONY. What a phlegmatic sot it is! Why, sirrah, you're an anchorite,[19] a vile, insensible stock![20] You, a soldier? You're a walking block, fit only to dust the company's regimentals on! Odd's life, I've a great mind to marry the girl myself!

JACK. I am entirely at your disposal, sir. If you should think of addressing Miss Languish yourself, I suppose you would have me marry the aunt. Or, if you change your mind and

[19] **anchorite:** recluse.

[20] **stock:** senseless or stupid person.

take the old lady, 'tis the same to me, I'll marry the niece.

SIR ANTHONY. Upon my word, Jack, thou'rt either a very great hypocrite or—but come, I know your indifference on such a subject must be all a lie. I'm sure it must. Come now, damn your demure face! Come, confess, Jack, you have been lying, ha'n't you? You have been playing the hypocrite, hey? I'll never forgive you, if you ha'n't been lying and playing the hypocrite.

JACK. I'm sorry, sir, that the respect and duty which I bear to you should be so mistaken.

SIR ANTHONY. Hang your respect and duty! But come along with me, I'll write a note to Mrs. Malaprop and you shall visit the lady directly. Her eyes shall be the Promethean torch to you. Come along, I'll never forgive you if you don't come back stark mad with rapture and impatience. If you don't, egad, I'll marry the girl myself! (SIR ANTHONY *claps* JACK *on the shoulder and leads him away to meet his bride-to-be.*)

SCENE 2

FAULKLAND *is waiting for* JULIA *in her sitting room.*

FAULKLAND. They told me Julia would return directly. I wonder she is not yet come. How mean does this captious, unsatisfied temper of mine appear to my cooler judgment! Yet I know not that I indulge it in any other point. But on this one subject and to this one subject, whom I think I love beyond my life, I am ever ungenerously fretful and madly capricious. I am conscious of it, yet I cannot correct myself. What tender, honest joy sparkled in her eyes when we met! How delicate was the warmth of her expressions! I was ashamed to appear less happy, though I had come resolved to wear a face of coolness and upbraiding. Sir Anthony's presence prevented my proposed expostulations, yet I must be satisfied that she has not been so *very* happy in my absence. (*Listens*) She is coming? Yes, I know the nimbleness of her tread when she thinks her impatient Faulkland counts the moments of her stay.

Enter JULIA.

JULIA. I had not hoped to see you again so soon.

FAULKLAND. Could I, Julia, be contented with my first welcome, restrained as we were by the presence of a third person?

JULIA. Oh, Faulkland, when your kindness can make me thus happy, let me not think that I discovered something of coldness in your first salutation.

FAULKLAND. 'Twas but your fancy, Julia. I *was* rejoiced to see you, to see you—in such health. Sure I had no cause for coldness?

JULIA. Nay, then I see you have taken something ill. You must not conceal from me what it is. (*Sits.*)

FAULKLAND (*pacing*). Well then, shall I own to you that my joy at hearing of your—health—and arrival here, by your neighbor Acres, was somewhat damped by his dwelling much on the high spirits you had enjoyed in Devonshire, on your mirth, your singing, your dancing and I know not what! For such is my temper, Julia, that I should regard every mirthful moment in your absence as a treason to constancy. The mutual tear that steals down the cheek of parting lovers is a compact that no smile shall live there 'til they meet again.

JULIA. Must I never cease to tax my Faulkland with this teasing minute caprice? Can the idle reports of a silly boor weigh in your breast against my tried affection?

FAULKLAND. They have no weight with me, Julia. No, no, I am happy if you have been so. Yet only say that you did not sing with *mirth*, say that you thought of Faulkland in the dance.

JULIA. I never can be happy in your absence. If I wear a countenance of content, it is to show that my mind holds no doubt of my Faulkland's truth. If I seemed sad, it were to make malice triumph and say that I had fixed my heart on one who left me to lament his roving and my own credulity. Believe me, Faulkland, I mean not to upbraid you when I say that I have often dressed sorrow in smiles, lest my friends should guess whose unkindness had caused my tears.

FAULKLAND. You were ever all goodness to me. (*On his

knees.) Oh, I am a brute when I but admit a doubt of your true constancy!

JULIA. If ever, without such cause from you as I will not suppose possible, you find my affections veering but a point, may I become a proverbial scoff for levity and base ingratitude.

FAULKLAND (*rising*). Ah, Julia, that last word is grating to me. I would I had no title to your gratitude. Search your heart, Julia. Perhaps what you have mistaken for love is but the warm effusion of a too thankful heart!

JULIA (*bewildered*). For what quality must I love you?

FAULKLAND. For no quality! To regard me for any quality of mind or understanding were only to esteem me. And for person, I have often wished myself deformed to be convinced that I owned no obligation there for any part of your affection.

JULIA (*patiently*). Where Nature has bestowed a show of nice attention in the features of a man he should laugh at it as misplaced. I have seen men who in this vain article, perhaps, might rank above you, but my heart has never asked my eyes if it were so or not.

FAULKLAND (*looks at her carefully*). Now this is not well from you, Julia. I despise person in a man, yet if you loved me as I wish, though I were an Ethiop you'd think none so fair.

JULIA. I see you are determined to be unkind. The contract which my poor father bound us in gives you more than a lover's privilege.

FAULKLAND. Again, Julia, you raise ideas that feed and justify my doubts. I would not have been more free. No, I am proud of my restraint. Yet, perhaps your high respect alone for this solemn compact has fettered your inclinations which else had made a worthier choice. How shall I be sure, had you remained unbound in thought and promise, that I should still have been the object of your persevering love?

JULIA (*rises*). Then try me now. Let us be as free as strangers as to what is past. My heart will not feel more liberty!

FAULKLAND. There now, so hasty, Julia, so anxious to be free? If your love for me were fixed and ardent, you would not lose your hold, even though I wished it.

JULIA. Oh, you torture me to the heart! I cannot bear it!

FAULKLAND. I do not mean to distress you. If I loved you less, I should never give you an uneasy moment. But hear me. All my fretful doubts arise from this. Women are not used to weigh and separate the motives of their affections. The cold dictates of prudence, gratitude or filial duty may sometimes be mistaken for the pleadings of the heart. I would not boast, yet let me say that I have neither age, person or character to found dislike on. My fortune such, as few ladies could be charged with indiscretion in the match. Oh, Julia, when love receives such countenance from prudence, nice minds will be suspicious of its birth.

JULIA (*trying to control herself*). I know not whither your insinuations would tend. But as they seem pressing to insult me, I will spare you the regret of having done so. I have given you no cause for this. (*Exits, weeping.*)

FAULKLAND (*follows her*). In tears? Stay, Julia, stay but for a moment. (*Tries the door.*) The door is fastened! Julia, my soul, but for one moment! I hear her sobbing. 'Sdeath! What a brute am I to use her thus! Yet stay. (*Listens*) Aye, she is coming now. How little resolution there is in a woman! How a few soft words can turn them. (*Sits. Listens.*) No, faith, she is *not* coming either. (*Rushes to the door.*) Why, Julia, my love, say but that you forgive me, come but to tell me that. (*Pause*) Now, this is being too resentful. (*Listens*) Stay, she is coming, too. I thought she would. No steadiness in anything. Her going away must have been a mere trick. She sha'n't see that I was hurt by it. I'll affect indifference. (*He hums a tune, then stops, listens.*) No, zounds, she's *not* coming! Nor don't intend it, I suppose! This is not steadiness but obstinacy! (*Pause*) Yet I deserve it. What, after so long an absence, to quarrel with her tenderness? 'Twas barbarous and unmanly! I should be ashamed to see her now. I'll wait 'til her just resentment is abated. And when I distress her so again, may I lose her forever and be linked instead to some antique virago whose gnawing passions and long-hoarded spleen shall make me curse my folly half the day and all the night. (*Exits.*)

Scene 3

MRS. MALAPROP'*s lodgings.* JACK *has just presented a letter of introduction.*

MRS. MALAPROP. Your being Sir Anthony's son, captain, would itself be a sufficient accommodation, but from the ingenuity of your appearance I am convinced you deserve the character here given of you.

JACK. Permit me to say, madam, that as I never yet have had the pleasure of seeing Miss Languish, my principal inducement in this affair at present is the honor of being allied to Mrs. Malaprop of whose intellectual accomplishments, elegant manners and unaffected learning no tongue is silent.

MRS. MALAPROP. Sir, you do me infinite honor! I beg, captain, you'll be seated. (*They sit.*) Ah, few gentlemen nowadays know how to value the ineffectual qualities in a woman, few think how a little knowledge becomes a gentlewoman. Men have no sense now but for the worthless flower of beauty.

JACK. It is but too true, indeed, ma'am, yet I fear our ladies should share the blame. They think our admiration of beauty so great that knowledge in them would be superfluous. Thus, like garden trees, they seldom show fruit 'til time has robbed them of the more specious blossom. Few, like Mrs. Malaprop and the orange tree, are rich in both at once!

MRS. MALAPROP. Sir, you overpower me with good breeding. (*To herself*) He is the very pineapple of politeness! You are not ignorant, captain, that this giddy girl has somehow contrived to fix her affections on a beggarly, strolling, eavesdropping ensign, whom none of us have seen and nobody knows anything of?

JACK. Oh, I have heard the silly affair before. I'm not at all prejudiced against her on *that* account.

MRS. MALAPROP. You are very good and very considerate, captain. I am sure I have done everything in my power since I exploded the affair! Long ago I laid my positive conjunctions on her never to think on the fellow again. I have since laid Sir Anthony's preposition before her but, I am sorry to say, she seems resolved to decline every particle that I enjoin her.

JACK. It must be very distressing, indeed, ma'am.

MRS. MALAPROP. Oh, it gives me the hydrostatics to such a degree! I thought she had persisted from corresponding with him but, behold, this very day I have interceded another letter from the fellow. I believe I have it in my pocket.

JACK (*to himself*). Oh, the devil, my last note!

MRS. MALAPROP. Aye, here it is.

JACK (*to himself*). Aye, my note, indeed! Oh, the little traitress Lucy!

MRS. MALAPROP (*giving him the letter*). There, perhaps you may know the writing.

JACK. I think I have seen the hand before. Yes, I certainly must have seen this hand before.

MRS. MALAPROP. Nay, but read it, captain.

JACK (*reading*). "My soul's idol, my adored Lydia!" Very tender, indeed.

MRS. MALAPROP Tender! Aye, and profane, too, o' my conscience!

JACK. "I am excessively alarmed at the intelligence you send me, the more so as my new rival—"

MRS. MALAPROP. That's you, sir.

JACK. "—has universally the character of being an accomplished gentleman and a man of honor." Well, that's handsome enough.

MRS. MALAPROP. Oh, the fellow has some design in writing so.

JACK. That he had, I'll answer for him, ma'am.

MRS. MALAPROP. But go on, sir, you'll see presently.

JACK. "As for the old weather-beaten she-dragon who guards you—" Who can he mean by that?

MRS. MALAPROP. Me, sir, me, he means me there! What do you think now? But go on a little further.

JACK. Impudent scoundrel! "—it shall go hard but I will elude her vigilance, as I am told that the same ridiculous vanity, which makes her dress up her coarse features, and deck her dull chat with hard words which she don't understand—"

MRS. MALAPROP. There, sir, an attack upon my language, what do you think of that? An aspersion on my parts of speech! Was ever such a brute? Sure, if I reprehend anything in this world it is the use of my oracular tongue and a nice derangement of epitaphs.

JACK. He deserves to be hanged and quartered! Let me see. "—same ridiculous vanity—"

MRS. MALAPROP. You need not read it again, sir.

JACK. I beg pardon, ma'am. "—does also lay her open to the grossest deceptions from flattery and pretended admiration —" An impudent coxcomb! "—so that I have a scheme to see you shortly with the old harridan's consent, and even to make her a go-between in our interviews." Was ever such assurance?

MRS. MALAPROP. Did you ever hear anything like it? He'll elude my vigilance, will he? Yes, yes, ha, ha! He's very likely to enter these doors! We'll try who can plot best!

JACK (*to himself*). So we will, ma'am—so we will. Ha, ha, ha, a conceited puppy, ha, ha, ha! Well, but Mrs. Malaprop, as the girl seems so infatuated by this fellow, suppose you were to wink at her corresponding with him for a little time, let her even plot an elopement with him. Then do you connive at her escape while *I*, just in the nick, will have the fellow laid by the heels and fairly contrive to carry her off in his stead.

MRS. MALAPROP. I am delighted with the scheme. Never was anything better perpetrated!

JACK. But, pray, could not I see the lady for a few minutes now? I should like to try her temper a little.

MRS. MALAPROP. Why, I don't know, I doubt she is not prepared for a visit of this kind. There is a decorum in these matters.

JACK. Oh, Lord, she won't mind me. Only tell her Beverley—

MRS. MALAPROP. Sir?

JACK (*to himself*). Gently, good tongue.

MRS. MALAPROP. What did you say of Beverley?

JACK. Oh, I was going to propose that you should tell her, by way of jest, that it was Beverley who was below. She'd come down fast enough then—ha, ha, ha!

MRS. MALAPROP. 'Twould be a trick she well deserves. Besides, you know the fellow tells her he'll get my consent to see her—ha, ha! Let him if he can, I say again. (*Calls*) Lydia, come down here! He'll make me a go-between in their interviews—ha, ha! (*Calls*) Come down, I say, Lydia! I don't wonder at your laughing—ha, ha, ha! His impudence is truly ridiculous.

JACK. 'Tis very ridiculous, upon my soul, ma'am—ha, ha, ha!

MRS. MALAPROP. The little hussy won't hear. Well, I'll go and tell her at once who it is. She shall know that Captain Absolute is come to wait on her and I'll make her behave as becomes a young woman.

JACK. As you please, ma'am.

MRS. MALAPROP. For the present, captain, your servant. Ah, you've not done laughing yet, I see. Elude my vigilance, yes—ha, ha, ha! (*Exit.*)

JACK. Ha, ha, ha! One would think now that I might throw off all disguise at once and seize my prize with security. But such is Lydia's caprice that to undeceive were probably to lose her. I'll see whether she knows me. (JACK *moves to the other side of the room and pretends to admire the pictures on the wall as* LYDIA *enters.*)

LYDIA (*to herself*). What a scene am I now to go through! Surely nothing can be more dreadful than to be obliged to listen to the loathsome addresses of a stranger to one's heart. I have heard of girls persecuted as I am, who have appealed in behalf of their favored lover to the generosity of his rival. Suppose I were to try it? (*Looking at* JACK'*s back.*) There stands the hated rival. An officer, too! But, oh, how unlike my Beverley! (*Pause*) I wonder he don't begin? Truly he seems a very negligent wooer, quite at his ease, upon my word. I'll speak first. Mr. Absolute!

JACK (*turning*). Ma'am?

LYDIA. Oh, heavens, Beverley!

JACK. Hush, hush, my life! Softly, be not surprised!

LYDIA. I am so astonished! And so terrified! And so overjoyed! For heaven's sake, how came you here?

JACK. Briefly—I have deceived your aunt. I was informed that my new rival was to visit here this evening and, contriving to have him kept away, have passed myself on her for Captain Absolute.

LYDIA. Oh, charming! And she really takes you for young Absolute?

JACK. Oh, she's convinced of it.

LYDIA. Ha, ha, ha! I can't forbear laughing to think how her sagacity is overreached!

JACK. But we trifle with our precious moments. Such another

opportunity may not occur. Then let me now conjure my kind, my condescending angel, to fix the time that I may rescue her from undeserving persecution and with a licensed warmth plead for my reward.

LYDIA. Will you then, Beverley, consent to forfeit that portion of my paltry wealth, that burden on the wings of love?

JACK. Oh, come to me rich only thus—in loveliness. Bring no portion to me but thy love. 'Twill be generous in you, Lydia, for well you know it is the only dower your poor Beverley can repay.

LYDIA (*to herself*). How persuasive are his words! How charming will poverty be with him!

JACK. Ah, my soul, what a life will we then live! Love shall be our idol and support. We will worship him with a monastic strictness, abjuring all worldly toys to center every thought and action there. Proud of calamity, we will enjoy the wreck of wealth while the surrounding gloom of adversity shall make the flame of our pure love show doubly bright. By heavens, I would fling all good of fortune from me with a prodigal hand to enjoy the scene where I might clasp my Lydia to my bosom and say—the world affords no smile to me but here! (*He embraces her. Then, to himself*) If she holds out now, the devil is in it!

LYDIA (*to herself*). Now could I fly with him to the Antipodes! But my persecution is not yet come to a crisis.

As LYDIA *reluctantly breaks away from* JACK, MRS. MALAPROP *peers around the doorway, eavesdropping.*

MRS. MALAPROP (*to herself*). I am impatient to know how the little hussy deports herself.

JACK. So pensive, Lydia? Is then your warmth abated?

MRS. MALAPROP. Warmth abated! So, she has been in a passion, I suppose.

LYDIA. No, nor ever can while I have life.

MRS. MALAPROP. An ill-tempered little devil! She'll be in a passion all her life, will she?

LYDIA. Think not the idle threats of my ridiculous aunt can ever have any weight with me.

MRS. MALAPROP. Very dutiful, upon my word!

LYDIA. Let her choice be Captain Absolute, but Beverley is mine!

MRS. MALAPROP. I am astonished at her assurance! To his face, this to his face!

JACK (*kneeling*). Thus, then, let me enforce my suit.

MRS. MALAPROP. Aye, poor young man! Down on his knees entreating for pity! I can contain no longer! (*Charging into the room.*) Why, thou vixen! I have overheard you.

JACK (*to himself*). Oh, confound her vigilance!

MRS. MALAPROP. Captain Absolute, I know not how to apologize for her shocking rudeness.

JACK (*to himself*). So, all's safe, I find. I have hopes, madam, that time will bring the young lady—

MRS. MALAPROP. Oh, there's nothing to be hoped for from her! She's as headstrong as an allegory on the banks of Nile!

LYDIA. Nay, madam, what do you charge me with now?

MRS. MALAPROP. Why, thou unblushing rebel, didn't you tell this gentleman to his face that you loved another better! Didn't you say you never would be his?

LYDIA. No, madam, I did not.

MRS. MALAPROP. Good heavens, what assurance! Lydia, Lydia, you ought to know that lying don't become a young woman! Didn't you boast that Beverley, that stroller Beverley, possessed your heart? Tell me that, I say.

LYDIA. 'Tis true, ma'am, and none but Beverley—

MRS. MALAPROP. Hold, hold, assurance, you shall not be so rude!

JACK. Nay, pray, Mrs. Malaprop, don't stop the young lady's speech. She's very welcome to talk thus. It does not hurt me in the least, I assure you.

MRS. MALAPROP. You are too good, captain, too amiably patient. But come with me, miss. Let us see you again soon, captain. Remember what we have fixed.

JACK. I shall, ma'am.

MRS. MALAPROP. Come, take a graceful leave of the gentleman.

LYDIA. May every blessing wait on my Beverley, my loved Bev—

MRS. MALAPROP (*pulling* LYDIA *from the room*). Hussy! I'll choke the word in your throat! Come along, come along!

LYDIA, *flinging kisses at* JACK, *is forced from the room by* MRS. MALAPROP. JACK, *after returning a few kisses, leaves happily by another door.*

SCENE 4

ACRES' *lodgings.* DAVID, *a servant, is admiring* ACRES' *new clothes.*

ACRES. Indeed, David, do you think I become it so?

DAVID. You are quite another creature, believe me, master, by the mass! An' we've any luck we shall see the Devon monkeyrony[21] in all the print shops in Bath!

ACRES. Dress does make the difference, David.

DAVID. 'Tis all in all, I think! Difference! Why, an' you were to go now to Clod Hall, I am certain the old lady wouldn't know you. Master butler wouldn't believe his own eyes and Mrs. Pickle would cry, "Lard, presarve me!" Our dairymaid would come giggling to the door and I warrant Dolly Tester, your honor's favorite, would blush like my waistcoat. Oons! I'll hold a gallon there an't a dog in the house but would bark and I question whether Phyllis would wag a hair of her tail!

ACRES. Aye, David, there's nothing like polishing.

DAVID. So I says of your honor's boots but the boy never heeds me!

ACRES. But, David, has Mr. De-La-Grace been here? I must rub up my balancing and chasing and boring.[22]

DAVID. I'll call again, sir.

ACRES. Do, and see if there are any letters for me at the post office.

DAVID. I will. (*He starts to leave, stops.*) By the mass, I can't help looking at your head! If I hadn't been by at the cooking, I wish I may die if I should have known the dish again myself. (*Exit.*)

ACRES (*dancing*). Sink—slide—coupee![23] Confound the first

[21] **monkeyrony:** macaroni or fop.

[22] **balancing and chasing and boring:** dance movements; the latter are corruptions of "chassé" and "bourrée."

[23] **coupee:** dance step with one foot passing forward or backward.

inventors of cotillions, say I! They are as bad as algebra to us country gentlemen. I can walk a minuet easy enough when I am forced and I have been accounted a good stick in a country dance. Odd's jigs and tabors,[24] I never valued your cross-over to couple—figure in—right and left—and I'd foot it with e'er a captain in the country! But these outlandish heathen allemandes[25] and cotillions are quite beyond me! I shall never prosper to 'em, that's sure. Mine are true-born English legs, they don't understand their curst French lingo, their *pas* this, and *pas* that, and *pas* t'other! Damn me, my feet don't like to be called paws! No, 'tis certain, I have most anti-Gallican[26] toes!

A SERVANT *enters with* SIR LUCIUS O'TRIGGER.

SERVANT. Here is Sir Lucius O'Trigger to wait on you, sir (*Exits.*)

ACRES. Show him in.

SIR LUCIUS. Mr. Acres, I am delighted to embrace you.

ACRES. My dear Sir Lucius, I kiss your hands.

SIR LUCIUS. Pray, my friend, what has brought you so suddenly to Bath?

ACRES. Faith, I have followed Cupid's jack-o'-lantern and find myself in a quagmire at last. In short, I have been very ill-used, Sir Lucius. I don't choose to mention names but look on me as a very ill-used gentleman.

SIR LUCIUS. Pray, what is the case? I ask no names.

ACRES. Mark me, Sir Lucius. I fall as deep as need be in love with a young lady, her friends take my part, I follow her to Bath, send word of my arrival, and receive answer that the lady is to be otherwise disposed of. This, Sir Lucius, I call being ill-used.

SIR LUCIUS. Very ill, upon my conscience. Pray, can you divine the cause of it?

ACRES. Why, there's the matter—she has another lover, one Beverley who, I am told, is now in Bath. Odd's slanders and lies, he must be at the bottom of it!

[24] **tabors:** small drums.
[25] **allemandes:** various German dances.
[26] **anti-Gallican:** anti-French.

SIR LUCIUS. A rival in the case, is there? And do you think he has supplanted you unfairly?

ACRES. Unfairly? To be sure he has. He never could have done it fairly.

SIR LUCIUS. Then sure you know what is to be done?

ACRES. Not I, upon my soul.

SIR LUCIUS. We wear no swords here. But you understand me?

ACRES. What? Fight him?

SIR LUCIUS. Aye, to be sure. What can I mean else?

ACRES. But he has given me no provocation.

SIR LUCIUS. Now, I think he has given you the greatest provocation in the world. Can a man commit a more heinous offense against another than to fall in love with the same woman? Oh, by my soul, it is the most unpardonable breach of friendship.

ACRES. Breach of friendship, aye, aye! But I have no acquaintance with this man. I never saw him in my life.

SIR LUCIUS. That's no argument at all. He has the less right, then, to take such a liberty.

ACRES. Gad, that's true! I grow full of anger, Sir Lucius! I fire apace! Odd's hilts and blades, I find a man may have a deal of valor in him and not know it! But couldn't I contrive to have a little right on my side?

SIR LUCIUS. What the devil signifies right when your honor is concerned? Do you think Achilles or my little Alexander the Great ever inquired where the right lay? No, by my soul, they drew their broadswords and left the lazy sons of peace to settle the justice of it!

ACRES. Your words are a grenadier's march to my heart! I believe courage must be catching! I certainly do feel a kind of valor rising, as it were, a kind of courage, as I may say. Odd's flints, pans and triggers, I'll challenge him directly!

SIR LUCIUS. Ah, my little friend, if I had Blunderbuss Hall here I could show you a range of ancestry in the O'Trigger line that would furnish the New Room, every one of whom killed his man! For though the mansion house and dirty acres have slipped through my fingers, I thank heaven our honor and the family pictures are as fresh as ever.

ACRES. Oh, Sir Lucius, I have had ancestors, too, every man of 'em a colonel or a captain in the militia! Odd's balls and barrels, say no more, I am braced for it! The thunder of your words has soured the milk of human kindness in my breast. Zounds, as the man in the play says, "I could do such deeds—"

SIR LUCIUS. Come, come, there must be no passion at all in the case. These things should always be done civilly.

ACRES. I must be in a passion, Sir Lucius, I must be in a rage! Dear Sir Lucius, let me be in a rage, if you love me? Come, here's pen and paper. (*Sitting down to write.*) I would the ink were red! Indite, I say, indite! How shall I begin? Odd's bullets and blades, I'll write in a good bold hand, however!

SIR LUCIUS. Pray, compose yourself.

ACRES. Come now, shall I begin with an oath? Do, Sir Lucius, let me begin with a damn?

SIR LUCIUS. Pho, pho! Do the thing decently and like a Christian. Begin now. (*Dictating*) "Sir—"

ACRES. That's too civil by half.

SIR LUCIUS. "To prevent the confusion that might arise—"

ACRES (*writing*). Well—

SIR LUCIUS. "—from our both addressing the same lady—"

ACRES. Aye, there's the reason, "same lady." Well—

SIR LUCIUS. "—I shall expect the honor of your company—"

ACRES. Zounds! I'm not asking him to dinner.

SIR LUCIUS. Pray, be easy.

ACRES. Well, then, "honor of your company—"

SIR LUCIUS. "—to settle our pretensions—"

ACRES. Well—

SIR LUCIUS. Let me see. Aye, King's Mead Fields will do. "—in King's Mead Fields."

ACRES. So, that's done. Well, I'll fold it up presently. My own crest, a hand and a dagger, shall be the seal.

SIR LUCIUS. You see now this little explanation will put a stop at once to all confusion or misunderstanding that might arise between you?

ACRES. Aye, we fight to prevent any misunderstanding.

SIR LUCIUS. Now, I'll leave you to fix your own time. Take my advice and you'll do it this evening if you can. Then, let the worst come of it, 'twill be off your mind tomorrow.

ACRES. Very true.

SIR LUCIUS. So I shall see nothing more of you, unless it be by letter, 'til the evening. I would do myself the honor to carry your message but, to tell you a secret, I believe I shall have just such another affair on my own hands. There is a gay captain here who put a jest on me lately at the expense of my country and I want to fall in with the gentleman to call him out.

ACRES. By my valor, I should like to see you fight first! Odd's life, I should like to see you kill him, if it was only to get a little lesson!

SIR LUCIUS. I shall be very proud of instructing you. Well, for the present. (*Bows*) But remember now, when you meet your antagonist do everything in a mild and agreeable manner. Let your courage be as keen, but at the same time as polished, as your sword. (*Exit* SIR LUCIUS, *leaving* ACRES *to ponder his fate.*)

ACT FOUR

Scene 1

ACRES' *lodgings.* ACRES *and* DAVID *are talking.*

DAVID. Then, by the mass, sir, I would do no such thing! Ne'er a Sir Lucius O'Trigger in the kingdom should make me fight when I wa'n't so minded. Oons, what will the old lady say when she hears o't?

ACRES. Ah, David, if you had heard Sir Lucius! Odd's sparks and flames, he would have roused your valor!

DAVID. Not he, indeed, I hates such bloodthirsty cormorants.[27] Look'ee, master, if you'd wanted a bout at boxing, quarter-staff or short staff, I should never be the man to bid you cry off. But for your curst sharps and snaps,[28] I never knew any good come of 'em.

ACRES. But my honor, David, my honor. I must be very careful of my honor.

DAVID. Aye, by the mass, and I would be very careful of it.

[27] **cormorants:** insatiably greedy or predatory people.

[28] **sharps and snaps:** rapiers and pistols.

And I think in return my honor couldn't do less than to be very careful of me.

ACRES. Odd's blades, David, no gentleman will ever risk the loss of his honor!

DAVID. I say then, it would be but civil in honor never to risk the loss of a gentleman. Look'ee, master, this honor seems to me to be a marvelous false friend, aye, truly, a very courtier-like servant. Put the case I was a gentleman—which, thank God, no one can say of me. Well, my honor makes me quarrel with another gentleman of my acquaintance. So, we fight. Pleasant enough, that. Boh! I kill him—the more's my luck! Now, pray, who gets the profit of it? Why, my honor. But put the case that he kills me! By the mass, I go to the worms and my honor whips over to my enemy!

ACRES. No, David, in that case—odd's crowns and laurels!—your honor follows you to the grave.

DAVID. Now, that's just the place where I could make a shift to do without it.

ACRES. Zounds, David, you are a coward! It doesn't become my valor to listen to you. What, shall I disgrace my ancestors? Think of that, David! Think what it would be to disgrace my ancestors!

DAVID. Under favor, the surest way of not disgracing them is to keep as long as you can out of their company. Look'ee, now, master, to go to them in such haste, with an ounce of lead in your brains—I should think that might as well be let alone. Our ancestors are very good kind of folks but they are the last people I should choose to have a visiting acquaintance with.

ACRES. But, David, now, you don't think there is such very, very, *very* great danger, hey? Odd's life, people often fight without any mischief done.

DAVID. By the mass, I think 'tis ten to one against you! Oons! Here to meet some lion-headed fellow, I warrant, with his damned double-barrelled swords and cut-and-thrust pistols! Lord bless us, it makes me tremble to think o't. Those be such desperate, bloody-minded weapons! Well, I never could abide 'em, from a child I never could fancy 'em. I suppose there a'n't been so merciless a beast in the world as your loaded pistol!

ACRES. Zounds, I won't be afraid! Odd's fire and fury, you shan't make me afraid! (*Flourishing the letter.*) Here is the challenge and I have sent for my dear friend Jack Absolute to carry it for me!

DAVID. Aye, in the name of mischief, let him be the messenger. For my part, I wouldn't lend a hand to it for the best horse in your stable. By the mass, it don't look like another letter. It is, as I may say, a designing and malicious-looking letter and I warrant it smells of gunpowder like a soldier's pouch. Oons! I wouldn't swear it mayn't go off!

ACRES. Out, you poltroon! You ha'n't the valor of a grasshopper.

DAVID. Well, I say no more, 'twill be sad news, to be sure, at Clod Hall. But I ha' done. (*Whimpering*) How Phyllis will howl when she hears of it! Aye, poor bitch, she little thinks what shooting her master's going after. And I warrant old Crop, who has carried your honor, field and road, these ten years, will curse the hour he was born.

ACRES. It won't do, David. I am determined to fight, so get along, you coward, while I'm in the mind.

Enter a SERVANT.

SERVANT. Captain Absolute, sir.

ACRES. Oh, show him up.

Exit SERVANT.

DAVID. Well, heaven send we be all alive this time tomorrow.

ACRES. What's that? Don't provoke me, David.

DAVID. Good-by, master.

ACRES. Get along you cowardly, dastardly, croaking raven! (ACRES *chases* DAVID *out of the room, nearly capsizing* JACK, *who has just come in the door.*)

JACK. What's the matter, Bob?

ACRES. A vile, sheep-hearted blockhead. If I hadn't the valor of St. George and the dragon to boot—

JACK. But what do you want with me, Bob?

ACRES. Oh. (*Presenting the challenge.*) There!

ABSOLUTE (*to himself*). "To Ensign Beverley." So, what's going on now. (*To* ACRES) Well, what's this?

ACRES. A challenge!

JACK. Indeed! Why, you won't fight him, will you, Bob?

ACRES. Egad, but I will, Jack. Sir Lucius has wrought me to it. He has left me full of rage and I'll fight this evening that so much good passion mayn't be wasted.

JACK. But what have I to do with this?

ACRES. Why, as I think you know something of the fellow, I want you to find him out for me and give him this mortal defiance.

JACK. Well, give it to me and trust me he gets it.

ACRES. Thank you, my dear friend, my dear Jack. (*Pause*) But it is giving you a great deal of trouble.

JACK. Not in the least, I beg you won't mention it. No trouble in the world, I assure you.

ACRES. You are very kind. What it is to have a friend. (*Pause*) You couldn't be my second, could you, Jack?

JACK. Why no, Bob, not in this affair, it would not be quite so proper.

ACRES. Well, then, I must get my friend Sir Lucius. I shall have your good wishes, however, Jack?

JACK. Whenever he meets you, believe me.

Enter SERVANT.

SERVANT. Sir Anthony Absolute is below inquiring for the captain.

JACK. I'll come instantly.

Exit SERVANT.

JACK. Well, my little hero, success attend you. (*He starts for the door.*)

ACRES. Stay, stay, Jack. If Beverley should ask you what kind of a man your friend Acres is, do tell him I am a devil of a fellow, will you, Jack?

JACK. To be sure I shall. I'll say you are a determined dog, hey, Bob?

ACRES. Aye, aye, do, and if that frightens him, egad, perhaps he mayn't come. So tell him I generally kill a man a week, will you, Jack?

JACK. I will, I will. I'll say you are called in the country Fighting Bob.

ACRES. Right, right, 'tis all to prevent mischief, for I don't want to take his life if I clear my honor.

JACK. No. That's very kind of you.

ACRES. Why, you don't wish me to kill him, do you, Jack?

JACK. No, upon my soul, I do not. (*Starting to go.*) But a devil of a fellow, hey?

ACRES. True, true. But stay, stay, Jack. You may add that you never saw me in such a rage before, a most devouring rage.

JACK. I will, I will.

ACRES. Remember, Jack, a determined dog!

JACK (*as he leaves*). Aye, aye, Fighting Bob!

ACRES *thinks a moment and then stalks the room, growling terribly.*

SCENE 2

MRS. MALAPROP'S *lodgings.* LYDIA *enters, followed by* MRS. MALAPROP.

MRS. MALAPROP. Why, thou perverse one! Tell me what you can object to him? Isn't he a handsome man, tell me that? A genteel man? A pretty figure of a man?

LYDIA (*to herself*). She little thinks whom she is praising. So is Beverley, ma'am.

MRS. MALAPROP. No caparisons, miss, if you please. Caparisons don't become a young woman. No, Captain Absolute is indeed a fine gentleman.

LYDIA (*to herself*). Aye, the Captain Absolute *you* have seen.

MRS. MALAPROP. Then he's so well bred, so full of alacrity and adulation. And has so much to say for himself, in such good language. His physiognomy so grammatical! Then his presence is so noble! I protest, when I saw him I thought of what Hamlet says in the play—"Hesperian curls, the front of Job himself, an eye like March to threaten at command, a station like Harry Mercury, new—"[29] something about kissing—on a hill. However, the similitude struck me directly.

LYDIA (*to herself*). How enraged she'll be presently when she discovers her mistake!

Enter SERVANT.

[29] **Hesperian . . . new:** *Hamlet*, III, iv, 56–59.

SERVANT. Sir Anthony and Captain Absolute are below, ma'am.

MRS. MALAPROP. Show them up here.

Exit SERVANT

MRS. MALAPROP. Now, Lydia, I insist on your behaving as becomes a young woman. Show your good breeding, at least, though you have forgotten your duty.

LYDIA. Madam, I have told you my resolution. I shall not only give him no encouragement but I won't even speak to or look at him. (LYDIA *flings herself into a chair facing the wall. At this moment,* SIR ANTHONY *hauls* JACK *into the room.*)

SIR ANTHONY. Here we are, Mrs. Malaprop, come to mitigate the frowns of unrelenting beauty. And difficulty enough I had to bring this fellow. I don't know what's the matter but if I had not held him by force he'd have given me the slip.

MRS. MALAPROP. You have infinite trouble, Sir Anthony, in the affair. I am ashamed for my cause. (*To* LYDIA, *whispering*) Lydia, Lydia, rise I beseech you, pay your respects!

SIR ANTHONY. I hope, madam, that Miss Languish has reflected on the worth of this gentleman and the regard due to her aunt's choice and my alliance. (*Whispers to* JACK) Now, Jack, speak to her.

JACK (*to himself*). What the devil shall I do? (*Whispers to* SIR ANTHONY) You see, sir, she won't even look at me whilst you are here. I knew she wouldn't, I told you so. Let me entreat you, sir, to leave us together. (JACK *continues to whisper to* SIR ANTHONY.)

LYDIA (*to herself*). I wonder I ha'n't heard my aunt exclaim yet. Sure she can't have looked at him. Perhaps their regimentals are alike and she is something blind.

SIR ANTHONY. I say, sir, I won't stir a foot.

MRS. MALAPROP. I am sorry to say, Sir Anthony, that my affluence over my niece is very small. Turn round, Lydia, I blush for you.

SIR ANTHONY. May I not flatter myself that Miss Languish will assign what cause of dislike she can have to my son? (*To* JACK, *in a whisper*) Why don't you begin, Jack? Speak, you puppy, speak!

MRS. MALAPROP. It is impossible, Sir Anthony, she can have

any. She will not say she has. (*Whispers*) Answer, hussy, why don't you answer?

SIR ANTHONY. Then, madam, I trust that a childish and hasty predilection will be no bar to Jack's happiness. (*Whispers*) Zounds, sirrah, why don't you speak?

LYDIA (*to herself*). I think my lover seems as little inclined to conversation as myself. How strangely blind my aunt must be!

JACK (*trying to speak to* LYDIA). Hem, hem, madam—hem! (*Whispers*) Faith, sir, I am so confounded, and so—so—confused. I told you I should be so, sir, I knew it. The—the tremor of my passion entirely takes away my presence of mind.

SIR ANTHONY. But it don't take away your voice, fool, does it? Go up and speak to her directly.

Over SIR ANTHONY'*s head,* JACK *frantically signals* MRS. MALAPROP *to leave him alone with* LYDIA.

MRS. MALAPROP. Sir Anthony, shall we leave them together? (*Whispers*) Ah, you stubborn little vixen!

SIR ANTHONY. Not yet, ma'am, not yet. (*Whispers*) What the devil are you at? Unlock your jaws, sirrah, or—

JACK *moves reluctantly in* LYDIA'*s direction.*

JACK (*to himself*). Now heaven send she may be too sullen to look round! I must disguise my voice. (*Speaking in a low, hoarse voice.*) Will not Miss Languish lend an ear to the mild accents of true love? Will not—

SIR ANTHONY. What the devil ails the fellow? Why don't you speak out, not stand croaking like a frog in a quinsy?[30]

JACK (*hoarsely*). The—the excess of my awe and my—my—my modesty quite choke me!

SIR ANTHONY. Ah, your modesty again! I'll tell you what, Jack. If you don't speak out directly and glibly, too, I shall be in such a rage! Mrs. Malaprop, I wish the lady would favor us with something more than a side-front.

MRS. MALAPROP *shakes and scolds* LYDIA *to no avail.*

[30] **in a quinsy**: with tonsillitis.

JACK (*to himself*). So, all will out, I see.

As MRS. MALAPROP *moves away from* LYDIA *in despair,* JACK *whispers to her in his own voice.*

JACK. Be not surprised, my Lydia, suppress all surprise at present.

LYDIA (*to herself*). Heavens, 'tis Beverley's voice! Sure, he can't have imposed on Sir Anthony, too! (*She turns her head slowly, then jumps to her feet, exclaiming*) Is this possible? My Beverley! How can this be? My Beverley!

JACK. Ah, 'tis all over!

SIR ANTHONY. Beverley! The devil! Beverley! What can the girl mean? This is my son, Jack Absolute!

MRS. MALAPROP. For shame hussy, for shame! Your head runs so on that fellow that you have him always in your eyes. Beg Captain Absolute's pardon directly.

LYDIA. I see no Captain Absolute, but my loved Beverley!

SIR ANTHONY. Zounds, the girl's mad! Her brain's turned by reading!

MRS. MALAPROP. O' my conscience, I believe so. What do you mean by Beverley, hussy? You saw Captain Absolute before today. There he is, your husband that shall be.

LYDIA. With all my soul, ma'am. When I refuse my Beverley—

SIR ANTHONY. Oh, she's as mad as Bedlam! Or has this fellow been playing us a rogue's trick? Come here, sirrah, who the devil are you?

JACK. Faith, sir, I am not quite clear myself. But I'll endeavor to recollect.

SIR ANTHONY. Are you my son or not? Answer for your mother, you dog, if you won't for me!

MRS. MALAPROP. Aye, sir, who are you? Oh, mercy, I begin to suspect—

JACK (*to himself*). Ye powers of impudence, befriend me! Sir Anthony, most assuredly I am your wife's son and that I sincerely believe myself to be yours also, I hope my duty has always shown. Mrs. Malaprop, I am your most respectful admirer and shall be proud to add affectionate nephew. I need not tell my Lydia that she sees her faithful Beverley who, knowing the singular generosity of her temper, assumed that name and a station which has proved a test of the most disinterested love, which he now hopes to enjoy in a more elevated character.

LYDIA (*sullenly*). So! There will be no elopement after all!

SIR ANTHONY. Upon my soul, Jack, thou art a very impudent fellow. To do you justice, I think I never saw a piece of more consummate assurance.

JACK. Oh, you flatter me, sir, you compliment. 'Tis my modesty, you know, sir, my modesty that has stood in my way.

SIR ANTHONY. Well, I am glad you are not the dull, insensible varlet you pretended to be, however. I'm glad you have made a fool of your father, you dog, I am. So this was your penitence, your duty, and obedience. I thought it was damned sudden! You never heard their names before, not you! What, the Languishes of Worcestershire, hey? If you could please me in the affair, 'twas all you desired! Ah, you dissembling villain! What? (*Pointing to* LYDIA.) She squints, don't she? A little red-haired girl, hey? Why, you hypocritical young rascal, I wonder you an't ashamed to hold up your head!

JACK. 'Tis with difficulty, sir, I *am* confused, very much confused, as you must perceive.

MRS. MALAPROP. Oh, lud, Sir Anthony, a new light breaks in upon me! Hey! How! What! Captain! Did *you* write the letters, then? What? Am I to thank *you* for the elegant compilation of "an old weather-beaten she-dragon," hey? Oh, mercy! Was it *you* that reflected on my parts of speech?

JACK (*appealing to* SIR ANTHONY). Dear sir, my modesty will be overpowered at last, if you don't assist me. I shall certainly not be able to stand it.

SIR ANTHONY. Come, come, Mrs. Malaprop, we must forget and forgive. Odd's life, matters have taken so clever a turn all of a sudden that I could find in my heart to be so good-humored! And so gallant! (*Stalking* MRS. MALAPROP.) Hey, Mrs. Malaprop?

MRS. MALAPROP (*staying a step ahead of* SIR ANTHONY). Well, Sir Anthony, since *you* desire it, we will not anticipate the past. So mind, young people, our retrospection will now be all to the future.

SIR ANTHONY. Come, we must leave them together, Mrs. Malaprop, they long to fly into each other's arms, I warrant.

Jack, isn't the cheek as I said, hey? And the eye, you rogue, and the lip, hey? Come, Mrs. Malaprop, we'll not disturb their tenderness. Theirs is the time of life for happiness! (*Sings*) "Youth's the season made for joy—" (*Dances*) Hey! Odd's life, I'm in such spirits, I don't know what I could not do. (*Offers his arm to* MRS. MALAPROP.) Permit me, ma'am. (*Sings*) Tol-de-rol—gad, I should like to have a little fooling myself—tol-de-rol-de-rol! (SIR ANTHONY *skips out of the room, giddily accompanied by* MRS. MALAPROP. LYDIA *sits sullenly in her chair.*)

JACK (*to himself*). So much thought bodes me no good. So grave, Lydia?

LYDIA. Sir?

JACK (*to himself*). So, egad, I thought as much. That damned monosyllable has froze me! What, Lydia, now that we are as happy in our friends' consent as in our mutual vows—

LYDIA (*peevishly*). Friends' consent, indeed!

JACK. Come, come, we must lay aside some of our romance. A little wealth and comfort may be endured, after all. And for your fortune, the lawyers shall make such settlements as—

LYDIA. Lawyers! I hate lawyers!

JACK. Nay, then, we will not wait for their lingering forms, but instantly procure the license and—

LYDIA. The license! I hate license!

JACK. Oh, my love, be not so unkind. (*Kneels*) Thus let me entreat—

LYDIA. Pshaw! What signifies kneeling when you know I *must* have you?

JACK (*rising*). Nay, madam, there shall be no constraint upon your inclinations, I promise you. If I have lost your heart, I resign the rest. (*To himself*) Gad, I must try what a little spirit will do.

LYDIA (*rising*). Then, sir, let me tell you, the interest you had there was acquired by a mean, unmanly imposition and deserves the punishment of fraud. What, you have been treating me like a child! Humoring my romance! And laughing, I suppose, at your success!

JACK. You wrong me, Lydia, you wrong me, only hear—

LYDIA. So, while *I* fondly imagined we were deceiving my

relations and flattered myself that I should outwit and incense them all, behold—my hopes are to be crushed at once by my aunt's consent and approbation, and I am myself the only dupe at last! (*Walking about in a fury.*) But here, sir, here is the picture—(*taking a miniature from her bosom*) Beverley's picture, which I have worn night and day, in spite of threats and entreaties. (*Flings it at him.*) There, sir, and be assured I throw the original from my heart as easily.

JACK. Nay, nay, ma'am, we will not differ as to that. (*Removing a picture from inside his shirt.*) Here, here is Miss Lydia Languish. What a difference! Aye, *there* is the heavenly assenting smile that first gave soul and spirit to my hopes! Those are the lips which sealed a vow as yet scarce dry in Cupid's calendar. And there the half-resentful blush that would have checked the ardor of my thanks. Well, all that's past, all over indeed! There, madam, in beauty that copy is not equal to you, but in my mind its merit over the original, in being still the same, is such that I—(*puts back the picture*)—I cannot find in my heart to part with it.

LYDIA (*softening*). 'Tis your own doing, sir. I—I—I suppose you are perfectly satisfied.

JACK. Oh, most certainly. Sure now, this is much better than being in love! Ha, ha, ha! There's some spirit in this! What signifies breaking some scores of solemn promises? All that's of no consequence, you know. To be sure, people will say that Miss didn't know her own mind. But never mind that. Or, perhaps, they may be ill-natured enough to hint that the gentleman grew tired of the lady and forsook her. But don't let that fret you.

LYDIA (*bursting into tears*). There's no bearing his insolence!

Enter MRS. MALAPROP *and* SIR ANTHONY.

MRS. MALAPROP. Come, we must interrupt your billing and cooing a while.

LYDIA (*sobbing*). This is worse than your treachery and deceit, you base ingrate.

SIR ANTHONY. What the devil's the matter now? Zounds, Mrs. Malaprop, this is the oddest billing and cooing I ever heard! But what the deuce is the meaning of it? I'm quite astonished!

JACK. Ask the lady, sir.

MRS. MALAPROP. Oh, mercy! I'm quite analyzed, for my part! Why, Lydia, what is the reason of this?

LYDIA. Ask the gentleman, ma'am.

SIR ANTHONY. Zounds, I shall be in a frenzy! Why, Jack, you are not come out to be anyone else, are you?

MRS. MALAPROP. Aye, sir, there's no more trick, is there? You are not like Cerberus,[31] three gentlemen at once, are you?

JACK. You'll not let me speak. I say the lady can account for this much better than I can.

LYDIA. Ma'am, you once commanded me never to think of Beverley again. There is the man. I now obey you. For, from this moment I renounce him forever. (*Exit.*)

MRS. MALAPROP. Oh, mercy and miracles! What a turn here is. Why, sure, captain, you haven't behaved disrespectfully to my niece?

SIR ANTHONY. Ha, ha, ha! Ha, ha, ha! Now I see it. Ha, ha, ha! Now I see it. You have been too lively, Jack!

JACK. Nay, sir, upon my word—

SIR ANTHONY. Come, no lying, Jack, I'm sure 'twas so!

MRS. MALAPROP. Oh, lud, Sir Anthony! Oh, fie, captain!

JACK. Upon my soul, ma'am—

SIR ANTHONY. Come, no excuses, Jack. Why, your father, you rogue, was so before you. The blood of the Absolutes was always impatient. Ha, ha, ha, poor little Lydia! Why, you've frightened her, you dog, you have!

JACK. By all that's good, sir—

SIR ANTHONY. Zounds, say no more, I tell you. Mrs. Malaprop shall make your peace. You must make his peace, Mrs. Malaprop. You must tell her 'tis Jack's way, tell her 'tis all our ways, it runs in the blood of the family! Come away, Jack. Ha, ha, ha! Mrs. Malaprop, a young villain! (*Propels himself and* JACK *out the door.*)

MRS. MALAPROP (*horror-struck*). Oh, Sir Anthony! Oh, fie, captain!

[31] **Cerberus:** three-headed watch dog of the underworld, in Greek and Latin mythology.

Scene 3

The North Parade. Enter SIR LUCIUS O'TRIGGER.

SIR LUCIUS. I wonder where this Captain Absolute hides himself. Upon my conscience, these officers are always in one's way in love affairs. I remember I might have married Lady Dorothy Carmine, if it had not been for a little rogue of a major who ran away with her before she could get a sight of me! And I wonder, too, what it is the ladies can see in them to be so fond of them, unless it be a touch of the old serpent in 'em that makes the little creatures be caught like vipers with a bit of red cloth. Hah! Isn't this the captain coming? Faith, it is. There is a probability of succeeding about that fellow that is mighty provoking. Who the devil is he talking to? (*He steps aside.*)

JACK *enters, talking to himself.*

JACK. To what fine purpose I have been plotting! A noble reward for all my schemes, upon my soul. A little gypsy! I did not think her romance could have made her so damned absurd, either. 'Sdeath, I never was in a worse humor in my life. I could cut my own throat, or any other person's, with the greatest pleasure in the world!

SIR LUCIUS (*concealed*). Oh, faith, I'm in the luck of it. I never could have found him in a sweeter temper for my purpose. To be sure, I'm come in the nick! Now to enter into conversation with him and so quarrel genteely. (*He goes up to* JACK.) With regard to that matter, captain, I must beg leave to differ in opinion with you.

JACK. Upon my word, then, you must be a very subtle disputant, because, sir, I happened just then to be giving no opinion at all.

SIR LUCIUS. That's no reason. For give me leave to tell you, a man may *think* an untruth as well as speak one.

JACK. Very true, sir, but if a man never utters his thoughts, I should think they might stand a chance of escaping controversy.

SIR LUCIUS. Then, sir, you differ in opinion with me, which amounts to the same thing.

JACK. Hark'ee, Sir Lucius, if I had not before known you to be a gentleman, upon my soul, I should not have discovered it at this interview. For what you can drive at, unless you mean to quarrel with me, I cannot conceive!

SIR LUCIUS. I humbly thank you, sir, for the quickness of your apprehension. (*Bowing*) You have named the very thing I would be at.

JACK. Very well, sir, I shall certainly not balk your inclinations but I should be glad you would please to explain your motives.

SIR LUCIUS. Pray, sir, be easy. The quarrel is a very pretty quarrel as it stands. We should only spoil it by trying to explain it. However, your memory is very short or you could not have forgot an affront you passed on me within this week. So, no more, but name your time and place.

JACK. Well, sir, since you are so bent on it, the sooner, the better. Let it be this evening, here by the Spring Gardens. We shall scarcely be interrupted.

SIR LUCIUS. Faith, that same interruption in affairs of this nature shows very great ill breeding. I don't know what's the reason but in England, if a thing of this kind gets wind, people make such a pother that a gentleman can never fight in peace and quietness. However, if it's the same to you, captain, I should take it as a particular kindness if you'd let us meet in King's Mead Fields, as a little business will call me there about six o'clock and I may dispatch both matters at once.

JACK. 'Tis the same to me, exactly. A little after six, then, we will discuss this matter more seriously.

SIR LUCIUS. If you please, sir, there will be very pretty smallsword light, tho't won't do for a long shot. So that matter's settled and my mind's at ease. (*Exit.*)

Enter FAULKLAND.

JACK. Well met, I was going to look for you. Oh, Faulkland, all the demons of spite and disappointment have conspired against me. I'm so vexed that if I had not the prospect of a resource in being knocked o' the head by and by, I should scarce have spirits to tell you the cause!

FAULKLAND. What can you mean? Has Lydia changed her

mind? I should have thought her duty and inclination would now have pointed to the same object.

JACK. Aye, just as the eyes do of a person who squints. When her love eye was fixed on me, t'other—her eye of duty—was finely obliqued! But when duty bid her point that the same way, off t'other turned on a swivel and secured its retreat with a frown!

FAULKLAND. But what's the resource you—

JACK. Oh, to wind up the whole, a good-natured Irishman here has begged leave to have the pleasure of cutting my throat and I mean to indulge him, that's all.

FAULKLAND. Prithee, be serious.

JACK. 'Tis fact, upon my soul. Sir Lucius O'Trigger—you know him by sight—for some affront which I am sure I never intended has obliged me to meet him this evening at six o'clock. 'Tis on that account I wished to see you. You must go with me.

FAULKLAND. Nay, there must be some mistake, sure. Sir Lucius shall explain himself and I dare say matters may be accommodated. But this evening, did you say? I wish it had been any other time.

JACK. Why? There will be light enough. There will, as Sir Lucius says, "be very pretty smallsword light, tho't will not do for a long shot." Confound his long shots!

FAULKLAND. But I am myself a good deal ruffled by a difference I have had with Julia. My vile tormenting temper has made me treat her so cruelly that I shall not be myself 'til we are reconciled.

JACK. By heavens, Faulkland, you don't deserve her.

Enter SERVANT, *who gives* FAULKLAND *a letter and leaves.*

FAULKLAND. Oh, Jack, this is from Julia! I dread to open it. I fear it may be to take a last leave, perhaps to bid me return her letters and restore—oh, how I suffer for my folly!

JACK. Here, let me see. (*Takes the letter and opens it.*) Aye, a final sentence, indeed. 'Tis all over with you, faith!

FAULKLAND. Nay, Jack, don't keep me in suspense.

JACK. Hear, then. (*Reads*) "As I am convinced that my dear Faulkland's own reflections have already upbraided him for his last unkindness to me, I will not add a word on this subject. I wish to speak with you as soon as possible. Yours ever and truly, Julia." There's stubbornness and resentment for you! (*Gives* FAULKLAND *the letter.*) Why, man, you don't seem one whit the happier at this!

FAULKLAND. Oh, yes, I am, but—but—

JACK. Confound your "buts." You never hear anything that would make another man bless himself but you immediately damn it with a "but."

FAULKLAND. Now, Jack, as you are my friend, own honestly. Don't you think there is something forward, something indelicate in this haste to forgive? Women should never sue for reconciliation. That should always come from us. They should retain their coldness 'til wooed to kindness, and their pardon, like their love, should "not unsought be won."

JACK. I have not patience to listen to you! Thou'rt incorrigible! So say no more on the subject. I must go to settle a few matters. Let me see you before six, remember, at my lodgings. A poor, industrious devil like me, who have toiled and drudged and plotted to gain my ends and am at last disappointed by other people's folly may in pity be allowed to swear and grumble a little. (*Looking keenly at* FAULKLAND.) But a captious skeptic in love, a slave to fretfulness and whim, who has no difficulties but of his own creating, is a subject more fit for ridicule than compassion! (*Exit.*)

FAULKLAND. I feel his reproaches, yet I would not change this too exquisite nicety for the gross content with which he tramples on the thorns of love. His engaging me in this duel has started an idea in my head which I will instantly pursue. I'll use it as the touchstone of Julia's sincerity and disinterestedness. If her love prove pure and sterling ore, my name will rest on it with honor and once I've stamped it there I lay aside my doubts forever. But if the dross of selfishness, the ally of pride predominate, 'twill be best to leave her as a toy for some less cautious fool to sigh for. (*Exit.*)

ACT FIVE

SCENE 1

JULIA *is alone in her sitting room.*

JULIA. How this message has alarmed me! What dreadful accident can he mean? Why such charge to be alone? Oh, Faulkland, how many unhappy moments, how many tears you cost me!

Enter FAULKLAND, *wrapped in a large cloak.*

JULIA. What means this? Why this caution, Faulkland?

FAULKLAND. Alas, Julia, I am come to take a long farewell.

JULIA. Heavens, what do you mean?

FAULKLAND. You see before you a wretch whose life is forfeited. Nay, start not! The infirmity of my temper has drawn all this misery on me. I left you fretful and passionate. An untoward accident drew me into a quarrel. The event is that I must fly this kingdom instantly. Oh, Julia, had I been so fortunate as to have called you mine entirely before this mischance had fallen on me I should not so deeply dread my banishment.

JULIA. My soul is oppressed with sorrow at the nature of your misfortune. Had these adverse circumstances arisen from a less fatal cause, I should have felt strong comfort in the thought that I could now chase from your bosom every doubt of the warm sincerity of my love. My heart has long known no other guardian. (*Making a decision.*) I now entrust my person to your honor—we will fly together! When safe from pursuit, my father's will may be fulfilled and I receive a legal claim to be the partner of your sorrows and tenderest comforter. Then, on the bosom of your wedded Julia, you may lull your keen regret to slumbering, while virtuous love, with a cherub's hand, shall smooth the brow of upbraiding thought and pluck the thorn from compunction.

FAULKLAND. Oh, Julia, I am bankrupt in gratitude! But the time is so pressing, it calls on you for so hasty a resolution. Would you not wish some hours to weigh the advantages you forego and what little compensation poor Faulkland can make you beside his solitary love?

JULIA. I ask not a moment. No, Faulkland, I have loved you for yourself and if I now, more than ever, prize the solemn engagement which so long has pledged us to each other, it is because it leaves no room for hard aspersions on my fame and puts the seal of duty to an act of love. But let us not linger. Perhaps this delay—

FAULKLAND. 'Twill be better I should not venture out again 'til dark. Yet am I grieved to think what numberless distresses will press heavy on your gentle disposition.

JULIA. Perhaps your fortune may be forfeited by this unhappy act. I know not whether 'tis so. But, sure, that alone can never make us unhappy. The little I have will be sufficient to support us and exile never should be splendid.

FAULKLAND. Aye, but in such an abject state of life my wounded pride, perhaps, may increase the natural fretfulness of my temper 'til I become a rude, morose companion, beyond your patience to endure. Perhaps the recollection of a deed my conscience cannot justify may haunt me in such gloomy and unsocial fits that I shall hate the tenderness that would relieve me, break from your arms and quarrel with your fondness.

JULIA. If your thoughts should assume so unhappy a bent, you will the more want some mild and affectionate spirit to watch over and console you, one who, by bearing your infirmities with gentleness and resignation, may teach you so to bear the evils of your fortune.

FAULKLAND (*flinging off his cloak*). Julia, I have proved you to the quick and with this useless device I throw away all my doubts! How shall I plead to be forgiven this last unworthy effect of my restless, unsatisfied disposition?

JULIA (*staring at him*). Has no such disaster happened as you related?

FAULKLAND. I am ashamed to own that it was all pretended. Yet in pity, Julia, do not kill me with resenting a fault which never can be repeated, but sealing, this once, my pardon, let me tomorrow, in face of heaven, receive my future guide and monitress and expiate my past folly by years of tender adoration. (*He starts to embrace her.*)

JULIA (*preventing him*). Hold, Faulkland! That you are free from a crime which before I feared to name, heaven knows how sincerely I rejoice. These are tears of thankfulness for that. But that your cruel doubts should have urged you to an imposition that has wrung my heart gives me now a pang more keen than I can express!

FAULKLAND (*astonished*). By heavens, Julia—

JULIA. Yet hear me! My father loved you, Faulkland, and you preserved the life that tender parent gave me. In his presence I pledged my hand, joyfully pledged it, where before I had given my heart. When, soon after, I lost that parent, it seemed to me that Providence had, in Faulkland, shown me whither to transfer, without a pause, my grateful duty as well as my affection. Hence I have been content to bear from you what pride and delicacy would have forbid me from another. I will not upbraid you by repeating how you have trifled with my sincerity—

FAULKLAND. I confess it all! Yet, hear—

JULIA. After such a year of trial, I might have flattered myself that I should not have been insulted with a new probation of my sincerity, as cruel as unnecessary. I now see it is not in your nature to be content or confident in love. With this conviction—I never will be yours! While I had hopes that my persevering attention and unreproaching kindness might in time reform your temper, I should have been happy to have gained a dearer influence over you. But I will not furnish you with a licensed power to keep alive an incorrigible fault at the expense of one who never would contend with you.

FAULKLAND. Nay, but Julia, by my soul and honor, if after this—

JULIA. But one word more! As my faith has once been given to you, I never will barter it with another. I shall pray for your happiness with the truest sincerity, and the dearest blessing I can ask of heaven to send you will be to charm you from that unhappy temper which alone has prevented the performance of our solemn engagement. All I request of you is that you will yourself reflect upon this infirmity, and when you number up the many true delights it has deprived you of, let it not be your least regret that it lost you the love of one—who would have followed you in beggary through the world! (*Exit.*)

FAULKLAND. She's gone! Forever! There was an awful resolution in her manner that riveted me to my place. Oh, fool! Dolt! Barbarian! Curst as I am with more imperfections than my fellow wretches, kind Fortune sent a heaven-gifted cherub to my aid and, like a ruffian, I have driven her from my side! I must now haste to my appointment. Well my mind is tuned for such a scene. I shall wish only to become a principal in it and reverse the tale my cursed folly put me upon forging here. Oh, love—tormentor! fiend!—whose influence, like the moon's, acting on men of dull souls makes idiots of them but, meeting subtler spirits, betrays their course and urges sensibility to madness! (*Exit.*)

Enter a MAID, *followed by* LYDIA.

MAID. My mistress, ma'am, I know was here just now. Perhaps she is only in the next room. (*Exits.*)

LYDIA. Heigh ho! Though he has used me so, this fellow runs strangely in my head. I believe one lecture from my grave cousin will make me recall him.

Enter JULIA.

LYDIA. Oh, Julia, I am come to you with such an appetite for consolation. Lud, child, what's the matter with you? You have been crying! I'll be hanged if that Faulkland has not been tormenting you.

JULIA. You mistake the cause of my uneasiness. Something has flurried me a little. Nothing you can guess at. (*To herself*) I would not accuse Faulkland to a sister.

LYDIA. Ah, whatever vexations you may have I can assure you mine surpass them. You know who Beverley proves to be?

JULIA. I will now own to you, Lydia, that Mr. Faulkland had before informed me of the whole affair. Had young Absolute been the person you took him for, I should not have accepted your confidence on the subject without a serious endeavor to counteract your caprice.

LYDIA. So then, I see I have been deceived by everyone! But I don't care, I'll never have him.

JULIA. Nay, Lydia—

LYDIA. Why, is it not provoking? When I thought we were coming to the prettiest distress imaginable, to find myself made a mere Smithfield bargain[32] of at last. There had I projected one of the most sentimental elopements! So becoming a disguise! So amiable a ladder of ropes! Conscious moon, four horses, Scotch parson, with such surprise to Mrs. Malaprop and such paragraphs in the newspapers! Oh, I shall die with disappointment.

JULIA. I don't wonder at it.

LYDIA. Now, sad reverse! What have I to expect but, after a deal of flimsy preparation, with a bishop's license, and my aunt's blessing, to go simpering up to the altar or perhaps be cried three times in a country church and have an unmannerly fat clerk ask the consent of every butcher in the parish to join John Absolute and Lydia Languish, spinster! Oh, that I should live to hear myself called spinster!

JULIA. Melancholy, indeed!

LYDIA. How mortifying to remember the dear delicious shifts I used to be put to, to gain half a minute's conversation with this fellow! How often have I stole forth in the coldest night in January and found him in the garden, stuck like a dripping statue! There would he kneel to me in the snow and sneeze and cough so pathetically, he shivering with cold and I with apprehension! And while the freezing blast numbed our joints, how warmly would he press me to pity his flame, and glow with mutual ardor! Ah, Julia, that was something like being in love!

JULIA. If I were in spirits, Lydia, I should chide you only by laughing heartily at you. But it suits more the situation of my mind, at present, earnestly to entreat you not to let a man who loves you with sincerity suffer that unhappiness from your caprice which I know too well caprice can inflict.

The excited voice of MRS. MALAPROP *is heard suddenly outside the door.*

LYDIA. Oh, lud, what has brought my aunt here?

Enter MRS. MALAPROP, FAG *and* DAVID.

MRS. MALAPROP. So, so, here's fine work, here's suicide, parri-

[32] **Smithfield bargain:** marriage for money.

cide and simulation going on in the fields! And Sir Anthony not to be found to prevent the antistrophe!

JULIA. For heaven's sake, madam, what's the meaning of this?

MRS. MALAPROP (*indicating* FAG). That gentleman can tell you, 'twas he enveloped the affair to me.

LYDIA. Do, sir, will you inform us?

FAG (*carefully*). Ma'am, I should hold myself very deficient in every requisite that forms the man of breeding if I delayed a moment to give all the information in my power to a lady so deeply interested in the affair as you are.

LYDIA. But quick, quick, sir!

FAG. True, ma'am, as you say, one should be quick in divulging matters of this nature, for should we be tedious, perhaps while we are flourishing on the subject two or three lives may be lost!

LYDIA. Oh, patience! Do, ma'am, for heaven's sake, tell us what is the matter?

MRS. MALAPROP. Why, murder's the matter! Slaughter's the matter! Killing's the matter! But he can tell you the perpendiculars.

LYDIA. Then, prithee, sir, be brief.

FAG. Why then, ma'am, as to murder, I cannot take upon me to say. And as to slaughter, or manslaughter, that will be as the jury finds it.

LYDIA. But who sir, who are engaged in this?

FAG. Faith, ma'am, one is a young gentleman whom I should be very sorry anything was to happen to, a very pretty-behaved gentleman! We have lived much together and always on terms.

LYDIA. But who is this? Who, who, who?

FAG. My master, ma'am, my master! I speak of my master!

LYDIA. Heavens! What, Captain Absolute?

MRS. MALAPROP. Oh, to be sure, you are frightened now!

JULIA. But who are with him, sir?

FAG. As to the rest, ma'am, this gentleman can inform you better than I. (*Points to* DAVID.)

JULIA. Do speak, friend.

DAVID. Look'ee, my lady, by the mass, there's mischief going on. Folks don't use to meet for amusement with firearms, firelocks, fire engines, fire screens, fire office and the devil knows what other crackers beside! This, my lady, I say, has an angry favor.

JULIA. But who is there beside Captain Absolute, friend?

DAVID. My poor master, under favor for mentioning him first. You know me, my lady, I am David and my master, of course, is—or was—Squire Acres. Then comes Squire Faulkland.

JULIA. Do, ma'am, let us instantly endeavor to prevent mischief!

MRS. MALAPROP. Oh, fie, it would be very inelegant in us. We should only participate things.

DAVID. Ah, do, Mrs. Aunt, save a few lives. They are desperately given, believe me. Above all, there is that bloodthirsty Philistine, Sir Lucius O'Trigger.

MRS. MALAPROP. Sir Lucius O'Trigger! Oh, mercy, have they drawn poor little dear Sir Lucius into the scrape? (*To* LYDIA) Why, how you stand, girl! You have no more feeling than one of the Derbyshire putrefactions![33]

LYDIA. What are we to do, madam?

MRS. MALAPROP. Why fly with the utmost felicity, to be sure, to prevent mischief! (*To* FAG) Here, friend, you can show us the place?

FAG. If you please, ma'am, I will conduct you. David, do you look for Sir Anthony.

DAVID *exits.*

MRS. MALAPROP. Come, girls, this gentleman will exhort us. Come, sir, you're our envoy. Lead the way and we'll precede!

FAG (*with a bow*). Not a step before the ladies for the world!

MRS. MALAPROP (*leaving, escorted by* LYDIA *and* JULIA). You're sure you know the spot.

FAG. I think I can find it, ma'am. And one good thing is we shall hear report of the pistols as we draw near so we can't well miss them. Never fear, ma'am, never fear! (*He follows them, talking.*)

[33] **Derbyshire putrefactions:** probably the petrifactions (fossils and unusual rock formations) characteristic of Derbyshire's limestone region.

Scene 2

The South Parade. JACK *is trying to hide a sword beneath a bulky coat.*

JACK. A sword seen in the streets of Bath would raise as great an alarm as a mad dog. How provoking this is in Faulkland! Never punctual! I shall be obliged to go without him at last.

SIR ANTHONY *comes up the street.*

JACK. Oh, the devil, here's Sir Anthony! How shall I escape him? (*He turns up his coat collar and walks away.*)

SIR ANTHONY (*stops to look at* JACK). How one may be deceived at a little distance! Only that I see he don't know me, I could have sworn that was Jack! (*Looks again.*) Hey, gad's life, it is! Why, Jack, what are you afraid of, hey? Sure, I'm right! Why, Jack, Jack Absolute! (*Catching up with* JACK.)

JACK. Really, sir, you have the advantage of me. I don't remember ever to have had the honor. My name is Saunderson, at your service.

SIR ANTHONY. Sir, I beg your pardon. I took you—hey! Why, zounds, it is! Stay! (*Pushes* JACK*'s collar aside.*) So, so, your humble servant, Mr. Saunderson! Why, you scoundrel, what tricks are you after now?

JACK. Oh, a joke, sir, a joke. I came here on purpose to look for you, sir.

SIR ANTHONY. You did? Well, I am glad you were so lucky. But what are you muffled up so for? (*Tugging at* JACK*'s coat.*) What's this for, hey?

JACK. 'Tis cool, sir, isn't it? Rather chilly somehow. But I shall be late. I have a particular engagement. (*Starts to go.*)

SIR ANTHONY. Stay. Why, I thought you were looking for me. Pray, Jack, where is't you are going?

JACK. Going, sir?

SIR ANTHONY. Aye. Where are you going?

JACK. Where am I going?

SIR ANTHONY. You unmannerly puppy!

JACK. I was going, sir, to, to, to—to Lydia, sir, to Lydia, to make matters up if I could. And I was looking for you, sir, to, to—

SIR ANTHONY. To go with you, I suppose. Well, come along.

JACK. Oh, zounds, no, sir, not for the world! I wished to meet with you, sir, to, to, to—you find it cool, I'm sure, sir, you'd better not stay out.

SIR ANTHONY. Cool! Not at all. Well, Jack, and what will you say to Lydia?

JACK. Oh, beg her pardon, humor her, promise and vow. But I detain you, sir. Consider the cold air on your gout.

SIR ANTHONY. Oh, not at all, not at all. I'm in no hurry. Ah, Jack, you youngsters, when once you are wounded here—(*claps his hand on* JACK'*s chest*) hey! What the deuce have you got here?

JACK. Nothing, sir, nothing.

SIR ANTHONY. What's this? Here's something damned hard.

JACK. Oh, trinkets, sir, trinkets. A bauble for Lydia.

SIR ANTHONY. Nay, let me see your taste. (*Opens* JACK'*s coat. The sword falls to the ground with a clatter.*) Trinkets! A bauble for Lydia! Zounds, sirrah, you are not going to cut her throat, are you?

JACK. Ha, ha, ha! I thought it would divert you, sir, though I didn't mean to tell you 'til afterwards.

SIR ANTHONY. You didn't? Yes, this is a very diverting trinket, truly.

JACK. Sir, I'll explain to you. You know, sir, Lydia is romantic, devilish romantic, and very absurd, of course. Now, sir, I intend, if she refuses to forgive me, to unsheath this sword and swear I'll fall upon its point and expire at her feet!

SIR ANTHONY. Fall upon a fiddle-stick's end! Why, I suppose it is the very thing that would please her. Get along, you fool.

JACK. Well, sir, you shall hear of my success, you shall hear. "Oh, Lydia, forgive me or this pointed steel—" says I.

SIR ANTHONY. "Oh, booby, stab away and welcome!" says she. Get along! And your damned trinkets!

JACK *hurries off in one direction as* DAVID *runs in from another.*

DAVID. Stop him, stop him! Murder! Thief! Fire! Stop fire, stop fire! Oh, Sir Anthony, call! Call, bid'm stop! Murder! Fire!

SIR ANTHONY. Fire? Murder? Where?

DAVID. Oons! He's out of sight and I'm out of breath, for my part! Oh, Sir Anthony, why didn't you stop him, why didn't you stop him?

SIR ANTHONY. Zounds, the fellow's mad! Stop whom? Stop Jack?

DAVID. Aye, the captain, sir. There's murder and slaughter—

SIR ANTHONY. Murder!

DAVID. Aye, please you, Sir Anthony, there's all kinds of murder, all sorts of slaughter to be seen in the fields. There's fighting going on, sir, bloody sword-and-gun fighting!

SIR ANTHONY. Who are going to fight, dunce?

DAVID. Everybody that I know of, Sir Anthony, everybody is going to fight. My poor master, Sir Lucius O'Trigger, your son, the captain—

SIR ANTHONY. Oh, the dog! I see his tricks. Do you know the place?

DAVID. King's Mead Fields.

SIR ANTHONY. You know the way?

DAVID. Not an inch. But I'll call the mayor, aldermen, constables, churchwardens and beadles. We can't be too many to part them.

SIR ANTHONY. Come along, give me your shoulder. We'll get assistance as we go. The lying villain! Well, I shall be in such a frenzy. So, this was the history of his trinkets. I'll bauble him!

DAVID *helps* SIR ANTHONY *hurry away to the battleground.*

SCENE 3

King's Mead Fields. SIR LUCIUS *and* ACRES *are rehearsing for the duel.*

ACRES. By my valor, then, Sir Lucius, forty yards is a good distance. Odd's levels and aims, I say it is a good distance.

SIR LUCIUS. Is it for muskets or small field pieces? Upon my conscience, Mr. Acres, you must leave those things to me. Stay now, I'll show you. (*Measures off five or six paces.*) There now, that is a very pretty distance, a pretty gentleman's distance.

ACRES. Zounds, we might as well fight in a sentry box! I tell you, Sir Lucius, the farther he is off, the cooler I shall take my aim.

SIR LUCIUS. Faith, then, I suppose you would aim at him best of all if he was out of sight?

ACRES. No, Sir Lucius, but I should think forty or eight-and-thirty yards.

SIR LUCIUS. Pho, pho! Nonsense! Three or four feet between the mouths of your pistols is as good as a mile!

ACRES. Odd's bullets, no! By my valor, there is no merit in killing him so near. Do, my dear Sir Lucius, let me bring him down at a long shot, a long shot, Sir Lucius, if you love me?

SIR LUCIUS. Well, the gentleman's friend and I must settle that. But tell me now, Mr. Acres, in case of an accident is there any little will or commission I could execute for you?

ACRES. I am much obliged to you, Sir Lucius, but I don't understand?

SIR LUCIUS. Why, you may think there's no being shot at without a little risk. And if an unlucky bullet should carry a quietus[34] with it, I say it will be no time to be bothering you about family matters.

ACRES. A quietus?

SIR LUCIUS. For instance, now, if that should be the case, would you choose to be pickled and sent home or would it be the same to you to lie here in the Abbey? I am told there is very snug lying, in the Abbey.

ACRES. Pickled! Snug lying in the Abbey! Odd's tremors, Sir Lucius, don't talk so!

SIR LUCIUS. I suppose, Mr. Acres, you never were engaged in an affair of this kind before?

ACRES. No, Sir Lucius, never before.

SIR LUCIUS. Ah, that's a pity. There's nothing like being used to a thing. Pray now, how would you receive the gentleman's shot?

ACRES. Odd's files, I've practiced that! (*He stands in profile.*) There, Sir Lucius, there, a side-front, hey? Odd, I'll make myself small enough. I'll stand edgeways.

[34] **quietus**: death.

SIR LUCIUS. Now, you're quite out, for if you stand so when I take my aim—(*levels the pistol at* ACRES).

ACRES. Zounds, Sir Lucius, are you sure it is not cocked?

SIR LUCIUS. Never fear.

ACRES. But, but, you don't know—it may go off of its own head!

SIR LUCIUS. Pho, be easy. Well, now, if I hit you in the body, my bullet has a double chance, for if it misses a vital part of your right side, 'twill be very hard if it don't succeed on the left!

ACRES. A vital part?

SIR LUCIUS (*adjusting* ACRES' *posture*). But there, fix yourself so, let him see the broadside of your full front, there! Now, a ball or two may pass clean through your body and never do any harm at all.

ACRES. Clean through me? A ball or two clean through me?

SIR LUCIUS. Aye, may they, and it is much the genteelest attitude into the bargain.

ACRES. Look'ee, Sir Lucius, I'd just as lief be shot in an awkward posture as a genteel one. So, by my valor, I will stand edgeways!

SIR LUCIUS (*looking at his watch*). Sure they don't mean to disappoint us. Hah! No, faith, I think I see them coming.

ACRES. Hey, what? Coming?

SIR LUCIUS. Aye. Who are those yonder getting over the stile?

ACRES. There are two of them, indeed! Well, let them come, hey, Sir Lucius? We—we—we—we won't run.

SIR LUCIUS. Run!

ACRES. No! I say, we won't run, by my valor!

SIR LUCIUS. What the devil's the matter with you?

ACRES. Nothing, nothing, my dear friend, my dear Sir Lucius. But I—I—I don't feel quite so bold, somehow, as I did.

SIR LUCIUS. Oh, fie, consider your honor!

ACRES. Aye, true, my honor. Do, Sir Lucius, edge in a word or two every now and then about my honor.

SIR LUCIUS. Well, here, they're coming.

ACRES. Sir Lucius, if I wa'n't with you, I should almost think I was afraid. If my valor should leave me! Valor will come and go!

SIR LUCIUS. Then, pray, keep it fast while you have it.

ACRES. Sir Lucius? I doubt it is going. Yes. My valor is certainly going! It is sneaking off! I feel it oozing out, as it were at the palms of my hands!

SIR LUCIUS. Your honor, your honor! Here they are.

Enter JACK *and* FAULKLAND.

SIR LUCIUS. Gentlemen, your most obedient. (*Bows*) Hah, Captain Absolute! So, I suppose, sir, you are come here, just like myself, to do a kind of office, first for your friend, then to proceed to business on your own account?

ACRES. What, Jack? My dear Jack! My dear friend!

JACK. Hark'ee, Bob, Beverley's at hand.

SIR LUCIUS. Well, Mr. Acres, I don't blame your saluting the gentleman civilly. (*To* FAULKLAND) So, Mr. Beverley, if you'll choose your weapons, the captain and I will measure the ground.

FAULKLAND. My weapons, sir?

ACRES. Odd's life, Sir Lucius, I'm not going to fight Mr. Faulkland. These are my particular friends.

SIR LUCIUS. What, sir, did you not come here to fight Mr. Acres?

FAULKLAND. Not I, upon my word, sir.

SIR LUCIUS. Well, now, that's mighty provoking! But I hope, Mr. Faulkland, as there are three of us come on purpose for the game, you won't be so cantankerous as to spoil the party by sitting out?

JACK. Oh, pray, Faulkland, fight to oblige Sir Lucius.

FAULKLAND. Nay, if Mr. Acres is so bent on the matter.

ACRES. No, no, Mr. Faulkland, I'll bear my disappointment like a Christian. Look'ee, Sir Lucius, there's no occasion at all for me to fight and if it is the same to you, I'd as lief let it alone.

SIR LUCIUS (*sternly*). Observe me, Mr. Acres. I must not be trifled with. You have certainly challenged somebody and you came here to fight him. Now, if that gentleman is willing to represent him, I can't see, for my soul, why it isn't just the same thing?

ACRES. Why, no, Sir Lucius, I tell you, 'tis one Beverley I've challenged. A fellow, you see, that dare not show his face! If *he* were here, I'd make him give up his pretensions directly!

JACK. Hold, Bob, let me set you right. There is no such man as

Beverley in the case. The person who assumed that name is before you and as his pretensions are the same in both characters, he is ready to support them in whatever way you please.

SIR LUCIUS. Well, this is lucky. Now you have an opportunity—

ACRES. What, quarrel with my dear friend, Jack Absolute? Not if he were fifty Beverleys! Zounds, Sir Lucius, you would not have me be so unnatural!

SIR LUCIUS. Upon my conscience, Mr. Acres, your valor has oozed away with a vengeance!

ACRES. Not in the least! Odd's backs and abettors, I'll be *your* second with all my heart and if you should get a quietus, you may command me entirely. I'll get you snug lying in the Abbey here or pickle you and send you over to Blunderbuss Hall or anything of the kind with the greatest pleasure!

SIR LUCIUS. Pho! Pho! You are little better than a coward.

ACRES. Mind, gentlemen, he calls me a coward. Coward was the word, by my valor!

SIR LUCIUS. Well, sir?

ACRES. Look'ee, Sir Lucius, 'tisn't that I mind the word *coward. Coward* may be said in a joke. But if you had called me a poltroon, odd's daggers and balls—

SIR LUCIUS. Well, sir?

ACRES (*pauses*). I should have thought you a very ill-bred man.

SIR LUCIUS. Pho! You are beneath my notice.

JACK. Nay, Sir Lucius, you can't have a better second than my friend Acres. He is a most determined dog, called in the country Fighting Bob. He generally kills a man a week, don't you, Bob?

ACRES. Aye! At home!

SIR LUCIUS. Well, then, captain, 'tis *we* must begin. (*Drawing his sword.*) So, come out, my little counsellor and ask the gentleman whether he will resign the lady without forcing you to proceed against him.

JACK. Come on then, sir. Since you won't let it be an amicable suit, here's my reply. (*Draws.*)

Enter at a gallop SIR ANTHONY, MRS. MALAPROP, LYDIA, JULIA, LUCY, FAG, DAVID *and even* THOMAS, *the coachman.*

DAVID. Knock 'em all down, sweet Sir Anthony, knock down my master in particular and bind his hands over to their good behavior.

SIR ANTHONY (*brandishing his cane*). Put up, Jack, put up, or I shall be in a frenzy! How came you in a duel, sir?

JACK. Faith, sir, that gentleman can tell you better than I. (*Indicates* SIR LUCIUS.) 'Twas he called on me and you know, sir, I serve His Majesty.

SIR ANTHONY. Here's a pretty fellow! I catch him going to cut a man's throat and he tells me he serves His Majesty. Zounds, sirrah, then how durst you draw the King's sword against one of his subjects?

JACK. Sir, I tell you, that gentleman called me out without explaining his reasons.

SIR ANTHONY (*turning on* SIR LUCIUS). Gad, sir, how came you to call my son out without explaining your reasons?

SIR LUCIUS. Your son, sir, insulted me in a manner which my honor could not brook.

SIR ANTHONY (*turning on* JACK). Zounds, Jack, how durst you insult the gentleman in a manner which his honor could not brook?

MRS. MALAPROP. Come, come, let's have no honor before ladies. Captain Absolute, come here. How could you intimidate us so? Here's Lydia has been terrified to death for you.

JACK. For fear I should be killed or escape, ma'am?

MRS. MALAPROP. Nay, no delusions to the past. Lydia is convinced. Speak, child.

SIR LUCIUS. With your leave, ma'am, I must put in a word here. I believe I could interpret the young lady's silence. Now, mark—

LYDIA. What is it you mean, sir?

SIR LUCIUS (*to* LYDIA). Come, come, Delia, we must be serious now. This is no time for trifling.

LYDIA. 'Tis true, sir, and your reproof bids me offer this gentleman my hand and solicit the return of his affections. (*Goes to* JACK.)

JACK. Oh, my little angel, say you so? Sir Lucius, I perceive there must be some mistake here with regard to the affront which you affirm I have given you. I can only say that it could not have been intentional. And as you must be convinced that I should not fear to support a real injury, you shall now see that I am not ashamed to atone for an inadvertency. I ask your pardon. But for this lady, while honored with her approbation I will support my claim against any man whatsoever.

SIR ANTHONY. Well said, Jack, and I'll stand by you, my boy!

ACRES. Mind, I give up *all* my claim! I make no pretensions to anything in the world! And if I can't get a wife without fighting for her, by my valor, I'll live a bachelor!

SIR LUCIUS. Captain, give me your hand. An affront handsomely acknowledged becomes an obligation. And as for the lady, if she chooses to deny her own handwriting here—(*produces a bundle of letters*).

MRS. MALAPROP (*to herself*). Oh, he will dissolve my mystery! Sir Lucius, perhaps there's some mistake, perhaps I can illuminate—

SIR LUCIUS (*to* MRS. MALAPROP). Pray, old gentlewoman, don't interfere where you have no business. Miss Languish, are you my Delia, or not?

LYDIA. Indeed, Sir Lucius, I am not. (*She walks apart with* JACK.)

MRS. MALAPROP. Sir Lucius O'Trigger, ungrateful as you are, I own the soft impeachment. Pardon my blushes—*I* am Delia!

SIR LUCIUS (*examining her*). You, Delia? Pho, pho, be easy!

MRS. MALAPROP. Why, thou barbarous Vandyke![35] Those letters are mine. When you are more sensible of my benignity, perhaps I may be brought to encourage your addresses.

SIR LUCIUS. Mrs. Malaprop, I am extremely sensible of your condescension and whether you or Lucy have put this trick upon me, I am equally beholden to you. And to show you I am not ungrateful, Captain Absolute, since you have taken that lady from me, I'll give you my Delia into the bargain.

JACK. I am much obliged to you, Sir Lucius. But here's my friend, Fighting Bob, unprovided for.

[35] **Vandyke:** fashionable collar often depicted in portraits by Vandyke; here, probably *vandal*.

SIR LUCIUS. Hah, little valor. (*Indicating* MRS. MALAPROP.) Here, will you make your fortune?

ACRES. Odd's wrinkles, no! But give me your hand, Sir Lucius, forget and forgive. But if ever I give you a chance of pickling me again, say Bob Acres is a dunce, that's all.

SIR ANTHONY. Come, Mrs. Malaprop, don't be cast down. You are in your bloom yet.

MRS. MALAPROP. Oh, Sir Anthony! Men are all barbarians! (SIR ANTHONY *consoles her.*)

JULIA (*looking at* FAULKLAND). He seems dejected and unhappy, not sullen. There was some foundation, however, for the tale he told me. Oh, woman, how true should be your judgment when your resolution is so weak!

FAULKLAND (*coming to her*). Julia! How can I sue for what I so little deserve? I dare not presume. Yet hope is the child of penitence.

JULIA (*taking his hands*). Oh, Faulkland, you have not been more faulty in your unkind treatment of me than I am now in wanting inclination to resent it. As my heart honestly bids me place my weakness to the account of love, I should be ungenerous not to admit the same plea for yours.

FAULKLAND. Now I shall be blessed, indeed!

SIR ANTHONY. What's going on here? So, you have been quarreling, too, I warrant. Come, Julia, I never interfered before but let me have a hand in the matter at last. All the faults I have ever seen in my friend Faulkland seemed to proceed from what he calls the delicacy and warmth of his affection for you. There, marry him directly, Julia. You'll find he'll mend surprisingly.

SIR LUCIUS. Come now, I hope there is no dissatisfied person but what is content. For, as I have been disappointed myself, it will be very hard if I have not the satisfaction of seeing other people succeed better.

ACRES. You are right, Sir Lucius. So, Jack, I wish you joy. Mr. Faulkland, the same. Ladies, come now, to show you I am neither vexed nor angry, odd's tabors and pipes, I'll order the fiddles in half an hour to the New Room! And I insist on you all meeting me there!

SIR ANTHONY. Gad, sir, I like your spirit! And at night we single lads will drink a health to the young couples and a husband to Mrs. Malaprop!

FAULKLAND (*watching* JULIA *and* LYDIA *joyfully embracing*). Our partners are stolen from us, Jack, I hope to be congratulated by each other, yours for having checked in time the errors of an ill-directed imagination which might have betrayed an innocent heart, and mine for having, by her gentleness and candor, reformed the unhappy temper of one who by it made wretched whom he loved most and tortured the heart he ought to have adored.

JACK. Well, Faulkland, we have both tasted the bitters as well as the sweets of love, with this difference only—that you always prepared the bitter cup yourself, while I—

LYDIA (*overhearing*).—was always obliged to *me* for it, hey, Mr. Modesty? But come, no more of that. Our happiness is now as unallayed as general.

JULIA. Then let us study to preserve it so, and while hope pictures to us a flattering scene of future bliss, let us deny its pencil those colors which are too bright to be lasting. When hearts deserving happiness would unite their fortunes, virtue would crown them with an unfading garland of modest hurtless flowers. But ill-judging passion will force the gaudier rose into the wreath, whose thorn offends them, when its leaves are dropped.

General cheers and acclamation. All rally around ACRES *and follow him to the New Room for a celebration.*

INTERPRETATION

1. Comic writing is dependent on the vivid presentation of recognizable human types. Identify the various types in *The Rivals* by suggesting the names of actors or of your classmates, teachers, and parents who might play the parts. Does Sheridan ever resort to the use of stereotypes?

2. In many comedies the central conflict is between the older and younger generations over problems of marriage and inheritance. In *The Rivals* this generational conflict is present but the plot is complicated by conflicts between the lovers themselves. Identify the main obstacles to amorous and financial harmony. Are these obstacles removed by a change in situation or character? How logical is the ending, in terms of what has gone before?

Would a theater audience seeing this play for the first time be able to follow the story? Explain.

3. The eighteenth century was a very language-conscious era. It was the time in which English dictionaries first came to be written and a rising middle class was always eager to say the "right" thing. Several characters in *The Rivals* reflect this self-conscious preoccupation with language, the most conspicuous being Mrs. Malaprop, who prides herself on her "parts of speech." Sheridan shows how ridiculous such airs can be and, in creating the character of Mrs. Malaprop, added a new word to the language—*malapropism*. The following list contains words which Mrs. Malaprop intended to use at some point in the play but somehow could not find. Can you locate a malapropism for each of these words?

obliterate	superfluous	vernacular
extricate	ineligible	arrangement
misanthrope	benevolence	alligator
ironically	intellectual	comparisons
prodigy	pinnacle	paralyzed
contiguous	hysterics	catastrophe
orthography	desisted	particular
apprehend	intercepted	allusions

On page 51, Mrs. Malaprop misquotes Hamlet's description of his father. Compare her version with Shakespeare's (*Hamlet,* Act III, scene iv, lines 56–59). What is meant by "sentimental swearing"? What attitudes toward language are shared by Acres and Mrs. Malaprop? Find examples of how Sheridan differentiates one character from another through their habits of speech.

4. When it was first produced in 1775, *The Rivals* was not a period costume play. The actors on the stage wore the same style of clothing as members of the audience. If you were to present this comedy today, would you put actors in contemporary clothing or in the dress of 1775? What is the theatrical value of period costumes? To what extent is *The Rivals* dependent for its effect on an eighteenth-century look? (The movie *Tom Jones,* an excellent resource for eighteenth-century fashion, architecture, furniture, artifacts, and manners, may provide help in answering this question.)

5. Like most comedies, *The Rivals* celebrates desirable social values. The right men marry the right women, money is made available to the younger generation, and the crotchets and foibles of the antisocial characters are reformed or circumvented. At the final curtain, society is renewed and a happier life is born. What qualities of personality and character are valued in *The Rivals?* What qualities are ridiculed? Explain why or why not Sheridan's easy-going attitude toward folly and error is likely to be effective as social satire.

Arms and the Man

On November 13, 1887—a day which came to be known as "Bloody Sunday"—Bernard Shaw took part in a protest rally in Trafalgar Square in London together with masses of unemployed men and their families. When the demonstrators were set upon by mounted cavalry armed with bayonets, Shaw's comrades urged violent resistance. Shaw, however, refused to fight back, saying, "If we can hold our heads, and hold them high, we'll win." Although some accused him of cowardice, Shaw stuck to his non-violent strategy.

In the theater as well as in politics, Shaw was a peaceful revolutionary. For decades, a kind of play sometimes called the military melodrama had extolled the virtues and glories of war on the English stage. Not only were the plays silly, Shaw thought, but their depiction of soldiering was utterly false. In 1894, Shaw wrote his own version of one of these plays, exposing the sham of conventional heroism and revealing the virtues of the realistic man. Shaw knew well what the public expected of a military melodrama and he upset their expectations at every turn. The dashing cavalry officer marries a servant girl, not the romantic young lady. The great battle of Slivnitza is decided not by heroism but through a clerical error. And the professional soldier's secret to success is not cartridges but chocolate creams. The critics were furious—but the audience loved it.

Under the pretext of presenting a military melodrama Shaw had introduced to the stage a new kind of comedy—the comedy of ideas. To Shaw the greatest passions were those of the intellect. In order that man might evolve into higher forms his brain must be aroused and stimulated, and the theater—which Shaw called "a Temple to the Ascent of Man"—was a most effective instrument for that purpose. "It irks me," he wrote, "to see people comfortable when they ought to be uncomfortable." Unlike *The Rivals,* which accepts the basic mores of its time, *Arms and the Man* questions a number of important assumptions about life, love, and war. While this may give discomfort, it is a brisk, tingling, and ultimately pleasant discomfort.

Arms and the Man

GEORGE BERNARD SHAW

Characters

MAJOR PAUL PETKOFF
CATHERINE, his wife
RAINA, his daughter
LOUKA, their maid
NICOLA, their manservant
MAJOR SERGIUS SARANOFF
CAPTAIN BLUNTSCHLI
AN OFFICER

ACT ONE

Night. A lady's bedchamber in Bulgaria, in a small town near the Dragoman Pass. It is late in November in the year 1885, and through an open window with a little balcony on the left can be seen a peak of the Balkans, wonderfully white and beautiful in the starlit snow. The interior of the room is not like anything to be seen in the east of Europe. It is half rich Bulgarian, half cheap Viennese. The counterpane and hangings of the bed, the window curtains, the little carpet, and all the ornamental textile fabrics in the room are oriental and gorgeous: the paper on the walls is occidental and paltry. Above the head of the bed, which stands against a little wall cutting off the right hand corner of the room diagonally, is a painted wooden shrine, blue and gold, with an ivory image of Christ, and a light hanging before it in a pierced metal ball suspended by three chains. On the left, further forward, is an ottoman. The washstand, against the wall on the left, consists of an enamelled iron basin with a pail beneath it in a painted metal frame, and a single towel on the rail at the side. A chair near it is Austrian bent wood, with cane seat. The dressing table, between the bed and the window, is an ordinary pine table, covered with a cloth of many colors, but with an expensive toilet mirror on it. The door is on the right; and there is a chest of drawers between the door and the bed. This chest of drawers is also covered by a variegated native cloth, and on it there is a pile of paper backed novels, a box of chocolate creams, and a miniature easel, on which is a large photograph of an extremely handsome officer, whose lofty bearing and magnetic glance can be felt even from the portrait. The room is lighted by a candle on the chest of drawers, and another on the dressing table, with a box of matches beside it.

The window is hinged doorwise and stands wide open, folding back to the left. Outside a pair of wooden shutters, opening outwards, also stand open. On the balcony, a young lady, intensely conscious of the romantic beauty of the night, and of the fact that her own youth and beauty is a part of it, is on the balcony, gazing at the snowy Balkans. She is covered by a long mantle of furs, worth, on a moderate estimate, about three times the furniture of her room.

Her reverie is interrupted by her mother, Catherine Petkoff, a woman over forty, imperiously energetic, with magnificent black hair and eyes, who might be a very splendid specimen of the wife of a mountain farmer, but is determined to be a Viennese lady, and to that end wears a fashionable tea gown on all occasions.

CATHERINE (*entering hastily, full of good news*). Raina—(*she pronounces it Rah-eena, with the stress on the ee*) Raina—(*she goes to the bed, expecting to find Raina there*) Why, where— (*Raina looks into the room.*) Heavens! child, are you out in the night air instead of in your bed? You'll catch your death. Louka told me you were asleep.

RAINA (*coming in*). I sent her away. I wanted to be alone. The stars are so beautiful! What is the matter?

CATHERINE. Such news. There has been a battle!

RAINA (*her eyes dilating*). Ah! (*She throws the cloak on the ottoman, and comes eagerly to Catherine in her nightgown, a pretty garment, but evidently the only one she has on.*)

CATHERINE. A great battle at Slivnitza! A victory! And it was won by Sergius.

RAINA (*with a cry of delight*). Ah! (*Rapturously.*) Oh, mother! (*Then, with sudden anxiety*) Is father safe?

CATHERINE. Of course: he sent me the news. Sergius is the hero of the hour, the idol of the regiment.

RAINA. Tell me, tell me. How was it! (*Ecstatically.*) Oh, mother, mother, mother! (*Raina pulls her mother down on the ottoman; and they kiss one another frantically.*)

CATHERINE (*with surging enthusiasm*). You can't guess how splendid it is. A cavalry charge—think of that! He defied our Russian commanders—acted without orders—led a charge on his own responsibility—headed it himself—was the first man to sweep through their guns. Can't you see it, Raina; our gallant splendid Bulgarians with their swords and eyes flashing, thundering down like an avalanche and scattering the wretched Servian dandies[1] like chaff. And you—you kept Sergius waiting a year before you would be betrothed to him. Oh, if you have a drop of Bulgarian blood in your veins, you will worship him when he comes back.

RAINA. What will he care for my poor little worship after the acclamations of a whole army of heroes? But no matter: I am so happy—so proud! (*She rises and walks about excitedly.*) It proves that all our ideas were real after all.

CATHERINE (*indignantly*). Our ideas real! What do you mean?

RAINA. Our ideas of what Sergius would do—our patriotism—our heroic ideals. Oh, what faithless little creatures girls are!— I sometimes used to doubt whether they were anything but dreams. When I buckled on Sergius's sword he looked so noble: it was treason to think of disillusion or humiliation or failure. And yet—and yet— (*Quickly.*) Promise me you'll never tell him.

CATHERINE. Don't ask me for promises until I know what I am promising.

RAINA. Well, it came into my head just as he was holding me in his arms and looking into my eyes, that perhaps we only had our heroic ideas because we are so fond of reading Byron

[1] **Servian dandies:** troops from Serbia. Serbia's fear of Bulgarian expansion caused the Serbo-Bulgarian war, which forms the background for this play. The interminable quarrels among the Balkan states and the great European powers—all eager to control former Turkish lands—were only temporarily settled in 1886 at Bucharest, where Bulgaria surrendered no territory.

and Pushkin,[2] and because we were so delighted with the opera that season at Bucharest. Real life is so seldom like that —indeed never, as far as I knew it then. (*Remorsefully.*) Only think, mother, I doubted him: I wondered whether all his heroic qualities and his soldiership might not prove mere imagination when he went into a real battle. I had an uneasy fear that he might cut a poor figure there beside all those clever Russian officers.

CATHERINE. A poor figure! Shame on you! The Servians have Austrian officers who are just as clever as our Russians; but we have beaten them in every battle for all that.

RAINA (*laughing and sitting down again*). Yes, I was only a prosaic little coward. Oh, to think that it was all true—that Sergius is just as splendid and noble as he looks—that the world is really a glorious world for women who can see its glory and men who can act its romance! What happiness! what unspeakable fulfilment! Ah! (*She throws herself on her knees beside her mother and flings her arms passionately round her. They are interrupted by the entry of Louka, a handsome, proud girl in a pretty Bulgarian peasant's dress with double apron, so defiant that her servility to Raina is almost insolent. She is afraid of Catherine, but even with her goes as far as she dares. She is just now excited like the others; but she has no sympathy for Raina's raptures and looks contemptuously at the ecstasies of the two before she addresses them.*)

LOUKA. If you please, madam, all the windows are to be closed and the shutters made fast. They say there may be shooting in the streets. (*Raina and Catherine rise together, alarmed.*) The Servians are being chased right back through the pass; and they say they may run into the town. Our cavalry will be after them; and our people will be ready for them you may be sure, now that they are running away. (*She goes out on the balcony and pulls the outside shutters to; then steps back into the room.*)

RAINA. I wish our people were not so cruel. What glory is there in killing wretched fugitives?

[2] **Byron . . . Pushkin:** George Gordon, Lord Byron, was an English romantic poet who ardently joined Greece's war of independence from the Turks. Aleksandr Pushkin was an early nineteenth-century Russian poet whose early works reflected Byron's love of liberty and romantic melancholy.

CATHERINE (*business-like, her housekeeping instincts aroused*). I must see that everything is made safe downstairs.

RAINA (*to Louka*). Leave the shutters so that I can just close them if I hear any noise.

CATHERINE (*authoritatively, turning on her way to the door*). Oh, no, dear, you must keep them fastened. You would be sure to drop off to sleep and leave them open. Make them fast, Louka.

LOUKA. Yes, madam. (*She fastens them.*)

RAINA. Don't be anxious about me. The moment I hear a shot, I shall blow out the candles and roll myself up in bed with my ears well covered.

CATHERINE. Quite the wisest thing you can do, my love. Good-night.

RAINA. Good-night. (*They kiss one another, and Raina's emotion comes back for a moment.*) Wish me joy of the happiest night of my life—if only there are no fugitives.

CATHERINE. Go to bed, dear; and don't think of them. (*She goes out.*)

LOUKA (*secretly, to Raina*). If you would like the shutters open, just give them a push like this. (*She pushes them: they open: she pulls them to again.*) One of them ought to be bolted at the bottom; but the bolt's gone.

RAINA (*with dignity, reproving her*). Thanks, Louka; but we must do what we are told. (*Louka makes a grimace.*) Good-night.

LOUKA (*carelessly*). Good-night. (*She goes out, swaggering.*)

Raina, left alone, goes to the chest of drawers, and adores the portrait there with feelings that are beyond all expression. She does not kiss it or press it to her breast, or shew it any mark of bodily affection; but she takes it in her hands and elevates it like a priestess.

RAINA (*looking up at the picture with worship*). Oh, I shall never be unworthy of you any more, my hero—never, never, never. (*She replaces it reverently, and selects a novel from the little pile of books. She turns over the leaves dreamily; finds her page; turns the book inside out at it; and then, with a happy sigh, gets into bed and prepares to read herself to sleep. But before abandoning herself to fiction, she raises her eyes once more, thinking of the blessed reality and murmurs)* My hero! my hero! (*A distant shot breaks the quiet of the night outside. She starts, listening; and two more shots, much nearer, follow, startling her so that she scrambles out of bed, and hastily blows out the candle on the chest of drawers. Then, putting her fingers in her ears, she runs to the dressing-table and blows out the light there, and hurries back to bed. The room is now in darkness: nothing is visible but the glimmer of the light in the pierced ball before the image, and the starlight seen through the slits at the top of the shutters. The firing breaks out again: there is a startling fusillade quite close at hand. Whilst it is still echoing, the shutters disappear, pulled open from without, and for an instant the rectangle of snowy starlight flashes out with the figure of a man in black upon it. The shutters close immediately and the room is dark again. But the silence is now broken by the sound of panting. Then there is a scrape; and the flame of a match is seen in the middle of the room.*)

RAINA (*crouching on the bed*). Who's there? (*The match is out instantly.*) Who's there? Who is that?

A MAN'S VOICE (*in the darkness, subduedly, but threateningly*). Sh—sh! Don't call out or you'll be shot. Be good; and no harm will happen to you. (*She is heard leaving her bed, and making for the door.*) Take care, there's no use in trying to run away. Remember, if you raise your voice my pistol will go off. (*Commandingly.*) Strike a light and let me see you. Do you hear? (*Another moment of silence and darkness. Then she is heard retreating to the dressing-table. She lights a candle, and the mystery is at an end. A man of about 35, in a deplorable plight, bespattered with mud and blood and snow, his belt and the strap of his revolver case keeping together the torn ruins of the blue coat of a Servian artillery officer. As far as the candlelight and his unwashed, unkempt condition make it possible to judge, he is a man of middling stature and undistinguished appearance, with strong neck and shoulders, a roundish, obstinate looking head covered with short crisp bronze curls, clear quick blue eyes and good brows and mouth, a hopelessly prosaic nose like that of a strong-minded baby, trim soldierlike carriage and energetic manner, and with all his wits about him in spite of his desperate predicament—*

even with a sense of humor of it, without, however, the least intention of trifling with it or throwing away a chance. He reckons up what he can guess about Raina—her age, her social position, her character, the extent to which she is frightened—at a glance, and continues, more politely but still most determinedly) Excuse my disturbing you; but you recognise my uniform—Servian. If I'm caught I shall be killed. (*Determinedly.*) Do you understand that?

RAINA. Yes.

MAN. Well, I don't intend to get killed if I can help it. (*Still more determinedly.*) Do you understand that? (*He locks the door with a snap.*)

RAINA (*disdainfully*). I suppose not. (*She draws herself up superbly, and looks him straight in the face, saying with emphasis*) Some soldiers, I know, are afraid of death.

MAN (*with grim goodhumor*). All of them, dear lady, all of them, believe me. It is our duty to live as long as we can, and kill as many of the enemy as we can. Now if you raise an alarm—

RAINA (*cutting him short*). You will shoot me. How do you know that I am afraid to die?

MAN (*cunningly*). Ah; but suppose I don't shoot you, what will happen then? Why, a lot of your cavalry—the greatest blackguards in your army—will burst into this pretty room of yours and slaughter me here like a pig; for I'll fight like a demon: they shan't get me into the street to amuse themselves with: I know what they are. Are you prepared to receive that sort of company in your present undress? (*Raina, suddenly conscious of her nightgown, instinctively shrinks and gathers it more closely about her. He watches her, and adds, pitilessly*) It's rather scanty, eh? (*She turns to the ottoman. He raises his pistol instantly, and cries*) Stop! (*She stops.*) Where are you going?

RAINA (*with dignified patience*). Only to get my cloak.

MAN (*darting to the ottoman and snatching the cloak*). A good idea. No: I'll keep the cloak: and you will take care that nobody comes in and sees you without it. This is a better weapon than the pistol. (*He throws the pistol down on the ottoman.*)

RAINA (*revolted*). It is not the weapon of a gentleman!

MAN. It's good enough for a man with only you to stand between him and death. (*As they look at one another for a moment, Raina hardly able to believe that even a Servian officer can be so cynically and selfishly unchivalrous, they are startled by a sharp fusillade in the street. The chill of imminent death hushes the man's voice as he adds*) Do you hear? If you are going to bring those scoundrels in on me you shall receive them as you are. (*Raina meets his eye with unflinching scorn. Suddenly he starts, listening. There is a step outside. Someone tries the door, and then knocks hurriedly and urgently at it. Raina looks at the man, breathless. He throws up his head with the gesture of a man who sees that it is all over with him, and, dropping the manner which he has been assuming to intimidate her, flings the cloak to her, exclaiming, sincerely and kindly*) No use: I'm done for. Quick! wrap yourself up: they're coming!

RAINA (*catching the cloak eagerly*). Oh, thank you. (*She wraps herself up with great relief. He draws his sabre and turns to the door, waiting.*)

LOUKA (*outside, knocking*). My lady, my lady! Get up, quick, and open the door.

RAINA (*anxiously*). What will you do?

MAN (*grimly*). Never mind. Keep out of the way. It will not last long.

RAINA (*impulsively*). I'll help you. Hide yourself, oh, hide yourself, quick, behind the curtain. (*She seizes him by a torn strip of his sleeve, and pulls him towards the window.*)

MAN (*yielding to her*). There is just half a chance, if you keep your head. Remember: nine soldiers out of ten are born fools. (*He hides behind the curtain, looking out for a moment to say, finally*) If they find me, I promise you a fight—a devil of a fight! (*He disappears. Raina takes off the cloak and throws it across the foot of the bed. Then with a sleepy, disturbed air, she opens the door. Louka enters excitedly.*)

LOUKA. A man has been seen climbing up the waterpipe to your balcony—a Servian. The soldiers want to search for him; and they are so wild and drunk and furious. My lady says you are to dress at once.

RAINA (*as if annoyed at being disturbed*). They shall not search here. Why have they been let in?

CATHERINE (*coming in hastily*). Raina, darling, are you safe? Have you seen anyone or heard anything?

RAINA. I heard the shooting. Surely the soldiers will not dare come in here?

CATHERINE. I have found a Russian officer, thank Heaven: he knows Sergius. (*Speaking through the door to someone outside.*) Sir, will you come in now! My daughter is ready.

A young Russian officer, in Bulgarian uniform, enters, sword in hand.

THE OFFICER (*with soft, feline politeness and stiff military carriage*). Good evening, gracious lady; I am sorry to intrude, but there is a fugitive hiding on the balcony. Will you and the gracious lady your mother please to withdraw whilst we search?

RAINA (*petulantly*). Nonsense, sir, you can see that there is no one on the balcony. (*She throws the shutters wide open and stands with her back to the curtain where the man is hidden, pointing to the moonlit balcony. A couple of shots are fired right under the window, and a bullet shatters the glass opposite Raina, who winks and gasps, but stands her ground, whilst Catherine screams, and the officer rushes to the balcony.*)

THE OFFICER (*on the balcony, shouting savagely down to the street*). Cease firing there, you fools: do you hear? Cease firing, damn you. (*He glares down for a moment; then turns to Raina, trying to resume his polite manner.*) Could anyone have got in without your knowledge. Were you asleep?

RAINA. No, I have not been to bed.

THE OFFICER (*impatiently, coming back into the room*). Your neighbours have their heads so full of runaway Servians that they see them everywhere. (*Politely.*) Gracious lady, a thousand pardons. Good-night. (*Military bow, which Raina returns coldly. Another to Catherine, who follows him out. Raina closes the shutters. She turns and sees Louka, who has been watching the scene curiously.*)

RAINA. Don't leave my mother, Louka, whilst the soldiers are here. (*Louka glances at Raina, at the ottoman, at the curtain; then purses her lips secretively, laughs to herself, and goes out. Raina follows her to the door, shuts it behind her with a slam, and locks it violently. The man immediately steps out from behind the curtain, sheathing his sabre, and dismissing the danger from his mind in a businesslike way.)*

MAN. A narrow shave; but a miss is as good as a mile. Dear young lady, your servant until death. I wish for your sake I had joined the Bulgarian army instead of the Servian. I am not a native Servian.

RAINA (*haughtily*). No, you are one of the Austrians who set the Servians on to rob us of our national liberty, and who officer their army for them. We hate them!

MAN. Austrian! not I. Don't hate me, dear young lady. I am only a Swiss, fighting merely as a professional soldier. I joined Servia because it was nearest to me. Be generous: you've beaten us hollow.

RAINA. Have I not been generous?

MAN. Noble!—heroic! But I'm not saved yet. This particular rush will soon pass through; but the pursuit will go on all night by fits and starts. I must take my chance to get off during a quiet interval. You don't mind my waiting just a minute or two, do you?

RAINA. Oh, no: I am sorry you will have to go into danger again. (*Motioning towards ottoman.*) Won't you sit— (*She breaks off with an irrepressible cry of alarm as she catches sight of the pistol. The man, all nerves, shies like a frightened horse.*)

MAN (*irritably*). Don't frighten me like that. What is it?

RAINA. Your pistol! It was staring that officer in the face all the time. What an escape!

MAN (*vexed at being unnecessarily terrified*). Oh, is that all?

RAINA (*staring at him rather superciliously, conceiving a poorer and poorer opinion of him, and feeling proportionately more and more at her ease with him*). I am sorry I frightened you. (*She takes up the pistol and hands it to him.*) Pray take it to protect yourself against me.

MAN (*grinning wearily at the sarcasm as he takes the pistol*). No use, dear young lady: there's nothing in it. It's not loaded. (*He makes a grimace at it, and drops it disparagingly into his revolver case.*)

RAINA. Load it by all means.

MAN. I've no ammunition. What use are cartridges in battle?

I always carry chocolate instead; and I finished the last cake of that yesterday.

RAINA (*outraged in her most cherished ideals of manhood*). Chocolate! Do you stuff your pockets with sweets—like a schoolboy—even in the field?

MAN. Yes. Isn't it contemptible?

Raina stares at him, unable to utter her feelings. Then she sails away scornfully to the chest of drawers, and returns with the box of confectionery in her hand.

RAINA. Allow me. I am sorry I have eaten them all except these. (*She offers him the box.*)

MAN (*ravenously*). You're an angel! (*He gobbles the comfits.*) Creams! Delicious! (*He looks anxiously to see whether there are any more. There are none. He accepts the inevitable with pathetic goodhumor, and says, with grateful emotion*) Bless you, dear lady. You can always tell an old soldier by the inside of his holsters and cartridge boxes. The young ones carry pistols and cartridges; the old ones, grub. Thank you. (*He hands back the box. She snatches it contemptuously from him and throws it away. This impatient action is so sudden that he shies again.*) Ugh! Don't do things so suddenly, gracious lady. Don't revenge yourself because I frightened you just now.

RAINA (*superbly*). Frighten me! Do you know, sir, that though I am only a woman, I think I am at heart as brave as you.

MAN. I should think so. You haven't been under fire for three days as I have. I can stand two days without shewing it much; but no man can stand three days: I'm as nervous as a mouse. (*He sits down on the ottoman, and takes his head in his hands.*) Would you like to see me cry?

RAINA (*quickly*). No.

MAN. If you would, all you have to do is to scold me just as if I were a little boy and you my nurse. If I were in camp now they'd play all sorts of tricks on me.

RAINA (*a little moved*). I'm sorry. I won't scold you. (*Touched by the sympathy in her tone, he raises his head and looks gratefully at her: she immediately draws back and says stiffly*) You must excuse me: our soldiers are not like that. (*She moves away from the ottoman.*)

MAN. Oh, yes, they are. There are only two sorts of soldiers: old ones and young ones. I've served fourteen years: half of your fellows never smelt powder before. Why, how is it that you've just beaten us? Sheer ignorance of the art of war, nothing else. (*Indignantly.*) I never saw anything so unprofessional.

RAINA (*ironically*). Oh, was it unprofessional to beat you?

MAN. Well, come, is it professional to throw a regiment of cavalry on a battery of machine guns, with the dead certainty that if the guns go off not a horse or man will ever get within fifty yards of the fire? I couldn't believe my eyes when I saw it.

RAINA (*eagerly turning to him, as all her enthusiasm and her dream of glory rush back on her*). Did you see the great cavalry charge? Oh, tell me about it. Describe it to me.

MAN. You never saw a cavalry charge, did you?

RAINA. How could I?

MAN. Ah, perhaps not—of course. Well, it's a funny sight. It's like slinging a handful of peas against a window pane: first one comes; then two or three close behind him; and then all the rest in a lump.

RAINA (*her eyes dilating as she raises her clasped hands ecstatically*). Yes, first One!—the bravest of the brave!

MAN (*prosaically*). Hm! you should see the poor devil pulling at his horse.

RAINA. Why should he pull at his horse?

MAN (*impatient of so stupid a question*). It's running away with him, of course: do you suppose the fellow wants to get there before the others and be killed? Then they all come. You can tell the young ones by their wildness and their slashing. The old ones come bunched up under the number one guard: they know that they are mere projectiles, and that it's no use trying to fight. The wounds are mostly broken knees, from the horses cannoning together.

RAINA. Ugh! But I don't believe the first man is a coward. I believe he is a hero!

MAN (*goodhumoredly*). That's what you'd have said if you'd seen the first man in the charge to-day.

RAINA (*breathless*). Ah, I knew it! Tell me—tell me about him.

MAN. He did it like an operatic tenor—a regular handsome

fellow, with flashing eyes and lovely moustache, shouting a war-cry and charging like Don Quixote at the windmills.[3] We nearly burst with laughter at him; but when the sergeant ran up as white as a sheet, and told us they'd sent us the wrong cartridges, and that we couldn't fire a shot for the next ten minutes, we laughed at the other side of our mouths. I never felt so sick in my life, though I've been in one or two very tight places. And I hadn't even a revolver cartridge—nothing but chocolate. We'd no bayonets—nothing. Of course, they just cut us to bits. And there was Don Quixote flourishing like a drum major, thinking he'd done the cleverest thing ever known, whereas he ought to be courtmartialled for it. Of all the fools ever let loose on a field of battle, that man must be the very maddest. He and his regiment simply committed suicide—only the pistol missed fire, that's all.

RAINA (*deeply wounded, but steadfastly loyal to her ideals*). Indeed! Would you know him again if you saw him?

MAN. Shall I ever forget him. (*She again goes to the chest of drawers. He watches her with a vague hope that she may have something else for him to eat. She takes the portrait from its stand and brings it to him.*)

RAINA. That is a photograph of the gentleman—the patriot and hero—to whom I am betrothed.

MAN (*looking at it*). I'm really very sorry. (*Looking at her.*) Was it fair to lead me on? (*He looks at the portrait again.*) Yes: that's him: not a doubt of it. (*He stifles a laugh.*)

RAINA (*quickly*). Why do you laugh?

MAN (*shamefacedly, but still greatly tickled*). I didn't laugh, I assure you. At least I didn't mean to. But when I think of him charging the windmills and thinking he was doing the finest thing—(*chokes with suppressed laughter*).

RAINA (*sternly*). Give me back the portrait, sir.

MAN (*with sincere remorse*). Of course. Certainly. I'm really very sorry. (*She deliberately kisses it, and looks him straight in the face, before returning to the chest of drawers to replace it. He follows her, apologizing.*) Perhaps I'm quite wrong, you

[3] **Don Quixote at the windmills:** an allusion to Cervantes' *Don Quixote de la Mancha*, a satire of the ideals of knight-errantry. In one celebrated incident the fanciful hero charged full tilt against windmills mistaken for giants.

know: no doubt I am. Most likely he had got wind of the cartridge business somehow, and knew it was a safe job.

RAINA. That is to say, he was a pretender and a coward! You did not dare say that before.

MAN (*with a comic gesture of despair*). It's no use, dear lady: I can't make you see it from the professional point of view. (*As he turns away to get back to the ottoman, the firing begins again in the distance.*)

RAINA (*sternly, as she sees him listening to the shots*). So much the better for you.

MAN (*turning*). How?

RAINA. You are my enemy; and you are at my mercy. What would I do if I were a professional soldier?

MAN. Ah, true, dear young lady: you're always right. I know how good you have been to me: to my last hour I shall remember those three chocolate creams. It was unsoldierly; but it was angelic.

RAINA (*coldly*). Thank you. And now I will do a soldierly thing. You cannot stay here after what you have just said about my future husband; but I will go out on the balcony and see whether it is safe for you to climb down into the street. (*She turns to the window.*)

MAN (*changing countenance*). Down that waterpipe! Stop! Wait! I can't! I daren't! The very thought of it makes me giddy. I came up it fast enough with death behind me. But to face it now in cold blood!—(*He sinks on the ottoman.*) It's no use: I give up: I'm beaten. Give the alarm. (*He drops his head in his hands in the deepest dejection.*)

RAINA (*disarmed by pity*). Come, don't be disheartened. (*She stoops over him almost maternally: he shakes his head.*) Oh, you are a very poor soldier—a chocolate cream soldier. Come, cheer up: it takes less courage to climb down than to face capture—remember that.

MAN (*dreamily, lulled by her voice*). No, capture only means death; and death is sleep—oh, sleep, sleep, sleep, undisturbed sleep! Climbing down the pipe means doing something—exerting myself—thinking! Death ten times over first.

RAINA (*softly and wonderingly, catching the rhythm of his weariness*). Are you so sleepy as that?

MAN. I've not had two hours undisturbed sleep since the

war began. I'm on the staff: you don't know what that means. I haven't closed my eyes for thirty-six hours.

RAINA (*desperately*). But what am I to do with you.

MAN (*staggering up*). Of course I must do something. (*He shakes himself; pulls himself together; and speaks with rallied vigour and courage.*) You see, sleep or no sleep, hunger or no hunger, tired or not tired, you can always do a thing when you know it must be done. Well, that pipe must be got down—(*He hits himself on the chest, and adds*)—Do you hear that, you chocolate cream soldier? (*He turns to the window.*)

RAINA (*anxiously*). But if you fall?

MAN. I shall sleep as if the stones were a feather bed. Goodbye. (*He makes boldly for the window, and his hand is on the shutter when there is a terrible burst of firing in the street beneath.*)

RAINA (*rushing to him*). Stop! (*She catches him by the shoulder, and turns him quite round.*) They'll kill you.

MAN (*coolly, but attentively*). Never mind: this sort of thing is all in my day's work. I'm bound to take my chance. (*Decisively.*) Now do what I tell you. Put out the candles, so that they shan't see the light when I open the shutters. And keep away from the window, whatever you do. If they see me, they're sure to have a shot at me.

RAINA (*clinging to him*). They're sure to see you: it's bright moonlight. I'll save you—oh, how can you be so indifferent? You want me to save you, don't you?

MAN. I really don't want to be troublesome. (*She shakes him in her impatience.*) I am not indifferent, dear young lady, I assure you. But how is it to be done?

RAINA. Come away from the window—please. (*She coaxes him back to the middle of the room. He submits humbly. She releases him, and addresses him patronizingly.*) Now listen. You must trust to our hospitality. You do not yet know in whose house you are. I am a Petkoff.

MAN. What's that?

RAINA (*rather indignantly*). I mean that I belong to the family of the Petkoffs, the richest and best known in our country.

MAN. Oh, yes, of course. I beg your pardon. The Petkoffs, to be sure. How stupid of me!

RAINA. You know you never heard of them until this minute. How can you stoop to pretend?

MAN. Forgive me: I'm too tired to think; and the change of subject was too much for me. Don't scold me.

RAINA. I forgot. It might make you cry. (*He nods, quite seriously. She pouts and then resumes her patronizing tone.*) I must tell you that my father holds the highest command of any Bulgarian in our army. He is (*proudly*) a Major.

MAN (*pretending to be deeply impressed*). A Major! Bless me! Think of that!

RAINA. You shewed great ignorance in thinking that it was necessary to climb up to the balcony, because ours is the only private house that has two rows of windows. There is a flight of stairs inside to get up and down by.

MAN. Stairs! How grand! You live in great luxury indeed, dear young lady.

RAINA. Do you know what a library is?

MAN. A library? A roomful of books.

RAINA. Yes, we have one, the only one in Bulgaria.

MAN. Actually a real library! I should like to see that.

RAINA (*affectedly*). I tell you these things to shew you that you are not in the house of ignorant country folk who would kill you the moment they saw your Servian uniform, but among civilized people. We go to Bucharest every year for the opera season; and I have spent a whole month in Vienna.

MAN. I saw that, dear young lady. I saw at once that you knew the world.

RAINA. Have you ever seen the opera of Ernani?[4]

MAN. Is that the one with the devil in it in red velvet, and a soldiers' chorus?

RAINA (*contemptuously*). No!

MAN (*stifling a heavy sigh of weariness*). Then I don't know it.

RAINA. I thought you might have remembered the great scene where Ernani, flying from his foes just as you are tonight, takes refuge in the castle of his bitterest enemy, an old Castilian noble. The noble refuses to give him up. His guest is sacred to him.

[4] **Ernani:** by the nineteenth-century Italian composer Giuseppe Verdi.

MAN (*quickly waking up a little*). Have your people got that notion?

RAINA (*with dignity*). My mother and I can understand that notion, as you call it. And if instead of threatening me with your pistol as you did, you had simply thrown yourself as a fugitive on our hospitality, you would have been as safe as in your father's house.

MAN. Quite sure?

RAINA (*turning her back on him in disgust*). Oh, it is useless to try and make you understand.

MAN. Don't be angry: you see how awkward it would be for me if there was any mistake. My father is a very hospitable man: he keeps six hotels; but I couldn't trust him as far as that. What about your father?

RAINA. He is away at Slivnitza fighting for his country. I answer for your safety. There is my hand in pledge of it. Will that reassure you? (*She offers him her hand.*)

MAN (*looking dubiously at his own hand*). Better not touch my hand, dear young lady. I must have a wash first.

RAINA (*touched*). That is very nice of you. I see that you are a gentleman.

MAN (*puzzled*). Eh?

RAINA. You must not think I am surprised. Bulgarians of really good standing—people in our position—wash their hands nearly every day. But I appreciate your delicacy. You may take my hand. (*She offers it again.*)

MAN (*kissing it with his hands behind his back*). Thanks, gracious young lady: I feel safe at last. And now would you mind breaking the news to your mother? I had better not stay here secretly longer than is necessary.

RAINA. If you will be so good as to keep perfectly still whilst I am away.

MAN. Certainly. (*He sits down on the ottoman.*)

Raina goes to the bed and wraps herself in the fur cloak. His eyes close. She goes to the door, but on turning for a last look at him, sees that he is dropping off to sleep.

RAINA (*at the door*). You are not going asleep, are you? (*He murmurs inarticulately: she runs to him and shakes him.*) Do you hear? Wake up: you are falling asleep.

MAN. Eh? Falling aslee—? Oh, no, not the least in the world: I was only thinking. It's all right: I'm wide awake.

RAINA (*severely*). Will you please stand up while I am away. (*He rises reluctantly.*) All the time, mind.

MAN (*standing unsteadily*). Certainly—certainly: you may depend on me.

Raina looks doubtfully at him. He smiles foolishly. She goes reluctantly, turning again at the door, and almost catching him in the act of yawning. She goes out.

MAN (*drowsily*). Sleep, sleep, sleep, sleep, slee—(*The words trail off into a murmur. He wakes again with a shock on the point of falling.*) Where am I? That's what I want to know: where am I? Must keep awake. Nothing keeps me awake except danger—remember that—(*intently*) danger, danger, danger, dan—Where's danger? Must find it. (*He starts off vaguely around the room in search of it.*) What am I looking for? Sleep—danger—don't know. (*He stumbles against the bed.*) Ah, yes: now I know. All right now. I'm to go to bed, but not to sleep—be sure not to sleep—because of danger. Not to lie down, either, only sit down. (*He sits on the bed. A blissful expression comes into his face.*) Ah! (*With a happy sigh he sinks back at full length; lifts his boots into the bed with a final effort; and falls fast asleep instantly.*)

Catherine comes in, followed by Raina.

RAINA (*looking at the ottoman*). He's gone! I left him here.

CATHERINE. Here! Then he must have climbed down from the—

RAINA (*seeing him*). Oh! (*She points.*)

CATHERINE (*scandalized*). Well! (*She strides to the left side of the bed, Raina following and standing opposite her on the right.*) He's fast asleep. The brute!

RAINA (*anxiously*). Sh!

CATHERINE (*shaking him*). Sir! (*Shaking him again, harder.*) Sir!! (*Vehemently shaking very hard.*) Sir!!!

RAINA (*catching her arm*). Don't, mamma: the poor dear is worn out. Let him sleep.

CATHERINE (*letting him go and turning amazed to Raina*). The poor dear! Raina!!! (*She looks sternly at her daughter. The man sleeps profoundly.*)

ACT TWO

The sixth of March, 1886. In the garden of Major Petkoff's house. It is a fine spring morning; and the garden looks fresh and pretty. Beyond the paling the tops of a couple of minarets can be seen, shewing that there is a valley there, with the little town in it. A few miles further the Balkan mountains rise and shut in the view. Within the garden the side of the house is seen on the right, with a garden door reached by a little flight of steps. On the left the stable yard, with its gateway, encroaches on the garden. There are fruit bushes along the paling and house, covered with washing hung out to dry. A path runs by the house, and rises by two steps at the corner where it turns out of the sight along the front. In the middle a small table, with two bent wood chairs at it, is laid for breakfast with Turkish coffee pot, cups, rolls, etc.; but the cups have been used and the bread broken. There is a wooden garden seat against the wall on the left.

Louka, smoking a cigaret, is standing between the table and the house, turning her back with angry disdain on a manservant who is lecturing her. He is a middle-aged man of cool temperament and low but clear and keen intelligence, with the complacency of the servant who values himself on his rank in servility, and the imperturbability of the accurate calculator who has no illusions. He wears a white Bulgarian costume jacket with decorated border, sash, wide knickerbockers, and decorated gaiters. His head is shaved up to the crown, giving him a high Japanese forehead. His name is Nicola.

NICOLA. Be warned in time, Louka: mend your manners. I know the mistress. She is so grand that she never dreams that any servant could dare to be disrespectful to her; but if she once suspects that you are defying her, out you go.

LOUKA. I do defy her. I will defy her. What do I care for her?

NICOLA. If you quarrel with the family, I never can marry you. It's the same as if you quarrelled with me!

LOUKA. You take her part against me, do you?

NICOLA (*sedately*). I shall always be dependent on the good will of the family. When I leave their service and start a shop in Sofia, their custom will be half my capital: their bad word would ruin me.

LOUKA. You have no spirit. I should like to see them dare say a word against me!

NICOLA (*pityingly*). I should have expected more sense from you, Louka. But you're young, you're young!

LOUKA. Yes; and you like me the better for it, don't you? But I know some family secrets they wouldn't care to have told, young as I am. Let them quarrel with me if they dare!

NICOLA (*with compassionate superiority*). Do you know what they would do if they heard you talk like that?

LOUKA. What could they do?

NICOLA. Discharge you for untruthfulness. Who would believe any stories you told after that? Who would give you another situation? Who in this house would dare be seen speaking to you ever again? How long would your father be left on his little farm? (*She impatiently throws away the end of her cigaret, and stamps on it.*) Child, you don't know the power such high people have over the like of you and me when we try to rise out of our poverty against them. (*He goes close to her and lowers his voice.*) Look at me, ten years in their service. Do you think I know no secrets? I know things about the mistress that she wouldn't have the master know for a thousand levas. I know things about him that she wouldn't let him hear the last of for six months if I blabbed them to her. I know things about Raina that would break off her match with Sergius if—

LOUKA (*turning on him quickly*). How do you know? I never told you!

NICOLA (*opening his eyes cunningly*). So that's your little secret, is it? I thought it might be something like that. Well, you take my advice, and be respectful; and make the mistress feel that no matter what you know or don't know, they can depend on you to hold your tongue and serve the family faithfully. That's what they like; and that's how you'll make most out of them.

LOUKA (*with searching scorn*). You have the soul of a servant, Nicola.

NICOLA (*complacently*). Yes: that's the secret of success in service.

A loud knocking with a whip handle on a wooden door, outside on the left, is heard.

MALE VOICE OUTSIDE. Hollo! Hollo there! Nicola!

LOUKA. Master! back from the war!

NICOLA (*quickly*). My word for it, Louka, the war's over. Off with you and get some fresh coffee. (*He runs out into the stable yard.*)

LOUKA (*as she puts the coffee pot and the cups upon the tray, and carries it into the house*). You'll never put the soul of a servant into me.

Major Petkoff comes from the stable yard, followed by Nicola. He is a cheerful, excitable, insignificant, unpolished man of about 50, naturally unambitious except as to his income and his importance in local society, but just now greatly pleased with the military rank which the war has thrust on him as a man of consequence in his town. The fever of plucky patriotism which the Servian attack roused in all the Bulgarians has pulled him through the war; but he is obviously glad to be home again.

PETKOFF (*pointing to the table with his whip*). Breakfast out here, eh?

NICOLA. Yes, sir. The mistress and Miss Raina have just gone in.

PETKOFF (*sitting down and taking a roll*). Go in and say I've come; and get me some fresh coffee.

NICOLA. It's coming, sir. (*He goes to the house door. Louka, with fresh coffee, a clean cup, and a brandy bottle on her tray meets him.*) Have you told the mistress?

LOUKA. Yes: she's coming.

Nicola goes into the house. Louka brings the coffee to the table.

PETKOFF. Well, the Servians haven't run away with you, have they?

LOUKA. No, sir.

PETKOFF. That's right. Have you brought me some cognac?

LOUKA (*putting the bottle on the table*). Here, sir.

PETKOFF. That's right. (*He pours some into his coffee.*)

Catherine who has at this early hour made only a very perfunctory toilet, and wears a Bulgarian apron over a once brilliant, but now half worn out red dressing gown, and a colored handkerchief tied over her thick black hair, with Turkish slippers on her bare feet, comes from the house, looking astonishingly handsome and stately under all the circumstances. Louka goes into the house.

CATHERINE. My dear Paul, what a surprise for us. (*She stoops over the back of his chair to kiss him.*) Have they brought you fresh coffee?

PETKOFF. Yes, Louka's been looking after me. The war's over. The treaty was signed three days ago at Bucharest; and the decree for our army to demobilize was issued yesterday.

CATHERINE (*springing erect, with flashing eyes*). The war over! Paul: have you let the Austrians force you to make peace?

PETKOFF (*submissively*). My dear: they didn't consult me. What could *I* do? (*She sits down and turns away from him.*) But of course we saw to it that the treaty was an honorable one. It declares peace—

CATHERINE (*outraged*). Peace!

PETKOFF (*appeasing her*). —but not friendly relations: remember that. They wanted to put that in; but I insisted on its being struck out. What more could I do?

CATHERINE. You could have annexed Servia and made Prince Alexander Emperor of the Balkans. That's what I would have done.

PETKOFF. I don't doubt it in the least, my dear. But I should have had to subdue the whole Austrian Empire first; and that would have kept me too long away from you. I missed you greatly.

CATHERINE (*relenting*). Ah! (*Stretches her hand affectionately across the table to squeeze his.*)

PETKOFF. And how have you been, my dear?

CATHERINE. Oh, my usual sore throats, that's all.

PETKOFF (*with conviction*). That comes from washing your neck every day. I've often told you so.

CATHERINE. Nonsense, Paul!

PETKOFF (*over his coffee and cigaret*). I don't believe in going too far with these modern customs. All this washing can't be good for the health: it's not natural. There was an Englishman at Phillipopolis who used to wet himself all over with cold water every morning when he got up. Disgusting! It all comes from the English: their climate makes them so dirty that they have to be perpetually washing themselves. Look at my father: he never had a bath in his life; and he lived to be ninety-eight, the healthiest man in Bulgaria. I don't mind a good wash once a week to keep up my position; but once a day is carrying the thing to a ridiculous extreme.

CATHERINE. You are a barbarian at heart still, Paul. I hope you behaved yourself before all those Russian officers.

PETKOFF. I did my best. I took care to let them know that we had a library.

CATHERINE. Ah; but you didn't tell them that we have an electric bell in it? I have had one put up.

PETKOFF. What's an electric bell?

CATHERINE. You touch a button; something tinkles in the kitchen; and then Nicola comes up.

PETKOFF. Why not shout for him?

CATHERINE. Civilized people never shout for their servants. I've learnt that while you were away.

PETKOFF. Well, I'll tell you something I've learnt, too. Civilized people don't hang out their washing to dry where visitors can see it; so you'd better have all that (*indicating the clothes on the bushes*) put somewhere else.

CATHERINE. Oh, that's absurd, Paul: I don't believe really refined people notice such things.

Someone is heard knocking at the stable gates.

PETKOFF. There's Sergius. (*Shouting.*) Hollo, Nicola!

CATHERINE. Oh, don't shout, Paul: it really isn't nice.

PETKOFF. Bosh! (*He shouts louder than before.*) Nicola!

NICOLA (*appearing at the house door*). Yes, sir.

PETKOFF. If that is Major Saranoff, bring him round this way. (*He pronounces the name with the stress on the second syllable—Sarah noff.*)

NICOLA. Yes, sir. (*He goes into the stable yard.*)

PETKOFF. You must talk to him, my dear, until Raina takes him off our hands. He bores my life out about our not promoting him—over my head, mind you.

CATHERINE. He certainly ought to be promoted when he marries Raina. Besides, the country should insist on having at least one native general.

PETKOFF. Yes, so that he could throw away whole brigades instead of regiments. It's no use, my dear: he has not the slightest chance of promotion until we are quite sure that the peace will be a lasting one.

NICOLA (*at the gate, announcing*). Major Sergius Saranoff! (*He goes into the house and returns presently with a third chair, which he places at the table. He then withdraws.*)

Major Sergius Saranoff, the original of the portrait in Raina's room, is a tall, romantically handsome man, with the physical hardihood, the high spirit, and the susceptible imagination of an untamed mountaineer chieftain. But his remarkable personal distinction is of a characteristically civilized type. The ridges of his eyebrows, curving with a ram's-horn twist round the marked projections at the outer corners, his jealously observant eye, his nose, thin, keen, and apprehensive in spite of the pugnacious high bridge and large nostril, his assertive chin, would not be out of place in a Paris salon. In short, the clever, imaginative barbarian has an acute critical faculty which has been thrown into intense activity by the arrival of western civilization in the Balkans; and the result is precisely what the advent of nineteenth century thought first produced in England: to-wit, Byronism. By his brooding on the perpetual failure, not only of others, but of himself, to live up to his imaginative ideals, his consequent cynical scorn for humanity, the jejune credulity as to the absolute validity of his ideals and the unworthiness of the world in disregarding them, his mincings and mockeries under the sting of the petty disillusions which every hour spent among men brings to his infallibly quick observation, he has acquired the half tragic, half ironic air, the mysterious moodiness, the suggestion of a strange and terrible history that has left him nothing but undying remorse, by which Childe Harold[5] *fascinated the grandmothers of his English contemporaries. Altogether it is clear that here or nowhere is Raina's ideal hero. Catherine is hardly*

[5] **Childe Harold:** the lonely but gallant hero of Byron's poem "Childe Harold's Pilgrimage."

less enthusiastic, and much less reserved in shewing her enthusiasm. As he enters from the stable gate, she rises effusively to greet him. Petkoff is distinctly less disposed to make a fuss about him.

PETKOFF. Here already, Sergius. Glad to see you!

CATHERINE. My dear Sergius! (*She holds out both her hands.*)

SERGIUS (*kissing them with scrupulous gallantry*). My dear mother, if I may call you so.

PETKOFF (*drily*). Mother-in-law, Sergius; mother-in-law! Sit down, and have some coffee.

SERGIUS. Thank you, none for me. (*He gets away from the table with a certain distaste for Petkoff's enjoyment of it, and posts himself with conscious grace against the rail of the steps leading to the house.*)

CATHERINE. You look superb—splendid. The campaign has improved you. Everybody here is mad about you. We were all wild with enthusiasm about that magnificent cavalry charge.

SERGIUS (*with grave irony*). Madam: it was the cradle and the grave of my military reputation.

CATHERINE. How so?

SERGIUS. I won the battle the wrong way when our worthy Russian generals were losing it the right way. That upset their plans, and wounded their self-esteem. Two of their colonels got their regiments driven back on the correct principles of scientific warfare. Two major-generals got killed strictly according to military etiquette. Those two colonels are now major-generals; and I am still a simple major.

CATHERINE. You shall not remain so, Sergius. The women are on your side; and they will see that justice is done you.

SERGIUS. It is too late. I have only waited for the peace to send in my resignation.

PETKOFF (*dropping his cup in his amazement*). Your resignation!

CATHERINE. Oh, you must withdraw it!

SERGIUS (*with resolute, measured emphasis, folding his arms*). I never withdraw!

PETKOFF (*vexed*). Now who could have supposed you were going to do such a thing?

SERGIUS (*with fire*). Everyone that knew me. But enough of myself and my affairs. How is Raina; and where is Raina?

RAINA (*suddenly coming round the corner of the house and standing at the top of the steps in the path*). Raina is here. (*She makes a charming picture as they all turn to look at her. She wears an underdress of pale green silk, draped with an overdress of thin ecru canvas embroidered with gold. On her head she wears a pretty Phrygian cap*[6] *of gold tinsel. Sergius, with an exclamation of pleasure, goes impulsively to meet her. She stretches out her hand: he drops chivalrously on one knee and kisses it.*)

PETKOFF (*aside to Catherine, beaming with parental pride*). Pretty, isn't it? She always appears at the right moment.

CATHERINE (*impatiently*). Yes: she listens for it. It is an abominable habit.

Sergius leads Raina forward with splendid gallantry, as if she were a queen. When they come to the table, she turns to him with a bend of the head; he bows; and thus they separate, he coming to his place, and she going behind her father's chair.

RAINA (*stooping and kissing her father*). Dear father! Welcome home!

PETKOFF (*patting her cheek*). My little pet girl. (*He kisses her; she goes to the chair left by Nicola for Sergius, and sits down.*)

CATHERINE. And so you're no longer a soldier, Sergius.

SERGIUS. I am no longer a soldier. Soldiering, my dear madam, is the coward's art of attacking mercilessly when you are strong, and keeping out of harm's way when you are weak. That is the whole secret of successful fighting. Get your enemy at a disadvantage; and never, on any account, fight him on equal terms. Eh, Major!

PETKOFF. They wouldn't let us make a fair stand-up fight of it. However, I suppose soldiering has to be a trade like any other trade.

SERGIUS. Precisely. But I have no ambition to succeed as a tradesman; so I have taken the advice of that bagman of a captain that settled the exchange of prisoners with us at Peerot, and given it up.

[6] **Phrygian cap:** conical cap or bonnet with a folded peak.

PETKOFF. What, that Swiss fellow? Sergius: I've often thought of that exchange since. He over-reached us about those horses.

SERGIUS. Of course he over-reached us. His father was a hotel and livery stable keeper; and he owed his first step to his knowledge of horse-dealing. (*With mock enthusiasm.*) Ah, he was a soldier—every inch a soldier! If only I had bought the horses for my regiment instead of foolishly leading it into danger, I should have been a field-marshal now!

CATHERINE. A Swiss? What was he doing in the Servian army?

PETKOFF. A volunteer of course—keen on picking up his profession. (*Chuckling.*) We shouldn't have been able to begin fighting if these foreigners hadn't shewn us how to do it: we knew nothing about it; and neither did the Servians. Egad, there'd have been no war without them.

RAINA. Are there many Swiss officers in the Servian army?

PETKOFF. No—all Austrians, just as our officers were all Russians. This was the only Swiss I came across. I'll never trust a Swiss again. He cheated us—humbugged us into giving him fifty able bodied men for two hundred confounded worn out chargers. They weren't even eatable!

SERGIUS. We were two children in the hands of that consummate soldier, Major: simply two innocent little children.

RAINA. What was he like?

CATHERINE. Oh, Raina, what a silly question!

SERGIUS. He was like a commercial traveller in uniform. Bourgeois to his boots.

PETKOFF (*grinning*). Sergius: tell Catherine that queer story his friend told us about him—how he escaped after Slivnitza. You remember?—about his being hid by two women.

SERGIUS (*with bitter irony*). Oh, yes, quite a romance. He was serving in the very battery I so unprofessionally charged. Being a thorough soldier, he ran away like the rest of them, with our cavalry at his heels. To escape their attentions, he had the good taste to take refuge in the chamber of some patriotic young Bulgarian lady. The young lady was enchanted by his persuasive commercial traveller's manners. She very modestly entertained him for an hour or so and then called in her mother lest her conduct should appear unmaidenly. The old lady was equally fascinated; and the fugitive was sent on his way in the morning, disguised in an old coat belonging to the master of the house, who was away at the war.

RAINA (*rising with marked stateliness*). Your life in the camp has made you coarse, Sergius. I did not think you would have repeated such a story before me. (*She turns away coldly.*)

CATHERINE (*also rising*). She is right, Sergius. If such women exist, we should be spared the knowledge of them.

PETKOFF. Pooh! nonsense! what does it matter?

SERGIUS (*ashamed*). No, Petkoff: I was wrong. (*To Raina, with earnest humility.*) I beg your pardon. I have behaved abominably. Forgive me, Raina. (*She bows reservedly.*) And you, too, madam. (*Catherine bows graciously and sits down. He proceeds solemnly, again addressing Raina.*) The glimpses I have had of the seamy side of life during the last few months have made me cynical; but I should not have brought my cynicism here—least of all into your presence, Raina. I— (*Here, turning to the others, he is evidently about to begin a long speech when the Major interrupts him.*)

PETKOFF. Stuff and nonsense, Sergius. That's quite enough fuss about nothing: a soldier's daughter should be able to stand up without flinching to a little strong conversation. (*He rises.*) Come: it's time for us to get to business. We have to make up our minds how those three regiments are to get back to Phillipopolis:—there's no forage for them on the Sophia route. (*He goes towards the house.*) Come along. (*Sergius is about to follow him when Catherine rises and intervenes.*)

CATHERINE. Oh, Paul, can't you spare Sergius for a few moments? Raina has hardly seen him yet. Perhaps I can help you to settle about the regiments.

SERGIUS (*protesting*). My dear madam, impossible: you——

CATHERINE (*stopping him playfully*). You stay here, my dear Sergius: there's no hurry. I have a word or two to say to Paul. (*Sergius instantly bows and steps back.*) Now, dear (*taking Petkoff's arm*), come and see the electric bell.

PETKOFF. Oh, very well, very well. (*They go into the house together affectionately. Sergius, left alone with Raina, looks anxiously at her, fearing that she may be still offended. She smiles, and stretches out her arms to him.*)

Exit R. into house, followed by Catherine.

SERGIUS (*hastening to her, but refraining from touching her without express permission*). Am I forgiven?

RAINA (*placing her hands on his shoulder as she looks up at him with admiration and worship*). My hero! My king.

SERGIUS. My queen! (*He kisses her on the forehead with holy awe.*)

RAINA. How I have envied you, Sergius! You have been out in the world, on the field of battle, able to prove yourself there worthy of any woman in the world; whilst I have had to sit at home inactive,—dreaming—useless—doing nothing that could give me the right to call myself worthy of any man.

SERGIUS. Dearest, all my deeds have been yours. You inspired me. I have gone through the war like a knight in a tournament with his lady looking on at him!

RAINA. And you have never been absent from my thoughts for a moment. (*Very solemnly.*) Sergius: I think we two have found the higher love. When I think of you, I feel that I could never do a base deed, or think an ignoble thought.

SERGIUS. My lady, and my saint! (*Clasping her reverently.*)

RAINA (*returning his embrace*). My lord and my g——

SERGIUS. Sh—sh! Let me be the worshipper, dear. You little know how unworthy even the best man is of a girl's pure passion!

RAINA. I trust you. I love you. You will never disappoint me, Sergius. (*Louka is heard singing within the house. They quickly release each other.*) Hush! I can't pretend to talk indifferently before her: my heart is too full. (*Louka comes from the house with her tray. She goes to the table, and begins to clear it, with her back turned to them.*) I will go and get my hat; and then we can go out until lunch time. Wouldn't you like that?

SERGIUS. Be quick. If you are away five minutes, it will seem five hours. (*Raina runs to the top of the steps and turns there to exchange a look with him and wave him a kiss with both hands. He looks after her with emotion for a moment, then turns slowly away, his face radiant with the exultation of the scene which has just passed. The movement shifts his field of vision, into the corner of which there now comes the tail of Louka's double apron. His eye gleams at once. He takes a stealthy look at her, and begins to twirl his moustache nervously, with his left hand akimbo on his hip. Finally, striking the ground with his heels in something of a cavalry swagger, he strolls over to the left of the table, opposite her, and says*) Louka: do you know what the higher love is?

LOUKA (*astonished*). No, sir.

SERGIUS. Very fatiguing thing to keep up for any length of time, Louka. One feels the need of some relief after it.

LOUKA (*innocently*). Perhaps you would like some coffee, sir? (*She stretches her hand across the table for the coffee pot.*)

SERGIUS (*taking her hand*). Thank you, Louka.

LOUKA (*pretending to pull*). Oh, sir, you know I didn't mean that. I'm surprised at you!

SERGIUS (*coming clear of the table and drawing her with him*). I am surprised at myself, Louka. What would Sergius, the hero of Slivnitza, say if he saw me now? What would Sergius, the apostle of the higher love, say if he saw me now? What would the half dozen Sergiuses who keep popping in and out of this handsome figure of mine say if they caught us here? (*Letting go her hand and slipping his arm dexterously round her waist.*) Do you consider my figure handsome, Louka?

LOUKA. Let me go, sir. I shall be disgraced. (*She struggles: he holds her inexorably.*) Oh, will you let go?

SERGIUS (*looking straight into her eyes*). No.

LOUKA. Then stand back where we can't be seen. Have you no common sense?

SERGIUS. Ah, that's reasonable. (*He takes her into the stableyard gateway, where they are hidden from the house.*)

LOUKA (*complaining*). I may have been seen from the windows: Miss Raina is sure to be spying about after you.

SERGIUS (*stung—letting her go*). Take care, Louka. I may be worthless enough to betray the higher love; but do not you insult it.

LOUKA (*demurely*). Not for the world, sir, I'm sure. May I go on with my work please, now?

SERGIUS (*again putting his arm round her*). You are a provoking little witch, Louka. If you were in love with me, would you spy out of windows on me?

LOUKA. Well, you see, sir, since you say you are half a dozen different gentlemen all at once, I should have a great deal to look after.

SERGIUS (*charmed*). Witty as well as pretty. (*He tries to kiss her.*)

LOUKA (*avoiding him*). No, I don't want your kisses. Gentlefolk are all alike—you making love to me behind Miss Raina's back, and she doing the same behind yours.

SERGIUS (*recoiling a step*). Louka!

LOUKA. It shews how little you really care!

SERGIUS (*dropping his familiarity and speaking with freezing politeness*). If our conversation is to continue, Louka, you will please remember that a gentleman does not discuss the conduct of the lady he is engaged to with her maid.

LOUKA. It's so hard to know what a gentleman considers right. I thought from your trying to kiss me that you had given up being so particular.

SERGIUS (*turning from her and striking his forehead as he comes back into the garden from the gateway*). Devil! devil!

LOUKA. Ha! ha! I expect one of the six of you is very like me, sir, though I am only Miss Raina's maid. (*She goes back to her work at the table, taking no further notice of him.*)

SERGIUS (*speaking to himself*). Which of the six is the real man?—that's the question that torments me. One of them is a hero, another a buffoon, another a humbug, another perhaps a bit of a blackguard. (*He pauses and looks furtively at Louka, as he adds with deep bitterness.*) And one, at least, is a coward—jealous, like all cowards. (*He goes to the table.*) Louka.

LOUKA. Yes?

SERGIUS. Who is my rival?

LOUKA. You shall never get that out of me, for love or money.

SERGIUS. Why?

LOUKA. Never mind why. Besides, you would tell that I told you; and I should lose my place.

SERGIUS (*holding out his right hand in affirmation*). No; on the honor of a— (*He checks himself, and his hand drops nerveless as he concludes, sardonically*) —of a man capable of behaving as I have been behaving for the last five minutes. Who is he?

LOUKA. I don't know. I never saw him. I only heard his voice through the door of her room.

SERGIUS. Damnation! How dare you?

LOUKA (*retreating*). Oh, I mean no harm: you've no right to take up my words like that. The mistress knows all about it.

And I tell you that if that gentleman ever comes here again, Miss Raina will marry him, whether he likes it or not. I know the difference between the sort of manner you and she put on before one another and the real manner. (*Sergius shivers as if she had stabbed him. Then, setting his face like iron, he strides grimly to her, and grips her above the elbows with both hands.*)

SERGIUS. Now listen you to me!

LOUKA (*wincing*). Not so tight: you're hurting me!

SERGIUS. That doesn't matter. You have stained my honor by making me a party to your eavesdropping. And you have betrayed your mistress——

LOUKA (*writhing*). Please——

SERGIUS. That shews that you are an abominable little clod of common clay, with the soul of a servant. (*He lets her go as if she were an unclean thing, and turns away, dusting his hands of her, to the bench by the wall, where he sits down with averted head, meditating gloomily.*)

LOUKA (*whimpering angrily with her hands up her sleeves, feeling her bruised arms*). You know how to hurt with your tongue as well as with your hands. But I don't care, now I've found out that whatever clay I'm made of, you're made of the same. As for her, she's a liar; and her fine airs are a cheat; and I'm worth six of her. (*She shakes the pain off hardily; tosses her head; and sets to work to put the things on the tray. He looks doubtfully at her once or twice. She finishes packing the tray, and laps the cloth over the edges, so as to carry all out together. As she stoops to lift it, he rises.*)

SERGIUS. Louka! (*She stops and looks defiantly at him with the tray in her hands.*) A gentleman has no right to hurt a woman under any circumstances. (*With profound humility, uncovering his head.*) I beg your pardon.

LOUKA. That sort of apology may satisfy a lady. Of what use is it to a servant?

SERGIUS (*thus rudely crossed in his chivalry, throws it off with a bitter laugh and says slightingly*). Oh, you wish to be paid for the hurt? (*He puts on his shako, and takes some money from his pocket.*)

LOUKA (*her eyes filling with tears in spite of herself*). No, I want my hurt made well.

SERGIUS (*sobered by her tone*). How? (*She rolls up her left sleeve; clasps her arm with the thumb and fingers of her right hand; and looks down at the bruise. Then she raises her head and looks straight at him. Finally, with a superb gesture she presents her arm to be kissed. Amazed, he looks at her; at the arm; at her again; hesitates; and then, with shuddering intensity, exclaims*) Never! (*and gets away as far as possible from her.*)

Her arm drops. Without a word, and with unaffected dignity, she takes her tray, and is approaching the house when Raina returns wearing a hat and jacket in the height of the Vienna fashion of the previous year, 1885. Louka makes way proudly for her, and then goes into the house.

RAINA. I'm ready! What's the matter? (*Gaily.*) Have you been flirting with Louka?

SERGIUS (*hastily*). No, no. How can you think such a thing?

RAINA (*ashamed of herself*). Forgive me, dear: it was only a jest. I am so happy to day.

He goes quickly to her, and kisses her hand remorsefully. Catherine comes out and calls to them from the top of the steps.

CATHERINE (*coming down to them*). I am sorry to disturb you, children; but Paul is distracted over those three regiments. He does not know how to get them to Phillipopolis; and he objects to every suggestion of mine. You must go and help him, Sergius. He is in the library.

RAINA (*disappointed*). But we are just going out for a walk.

SERGIUS. I shall not be long. Wait for me just five minutes. (*He runs up the steps to the door.*)

RAINA (*following him to the foot of the steps and looking up at him with timid coquetry*). I shall go round and wait in full view of the library windows. Be sure you draw father's attention to me. If you are a moment longer than five minutes, I shall go in and fetch you, regiments or no regiments.

SERGIUS (*laughing*). Very well. (*He goes in. Raina watches him until he is out of her sight. Then, with a perceptible relaxation of manner, she begins to pace up and down about the garden in a brown study.*)

CATHERINE. Imagine their meeting that Swiss and hearing the whole story! The very first thing your father asked for was the old coat we sent him off in. A nice mess you have got us into!

RAINA (*gazing thoughtfully at the gravel as she walks*). The little beast!

CATHERINE. Little beast! What little beast?

RAINA. To go and tell. Oh, if I had him here, I'd stuff him with chocolate creams till he couldn't ever speak again!

CATHERINE. Don't talk nonsense. Tell me the truth, Raina. How long was he in your room before you came to me?

RAINA (*whisking round and recommencing her march in the opposite direction*). Oh, I forget.

CATHERINE. You cannot forget! Did he really climb up after the soldiers were gone, or was he there when that officer searched the room?

RAINA. No. Yes, I think he must have been there then.

CATHERINE. You think! Oh, Raina, Raina! Will anything ever make you straightforward? If Sergius finds out, it is all over between you.

RAINA (*with cool impertinence*). Oh, I know Sergius is your pet. I sometimes wish you could marry him instead of me. You would just suit him. You would pet him, and spoil him, and mother him to perfection.

CATHERINE (*opening her eyes very widely indeed*). Well, upon my word!

RAINA (*capriciously—half to herself*). I always feel a longing to do or say something dreadful to him—to shock his propriety—to scandalize the five senses out of him! (*To Catherine perversely.*) I don't care whether he finds out about the chocolate cream soldier or not. I half hope he may. (*She again turns flippantly away and strolls up the path to the corner of the house.*)

CATHERINE. And what should I be able to say to your father, pray?

RAINA (*over her shoulder, from the top of the two steps*). Oh, poor father! As if he could help himself! (*She turns the corner and passes out of sight.*)

CATHERINE (*looking after her, her fingers itching*). Oh, if you were only ten years younger! (*Louka comes from the house with a salver, which she carries hanging down by her side.*) Well?

LOUKA. There's a gentleman just called, madam—a Servian officer——

CATHERINE (*flaming*). A Servian! How dare he—(*Checking herself bitterly.*) Oh, I forgot. We are at peace now. I suppose we shall have them calling every day to pay their compliments. Well, if he is an officer why don't you tell your master? He is in the library with Major Saranoff. Why do you come to me?

LOUKA. But he asks for you, madam. And I don't think he knows who you are: he said the lady of the house. He gave me this little ticket for you. (*She takes a card out of her bosom; puts it on the salver and offers it to Catherine.*)

CATHERINE (*reading*). "Captain Bluntschli!" That's a German name.

LOUKA. Swiss, madam, I think.

CATHERINE (*with a bound that makes Louka jump back*). Swiss! What is he like?

LOUKA (*timidly*). He has a big carpet bag, madam.

CATHERINE. Oh, Heavens, he's come to return the coat! Send him away—say we're not at home—ask him to leave his address and I'll write to him— Oh, stop: that will never do. Wait! (*She throws herself into a chair to think it out. Louka waits.*) The master and Major Saranoff are busy in the library, aren't they?

LOUKA. Yes, madam.

CATHERINE (*decisively*). Bring the gentleman out here at once. (*Imperatively.*) And be very polite to him. Don't delay. Here (*impatiently snatching the salver from her*): leave that here; and go straight back to him.

LOUKA. Yes, madam. (*Going.*)

CATHERINE. Louka!

LOUKA (*stopping*). Yes, madam.

CATHERINE. Is the library door shut?

LOUKA. I think so, madam.

CATHERINE. If not, shut it as you pass through.

LOUKA. Yes, madam. (*Going.*)

CATHERINE. Stop! (*Louka stops.*) He will have to go out that way (*indicating the gate of the stable yard*). Tell Nicola to bring his bag here after him. Don't forget.

LOUKA (*surprised*). His bag?

CATHERINE. Yes, here, as soon as possible. (*Vehemently.*) Be quick! (*Louka runs into the house. Catherine snatches the apron off and throws it behind a bush. She then takes up the salver and uses it as a mirror, with the result that the handkerchief tied round her head follows the apron. A touch to her hair and a shake to her dressing gown makes her presentable.*) Oh, how—how—how can a man be such a fool! Such a moment to select! (*Louka appears at the door of the house, announcing* "Captain Bluntschli;" *and standing aside at the top of the steps to let him pass before she goes in again. He is the man of the adventure in Raina's room. He is now clean, well brushed, smartly uniformed, and out of trouble, but still unmistakably the same man. The moment Louka's back is turned, Catherine swoops on him with hurried, urgent, coaxing appeal.*) Captain Bluntschli, I am very glad to see you; but you must leave this house at once. (*He raises his eyebrows.*) My husband has just returned, with my future son-in-law; and they know nothing. If they did, the consequences would be terrible. You are a foreigner: you do not feel our national animosities as we do. We still hate the Servians: the only effect of the peace on my husband is to make him feel like a lion baulked of his prey. If he discovered our secret, he would never forgive me; and my daughter's life would hardly be safe. Will you, like the chivalrous gentleman and soldier you are, leave at once before he finds you here?

BLUNTSCHLI (*disappointed, but philosophical*). At once, gracious lady. I only came to thank you and return the coat you lent me. If you will allow me to take it out of my bag and leave it with your servant as I pass out, I need detain you no further. (*He turns to go into the house.*)

CATHERINE (*catching him by the sleeve*). Oh, you must not think of going back that way. (*Coaxing him across to the stable gates.*) This is the shortest way out. Many thanks. So glad to have been of service to you. Good-bye.

BLUNTSCHLI. But my bag?

CATHERINE. It will be sent on. You will leave me your address.

BLUNTSCHLI. True. Allow me. (*He takes out his card-case, and stops to write his address, keeping Catherine in an agony of impatience. As he hands her the card, Petkoff, hatless, rushes from the house in a fluster of hospitality, followed by Sergius.*)

PETKOFF (*as he hurries down the steps*). My dear Captain Bluntschli——

CATHERINE. Oh Heavens! (*She sinks on the seat against the wall.*)

PETKOFF (*too preoccupied to notice her as he shakes Bluntschli's hand heartily*). Those stupid people of mine thought I was out here, instead of in the—haw!—library. (*He cannot mention the library without betraying how proud he is of it.*) I saw you through the window. I was wondering why you didn't come in. Saranoff is with me: you remember him, don't you?

SERGIUS (*saluting humorously, and then offering his hand with great charm of manner*). Welcome, our friend the enemy!

PETKOFF. No longer the enemy, happily. (*Rather anxiously.*) I hope you've come as a friend, and not on business.

CATHERINE. Oh, quite as a friend, Paul. I was just asking Captain Bluntschli to stay to lunch; but he declares he must go at once.

SERGIUS (*sardonically*). Impossible, Bluntschli. We want you here badly. We have to send on three cavalry regiments to Phillipopolis; and we don't in the least know how to do it.

BLUNTCHLI (*suddenly attentive and business-like*). Phillipopolis! The forage is the trouble, eh?

PETKOFF (*eagerly*). Yes, that's it. (*To Sergius.*) He sees the whole thing at once.

BLUNTSCHLI. I think I can shew you how to manage that.

SERGIUS. Invaluable man! Come along! (*Towering over Bluntschli, he puts his hand on his shoulder and takes him to the steps, Petkoff following. As Bluntschli puts his foot on the first step, Raina comes out of the house.*)

RAINA (*completely losing her presence of mind*). Oh, the chocolate cream soldier!

Bluntschli stands rigid. Sergius, amazed, looks at Raina, then at Petkoff, who looks back at him and then at his wife.

CATHERINE (*with commanding presence of mind*). My dear Raina, don't you see that we have a guest here—Captain Bluntschli, one of our new Servian friends? (*Raina bows; Bluntschli bows.*)

RAINA. How silly of me! (*She comes down into the centre of the group, between Bluntschli and Petkoff.*) I made a beautiful ornament this morning for the ice pudding; and that stupid Nicola has just put down a pile of plates on it and spoiled it. (*To Bluntschli, winningly.*) I hope you didn't think that you were the chocolate cream soldier, Captain Bluntschli.

BLUNTSCHLI (*laughing*). I assure you I did. (*Stealing a whimsical glance at her.*) Your explanation was a relief.

PETKOFF (*suspiciously, to Raina*). And since when, pray, have you taken to cooking?

CATHERINE. Oh, whilst you were away. It is her latest fancy.

PETKOFF (*testily*). And has Nicola taken to drinking? He used to be careful enough. First he shews Captain Bluntschli out here when he knew quite well I was in the—hum!—library; and then he goes downstairs and breaks Raina's chocolate soldier. He must— (*At this moment Nicola appears at the top of the steps R., with a carpet bag. He descends; places it respectfully before Bluntschli; and waits for further orders. General amazement. Nicola, unconscious of the effect he is producing, looks perfectly satisfied with himself. When Petkoff recovers his power of speech, he breaks out at him with*) Are you mad, Nicola?

NICOLA (*taken aback*). Sir?

PETKOFF. What have you brought that for?

NICOLA. My lady's orders, sir. Louka told me that——

CATHERINE (*interrupting him*). My orders! Why should I order you to bring Captain Bluntschli's luggage out here? What are you thinking of, Nicola?

NICOLA (*after a moment's bewilderment, picking up the bag as he addresses Bluntschli with the very perfection of servile discretion*). I beg your pardon, sir, I am sure. (*To Catherine.*) My fault, madam! I hope you'll overlook it! (*He bows, and is going to the steps with the bag, when Petkoff addresses him angrily.)*

PETKOFF. You'd better go and slam that bag, too, down on Miss Raina's ice pudding! (*This is too much for Nicola. The bag drops from his hands on Petkoff's corns, eliciting a roar of anguish from him.*) Begone, you butter-fingered donkey.

NICOLA (*snatching up the bag, and escaping into the house*). Yes, sir.

CATHERINE. Oh, never mind, Paul, don't be angry!

PETKOFF (*muttering*). Scoundrel. He's got out of hand while I was away. I'll teach him. (*Recollecting his guest.*) Oh, well, never mind. Come, Bluntschli, let's have no more nonsense about your having to go away. You know very well you're not going back to Switzerland yet. Until you do go back you'll stay with us.

RAINA. Oh, do, Captain Bluntschli.

PETKOFF (*to Catherine*). Now, Catherine, it's of you that he's afraid. Press him and he'll stay.

CATHERINE. Of course I shall be only too delighted if (*appealingly*) Captain Bluntschli really wishes to stay. He knows my wishes.

BLUNTSCHLI (*in his driest military manner*). I am at madame's orders.

SERGIUS (*cordially*). That settles it!

PETKOFF (*heartily*). Of course!

RAINA. You see, you must stay!

BLUNTSCHLI (*smiling*). Well, if I must, I must!

Gesture of despair from Catherine.

ACT THREE

In the library after lunch. It is not much of a library, its literary equipment consisting of a single fixed shelf stocked with old paper covered novels, broken backed, coffee stained, torn and thumbed, and a couple of little hanging shelves with a few gift books on them, the rest of the wall space being occupied by trophies of war and the chase. But it is a most com-

fortable sitting-room. A row of three large windows in the front of the house shew a mountain panorama, which is just now seen in one of its softest aspects in the mellowing afternoon light. In the left hand corner, a square earthenware stove, a perfect tower of colored pottery, rises nearly to the ceiling and guarantees plenty of warmth. The ottoman in the middle is a circular bank of decorated cushions, and the window seats are well upholstered divans. Little Turkish tables, one of them with an elaborate hookah on it, and a screen to match them, complete the handsome effect of the furnishing. There is one object, however, which is hopelessly out of keeping with its surroundings. This is a small kitchen table, much the worse for wear, fitted as a writing table with an old canister full of pens, an eggcup filled with ink, and a deplorable scrap of severely used pink blotting paper.

At the side of this table, which stands on the right, Bluntschli is hard at work, with a couple of maps before him, writing orders. At the head of it sits Sergius, who is also supposed to be at work, but who is actually gnawing the feather of a pen, and contemplating Bluntschli's quick, sure, businesslike progress with a mixture of envious irritation at his own incapacity, and awestruck wonder at an ability which seems to him almost miraculous, though its prosaic character forbids him to esteem it. The major is comfortably established on the ottoman, with a newspaper in his hand and the tube of the hookah within his reach. Catherine sits at the stove with her back to them, embroidering. Raina, reclining on the divan under the left hand window, is gazing in a daydream out at the Balkan landscape, with a neglected novel in her lap.

The door is on the left. The button of the electric bell is between the door and the fireplace.

PETKOFF (*looking up from his paper to watch how they are getting on at the table*). Are you sure I can't help you in any way, Bluntschli?

BLUNTSCHLI (*without interrupting his writing or looking up*). Quite sure, thank you. Saranoff and I will manage it.

SERGIUS (*grimly*). Yes: we'll manage it. He finds out what to do; draws up the orders; and I sign 'em. Division of labour, Major. (*Bluntschli passes him a paper.*) Another one? Thank you. (*He plants the papers squarely before him; sets his chair carefully parallel to them; and signs with the air of a man resolutely performing a difficult and dangerous feat.*) This hand is more accustomed to the sword than to the pen.

PETKOFF. It's very good of you, Bluntschli, it is indeed, to let yourself be put upon in this way. Now are you quite sure I can do nothing?

CATHERINE (*in a low, warning tone*). You can stop interrupting, Paul.

PETKOFF (*starting and looking round at her*). Eh? Oh! Quite right, my love, quite right. (*He takes his newspaper up, but lets it drop again.*) Ah, you haven't been campaigning, Catherine: you don't know how pleasant it is for us to sit here, after a good lunch, with nothing to do but enjoy ourselves. There's only one thing I want to make me thoroughly comfortable.

CATHERINE. What is that?

PETKOFF. My old coat. I'm not at home in this one: I feel as if I were on parade.

CATHERINE. My dear Paul, how absurd you are about that old coat! It must be hanging in the blue closet where you left it.

PETKOFF. My dear Catherine, I tell you I've looked there. Am I to believe my own eyes or not? (*Catherine quietly rises and presses the button of the electric bell by the fireplace.*) What are you shewing off that bell for. (*She looks at him majestically, and silently resumes her chair and her needlework.*) My dear: if you think the obstinacy of your sex can make a coat out of two old dressing gowns of Raina's, your waterproof, and my mackintosh, you're mistaken. That's exactly what the blue closet contains at present. (*Nicola presents himself.*)

CATHERINE (*unmoved by Petkoff's sally*). Nicola: go to the blue closet and bring your master's old coat here—the braided one he usually wears in the house.

NICOLA. Yes, madam. (*Nicola goes out.*)

PETKOFF. Catherine.

CATHERINE. Yes, Paul?

PETKOFF. I bet you any piece of jewellery you like to order from Sophia against a week's housekeeping money, that the coat isn't there.

CATHERINE. Done, Paul.

PETKOFF (*excited by the prospect of a gamble*). Come: here's an opportunity for some sport. Who'll bet on it? Bluntschli: I'll give you six to one.

BLUNTSCHLI (*imperturbably*). It would be robbing you, Major. Madame is sure to be right. (*Without looking up, he passes another batch of papers to Sergius.*)

SERGIUS (*also excited*). Bravo, Switzerland! Major: I bet my best charger against an Arab mare for Raina that Nicola finds the coat in the blue closet.

PETKOFF (*eagerly*). Your best char——

CATHERINE (*hastily interrupting him*). Don't be foolish, Paul. An Arabian mare will cost you 50,000 levas.

RAINA (*suddenly coming out of her picturesque revery*). Really, mother, if you are going to take the jewellery, I don't see why you should grudge me my Arab.

Nicola comes back with the coat and brings it to Petkoff, who can hardly believe his eyes.

CATHERINE. Where was it, Nicola?

NICOLA. Hanging in the blue closet, madam.

PETKOFF. Well, I am d——

CATHERINE (*stopping him*). Paul!

PETKOFF. I could have sworn it wasn't there. Age is beginning to tell on me. I'm getting hallucinations. (*To Nicola.*) Here: help me to change. Excuse me, Bluntschli. (*He begins changing coats, Nicola acting as valet.*) Remember: I didn't take that bet of yours, Sergius. You'd better give Raina that Arab steed yourself, since you've roused her expectations. Eh, Raina? (*He looks round at her; but she is again rapt in the landscape. With a little gush of paternal affection and pride, he points her out to them and says*) She's dreaming, as usual.

SERGIUS. Assuredly she shall not be the loser.

PETKOFF. So much the better for her. *I* shan't come off so cheap, I expect. (*The change is now complete. Nicola goes out with the discarded coat.*) Ah, now I feel at home at last. (*He sits down and takes his newspaper with a grunt of relief.*)

BLUNTSCHLI (*to Sergius, handing a paper*). That's the last order.

PETKOFF (*jumping up*). What! finished?

BLUNTSCHLI. Finished. (*Petkoff goes beside Sergius; looks curiously over his left shoulder as he signs; and says with childlike envy*) Haven't you anything for me to sign?

BLUNTSCHLI. Not necessary. His signature will do.

PETKOFF. Ah, well, I think we've done a thundering good day's work. (*He goes away from the table.*) Can I do anything more?

BLUNTSCHLI. You had better both see the fellows that are to take these. (*To Sergius.*) Pack them off at once; and shew them that I've marked on the orders the time they should hand them in by. Tell them that if they stop to drink or tell stories—if they're five minutes late, they'll have the skin taken off their backs.

SERGIUS (*rising indignantly*). I'll say so. And if one of them is man enough to spit in my face for insulting him, I'll buy his discharge and give him a pension. (*He strides out, his humanity deeply outraged.*)

BLUNTSCHLI (*confidentially*). Just see that he talks to them properly, Major, will you?

PETKOFF (*officiously*). Quite right, Bluntschli, quite right. I'll see to it. (*He goes to the door importantly, but hesitates on the threshold.*) By the bye, Catherine, you may as well come, too. They'll be far more frightened of you than of me.

CATHERINE (*putting down her embroidery*). I daresay I had better. You will only splutter at them. (*She goes out, Petkoff holding the door for her and following her.*)

BLUNTSCHLI. What a country! They make cannons out of cherry trees; and the officers send for their wives to keep discipline! (*He begins to fold and docket the papers. Raina, who has risen from the divan, strolls down the room with her hands clasped behind her, and looks mischievously at him.*)

RAINA. You look ever so much nicer than when we last met. (*He looks up, surprised.*) What have you done to yourself?

BLUNTSCHLI. Washed; brushed; good night's sleep and breakfast. That's all.

RAINA. Did you get back safely that morning?

BLUNTSCHLI. Quite, thanks.

RAINA. Were they angry with you for running away from Sergius's charge?

BLUNTSCHLI. No, they were glad; because they'd all just run away themselves.

RAINA (*going to the table, and leaning over it towards him*). It must have made a lovely story for them—all that about me and my room.

BLUNTSCHLI. Capital story. But I only told it to one of them —a particular friend.

RAINA. On whose discretion you could absolutely rely?

BLUNTSCHLI. Absolutely.

RAINA. Hm! He told it all to my father and Sergius the day you exchanged the prisoners. (*She turns away and strolls carelessly across to the other side of the room.*)

BLUNTSCHLI (*deeply concerned and half incredulous*). No! you don't mean that, do you?

RAINA (*turning, with sudden earnestness*). I do indeed. But they don't know that it was in this house that you hid. If Sergius knew, he would challenge you and kill you in a duel.

BLUNTSCHLI. Bless me! then don't tell him.

RAINA (*full of reproach for his levity*). Can you realize what it is to me to deceive him? I want to be quite perfect with Sergius—no meanness, no smallness, no deceit. My relation to him is the one really beautiful and noble part of my life. I hope you can understand that.

BLUNTSCHLI (*sceptically*). You mean that you wouldn't like him to find out that the story about the ice pudding was a—a— a— You know.

RAINA (*wincing*). Ah, don't talk of it in that flippant way. I lied: I know it. But I did it to save your life. He would have killed you. That was the second time I ever uttered a falsehood. (*Bluntschli rises quickly and looks doubtfully and somewhat severely at her.*) Do you remember the first time?

BLUNTSCHLI. I! No. Was I present?

RAINA. Yes; and I told the officer who was searching for you that you were not present.

BLUNTSCHLI. True. I should have remembered it.

RAINA (*greatly encouraged*). Ah, it is natural that you should forget it first. It cost you nothing: it cost me a lie!—a lie!! (*She *sits down on the ottoman, looking straight before her with her hands clasped on her knee. Bluntschli, quite touched, goes to the ottoman with a particularly reassuring and considerate air, and sits down beside her.*)

BLUNTSCHLI. My dear young lady, don't let this worry you. Remember: I'm a soldier. Now what are the two things that happen to a soldier so often that he comes to think nothing of them? One is hearing people tell lies (*Raina recoils*): the other is getting his life saved in all sorts of ways by all sorts of people.

RAINA (*rising in indignant protest*). And so he becomes a creature incapable of faith and of gratitude.

BLUNTSCHLI (*making a wry face*). Do you like gratitude? I don't. If pity is akin to love, gratitude is akin to the other thing.

RAINA. Gratitude! (*Turning on him.*) If you are incapable of gratitude you are incapable of any noble sentiment. Even animals are grateful. Oh, I see now exactly what you think of me! You were not surprised to hear me lie. To you it was something I probably did every day—every hour. That is how men think of women. (*She walks up the room melodramatically.*)

BLUNTSCHLI (*dubiously*). There's reason in everything. You said you'd told only two lies in your whole life. Dear young lady: isn't that rather a short allowance? I'm quite a straightforward man myself; but it wouldn't last me a whole morning.

RAINA (*staring haughtily at him*). Do you know, sir, that you are insulting me?

BLUNTSCHLI. I can't help it. When you get into that noble attitude and speak in that thrilling voice, I admire you; but I find it impossible to believe a single word you say.

RAINA (*superbly*). Captain Bluntschli!

BLUNTSCHLI (*unmoved*). Yes?

RAINA (*coming a little towards him, as if she could not believe her senses*). Do you mean what you said just now? Do you know what you said just now?

BLUNTSCHLI. I do.

RAINA (*gasping*). I! I!!! (*She points to herself incredulously, meaning "I, Raina Petkoff, tell lies!" He meets her gaze un-*

flinchingly. She suddenly sits down beside him, and adds, with a complete change of manner from the heroic to the familiar) How did you find me out?

BLUNTSCHLI (*promptly*). Instinct, dear young lady. Instinct, and experience of the world.

RAINA (*wonderingly*). Do you know, you are the first man I ever met who did not take me seriously?

BLUNTSCHLI. You mean, don't you, that I am the first man that has ever taken you quite seriously?

RAINA. Yes, I suppose I do mean that. (*Cosily, quite at her ease with him.*) How strange it is to be talked to in such a way! You know, I've always gone on like that—I mean the noble attitude and the thrilling voice. I did it when I was a tiny child to my nurse. She believed in it. I do it before my parents. They believe in it. I do it before Sergius. He believes in it.

BLUNTSCHLI. Yes: he's a little in that line himself, isn't he?

RAINA (*startled*). Do you think so?

BLUNTSCHLI. You know him better than I do.

RAINA. I wonder—I wonder is he? If I thought that—! (*Discouraged.*) Ah, well, what does it matter? I suppose, now that you've found me out, you despise me.

BLUNTSCHLI (*warmly, rising*). No, my dear young lady, no, no, no a thousand times. It's part of your youth—part of your charm. I'm like all the rest of them—the nurse—your parents —Sergius: I'm your infatuated admirer.

RAINA (*pleased*). Really?

BLUNTSCHLI (*slapping his breast smartly with his hand, German fashion*). Hand aufs Herz![7] Really and truly.

RAINA (*very happy*). But what did you think of me for giving you my portrait?

BLUNTSCHLI (*astonished*). Your portrait! You never gave me your portrait.

RAINA (*quickly*). Do you mean to say you never got it?

BLUNTSCHLI. No. (*He sits down beside her, with renewed interest, and says, with some complacency.*) When did you send it to me?

RAINA (*indignantly*). I did not send it to you. (*She turns her head away, and adds, reluctantly.*) It was in the pocket of that coat.

[7] **Hand aufs Herz:** Cross your heart.

BLUNTSCHLI (*pursing his lips and rounding his eyes*). Oh-o-oh! I never found it. It must be there still.

RAINA (*springing up*). There still!—for my father to find the first time he puts his hand in his pocket! Oh, how could you be so stupid?

BLUNTSCHLI (*rising also*). It doesn't matter: it's only a photograph: how can he tell who it was intended for? Tell him he put it there himself.

RAINA (*impatiently*). Yes, that is so clever—so clever! What shall I do?

BLUNTSCHLI. Ah, I see. You wrote something on it. That was rash!

RAINA (*annoyed almost to tears*). Oh, to have done such a thing for you, who care no more—except to laugh at me—oh! Are you sure nobody has touched it?

BLUNTSCHLI. Well, I can't be quite sure. You see I couldn't carry it about with me all the time: one can't take much luggage on active service.

RAINA. What did you do with it?

BLUNTSCHLI. When I got through to Peerot I had to put it in safe keeping somehow. I thought of the railway cloak room; but that's the surest place to get looted in modern warfare. So I pawned it.

RAINA. Pawned it!!!

BLUNTSCHLI. I know it doesn't sound nice; but it was much the safest plan. I redeemed it the day before yesterday. Heaven only knows whether the pawnbroker cleared out the pockets or not.

RAINA (*furious—throwing the words right into his face*). You have a low, shopkeeping mind. You think of things that would never come into a gentleman's head.

BLUNTSCHLI (*phlegmatically*). That's the Swiss national character, dear lady.

RAINA. Oh, I wish I had never met you. (*She flounces away and sits at the window fuming.*)

Louka comes in with a heap of letters and telegrams on her salver, and crosses, with her bold, free gait, to the table. Her left sleeve is looped up to the shoulder with a brooch, shewing her naked arm, with a broad gilt bracelet covering the bruise.

LOUKA (*to Bluntschli*). For you. (*She empties the salver recklessly on the table.*) The messenger is waiting. (*She is determined not to be civil to a Servian, even if she must bring him his letters.*)

BLUNTSCHLI (*to Raina*). Will you excuse me: the last postal delivery that reached me was three weeks ago. These are the subsequent accumulations. Four telegrams—a week old. (*He opens one.*) Oho! Bad news!

RAINA (*rising and advancing a little remorsefully*). Bad news?

BLUNTSCHLI. My father's dead. (*He looks at the telegram with his lips pursed, musing on the unexpected change in his arrangements.*)

RAINA. Oh, how very sad!

BLUNTSCHLI. Yes: I shall have to start for home in an hour. He has left a lot of big hotels behind him to be looked after. (*Takes up a heavy letter in a long blue envelope.*) Here's a whacking letter from the family solicitor. (*He pulls out the enclosures and glances over them.*) Great Heavens! Seventy! Two hundred! (*In a crescendo of dismay.*) Four hundred! Four thousand!! Nine thousand six hundred!!! What on earth shall I do with them all?

RAINA (*timidly*). Nine thousand hotels?

BLUNTSCHLI. Hotels! Nonsense. If you only knew!—oh, it's too ridiculous! Excuse me: I must give my fellow orders about starting. (*He leaves the room hastily, with the documents in his hand.*)

LOUKA (*tauntingly*). He has not much heart, that Swiss, though he is so fond of the Servians. He has not a word of grief for his poor father.

RAINA (*bitterly*). Grief!—a man who has been doing nothing but killing people for years! What does he care? What does any soldier care? (*She goes to the door, evidently restraining her tears with difficulty.*)

LOUKA. Major Saranoff has been fighting, too; and he has plenty of heart left. (*Raina, at the door, looks haughtily at her and goes out.*) Aha! I thought you wouldn't get much feeling out of your soldier. (*She is following Raina when Nicola enters with an armful of logs for the fire.*)

NICOLA (*grinning amorously at her*). I've been trying all the afternoon to get a minute alone with you, my girl. (*His countenance changes as he notices her arm.*) Why, what fashion is that of wearing your sleeve, child?

LOUKA (*proudly*). My own fashion.

NICOLA. Indeed! If the mistress catches you, she'll talk to you. (*He throws the logs down on the ottoman, and sits comfortably beside them.*)

LOUKA. Is that any reason why you should take it on yourself to talk to me?

NICOLA. Come: don't be so contrary with me. I've some good news for you. (*He takes out some paper money. Louka, with an eager gleam in her eyes, comes close to look at it.*) See, a twenty leva bill! Sergius gave me that out of pure swagger. A fool and his money are soon parted. There's ten levas more. The Swiss gave me that for backing up the mistress's and Raina's lies about him. He's no fool, he isn't. You should have heard old Catherine downstairs as polite as you please to me, telling me not to mind the Major being a little impatient; for they knew what a good servant I was—after making a fool and a liar of me before them all! The twenty will go to our savings; and you shall have the ten to spend if you'll only talk to me so as to remind me I'm a human being. I get tired of being a servant occasionally.

LOUKA (*scornfully*). Yes: sell your manhood for thirty levas, and buy me for ten! Keep your money. You were born to be a servant. I was not. When you set up your shop you will only be everybody's servant instead of somebody's servant.

NICOLA (*picking up his logs, and going to the stove*). Ah, wait till you see. We shall have our evenings to ourselves; and I shall be master in my own house, I promise you. (*He throws the logs down and kneels at the stove.*)

LOUKA. You shall never be master in mine. (*She sits down on Sergius's chair.*)

NICOLA (*turning, still on his knees, and squatting down rather forlornly, on his calves, daunted by her implacable disdain*). You have a great ambition in you, Louka. Remember: if any luck comes to you, it was I that made a woman of you.

LOUKA. You!

NICOLA (*with dogged self-assertion*). Yes, me. Who was it made you give up wearing a couple of pounds of false black hair on your head and reddening your lips and cheeks like any other Bulgarian girl? I did. Who taught you to trim your nails, and keep your hands clean, and be dainty about yourself, like a fine Russian lady? Me! do you hear that? me! (*She tosses her head defiantly; and he rises, illhumoredly, adding more coolly*) I've often thought that if Raina were out of the way, and you just a little less of a fool and Sergius just a little more of one, you might come to be one of my grandest customers, instead of only being my wife and costing me money.

LOUKA. I believe you would rather be my servant than my husband. You would make more out of me. Oh, I know that soul of yours.

NICOLA (*going up close to her for greater emphasis*). Never you mind my soul; but just listen to my advice. If you want to be a lady, your present behaviour to me won't do at all, unless when we're alone. It's too sharp and impudent; and impudence is a sort of familiarity: it shews affection for me. And don't you try being high and mighty with me either. You're like all country girls: you think it's genteel to treat a servant the way I treat a stable-boy. That's only your ignorance; and don't you forget it. And don't be so ready to defy everybody. Act as if you expected to have your own way, not as if you expected to be ordered about. The way to get on as a lady is the same as the way to get on as a servant: you've got to know your place; that's the secret of it. And you may depend on me to know my place if you get promoted. Think over it, my girl. I'll stand by you: one servant should always stand by another.

LOUKA (*rising impatiently*). Oh, I must behave in my own way. You take all the courage out of me with your cold-blooded wisdom. Go and put those logs on the fire: that's the sort of thing you understand. (*Before Nicola can retort, Sergius comes in. He checks himself a moment on seeing Louka; then goes to the stove.*)

SERGIUS (*to Nicola*). I am not in the way of your work, I hope.

NICOLA (*in a smooth, elderly manner*). Oh, no, sir, thank you kindly. I was only speaking to this foolish girl about her habit of running up here to the library whenever she gets a chance, to look at the books. That's the worst of her education, sir: it gives her habits above her station. (*To Louka.*) Make that table tidy, Louka, for the Major. (*He goes out sedately.*)

Louka, without looking at Sergius, begins to arrange the papers on the table. He crosses slowly to her, and studies the arrangement of her sleeve reflectively.

SERGIUS. Let me see: is there a mark there? (*He turns up the bracelet and sees the bruise made by his grasp. She stands motionless, not looking at him: fascinated, but on her guard.*) Ffff! Does it hurt?

LOUKA. Yes.

SERGIUS. Shall I cure it?

LOUKA (*instantly withdrawing herself proudly, but still not looking at him*). No. You cannot cure it now.

SERGIUS (*masterfully*). Quite sure? (*He makes a movement as if to take her in his arms.*)

LOUKA. Don't trifle with me, please. An officer should not trifle with a servant.

SERGIUS (*touching the arm with a merciless stroke of his forefinger*). That was no trifle, Louka.

LOUKA. No. (*Looking at him for the first time.*) Are you sorry?

SERGIUS (*with measured emphasis, folding his arms*). I am never sorry.

LOUKA (*wistfully*). I wish I could believe a man could be so unlike a woman as that. I wonder are you really a brave man?

SERGIUS (*unaffectedly, relaxing his attitude*). Yes: I am a brave man. My heart jumped like a woman's at the first shot; but in the charge I found that I was brave. Yes: that at least is real about me.

LOUKA. Did you find in the charge that the men whose fathers are poor like mine were any less brave than the men who are rich like you?

SERGIUS (*with bitter levity*). Not a bit. They all slashed and cursed and yelled like heroes. Psha! the courage to rage and kill is cheap. I have an English bull terrier who has as much of that sort of courage as the whole Bulgarian nation, and the whole Russian nation at its back. But he lets my groom thrash him, all the same. That's your soldier all over! No, Louka, your poor men can cut throats; but they are afraid of their officers; they put up with insults and blows; they stand by and see one another punished like children—aye, and help to do it when they are ordered. And the officers!—well (*with a short, bitter laugh*) *I* am an officer. Oh, (*fervently*) give me the man who will defy to the death any power on earth or in heaven that sets itself up against his own will and conscience: he alone is the brave man.

LOUKA. How easy it is to talk! Men never seem to me to grow up: they all have schoolboy's ideas. You don't know what true courage is.

SERGIUS (*ironically*). Indeed! I am willing to be instructed.

LOUKA. Look at me! how much am I allowed to have my own will? I have to get your room ready for you—to sweep and dust, to fetch and carry. How could that degrade me if it did not degrade you to have it done for you? But (*with subdued passion*) if I were Empress of Russia, above everyone in the world, then—ah, then, though according to you I could shew no courage at all; you should see, you should see.

SERGIUS. What would you do, most noble Empress?

LOUKA. I would marry the man I loved, which no other queen in Europe has the courage to do. If I loved you, though you would be as far beneath me as I am beneath you, I would dare to be the equal of my inferior. Would you dare as much if you loved me? No: if you felt the beginnings of love for me you would not let it grow. You dare not: you would marry a rich man's daughter because you would be afraid of what other people would say of you.

SERGIUS (*carried away*). You lie: it is not so, by all the stars! If I loved you, and I were the Czar himself, I would set you on the throne by my side. You know that I love another woman, a woman as high above you as heaven is above earth. And you are jealous of her.

LOUKA. I have no reason to be. She will never marry you now. The man I told you of has come back. She will marry the Swiss.

SERGIUS (*recoiling*). The Swiss!

LOUKA. A man worth ten of you. Then you can come to me; and I will refuse you. You are not good enough for me. (*She turns to the door.*)

SERGIUS (*springing after her and catching her fiercely in his arms*). I will kill the Swiss; and afterwards I will do as I please with you.

LOUKA (*in his arms, passive and steadfast*). The Swiss will kill you, perhaps. He has beaten you in love. He may beat you in war.

SERGIUS (*tormentedly*). Do you think I believe that she—she! whose worst thoughts are higher than your best ones, is capable of trifling with another man behind my back?

LOUKA. Do you think she would believe the Swiss if he told her now that I am in your arms?

SERGIUS (*releasing her in despair*). Damnation! Oh, damnation! Mockery, mockery everywhere: everything I think is mocked by everything I do. (*He strikes himself frantically on the breast.*) Coward, liar, fool! Shall I kill myself like a man, or live and pretend to laugh at myself? (*She again turns to go.*) Louka! (*She stops near the door.*) Remember: you belong to me.

LOUKA (*quietly*). What does that mean—an insult?

SERGIUS (*commandingly*). It means that you love me, and that I have had you here in my arms, and will perhaps have you there again. Whether that is an insult I neither know nor care: take it as you please. But (*vehemently*) I will not be a coward and a trifler. If I choose to love you, I dare marry you, in spite of all Bulgaria. If these hands ever touch you again, they shall touch my affianced bride.

LOUKA. We shall see whether you dare keep your word. But take care. I will not wait long.

SERGIUS (*again folding his arms and standing motionless in the middle of the room*). Yes, we shall see. And you shall wait my pleasure.

Bluntschli, much preoccupied, with his papers still in his hand, enters, leaving the door open for Louka to go out. He goes across to the table, glancing at her as he passes. Sergius, without altering his resolute attitude, watches him steadily. Louka goes out, leaving the door open.

BLUNTSCHLI (*absently, sitting at the table as before, and putting down his papers*). That's a remarkable looking young woman.

SERGIUS (*gravely, without moving*). Captain Bluntschli.

BLUNTSCHLI. Eh?

SERGIUS. You have deceived me. You are my rival. I brook

no rivals. At six o'clock I shall be in the drilling-ground on the Klissoura road, alone, on horseback, with my sabre. Do you understand?

BLUNTSCHLI (*staring, but sitting quite at his ease*). Oh, thank you: that's a cavalry man's proposal. I'm in the artillery; and I have the choice of weapons. If I go, I shall take a machine gun. And there shall be no mistake about the cartridges this time.

SERGIUS (*flushing, but with deadly coldness*). Take care, sir. It is not our custom in Bulgaria to allow invitations of that kind to be trifled with.

BLUNTSCHLI (*warmly*). Pooh! don't talk to me about Bulgaria. You don't know what fighting is. But have it your own way. Bring your sabre along. I'll meet you.

SERGIUS (*fiercely delighted to find his opponent a man of spirit*). Well said, Switzer. Shall I lend you my best horse?

BLUNTSCHLI. No: damn your horse!—thank you all the same, my dear fellow. (*Raina comes in, and hears the next sentence.*) I shall fight you on foot. Horseback's too dangerous: I don't want to kill you if I can help it.

RAINA (*hurrying forward anxiously*). I have heard what Captain Bluntschli said, Sergius. You are going to fight. Why? (*Sergius turns away in silence, and goes to the stove, where he stands watching her as she continues, to Bluntschli*) What about?

BLUNTSCHLI. I don't know: he hasn't told me. Better not interfere, dear young lady. No harm will be done: I've often acted as sword instructor. He won't be able to touch me; and I'll not hurt him. It will save explanations. In the morning I shall be off home; and you'll never see me or hear of me again. You and he will then make it up and live happily ever after.

RAINA (*turning away deeply hurt, almost with a sob in her voice*). I never said I wanted to see you again.

SERGIUS (*striding forward*). Ha! That is a confession.

RAINA (*haughtily*). What do you mean?

SERGIUS. You love that man!

RAINA (*scandalized*). Sergius!

SERGIUS. You allow him to make love to you behind my back, just as you accept me as your affianced husband behind his. Bluntschli: you knew our relations; and you deceived me.

It is for that that I call you to account, not for having received favours that I never enjoyed.

BLUNTSCHLI (*jumping up indignantly*). Stuff! Rubbish! I have received no favours. Why, the young lady doesn't even know whether I'm married or not.

RAINA (*forgetting herself*). Oh! (*Collapsing on the ottoman.*) Are you?

SERGIUS. You see the young lady's concern, Captain Bluntschli. Denial is useless. You have enjoyed the privilege of being received in her own room, late at night——

BLUNTSCHLI (*interrupting him pepperily*). Yes; you blockhead! She received me with a pistol at her head. Your cavalry were at my heels. I'd have blown out her brains if she'd uttered a cry.

SERGIUS (*taken aback*). Bluntschli! Raina: is this true?

RAINA (*rising in wrathful majesty*). Oh, how dare you, how dare you?

BLUNTSCHLI. Apologize, man, apologize! (*He resumes his seat at the table.*)

SERGIUS (*with the old measured emphasis, folding his arms*). I never apologize.

RAINA (*passionately*). This is the doing of that friend of yours, Captain Bluntschli. It is he who is spreading this horrible story about me. (*She walks about excitedly.*)

BLUNTSCHLI. No: he's dead—burnt alive.

RAINA (*stopping, shocked*). Burnt alive!

BLUNTSCHLI. Shot in the hip in a wood-yard. Couldn't drag himself out. Your fellows' shells set the timber on fire and burnt him, with half a dozen other poor devils in the same predicament.

RAINA. How horrible!

SERGIUS. And how ridiculous! Oh, war! war! the dream of patriots and heroes! A fraud, Bluntschli, a hollow sham, like love.

RAINA (*outraged*). Like love! You say that before me.

BLUNTSCHLI. Come, Saranoff: that matter is explained.

SERGIUS. A hollow sham, I say. Would you have come back here if nothing had passed between you, except at the muzzle of your pistol? Raina is mistaken about our friend who was burnt. He was not my informant.

RAINA. Who then? (*Suddenly guessing the truth.*) Ah, Louka! my maid, my servant! You were with her this morning all that time after—after— Oh, what sort of god is this I have been worshipping! (*He meets her gaze with sardonic enjoyment of her disenchantment. Angered all the more, she goes closer to him, and says, in a lower, intenser tone*) Do you know that I looked out of the window as I went upstairs, to have another sight of my hero; and I saw something that I did not understand then. I know now that you were making love to her.

SERGIUS (*with grim humor*). You saw that?

RAINA. Only too well. (*She turns away, and throws herself on the divan under the centre window, quite overcome.*)

SERGIUS (*cynically*). Raina: our romance is shattered. Life's a farce.

BLUNTSCHLI (*to Raina, goodhumoredly*). You see: he's found himself out now.

SERGIUS. Bluntschli: I have allowed you to call me a blockhead. You may now call me a coward as well. I refuse to fight you. Do you know why?

BLUNTSCHLI. No; but it doesn't matter. I didn't ask the reason when you cried on; and I don't ask the reason now that you cry off. I'm a professional soldier. I fight when I have to, and am very glad to get out of it when I haven't to. You're only an amateur: you think fighting's an amusement.

SERGIUS. You shall hear the reason all the same, my professional. The reason is that it takes two men—real men—men of heart, blood and honor—to make a genuine combat. I could no more fight with you than I could make love to an ugly woman. You've no magnetism: you're not a man, you're a machine.

BLUNTSCHLI (*apologetically*). Quite true, quite true. I always was that sort of chap. I'm very sorry. But now that you've found that life isn't a farce, but something quite sensible and serious, what further obstacle is there to your happiness?

RAINA (*rising*). You are very solicitous about my happiness and his. Do you forget his new love—Louka? It is not you that he must fight now, but his rival, Nicola.

SERGIUS. Rival!! (*Striking his forehead.*)

RAINA. Did you not know that they are engaged?

SERGIUS. Nicola! Are fresh abysses opening! Nicola!!

RAINA (*sarcastically*). A shocking sacrifice, isn't it? Such beauty, such intellect, such modesty, wasted on a middle-aged servant man! Really, Sergius, you cannot stand by and allow such a thing. It would be unworthy of your chivalry.

SERGIUS (*losing all self-control*). Viper! Viper! (*He rushes to and fro, raging.*)

BLUNTSCHLI. Look here, Saranoff; you're getting the worst of this.

RAINA (*getting angrier*). Do you realize what he has done, Captain Bluntschli? He has set this girl as a spy on us; and her reward is that he makes love to her.

SERGIUS. False! Monstrous!

RAINA. Monstrous! (*Confronting him.*) Do you deny that she told you about Captain Bluntschli being in my room?

SERGIUS. No; but——

RAINA (*interrupting*). Do you deny that you were making love to her when she told you?

SERGIUS. No; but I tell you——

RAINA (*cutting him short contemptuously*). It is unnecessary to tell us anything more. That is quite enough for us. (*She turns her back on him and sweeps majestically back to the window.*)

BLUNTSCHLI (*quietly, as Sergius, in an agony of mortification, sinks on the ottoman, clutching his averted head between his fists*). I told you you were getting the worst of it, Saranoff.

SERGIUS. Tiger cat!

RAINA (*running excitedly to Bluntschli*). You hear this man calling me names, Captain Bluntschli?

BLUNTSCHLI. What else can he do, dear lady? He must defend himself somehow. Come (*very persuasively*), don't quarrel. What good does it do? (*Raina, with a gasp, sits down on the ottoman, and after a vain effort to look vexedly at Bluntschli, she falls a victim to her sense of humor, and is attacked with a disposition to laugh.*)

SERGIUS. Engaged to Nicola! (*He rises.*) Ha! ha! (*Going to the stove and standing with his back to it.*) Ah, well, Bluntschli, you are right to take this huge imposture of a world coolly.

RAINA (*to Bluntschli with an intuitive guess at his state of mind*). I daresay you think us a couple of grown up babies, don't you?

SERGIUS (*grinning a little*). He does, he does. Swiss civilization nursetending Bulgarian barbarism, eh?

BLUNTSCHLI (*blushing*). Not at all, I assure you. I'm only very glad to get you two quieted. There now, let's be pleasant and talk it over in a friendly way. Where is this other young lady?

RAINA. Listening at the door, probably.

SERGIUS (*shivering as if a bullet had struck him, and speaking with quiet but deep indignation*). I will prove that that, at least, is a calumny. (*He goes with dignity to the door and opens it. A yell of fury bursts from him as he looks out. He darts into the passage, and returns dragging in Louka, whom he flings against the table, R., as he cries*) Judge her, Bluntschli—you, the moderate, cautious man: judge the eavesdropper.

Louka stands her ground, proud and silent.

BLUNTSCHLI (*shaking his head*). I mustn't judge her. I once listened myself outside a tent when there was a mutiny brewing. It's all a question of the degree of provocation. My life was at stake.

LOUKA. My love was at stake. (*Sergius flinches, ashamed of her in spite of himself.*) I am not ashamed.

RAINA (*contemptuously*). Your love! Your curiosity, you mean.

LOUKA (*facing her and retorting her contempt with interest*). My love, stronger than anything you can feel, even for your chocolate cream soldier.

SERGIUS (*with quick suspicion—to Louka*). What does that mean?

LOUKA (*fiercely*). It means——

SERGIUS (*interrupting her slightingly*). Oh, I remember, the ice pudding. A paltry taunt, girl.

Major Petkoff enters, in his shirtsleeves.

PETKOFF. Excuse my shirtsleeves, gentlemen. Raina: somebody has been wearing that coat of mine: I'll swear it—somebody with bigger shoulders than mine. It's all burst open at the back. Your mother is mending it. I wish she'd make haste. I shall catch cold. (*He looks more attentively at them.*) Is anything the matter?

RAINA. No. (*She sits down at the stove with a tranquil air.*)

SERGIUS. Oh, no! (*He sits down at the end of the table, as at first.*)

BLUNTSCHLI (*who is already seated*). Nothing, nothing.

PETKOFF (*sitting down on the ottoman in his old place*). That's all right. (*He notices Louka.*) Anything the matter, Louka?

LOUKA. No, sir.

PETKOFF (*genially*). That's all right. (*He sneezes.*) Go and ask your mistress for my coat, like a good girl, will you? (*She turns to obey; but Nicola enters with the coat; and she makes a pretence of having business in the room by taking the little table with the hookah away to the wall near the windows.*)

RAINA (*rising quickly, as she sees the coat on Nicola's arm*). Here it is, papa. Give it to me, Nicola; and do you put some more wood on the fire. (*She takes the coat, and brings it to the Major, who stands up to put it on. Nicola attends to the fire.*)

PETKOFF (*to Raina, teasing her affectionately*). Aha! Going to be very good to poor old papa just for one day after his return from the wars, eh?

RAINA (*with solemn reproach*). Ah, how can you say that to me, father?

PETKOFF. Well, well, only a joke, little one. Come, give me a kiss. (*She kisses him.*) Now give me the coat.

RAINA. Now, I am going to put it on for you. Turn your back. (*He turns his back and feels behind him with his arms for the sleeves. She dexterously takes the photograph from the pocket and throws it on the table before Bluntschli, who covers it with a sheet of paper under the very nose of Sergius, who looks on amazed, with his suspicions roused in the highest degree. She then helps Petkoff on with his coat.*) There, dear! Now are you comfortable?

PETKOFF. Quite, little love. Thanks. (*He sits down; and Raina returns to her seat near the stove.*) Oh, by the bye, I've found something funny. What's the meaning of this? (*He puts his hand into the picked pocket.*) Eh? Hallo! (*He tries the other pocket.*) Well, I could have sworn— (*Much puzzled, he tries the breast pocket.*) I wonder— (*Tries the original pocket.*) where can it— (*A light flashes on him; he rises, exclaiming*) Your mother's taken it.

RAINA (*very red*). Taken what?

PETKOFF. Your photograph, with the inscription: "Raina, to her Chocolate Cream Soldier—a souvenir." Now you know there's something more in this than meets the eye; and I'm going to find it out. (*Shouting.*) Nicola!

NICOLA (*dropping a log, and turning*). Sir!

PETKOFF. Did you spoil any pastry of Miss Raina's this morning?

NICOLA. You heard Miss Raina say that I did, sir.

PETKOFF. I know that, you idiot. Was it true?

NICOLA. I am sure Miss Raina is incapable of saying anything that is not true, sir.

PETKOFF. Are you? Then I'm not. (*Turning to the others.*) Come: do you think I don't see it all? (*Goes to Sergius, and slaps him on the shoulder.*) Sergius: you're the chocolate cream soldier, aren't you?

SERGIUS (*starting up*). I! a chocolate cream soldier! Certainly not.

PETKOFF. Not! (*He looks at them. They are all very serious and very conscious.*) Do you mean to tell me that Raina sends photographic souvenirs to other men?

SERGIUS (*enigmatically*). The world is not such an innocent place as we used to think, Petkoff.

BLUNTSCHLI (*rising*). It's all right, Major. I'm the chocolate cream soldier. (*Petkoff and Sergius are equally astonished.*) The gracious young lady saved my life by giving me chocolate creams when I was starving—shall I ever forget their flavour! My late friend Stolz told you the story at Peerot. I was the fugitive.

PETKOFF. You! (*He gasps.*) Sergius: do you remember how those two women went on this morning when we mentioned it? (*Sergius smiles cynically. Petkoff confronts Raina severely.*) You're a nice young woman, aren't you?

RAINA (*bitterly*). Major Saranoff has changed his mind. And when I wrote that on the photograph, I did not know that Captain Bluntschli was married.

BLUNTSCHLI (*much startled—protesting vehemently*). I'm not married.

RAINA (*with deep reproach*). You said you were.

BLUNTSCHLI. I did not. I positively did not. I never was married in my life.

PETKOFF (*exasperated*). Raina: will you kindly inform me, if I am not asking too much, which gentleman you are engaged to?

RAINA. To neither of them. This young lady (*introducing Louka, who faces them all proudly*) is the object of Major Saranoff's affections at present.

PETKOFF. Louka! Are you mad, Sergius? Why, this girl's engaged to Nicola.

NICOLA (*coming forward*). I beg your pardon, sir. There is a mistake. Louka is not engaged to me.

PETKOFF. Not engaged to you, you scoundrel! Why, you had twenty-five levas from me on the day of your betrothal; and she had that gilt bracelet from Miss Raina.

NICOLA (*with cool unction*). We gave it out so, sir. But it was only to give Louka protection. She had a soul above her station; and I have been no more than her confidential servant. I intend, as you know, sir, to set up a shop later on in Sofia; and I look forward to her custom and recommendation should she marry into the nobility. (*He goes out with impressive discretion, leaving them all staring after him.*)

PETKOFF (*breaking the silence*). Well, I am—hm!

SERGIUS. This is either the finest heroism or the most crawling baseness. Which is it, Bluntschli?

BLUNTSCHLI. Never mind whether it's heroism or baseness. Nicola's the ablest man I've met in Bulgaria. I'll make him manager of a hotel if he can speak French and German.

LOUKA (*suddenly breaking out at Sergius*). I have been insulted by everyone here. You set them the example. You owe me an apology. (*Sergius immediately, like a repeating clock of which the spring has been touched, begins to fold his arms.*)

BLUNTSCHLI (*before he can speak*). It's no use. He never apologizes.

LOUKA. Not to you, his equal and his enemy. To me, his poor servant, he will not refuse to apologize.

SERGIUS (*approvingly*). You are right. (*He bends his knee in his grandest manner.*) Forgive me!

LOUKA. I forgive you. (*She timidly gives him her hand, which he kisses.*) That touch makes me your affianced wife.

SERGIUS (*springing up*). Ah, I forgot that!

LOUKA (*coldly*). You can withdraw if you like.

SERGIUS. Withdraw! Never! You belong to me! (*He puts his arm about her and draws her to him.*)

Catherine comes in and finds Louka in Sergius's arms, and all the rest gazing at them in bewildered astonishment.

CATHERINE. What does this mean? (*Sergius releases Louka.*)

PETKOFF. Well, my dear, it appears that Sergius is going to marry Louka instead of Raina. (*She is about to break out indignantly at him: he stops her by exclaiming testily.*) Don't blame me: I've nothing to do with it. (*He retreats to the stove.*)

CATHERINE. Marry Louka! Sergius: you are bound by your word to us!

SERGIUS (*folding his arms*). Nothing binds me.

BLUNTSCHLI (*much pleased by this piece of common sense*). Saranoff: your hand. My congratulations. These heroics of yours have their practical side after all. (*To Louka.*) Gracious young lady: the best wishes of a good Republican! (*He kisses her hand, to Raina's great disgust.*)

CATHERINE (*threateningly*). Louka: you have been telling stories.

LOUKA. I have done Raina no harm.

CATHERINE (*haughtily*). Raina! (*Raina is equally indignant at the liberty.*)

LOUKA. I have a right to call her Raina: she calls me Louka. I told Major Saranoff she would never marry him if the Swiss gentleman came back.

BLUNTSCHLI (*surprised*). Hallo!

LOUKA (*turning to Raina*). I thought you were fonder of him than of Sergius. You know best whether I was right.

BLUNTSCHLI. What nonsense! I assure you, my dear Major, my dear Madame, the gracious young lady simply saved my life, nothing else. She never cared two straws for me. Why, bless my heart and soul, look at the young lady and look at me. She, rich, young, beautiful, with her imagination full of fairy princes and noble natures and cavalry charges and goodness knows what! And I, a commonplace Swiss soldier who hardly knows what a decent life is after fifteen years of barracks and battles—a vagabond—a man who has spoiled all his chances in life through an incurably romantic disposition—a man——

SERGIUS (*starting as if a needle has pricked him and interrupting Bluntschli in incredulous amazement*). Excuse me, Bluntschli: what did you say had spoiled your chances in life?

BLUNTSCHLI (*promptly*). An incurably romantic disposition. I ran away from home twice when I was a boy. I went into the army instead of into my father's business. I climbed the balcony of this house when a man of sense would have dived into the nearest cellar. I came sneaking back here to have another look at the young lady when any other man of my age would have sent the coat back——

PETKOFF. My coat!

BLUNTSCHLI. —Yes: that's the coat I mean—would have sent it back and gone quietly home. Do you suppose I am the sort of fellow a young girl falls in love with? Why, look at our ages! I'm thirty-four: I don't suppose the young lady is much over seventeen. (*This estimate produces a marked sensation, all the rest turning and staring at one another. He proceeds innocently.*) All that adventure which was life or death to me, was only a schoolgirl's game to her—chocolate creams and hide and seek. Here's the proof! (*He takes the photograph from the table.*) Now, I ask you, would a woman who took the affair seriously have sent me this and written on it: "Raina, to her Chocolate Cream Soldier—a souvenir?" (*He exhibits the photograph triumphantly, as if it settled the matter beyond all possibility of refutation.*)

PETKOFF. That's what I was looking for. How the deuce did it get there?

BLUNTSCHLI (*to Raina complacently*). I have put everything right, I hope, gracious young lady!

RAINA (*in uncontrollable vexation*). I quite agree with your account of yourself. You are a romantic idiot. (*Bluntschli is unspeakably taken aback.*) Next time I hope you will know the difference between a schoolgirl of seventeen and a woman of twenty-three.

BLUNTSCHLI (*stupefied*). Twenty-three! (*She snaps the photograph contemptuously from his hand; tears it across; and throws the pieces at his feet.*)

SERGIUS (*with grim enjoyment of Bluntschli's discomfiture*). Bluntschli: my one last belief is gone. Your sagacity is a fraud, like all the other things. You have less sense than even I have.

BLUNTSCHLI (*overwhelmed*). Twenty-three! Twenty-three!!

(*He considers.*) Hm! (*Swiftly making up his mind.*) In that case, Major Petkoff, I beg to propose formally to become a suitor for your daughter's hand, in place of Major Saranoff retired.

RAINA. You dare!

BLUNTSCHLI. If you were twenty-three when you said those things to me this afternoon, I shall take them seriously.

CATHERINE (*loftily polite*). I doubt, sir, whether you quite realize either my daughter's position or that of Major Sergius Saranoff, whose place you propose to take. The Petkoffs and the Saranoffs are known as the richest and most important families in the country. Our position is almost historical: we can go back for nearly twenty years.

PETKOFF. Oh, never mind that, Catherine. (*To Bluntschli.*) We should be most happy, Bluntschli, if it were only a question of your position; but hang it, you know, Raina is accustomed to a very comfortable establishment. Sergius keeps twenty horses.

BLUNTSCHLI. But what on earth is the use of twenty horses? Why, it's a circus.

CATHERINE (*severely*). My daughter, sir, is accustomed to a first-rate stable.

RAINA. Hush, mother, you're making me ridiculous.

BLUNTSCHLI. Oh, well, if it comes to a question of an establishment, here goes! (*He goes impetuously to the table and seizes the papers in the blue envelope.*) How many horses did you say?

SERGIUS. Twenty, noble Switzer!

BLUNTSCHLI. I have two hundred horses. (*They are amazed.*) How many carriages?

SERGIUS. Three.

BLUNTSCHLI. I have seventy. Twenty-four of them will hold twelve inside, besides two on the box, without counting the driver and conductor. How many tablecloths have you?

SERGIUS. How the deuce do I know?

BLUNTSCHLI. Have you four thousand?

SERGIUS. No.

BLUNTSCHLI. I have. I have nine thousand six hundred pairs of sheets and blankets, with two thousand four hundred eiderdown quilts. I have ten thousand knives and forks, and the same quantity of dessert spoons. I have six hundred servants.

I have six palatial establishments, besides two livery stables, a tea garden and a private house. I have four medals for distinguished services; I have the rank of an officer and the standing of a gentleman; and I have three native languages. Show me any man in Bulgaria that can offer as much.

PETKOFF (*with childish awe*). Are you Emperor of Switzerland?

BLUNTSCHLI. My rank is the highest known in Switzerland: I'm a free citizen.

CATHERINE. Then Captain Bluntschli, since you are my daughter's choice, I shall not stand in the way of her happiness. (*Petkoff is about to speak.*) That is Major Petkoff's feeling also.

PETKOFF. Oh, I shall be only too glad. Two hundred horses! Whew!

SERGIUS. What says the lady?

RAINA (*pretending to sulk*). The lady says that he can keep his tablecloths and his omnibuses. I am not here to be sold to the highest bidder.

BLUNTSCHLI. I won't take that answer. I appealed to you as a fugitive, a beggar, and a starving man. You accepted me. You gave me your hand to kiss, your bed to sleep in, and your roof to shelter me——

RAINA (*interrupting him*). I did not give them to the Emperor of Switzerland!

BLUNTSCHLI. That's just what I say. (*He catches her hand quickly and looks her straight in the face as he adds, with confident mastery*) Now tell us who you did give them to.

RAINA (*succumbing with a shy smile*). To my chocolate cream soldier!

BLUNTSCHLI (*with a boyish laugh of delight*). That'll do. Thank you. (*Looks at his watch and suddenly becomes businesslike.*) Time's up, Major. You've managed those regiments so well that you are sure to be asked to get rid of some of the Infantry of the Teemok division. Send them home by way of Lom Palanka. Saranoff: don't get married until I come back: I shall be here punctually at five in the evening on Tuesday fortnight. Gracious ladies—good evening. (*He makes them a military bow, and goes.*)

SERGIUS. What a man! What a man!

INTERPRETATION

1. In a letter to the famous actor-manager, Harley Granville-Barker, Shaw described the kind of actors he wanted to perform his plays as "stagey, brassbowelled barnstormers." This vivid method of characterization provides the heartiest kind of raw material for an actor as well as a strongly contrasting array of temperaments for dramatic interaction. Each character in the play has a different "voice," like the different instruments in a band. What musical instrument best fits the personality of each character? Which characters exhibit the most self-knowledge? Which characters achieve inner harmony? Which characters seem likely to continue to develop after the final curtain?

2. The basic conflict in *Arms and the Man* is between the melodramatic and realistic views of life, Sergius being the hero of melodrama and Bluntschli the hero of reality. If the play were a melodrama, how would it end? Bluntschli, after all, is an enemy soldier. What would be his fate in a melodrama? Raina's "noble attitude" and "thrilling voice" is standard equipment for the heroine of melodrama. How is it exposed as sham? In what way does it become an obstacle to the play's resolution? Does the happy ending resolve all future problems for the betrothed couples? What is the price of their happiness?

3. Shaw's descriptions of the settings for *Arms and the Man* are very detailed. What visual elements are essential to the story of the play? Which are essential to revealing character? Which are decorative in function? If you were designing a production of *Arms and the Man,* how would you emphasize the theme of illusion versus reality in your scenery and costumes?

4. You have been considering *Arms and the Man* as a comedy of ideas; it can also be seen as a comedy of disillusionment. What illusions are attacked in the play? What are the dangers of these illusions? Attitudes toward war have greatly changed since this play was first performed in 1894. Do you think Shaw would approve of these changes? What kind of play do you imagine Shaw would write on this theme today?

The Time of Your Life

The action of *The Time of Your Life* is set in October, 1939, which is also the month in which the play was first performed. The author, William Saroyan, of Fresno, California, presented his audience with a view of the time of their lives which is both despairing and sentimental.

In the first moments of the play the hero, Joe, is reading a newspaper which he soon throws away in disgust. No doubt Saroyan's first-night audience was wearily familiar with the contents of Joe's paper, for 1939 was a dangerous time for America. Hitler was on the march in Europe and at home American society was beset by strife and division. The troubles which penetrate Nick's Pacific Street Saloon in San Francisco, where the play is set, were the troubles of the world beyond the theater. And they are not so different from our troubles today.

However, despite the rumblings of war from across the seas and the clash of police and strikers not far from Nick's, the sweetness of life and the goodness of people endure. If Saroyan's characters despair of finding meaning in a world that is out of joint, they are ready to take the goodness of life where they find it: in the simple fact of being alive, in the everyday pleasures of drink, talk, music, memories, love. But more fundamentally, the denizens of Nick's place are there in search of some kind of satisfaction which the drudgery of living cannot supply—serenity, fellowship, pleasing idleness, even sometimes a glimpse of abiding truth. At Nick's there are few serious conflicts. Joe expresses the spirit of the place when he says—on being asked whose side he takes in a dispute—"I'm with everybody, one at a time."

The exception to Joe's rule is Blick, an overbearing, righteous-minded, killjoy cop who likes to bully the helpless. In the slapstick tradition, Blick would get a custard pie in the eye. What really happens to him, however, is not so harmless, and his fate throws into sharp relief the comedy of *The Time of Your Life*.

The humor of this play has a slightly different quality from that of the other plays in this collection. Although we are invited to laugh at the antics and pretensions of the human animal, we feel a bond of sympathetic attachment to these muddled, yearning people who so resemble our secret selves. Yet, despite the sentimental haze through which these characters are seen, they are not beyond the criticism which laughter implies. The incongruities of life, the gaps between human aspiration and capability, come through in almost every line of this sad, tender, funny play.

In the time of your life, live—so that in that good time there shall be no ugliness or death for yourself or for any life your life touches. Seek goodness everywhere, and when it is found, bring it out of its hiding-place and let it be free and unashamed. Place in matter and in flesh the least of the values, for these are the things that hold death and must pass away. Discover in all things that which shines and is beyond corruption. Encourage virtue in whatever heart it may have been driven into secrecy and sorrow by the shame and terror of the world. Ignore the obvious, for it is unworthy of the clear eye and the kindly heart. Be the inferior of no man, nor of any man be the superior. Remember that every man is a variation of yourself. No man's guilt is not yours, nor is any man's innocence a thing apart. Despise evil and ungodliness, but not men of ungodliness or evil. These, understand. Have no shame in being kindly and gentle, but if the time comes in the time of your life to kill, kill and have no regret. In the time of your life, live—so that in that wondrous time you shall not add to the misery and sorrow of the world, but shall smile to the infinite delight and mystery of it.

William Saroyan

The Time of Your Life

WILLIAM SAROYAN

The People

JOE, a young loafer with money and a good heart

TOM, his admirer, disciple, errand boy, stooge and friend

KITTY DUVAL, a young woman with memories

NICK, owner of Nick's Pacific Street Saloon, Restaurant, and Entertainment Palace

ARAB, an Eastern philosopher and harmonica-player

KIT CARSON, an old Indian-fighter

MCCARTHY, an intelligent and well-read longshoreman

KRUPP, his boyhood friend, a waterfront cop who hates his job but doesn't know what else to do instead

HARRY, a natural-born hoofer who wants to make people laugh but can't

WESLEY, a colored boy who plays a mean and melancholy boogie-woogie piano

DUDLEY, a young man in love

ELSIE, a nurse, the girl he loves

LORENE, an unattractive woman

MARY L., an unhappy woman of quality and great beauty

WILLIE, a marble-game maniac

BLICK, a heel

MA, Nick's mother

A KILLER

HER SIDE-KICK

A COP

ANOTHER COP

A SAILOR

A SOCIETY GENTLEMAN

A SOCIETY LADY

THE DRUNKARD

THE NEWSBOY

ANNA, Nick's daughter

THE PLACE: *Nick's Pacific Street Saloon, Restaurant, and Entertainment Palace at the foot of Embarcadero, in San Francisco. A suggestion of room 21 at The New York Hotel, upstairs, around the corner.*

THE TIME: *Afternoon and night of a day in October, 1939.*

ACT ONE

Nick's is an American place: a San Francisco waterfront honky-tonk.

At a table, JOE: *always calm, always quiet, always thinking, always eager, always bored, always superior. His expensive clothes are casually and youthfully worn and give him an almost boyish appearance. He is thinking.*

Behind the bar, NICK: *a big red-headed young Italian-American with an enormous naked woman tattooed in red on the inside of his right arm. He is studying The Racing Form.*

The ARAB, *at his place at the end of the bar. He is a lean old man with a rather ferocious old-country mustache, with the ends twisted up. Between the thumb and forefinger of his left hand is the Mohammedan tatoo indicating that he has been to Mecca. He is sipping a glass of beer.*

It is about eleven-thirty in the morning. SAM *is sweeping out. We see only his back. He disappears into the kitchen.*

The SAILOR *at the bar finishes his drink and leaves, moving thoughtfully, as though he were trying very hard to discover how to live.*

The NEWSBOY *comes in.*

NEWSBOY (*cheerfully*). Good morning, everybody. (*No answer. To* NICK) Paper, Mister? (NICK *shakes his head, no. The* NEWSBOY *goes to* JOE.) Paper, Mister?

JOE *shakes his head, no. The* NEWSBOY *walks away, counting papers.*

JOE (*noticing him*). How many you got?

NEWSBOY. Five.

JOE *gives him a quarter, takes all the papers, glances at the headlines with irritation, throws them away. The* NEWSBOY *watches carefully, then goes.*

ARAB (*picks up paper, looks at headlines, shakes head as if rejecting everything else a man might say about the world*). No foundation. All the way down the line.

The DRUNK *comes in. Walks to the telephone, looks for a nickel in the chute, sits down at* JOE'*s table.* NICK *takes the* DRUNK *out. The* DRUNK *returns.*

DRUNK (*champion of the Bill of Rights*). This is a free country, ain't it?

WILLIE, *the marble-game maniac, explodes through the swinging doors and lifts the forefinger of his right hand comically, indicating one beer. He is a very young man, not more than twenty. He is wearing heavy shoes, a pair of old and dirty corduroys, a light green turtle-neck jersey with a large letter "F" on the chest, an oversize two-button tweed coat, and a green hat, with the brim up.* NICK *sets out a glass of beer for him, he drinks it, straightens up vigorously, saying Aaah, makes a solemn face, gives* NICK *a one-finger salute of adieu, and begins to leave, refreshed and restored in spirit. He walks by the marble game, halts suddenly, turns, studies the contraption, gestures as if to say, Oh, no. Turns to go, stops, re-*

turns to the machine, studies it, takes a handful of small coins out of his pants pocket, lifts a nickel, indicates with a gesture, One game, no more. Puts the nickel in the slot, pushes in the slide, making an interesting noise.

NICK. You can't beat that machine.
WILLIE. Oh, yeah?

The marbles fall, roll, and take their place. He pushes down the lever, placing one marble in position. Takes a very deep breath, walks in a small circle, excited at the beginning of great drama. Stands straight and pious before the contest. Himself vs. the machine. WILLIE *vs. Destiny. His skill and daring vs. the cunning and trickery of the novelty industry of America, and the whole challenging world. He is the last of the American pioneers, with nothing more to fight but the machine, with no other reward than lights going on and off, and six nickels for one. Before him is the last champion, the machine. He is the last challenger, the young man with nothing to do in the world.* WILLIE *grips the knob delicately, studies the situation carefully, draws the knob back, holds it a moment, and then releases it. The first marble rolls out among the hazards, and the contest is on. At the very beginning of the play "The Missouri Waltz" is coming from the phonograph. The music ends here.*

This is the signal for the beginning of the play.

JOE *suddenly comes out of his reverie. He whistles the way people do who are calling a cab that's about a block away, only he does it quietly.* WILLIE *turns around, but* JOE *gestures for him to return to his work.* NICK *looks up from The Racing Form.*

JOE (*calling*). Tom. (*To himself*) Where the hell is he, every time I need him? (*He looks around calmly: the nickel-in-the-slot phonograph in the corner; the open public telephone; the stage; the marble game; the bar; and so on. He calls again, this time very loud.*) Hey, Tom.
NICK (*with morning irritation*). What do you want?
JOE (*without thinking*). I want the boy to get me a watermelon, that's what I want. What do you want? Money, or love, or

fame, or what? You won't get them studying The Racing Form.

NICK. I like to keep abreast of the times.

TOM *comes hurrying in. He is a great big man of about thirty or so who appears to be much younger because of the childlike expression of his face: handsome, dumb, innocent, troubled, and a little bewildered by everything. He is obviously adult in years, but it seems as if by all rights he should still be a boy. He is defensive as clumsy, self-conscious, overgrown boys are. He is wearing a flashy cheap suit.* JOE *leans back and studies him with casual disapproval.* TOM *slackens his pace and becomes clumsy and embarrassed, waiting for the bawling-out he's going to get.*

JOE (*objectively, severely, but a little amused*). Who saved your life?

TOM (*sincerely*). You did, Joe. Thanks.

JOE (*interested*). How'd I do it?

TOM (*confused*). What?

JOE (*even more interested*). *How'd I do it?*

TOM. Joe, you know how you did it.

JOE (*softly*). I want you to answer me. How'd I save your life? I've forgotten.

TOM (*remembering, with a big sorrowful smile*). You made me eat all that chicken soup three years ago when I was sick and hungry.

JOE (*fascinated*). *Chicken soup?*

TOM (*eagerly*). Yeah.

JOE. Three years? Is it that long?

TOM (*delighted to have the information*). Yeah, sure. 1937. 1938. 1939. This is 1939, Joe.

JOE (*amused*). Never mind what year it is. Tell me the whole story.

TOM. You took me to the doctor. You gave me money for food and clothes, and paid my room rent. Aw, Joe, you know all the different things you did. (JOE *nods, turning away from* TOM *after each question.*)

JOE. You in good health now?

TOM. Yeah, Joe.

JOE. You got clothes?

TOM. Yeah, Joe.

JOE. You eat three times a day. Sometimes four?

TOM. Yeah, Joe. Sometimes five.

JOE. You got a place to sleep?

TOM. Yeah, Joe. (JOE *nods. Pauses. Studies* TOM *carefully.*)

JOE. Then, where the hell have you been?

TOM (*humbly*). Joe, I was out in the street listening to the boys. They're talking about the trouble down here on the waterfront.

JOE (*sharply*). I want you to be around when I need you.

TOM (*pleased that the bawling-out is over*). I won't do it again. Joe, one guy out there says there's got to be a revolution before anything will ever be all right.

JOE (*impatient*). I know all about it. Now, here. Take this money. Go up to the Emporium. You know where the Emporium is?

TOM. Yeah, sure, Joe.

JOE. All right. Take the elevator and go up to the fourth floor. Walk around to the back, to the toy department. Buy me a couple of dollars' worth of toys and bring them here.

TOM (*amazed*). Toys? What *kind* of toys, Joe?

JOE. Any kind of toys. Little ones that I can put on this table.

TOM. What do you want toys for, Joe?

JOE (*mildly angry*). *What?*

TOM. All right, all right. You don't have to get sore at *everything*. What'll people think, a big guy like me buying toys?

JOE. *What people?*

TOM. Aw, Joe, you're always making me do crazy things for you, and *I'm* the guy that gets embarrassed. You just sit in this place and make me do all the dirty work.

JOE (*looking away*). Do what I tell you.

TOM. O.K., but I wish I knew *why*. (*He makes to go.*)

JOE. Wait a minute. Here's a nickel. Put it in the phonograph. Number seven. I want to hear that waltz again.

TOM. Boy, I'm glad *I* don't have to stay and listen to it. Joe, what do you hear in that song anyway? We listen to that song ten times a day. Why can't we hear number six, or two, or nine? There are a lot of other numbers.

JOE (*emphatically*). Put the nickel in the phonograph. (*Pause*)

Sit down and wait till the music's over. Then go get me some toys.

TOM. O.K. O.K.

JOE (*loudly*). Never mind being a martyr about it either. The cause isn't worth it.

TOM *puts the nickel into the machine, with a ritual of impatient and efficient movement which plainly shows his lack of sympathy or enthusiasm. His manner also reveals, however, that his lack of sympathy is spurious and exaggerated. Actually, he is fascinated by the music, but is so confused by it that he tries to pretend he dislikes it.*

The music begins. It is another variation of "The Missouri Waltz," played dreamily and softly, with perfect orchestral form, and with a theme of weeping in the horns repeated a number of times.

At first TOM *listens with something close to irritation, since he can't understand what is so attractive in the music to* JOE, *and what is so painful and confusing in it to himself. Very soon, however, he is carried away by the melancholy story of grief and nostalgia of the song. He stands, troubled by the grief and confusion in himself.*

JOE, *on the other hand, listens as if he were not listening, indifferent and unmoved. What he's interested in is* TOM. *He turns and glances at* TOM.

KITTY DUVAL, *who lives in a room in The New York Hotel, around the corner, comes beyond the swinging doors quietly, and walks slowly to the bar, her reality and rhythm a perfect accompaniment to the sorrowful American music, which is her music, as it is* TOM's. *Which the world drove out of her, putting in its place brokenness and all manner of spiritually crippled forms. She seems to understand this, and is angry. Angry with herself, full of hate for the poor world, and full of pity and contempt for its tragic, unbelievable, confounded people. She is a small powerful girl, with that kind of delicate and rugged beauty which no circumstance of evil or ugly reality can destroy. This beauty is that element of the immortal which is in the seed of good and common people, and which is kept alive in some of the female of our kind, no matter how accidentally or pointlessly they may have entered the world.* KITTY DUVAL *is somebody. There is an angry purity, and a fierce pride, in her.*

In her stance, and way of walking, there is grace and arrogance. JOE *recognizes her as a great person immediately. She goes to the bar.*

KITTY. Beer.

NICK *places a glass of beer before her mechanically. She swallows half the drink, and listens to the music again.* TOM *turns and sees her. He becomes dead to everything in the world but her. He stands like a lump, fascinated and undone by his almost religious adoration for her.* JOE *notices* TOM.

JOE (*gently*). Tom. (TOM *begins to move toward the bar, where* KITTY *is standing. Loudly*) Tom. (TOM *halts, then turns, and* JOE *motions to him to come over to the table.* TOM *goes over. Quietly*) Have you got everything straight?

TOM (*out of the world*). What?

JOE. What do you mean, what? I just gave you some instructions.

TOM (*pathetically*). What do you want, Joe?

JOE. I want you to come to your senses. (*He stands up quietly and knocks* TOM*'s hat off.* TOM *picks up his hat quickly.*)

TOM. I got it, Joe. I got it. The Emporium. Fourth floor. In the back. The toy department. Two dollars' worth of toys. That you can put on a table.

KITTY (*to herself*). Who the hell is he to push a big man like that around?

JOE. I'll expect you back in a half hour. Don't get side-tracked anywhere. Just do what I tell you.

TOM (*pleading*). Joe? Can't I bet four bits on a horse race? There's a long shot—Precious Time—that's going to win by ten lengths. I got to have money.

JOE *points to the street.* TOM *goes out.* NICK *is combing his hair, looking in the mirror.*

NICK. I thought you wanted him to get you a watermelon.

JOE. I forgot. (*He watches* KITTY *a moment. To* KITTY, *clearly, slowly, with great compassion*) What's the dream?

KITTY (*moving to* JOE, *coming to*). What?

JOE (*holding the dream for her*). What's the dream, *now?*

KITTY (*coming still closer*). What dream?

JOE. What dream! The dream you're dreaming.

NICK. Suppose he did bring you a watermelon? What the hell would you do with it?

JOE (*irritated*). I'd put it on this table. I'd look at it. Then I'd eat it. What do you *think* I'd do with it, sell it for a profit?

NICK. How should I know what *you'd* do with *anything?* What I'd like to know is, where do you get your money from? What work do you do?

JOE (*looking at* KITTY). Bring us a bottle of champagne.

KITTY. Champagne?

JOE (*simply*). Would you rather have something else?

KITTY. What's the big idea?

JOE. I thought you might like some champagne. I myself am very fond of it.

KITTY. Yeah, but what's the big idea? You can't push me around.

JOE (*gently but severely*). It's not in my nature to be unkind to another human being. I have only contempt for wit. Otherwise I might say something obvious, therefore cruel, and perhaps untrue.

KITTY. You be careful what you think about me.

JOE (*slowly, not looking at her*). I have only the noblest thoughts for both your person, and your spirit.

NICK (*having listened carefully and not being able to make it out*). What are you talking about?

KITTY. You shut up. You—

JOE. He owns this place. He's an important man. All kinds of people come to him looking for work. Comedians. Singers. Dancers.

KITTY. I don't care. He can't call me names.

NICK. All right, sister. I know how it is with a two-dollar whore in the morning.

KITTY (*furiously*). Don't you dare call me names. I used to be in burlesque.

NICK. If you were ever in burlesque, I used to be Charlie Chaplin.

KITTY (*angry and a little pathetic*). I *was* in burlesque. I played the burlesque circuit from coast to coast. I've had flowers sent to me by European royalty. I've had dinner with young men of wealth and social position.

NICK. You're dreaming.

KITTY (*to* JOE). I *was* in burlesque. Kitty Duval. That was my name. Lifesize photographs of me in costume in front of burlesque theaters all over the country.

JOE (*gently, coaxingly*). I believe you. Have some champagne.

NICK (*going to table, with champagne bottle and glasses*). There he goes again.

JOE. Miss Duval?

KITTY (*sincerely, going over*). That's not my real name. That's my stage name.

JOE. I'll call you by your stage name.

NICK (*pouring*). All right, sister, make up your mind. Are you going to have champagne with him, or not?

JOE. Pour the lady some wine.

NICK. O.K., Professor. Why you come to this joint instead of one of the high-class dumps uptown is more than I can understand. Why don't you have champagne at the St. Francis? Why don't you drink with a lady?

KITTY (*furiously*). Don't you call me names—you dentist.

JOE. Dentist?

NICK (*amazed, loudly*). What kind of cussing is that? (*Pause. Looking at* KITTY, *then at* JOE, *bewildered.*) This guy doesn't belong here. The only reason I've got champagne is because *he* keeps ordering it all the time. (*To* KITTY) Don't think you're the only one he drinks champagne with. He drinks with *all* of them. (*Pause*) He's crazy. Or something.

JOE (*confidentially*). Nick, I think you're going to be all right in a couple of centuries.

NICK. I'm sorry, I don't understand your English.

JOE *lifts his glass.* KITTY *slowly lifts hers, not quite sure of what's going on.*

JOE (*sincerely*). To the spirit, Kitty Duval.

KITTY (*beginning to understand, and very grateful, looking at him*). Thank you. (*They drink.*)

JOE (*calling*). Nick.

NICK. Yeah?

JOE. Would you mind putting a nickel in the machine again? Number—

NICK. Seven. I know. I know. I don't mind at all, Your Highness, although, personally, I'm not a lover of music. (*Going to the machine.*) As a matter of fact I think Tchaikowsky was a dope.

JOE. Tchaikowsky? Where'd you ever hear of Tchaikowsky?

NICK. He was a dope.

JOE. Yeah. Why?

NICK. They talked about him on the radio one Sunday morning. He was a sucker. He let a woman drive him crazy.

JOE. I see.

NICK. I stood behind that bar listening to the God damn stuff and cried like a baby. *None but the lonely heart!* He was a dope.

JOE. What made you cry?

NICK. What?

JOE (*sternly*). What made you cry, Nick?

NICK (*angry with himself*). I don't know.

JOE. I've been underestimating you, Nick. Play number seven.

NICK. They get everybody worked up. They give everybody stuff they shouldn't have. (*He puts the nickel into the machine and the Waltz begins again. He listens to the music. Then studies The Racing Form.*)

KITTY (*to herself, dreaming*). I like champagne, and everything that goes with it. Big houses with big porches, and big rooms with big windows, and big lawns, and big trees, and flowers growing everywhere, and big shepherd dogs sleeping in the shade.

NICK. I'm going next door to Frankie's to make a bet. I'll be right back.

JOE. Make one for me.

NICK (*going to* JOE). Who do you like?
JOE (*giving him money*). Precious Time.
NICK. *Ten dollars?* Across the board?
JOE. No. On the nose.
NICK. O.K. (*He goes.*)

DUDLEY R. BOSTWICK, *as he calls himself, breaks through the swinging doors, and practically flings himself upon the open telephone beside the phonograph.* DUDLEY *is a young man of about twenty-four or twenty-five, ordinary and yet extraordinary. He is smallish, as the saying is, neatly dressed in bargain clothes, over-worked and irritated by the routine and dullness and monotony of his life, apparently nobody and nothing, but in reality a great personality. The swindled young man. Educated, but without the least real understanding. A brave, dumb, salmon-spirit struggling for life in weary, stupefied flesh, dueling ferociously with a banal mind which has been only irritated by what it has been taught. He is a great personality because, against all these handicaps, what he wants is simple and basic: a woman. This urgent and violent need, common yet miraculous enough in itself, considering the unhappy environment of the animal, is the force which elevates him from nothingness to greatness. A ridiculous greatness, but in the nature of things beautiful to behold. All that he has been taught, and everything he believes, is phony, and yet he himself is real, almost super-real, because of this indestructible force in himself. His face is ridiculous. His personal rhythm is tense and jittery. His speech is shrill and violent. His gestures are wild. His ego is disjointed and epileptic. And yet deeply he possesses the same wholeness of spirit, and directness of energy, that is in all species of animals. There is little innate or cultivated spirit in him, but there is no absence of innocent animal force. He is a young man who has been taught that he has a chance, as a person, and believes it. As a matter of fact, he hasn't a chance in the world, and should have been told by somebody, or should not have had his natural and valuable ignorance spoiled by education, ruin-*

ing an otherwise perfectly good and charming member of the human race.

At the telephone he immediately begins to dial furiously, hesitates, changes his mind, stops dialing, hangs up furiously, and suddenly begins again.

Not more than half a minute after the firecracker arrival of DUDLEY R. BOSTWICK, *occurs the polka-and-waltz arrival of* HARRY. HARRY *is another story.*

He comes in timidly, turning about uncertainly, awkward, out of place everywhere, embarrassed and encumbered by the contemporary costume, sick at heart, but determined to fit in somewhere. His arrival constitutes a dance. His clothes don't fit. The pants are a little too large. The coat, which doesn't match, is also a little too large, and loose. He is a dumb young fellow, but he has ideas. A philosophy, in fact. His philosophy is simple and beautiful. The world is sorrowful. The world needs laughter. HARRY *is funny. The world needs* HARRY. HARRY *will make the world laugh. He has probably had a year or two of high school. He has also listened to the boys at the pool room.*

He's looking for NICK. *He goes to the* ARAB, *and says, Are you Nick? The* ARAB *shakes his head. He stands at the bar, waiting. He waits very busily.*

HARRY (*as* NICK *returns*). You Nick?

NICK (*very loudly*). *I am Nick.*

HARRY (*acting*). Can you use a great comedian?

NICK (*behind the bar*). Who, for instance?

HARRY (*almost angry*). Me.

NICK. You? What's funny about you?

DUDLEY *at the telephone, is dialing. Because of some defect in the apparatus the dialing is very loud.*

DUDLEY. Hello. Sunset 7349? May I speak to Miss Elsie Mandelspiegel? (*Pause.*)

HARRY (*with spirit and noise, dancing*). I dance and do gags and stuff.

NICK. In costume? Or are you wearing your costume?

DUDLEY. All I need is a cigar.

KITTY (*continuing the dream of grace*). I'd walk out of the house, and stand on the porch, and look at the trees, and smell the flowers, and run across the lawn, and lie down under a tree, and read a book. (*Pause*) A book of poems, maybe.

DUDLEY (*very, very clearly*). Elsie Mandelspiegel. (*Impatiently*) She has a room on the fourth floor. She's a nurse at the Southern Pacific Hospital. Elsie Mandelspiegel. She works at night. Elsie. Yes. (*He begins waiting again.*)

WESLEY, *a colored boy, comes to the bar and stands near* HARRY, *waiting.*

NICK. Beer?

WESLEY. No, sir. I'd like to talk to you.

NICK (*to* HARRY). All right. Get funny.

HARRY (*getting funny, an altogether different person, an actor with great energy, both in power of voice, and in force and speed of physical gesture*). Now, I'm standing on the corner of Third and Market. I'm looking around. I'm figuring it out. There it is. Right in front of me. The whole city. The whole world. People going by. They're going somewhere. I don't know where, but they're going. I ain't going *anywhere.* Where the hell can you go? I'm figuring it out. All right, I'm a citizen. A fat guy bumps his stomach into the face of an old lady. They were in a hurry. Fat and old. *They bumped.* Boom. I don't know. It may mean war. *War.* Germany. England. Russia. I don't know for sure. (*Loudly, dramatically, he salutes, about faces, presents arms, aims, and fires.*) WAAAAAR. (*He blows a call to arms.* NICK *gets sick of this, indicates with a gesture that* HARRY *should hold it, and goes to* WESLEY.)

NICK. What's on *your* mind?

WESLEY (*confused*). Well—

NICK. Come on. Speak up. Are you hungry, or what?

WESLEY. Honest to God, I ain't hungry. All I want is a job. I don't want no charity.

NICK. Well, what can you do, and how good are you?

WESLEY. I can run errands, clean up, wash dishes, anything.

DUDLEY (*on the telephone, very eagerly*). Elsie? Elsie, this is

Dudley. Elsie, I'll jump in the bay if you don't marry me. Life isn't worth living without you. I can't sleep. I can't think of anything but you. All the time. Day and night and night and day. Elsie, I love you. I love you. What? (*Burning up*) Is this Sunset 7-3-4-9? (*Pause*) 7943? (*Calmly, while* WILLIE *begins making a small racket*) Well, what's *your* name? *Lorene?* Lorene Smith? I thought you were Elsie Mandelspiegel. What? Dudley. Yeah. Dudley R. Bostwick. Yeah. R. It stands for Raoul, but I never spell it out. I'm pleased to meet *you,* too. What? There's a lot of noise around here. (WILLIE *stops hitting the marble game.*) Where am I? At Nick's, on Pacific Street. I work at the S. P. I told them I was sick and they gave me the afternoon off. Wait a minute. I'll ask them. I'd like to meet *you,* too. Sure I'll ask them. (*Turns around to* NICK.) What's this address?

NICK. Number 3 Pacific Street, you cad.

DUDLEY. Cad? You don't know how I've been suffering on account of Elsie. I take things too ceremoniously. I've got to be more lackadaisical. (*Into telephone*) Hello, Elenore? I mean, Lorene? It's number 3 Pacific Street. Yeah. Sure. I'll wait for you. How'll you know me? You'll *know* me. I'll recognize *you.* Good-by, now. (*He hangs up.*)

HARRY (*continuing his monologue, with gestures, movements, and so on*). I'm standing there. I didn't do anything to anybody. Why should *I* be a soldier? (*Sincerely, insanely*) BOOOOOOOOOM. *WAR!* O.K. War. *I* retreat. *I* hate war. I move to Sacramento.

NICK (*shouting*). All right, Comedian. Lay off a minute.

HARRY (*broken-hearted, going to* WILLIE). Nobody's got a sense of humor any more. The world's dying for comedy like never before, but nobody knows how to *laugh.*

NICK (*to* WESLEY). Do you belong to the union?

WESLEY. What union?

NICK. For the love of Mike, where've you been? Don't you know you can't come into a place and ask for a job and get one and go to work, just like that. You've got to belong to one of the unions.

WESLEY. I didn't know. I got to have a job. Real soon.

NICK. Well, you've got to belong to a union.

WESLEY. I don't want any favors. All I want is a chance to earn a living.

NICK. Go on into the kitchen and tell Sam to give you some lunch.

WESLEY. Honest, I ain't hungry.

DUDLEY (*shouting*). What I've gone through for Elsie.

HARRY. I've got all kinds of funny ideas in my head to help make the world happy again.

NICK (*holding* WESLEY). No, he isn't hungry.

WESLEY *almost faints from hunger.* NICK *catches him just in time. The* ARAB *and* NICK *go off with* WESLEY *into the kitchen.*

HARRY (*to* WILLIE). See if you think this is funny. It's my own idea. I created this dance myself. It comes after the monologue.

HARRY *begins to dance.* WILLIE *watches a moment, and then goes back to the game. It's a goofy dance, which* HARRY *does with great sorrow, but much energy.*

DUDLEY. Elsie. Aw, gee, Elsie. What the hell do I want to see Lorene Smith for? Some girl I don't know.

JOE *and* KITTY *have been drinking in silence. There is no sound now except the soft shoe shuffling of* HARRY, *the Comedian.*

JOE. What's the dream now, Kitty Duval?

KITTY (*dreaming the words and pictures*). I dream of home. Christ, I always dream of home. I've no *home.* I've no place. But I always dream of all of us together again. We had a farm in Ohio. There was nothing good about it. It was always sad. There was always trouble. But I always dream about it as if I could go back and Papa would be there and Mamma and Louie and my little brother Stephen and my sister Mary. I'm Polish. Duval! My name isn't Duval, it's Koranovsky. Katerina Koranovsky. We lost everything. The house, the farm, the trees, the horses, the cows, the chickens. Papa died. He was old. He was thirteen years older than Mamma. We moved to Chicago. We tried to work. We tried to stay together. Louie got in trouble. The fellows he was with killed him for something. I don't know what. Stephen ran away from home. Seventeen years old. I don't know where he is. Then Mamma died. (*Pause*) What's the dream? I dream of home.

NICK *comes out of the kitchen with* WESLEY.

NICK. Here. Sit down here and rest. That'll hold you for a *while*. Why didn't you tell me you were hungry? You all right now?

WESLEY (*sitting down in the chair at the piano*). Yes, I am. Thank you. I didn't know I was that hungry.

NICK. Fine. (*to* HARRY, *who is dancing*) Hey. What the hell do you think you're doing?

HARRY (*stopping*). That's my own idea. I'm a natural-born dancer and comedian.

WESLEY *begins slowly, one note, one chord at a time, to play the piano.*

NICK. You're no good. Why don't you try some other kind of work? Why don't you get a job in a store, selling something? What do you want to be a comedian for?

HARRY. I've got something for the world and they haven't got sense enough to let me give it to them. Nobody knows me.

DUDLEY. Elsie. Now I'm waiting for some dame I've never seen before. Lorene Smith. Never saw her in my life. Just happened to get the wrong number. She turns on the personality, and I'm a cooked Indian. Give me a beer, please.

HARRY. Nick, you've got to see my act. It's the greatest thing of its kind in America. All I want is a chance. No salary to begin. Let me try it out tonight. If I don't wow 'em, O.K., I'll go home. If vaudeville wasn't dead, a guy like me would have a chance.

NICK. You're not funny. You're a sad young punk. What the hell do you want to try to be funny for? You'll break everybody's heart. What's there for you to be funny about? You've been poor all your life, haven't you?

HARRY. I've been poor all right, but don't forget that some things count more than some other things.

NICK. What counts more, for instance, than what else, for instance?

HARRY. Talent, for instance, counts more than money, for instance, that's what, and I've got talent. I get new ideas night and day. Everything comes natural to me. I've got style, but it'll take me a little time to round it out. That's all.

By now WESLEY *is playing something of his own which is very good and out of the world. He plays about half a minute, after which* HARRY *begins to dance.*

NICK (*watching*). I run the lousiest dive in Frisco, and a guy arrives and makes me stock up with champagne. The whores come in and holler at me that they're ladies. Talent comes in and begs me for a chance to show itself. Even society people come here once in a while. I don't know what for. Maybe it's liquor. Maybe it's the location. Maybe it's my personality. Maybe it's the crazy personality of the joint. The old honky-tonk. (*Pause*) Maybe they can't feel at home anywhere else.

By now WESLEY *is really playing, and* HARRY *is going through a new routine.* DUDLEY *grows sadder and sadder.*

KITTY. Please dance with me.

JOE (*loudly*). I never learned to dance.

KITTY. Anybody can dance. Just hold me in your arms.

JOE. I'm very fond of you. I'm *sorry*. I *can't* dance. I wish to God I could.

KITTY. Oh, please.

JOE. Forgive me. I'd like to very much.

KITTY *dances alone.* TOM *comes in with a package. He sees* KITTY *and goes ga-ga again. He comes out of the trance and puts the bundle on the table in front of* JOE.

JOE (*taking the package*). What'd you get?

TOM. Two dollars' worth of toys. That's what you sent me for. The girl asked me what I wanted with toys. I didn't know what to tell her. (*He stares at* KITTY, *then back at* JOE.) Joe? I've got to have some money. After all you've done for me, I'll do anything in the world for you, but, Joe, you got to give me some money once in a while.

JOE. What do you want it for?

TOM *turns and stares at* KITTY *dancing.*

JOE (*noticing*). Sure. Here. Here's five. (*Shouting*) Can you dance?

TOM (*proudly*). I got second prize at the Palomar in Sacramento five years ago.

JOE (*loudly, opening package*). O.K., dance with her.

TOM. You mean *her?*

JOE (*loudly*). I mean Kitty Duval, the burlesque queen. I mean the queen of the world burlesque. Dance with her. She wants to dance.

TOM (*worshiping the name* KITTY DUVAL, *helplessly*). Joe, can I tell you something?

JOE (*he brings out a toy and winds it*). You don't have to. I know. You love her. You *really* love her. I'm not blind. I know. But take care of yourself. Don't get sick that way again.

NICK (*looking at and listening to* WESLEY *with amazement*). Comes in here and wants to be a dish-washer. Faints from hunger. And then sits down and plays better than Heifetz.

JOE. Heifetz plays the violin.

NICK. All right, don't get careful. He's good, ain't he?

TOM (*to* KITTY). Kitty.

JOE (*he lets the toy go, loudly*). Don't *talk.* Just *dance.*

TOM *and* KITTY *dance.* NICK *is at the bar, watching everything.* HARRY *is dancing.* DUDLEY *is grieving into his beer.* LORENE SMITH, *about thirty-seven, very overbearing and funny-looking, comes to the bar.*

NICK. What'll it be, lady?

LORENE (*looking about and scaring all the young men*). I'm looking for the young man I talked to on the telephone. Dudley R. Bostwick.

DUDLEY (*jumping, running to her, stopping, shocked*). Dudley R. (*Slowly*) Bostwick? Oh, yeah. He left here ten minutes ago. You mean Dudley Bostwick, that poor man on crutches?

LORENE. Crutches?

DUDLEY. Yeah. Dudley Bostwick. That's what he *said* his name was. He said to tell you not to wait.

LORENE. Well. (*She begins to go, turns around*) Are you sure *you're* not Dudley Bostwick?

DUDLEY. Who—me? (*Grandly*) My name is Roger Tenefrancia. I'm a French-Canadian. I never saw the poor fellow before.

LORENE. It seems to me your voice is like the voice I heard over the telephone.

DUDLEY. A coincidence. An accident. A quirk of fate. One of those things. Dismiss the thought. That poor cripple hobbled out of here ten minutes ago.

LORENE. He said he was going to commit suicide. I only wanted to be of help. (*She goes.*)

DUDLEY. Be of help? What kind of help could she be, of? (*He runs to the telephone in the corner.*) Gee whiz, Elsie. Gee whiz. I'll never leave you again. (*He turns the pages of a little address book.*) Why do I always forget the number? I've tried to get her on the phone a hundred times this week and I still forget the number. She won't come to the phone, but I keep trying anyway. She's out. She's not in. She's working. I get the wrong number. Everything goes haywire. I can't sleep. (*Defiantly*) She'll come to the phone one of these days. If there's anything to true love at all. She'll come to the phone. Sunset 7349.

He dials the number, as JOE *goes on studying the toys. They are one big mechanical toy, whistles, and a music box.* JOE *blows into the whistles, quickly, by way of getting casually acquainted with them.* TOM *and* KITTY *stop dancing.* TOM *stares at her.*

DUDLEY. Hello. Is this Sunset 7349? May I speak to Elsie? Yes. (*Emphatically, and bitterly*) No, this is *not* Dudley Bostwick. This is Roger Tenefrancia of Montreal, Canada. I'm a childhood friend of Miss Mandelspiegel. We went to kindergarten together. (*Hand over phone.*) God damn it. (*Into phone*) Yes. I'll wait, thank you.

TOM. I love you.

KITTY. You want to go to my room? (TOM *can't answer.*) Have you got two dollars?

TOM (*shaking his head with confusion*). I've got *five* dollars, but I *love* you.

KITTY (*looking at him*). You want to spend *all* that money?

TOM *embraces her. They go.* JOE *watches. Goes back to the toy.*

JOE. Where's that longshoreman, McCarthy?

NICK. He'll be around.

JOE. What do you think he'll have to say today?

NICK. Plenty, as usual. I'm going next door to see who won that third race at Laurel.

JOE. Precious Time won it.

NICK. That's what you think. (*He goes.*)

JOE (*to himself*). A horse named McCarthy is running in the sixth race today.

DUDLEY (*on the phone*). Hello. Hello, Elsie? Elsie? (*His voice weakens; also his limbs.*) My God. She's come to the phone. Elsie, I'm at Nick's on Pacific Street. You've got to come here and talk to me. Hello. Hello, Elsie? (*Amazed*) Did she hang up? Or was I disconnected? (*He hangs up and goes to bar.*)

WESLEY *is still playing the piano.* HARRY *is still dancing.* JOE *has wound up the big mechanical toy and is watching it work.* NICK *returns.*

NICK (*watching the toy*). Say. That's some gadget.

JOE. How much did I win?

NICK. How do you know you *won*?

JOE. Don't be silly. He said Precious Time was going to win by ten lengths, didn't he? He's in love, isn't he?

NICK. O.K. I don't know why, but Precious Time won. You got eighty for ten. How do you do it?

JOE (*roaring*). Faith. Faith. How'd he win?

NICK. By a nose. Look him up in The Racing Form. The slowest, the cheapest, the worst horse in the race, and the worst jockey. What's the matter with my luck?

JOE. How much did you lose?

NICK. Fifty cents.

JOE. You should never gamble.

NICK. Why not?

JOE. You always bet fifty cents. You've got no more faith than a flea, that's why.

HARRY (*shouting*). How do you like this, Nick? (*He is really busy now, all legs and arms.*)

NICK (*turning and watching*). Not bad. Hang around. You can wait table. (*To* WESLEY) Hey. Wesley. Can you play that again tonight?

WESLEY (*turning, but still playing the piano*). I don't know for sure, Mr. Nick. I can play *something*.

NICK. Good. *You* hang around, too. (*He goes behind the bar.*)

The atmosphere is now one of warm, natural, American ease; every man innocent and good; each doing what he believes he should do, or what he must do. There is deep American naïveté and faith in the behavior of each person. No one is competing with anyone else. No one hates anyone else. Every man is living, and letting live. Each man is following his destiny as he feels it should be followed; or is abandoning it as he feels it must, by now, be abandoned; or is forgetting it for the moment as he feels he should forget it. Although everyone is dead serious, there is unmistakable smiling and humor in the scene; a sense of the human body and spirit emerging from the world-imposed state of stress and fretfulness, fear and awkwardness, to the more natural state of casualness and grace. Each person belongs to the environment, in his own person, as himself: WESLEY *is playing better than ever.* HARRY *is hoofing better than ever.* NICK *is behind the bar shining glasses.* JOE *is smiling at the toy and studying it.* DUDLEY, *although still troubled, is at least calm now and full of melancholy poise.* WILLIE, *at the marble game, is happy. The* ARAB *is deep in his memories, where he wants to be.*

Into this scene and atmosphere comes BLICK. BLICK *is the sort of human being you dislike at sight. He is no different from anybody else physically. His face is an ordinary face. There is nothing obviously wrong with him, and yet you know that it is impossible, even by the most generous expansion of understanding, to accept him as a human being. He is the strong man without strength—strong only among the weak—the weakling who uses force on the weaker.*

BLICK *enters casually, as if he were a customer, and immediately* HARRY *begins slowing down.*

BLICK (*oily, and with mock-friendliness*). Hello, Nick.

NICK (*stopping his work and leaning across the bar*). What do you want to come here for? You're too big a man for a little honky-tonk.

BLICK (*flattered*). Now, Nick.

NICK. Important people never come here. *Here*. Have a drink. (*Whiskey bottle.*)

BLICK. Thanks, I don't drink.

NICK (*drinking the drink himself*). Well, why don't you?

BLICK. I have responsibilities.

NICK. You're head of the lousy Vice Squad. There's no vice here.

BLICK (*sharply*). Street-walkers are working out of this place.

NICK (*angry*). What do you want?

BLICK (*loudly*). I just want you to know that it's got to *stop*.

The music stops. The mechanical toy runs down. There is absolute silence, and a strange fearfulness and disharmony in the atmosphere now. HARRY *doesn't know what to do with his hands or feet.* WESLEY'*s arms hang at his sides.* JOE *quietly pushes the toy to one side of the table eager to study what is happening.* WILLIE *stops playing the marble game, turns around and begins to wait.* DUDLEY *straightens up very, very vigorously, as if to say: "Nothing can scare me. I know love is the only thing." The* ARAB *is the same as ever, but watchful.* NICK *is arrogantly aloof. There is a moment of this silence and tension, as though* BLICK *were waiting for everybody to acknowledge his presence. He is obviously flattered by the acknowledgment of* HARRY, DUDLEY, WESLEY, *and* WILLIE, *but a little irritated by* NICK'*s aloofness and unfriendliness.*

NICK. Don't look at me. I can't tell a street-walker from a lady. You married?

BLICK. You're not asking *me* questions. *I'm* telling *you*.

NICK (*interrupting*). You're a man of about forty-five or so. You *ought* to know better.

BLICK (*angry*). Street-walkers are working out of this place.

NICK (*beginning to shout*). Now, don't start any trouble with me. People come here to drink and loaf around. I don't care who they are.

BLICK. Well, I do.

NICK. The only way to find out if a lady is a street-walker is to walk the streets with her, go to bed, and make sure. You wouldn't want to do that. You'd *like* to, of course.

BLICK. Any more of it, and I'll have your joint closed.

NICK (*very casually, without ill-will*). Listen. I've got no use for you, or anybody like you. You're out to change the world from something bad to something worse. Something like yourself.

BLICK (*furious pause, and contempt*). I'll be back tonight. (*He begins to go.*)

NICK (*very angry but very calm*). Do yourself a big favor and don't come back tonight. Send somebody else. I don't like your personality.

BLICK (*casually, but with contempt*). Don't break any laws. I don't like yours, either. (*He looks the place over, and goes.*)

There is a moment of silence. Then WILLIE *turns and puts a new nickel in the slot and starts a new game.* WESLEY *turns to the piano and rather falteringly begins to play. His heart really isn't in it.* HARRY *walks about, unable to dance.* DUDLEY *lapses into his customary melancholy, at a table.* NICK *whistles a little: suddenly stops.* JOE *winds the toy.*

JOE (*comically*). Nick. You going to kill that man?

NICK. I'm disgusted.

JOE. Yeah? Why?

NICK. Why should I get worked up over a guy like that? Why should I hate *him?* He's nothing. He's nobody. He's a mouse. But every time he comes into this place I get burned up. He doesn't want to drink. He doesn't want to sit down. He doesn't want to take things easy. Tell me one thing?

JOE. Do my best.

NICK. What's a punk like *that* want to go out and try to change the world for?

JOE (*amazed*). Does *he* want to change the world, too?

NICK (*irritated*). You know what I mean. What's he want to bother people for? He's *sick.*

JOE (*almost to himself, reflecting on the fact that* BLICK *too wants to change the world*). I guess he wants to change the world at that.

NICK. So I go to work and hate him.

JOE. It's not him, Nick. It's everything.

NICK. Yeah, *I know.* But I've still got no use for him. He's no good. You know what I mean? He hurts little people. (*Confused*) One of the girls tried to commit suicide on account of him. (*Furiously*) I'll break his head if he hurts anybody around here. This is *my* joint. (*Afterthought*) Or anybody's *feelings,* either.

JOE. He may not be so bad, deep down underneath.

NICK. I know all about him. He's no good.

During this talk WESLEY *has really begun to play the piano, the toy is rattling again, and little by little* HARRY *has begun to dance.* NICK *has come around the bar, and now, very much like a child—forgetting all his anger—is watching the toy work. He begins to smile at everything: turns and listens to* WESLEY: *watches* HARRY: *nods at the* ARAB: *shakes his head at* DUDLEY: *and gestures amiably about* WILLIE. *It's* his *joint all right.*

It's a good, low down, honky-tonk American place that lets people alone.

NICK. I've got a good joint. There's nothing wrong here. Hey. Comedian. Stick to the dancing tonight. I think you're O.K. Wesley? Do some more of that tonight. That's fine!

HARRY. Thanks, Nick. Gosh, I'm on my way at last. (*On telephone*) Hello, Ma? Is that you, Ma? Harry. I got the job. (*He hangs up and walks around, smiling.*)

NICK (*watching the toy all this time*). Say, that really is something. What is that, anyway?

MARY L. *comes in.*

JOE (*holding it toward* NICK, *and* MARY L.). Nick, this is a toy. A contraption devised by the cunning of man to drive boredom, or grief, or anger out of children. A noble gadget. A gadget, I might say, infinitely nobler than any other I can think of at the moment. (*Everybody gathers around* JOE's *table to look at the toy. The toy stops working.* JOE *winds the music box. Lifts a whistle: blows it, making a very strange, funny and sorrowful sound.*) Delightful. Tragic, but delightful.

WESLEY *plays the music-box theme on the piano.* MARY L. *takes a table.*

NICK. Joe. That girl, Kitty. What's she mean, calling me a dentist? I wouldn't hurt anybody, let alone a tooth. (*He goes to* MARY L.'*s table.*)

HARRY *imitates the toy. Dances. The piano music comes up, the light dims slowly, while the piano solo continues.*

ACT TWO

An hour later. All the people who were at Nick's when the curtain came down are still there. JOE *at his table, quietly shuffling and turning a deck of cards, and at the same time watching the face of the woman, and looking at the initials on her handbag, as though they were the symbols of the lost glory of the world. The* WOMAN, *in turn, very casually regards* JOE *occasionally. Or rather senses him; has sensed him in fact the whole hour. She is mildly tight on beer, and* JOE *himself is tight, but as always completely under control; simply sharper. The others are about, at tables, and so on.*

JOE. Is it Madge—Laubowitz?
MARY. Is what *what?*
JOE. Is the name Mabel Lepescu?
MARY. What name?
JOE. The name the initials M. L. stand for. The initials on your bag.

MARY. No.

JOE (*after a long pause, thinking deeply what the name might be, turning a card, looking into the beautiful face of the woman*). Margie Longworthy?

MARY (*all this is very natural and sincere, no comedy on the part of the people involved: they are both solemn, being drunk*). No.

JOE (*his voice higher-pitched, as though he were growing a little alarmed*). Midge Laurie? (MARY *shakes her head.*) My initials are J. T.

MARY (*pause*). John?

JOE. No. (*Pause*) Martha Lancaster?

MARY. No. (*Slight pause*) Joseph?

JOE. Well, not exactly. That's my first name, but everybody calls me Joe. The last name is the tough one. I'll help you a little. I'm Irish. (*Pause*) Is it just plain Mary?

MARY. Yes, it is. I'm Irish, too. At least on my father's side. English on my mother's side.

JOE. I'm Irish on both sides. Mary's one of my favorite names. I guess that's why I didn't think of it. I met a girl in Mexico City named Mary once. She was an American from Philadelphia. She got married there. In Mexico City, I mean. While I was *there*. We were in love, too. At least *I* was. You never know about anyone else. They were engaged, you see, and her mother was with her, so they went through with it. Must have been six or seven years ago. She's probably got three or four children by this time.

MARY. Are you still in love with her?

JOE. Well—no. To tell you the truth, I'm not sure. I guess I am. I didn't even know she was engaged until a couple of days before they got married. I thought *I* was going to marry her. I kept thinking all the time about the kind of kids we would be likely to have. My favorite was the third one. The first two were fine. Handsome and fine and intelligent, but that third one was different. Dumb and goofy-looking. I liked *him* a lot. When she told me she was going to be married, I didn't feel so bad about the first two, it was that dumb one.

MARY (*after a pause of some few seconds*). What do you do?

JOE. Do? To tell you the truth, nothing.

MARY. Do you always drink a great deal?

JOE (*scientifically*). Not *always*. Only when I'm awake. I sleep seven or eight hours every night, you know.

MARY. How nice. I mean to drink when you're awake.

JOE (*thoughtfully*). It's a privilege.

MARY. Do you really *like* to drink?

JOE (*positively*). As much as I like to *breathe*.

MARY (*beautifully*). Why?

JOE (*dramatically*). Why do I like to drink? (*Pause*) Because I don't like to be gypped. Because I don't like to be dead most of the time and just a little alive every once in a long while. (*Pause*) If I don't drink, I become fascinated by unimportant things—like everybody else. I get busy. Do things. All kinds of little stupid things, for all kinds of little stupid reasons. Proud, selfish, *ordinary* things. I've done them. Now I don't do anything. *I live all the time*. Then I go to sleep. (*Pause*.)

MARY. Do you sleep well?

JOE (*taking it for granted*). Of course.

MARY (*quietly, almost with tenderness*). What are your plans?

JOE (*loudly, but also tenderly*). Plans? I haven't *got* any. *I just get up*.

MARY (*beginning to understand everything*). Oh, yes. Yes, of course.

DUDLEY *puts a nickel in the phonograph.*

JOE (*thoughtfully*). Why do I drink? (*Pause, while he thinks about it. The thinking appears to be profound and complex, and has the effect of giving his face a very comical and naive expression.*) That questions calls for a pretty complicated answer. (*He smiles abstractly*.)

MARY. Oh, I didn't mean—

JOE (*swiftly, gallantly*). No. No. I *insist*. I *know* why. It's just a matter of finding words. Little ones.

MARY. It really doesn't matter.

JOE (*seriously*). Oh, yes, it does. (*Clinically*) Now, why do I drink? (*Scientifically*) No. Why does *anybody* drink? (*Working it out*) Every day has twenty-four hours.

MARY (*sadly, but brightly*). Yes, that's true.

JOE. Twenty-four hours. Out of the twenty-four hours at *least* twenty-three and a half are—my God, I don't know why—dull, dead, boring, empty, and murderous. Minutes on the clock, *not time of living.* It doesn't make any difference who you are or what you do, twenty-three and a half hours of the twenty-four are spent *waiting.*

MARY. Waiting?

JOE (*gesturing, loudly*). And the more you wait, the less there is to wait *for.*

MARY (*attentively, beautifully his student*). Oh?

JOE (*continuing*). That goes on for days and days, and weeks and months and years, and years, and the first thing you know *all* the years are dead. All the minutes are dead. You yourself are dead. There's nothing to wait for any more. Nothing except *minutes* on the *clock.* No time of life. Nothing but minutes, and idiocy. Beautiful, bright, intelligent idiocy. (*Pause*) Does that answer your question?

MARY (*earnestly*). I'm afraid it does. Thank you. You shouldn't have gone to all the trouble.

JOE. No trouble at all. (*Pause*) You have children?

MARY. Yes. Two. A son and a daughter.

JOE (*delighted*). How swell. Do they look like you?

MARY. Yes.

JOE. Then why are you sad?

MARY. I was always sad. It's just that after I was married I was allowed to drink.

JOE (*eagerly*). Who are you waiting for?

MARY. No one.

JOE (*smiling*). I'm not waiting for anybody, either.

MARY. My husband, of course.

JOE. Oh, sure.

MARY. He's a lawyer.

JOE (*standing, leaning on the table*). He's a great guy. I like him. I'm very fond of him.

MARY (*listening*). You have responsibilities?

JOE (*loudly*). *One,* and *thousands.* As a matter of fact, I feel responsible to everybody. At least to everybody I meet. I've been trying for three years to find out if it's possible to live what I think is a civilized life. I mean a life that can't hurt any other life.

MARY. You're famous?

JOE. Very. Utterly unknown, but very famous. Would you like to dance?

MARY. All right.

JOE (*loudly*). I'm *sorry*. I don't dance. I didn't think you'd like to.

MARY. To tell you the truth. I don't like to dance at all.

JOE (*proudly. Commentator*). I can hardly walk.

MARY. You mean you're tight?

JOE (*smiling*). No. I mean *all* the time.

MARY (*looking at him closely*). Were you ever in Paris?

JOE. In 1929, and again in 1934.

MARY. What month of 1934?

JOE. Most of April, all of May, and a little of June.

MARY. I was there in November and December that year.

JOE. We were there almost at the same time. You were married?

MARY. Engaged. (*They are silent a moment, looking at one another. Quietly and with great charm*) Are you *really* in love with me?

JOE. Yes.

MARY. Is it the champagne?

JOE. Yes. Partly, at least. (*He sits down.*)

MARY. If you don't see me again, will you be very unhappy?

JOE. Very.

MARY (*getting up*). I'm so pleased. (JOE *is deeply grieved that she is going. In fact, he is almost panic-stricken about it, getting up in a way that is full of furious sorrow and regret.*) I must go now. Please don't get up. (JOE *is up, staring at her with amazement.*) Good-by.

JOE (*simply*). Good-by.

The WOMAN *stands looking at him a moment, then turns and goes.* JOE *stands staring after her for a long time. Just as he is slowly sitting down again, the* NEWSBOY *enters, and goes to* JOE*'s table.*

NEWSBOY. Paper, Mister?

JOE. How many you got this time?

NEWSBOY. Eleven.

JOE *buys them all, looks at the lousy headlines, throws them away. The* NEWSBOY *looks at* JOE, *amazed. He walks over to* NICK *at the bar.*

NEWSBOY (*troubled*). Hey, Mister, do you own this place?

NICK (*casually but emphatically*). I own this place.

NEWSBOY. Can you use a great lyric tenor?

NICK (*almost to himself*). Great lyric tenor? (*Loudly*) Who?

NEWSBOY (*loud and the least bit angry*). Me. I'm getting too big to sell papers. I don't want to holler headlines all the time. I want to *sing*. You can use a great lyric tenor, can't you?

NICK. What's lyric about you?

NEWSBOY (*voice high-pitched, confused*). My voice.

NICK. Oh. (*Slight pause, giving in*) All right, then—sing!

The NEWSBOY *breaks into swift and beautiful song: "When Irish Eyes Are Smiling."* NICK *and* JOE *listen carefully:* NICK *with wonder,* JOE *with amazement and delight.*

NEWSBOY (*singing*).

When Irish eyes are smiling,
Sure 'tis like a morn in Spring.
In the lilt of Irish laughter,
You can hear the angels sing.
When Irish hearts are happy,
All the world seems bright and gay.
But when Irish eyes are smiling—

NICK (*loudly, swiftly*). Are you Irish?

NEWSBOY (*speaking swiftly, loudly, a little impatient with the irrelevant question*). No. I'm Greek. (*He finishes the song, singing louder than ever.*) Sure they steal your heart away. (*He turns to* NICK *dramatically, like a vaudeville singer begging his audience for applause.* NICK *studies the* BOY *eagerly.* JOE *gets to his feet and leans toward the* BOY *and* NICK.)

NICK. Not bad. Let me hear you again about a year from now.

NEWSBOY (*thrilled*). Honest?

NICK. Yeah. Along about November 7th, 1940.

NEWSBOY (*happier than ever before in his life, running over to* JOE). Did you hear it too, Mister?

JOE. Yes, and it's great. What part of Greece?

NEWSBOY. Salonica. Gosh, Mister. Thanks.

JOE. Don't wait a year. Come back with some papers a little later. You're a great singer.

NEWSBOY (*thrilled and excited*). Aw, thanks, Mister. So long. (*Running, to* NICK) Thanks, Mister. (*He runs out.*)

JOE *and* NICK *look at the swinging doors.* JOE *sits down.* NICK *laughs.*

NICK. Joe, people are so wonderful. Look at that kid.
JOE. Of course they're wonderful. Every one of them is wonderful. (*Pause*) A nation like this can't go wrong.

MCCARTHY *and* KRUPP *come in, talking.* MCCARTHY *is a big man in work clothes, which make him seem very young. He is wearing black jeans, and a blue workman's shirt. No tie. No hat. He has broad shoulders, a lean intelligent face, thick black hair. In his right pocket is the longshoreman's hook. His arms are long and hairy. His sleeves are rolled up to just below his elbows. He is a casual man, easy-going in movement, sharp in perception, swift in appreciation of charm or innocence or comedy, and gentle in spirit. His speech is clear and full of warmth. His voice is powerful, but modulated. He enjoys the world, in spite of the mess it is, and he is fond of people, in spite of the mess they are.*

KRUPP *is not quite as tall or broad-shouldered as* MCCARTHY. *He is physically encumbered by his uniform, club, pistol, belt, and cap. And he is plainly not at home in the role of policeman. His movement is stiff and unintentionally pompous. He is a naive man, essentially good. His understanding is less than* MCCARTHY*'s, but he is honest and he doesn't try to bluff.*

KRUPP. You don't understand what I mean. Hi-ya, Joe.
JOE. Hello, Krupp.
MCCARTHY. Hi-ya, Joe.
JOE. Hello, McCarthy.
KRUPP. Two beers, Nick. (*To* MCCARTHY) All I do is carry out orders, carry out orders. I don't know what the idea is behind the order. Who it's for, or who it's against, or why. All I do is carry it out. (NICK *gives them beer.*)
MCCARTHY. You don't read enough.
KRUPP. I do read. I read *The Examiner* every morning. *The Call-Bulletin* every night.

MCCARTHY. And carry out orders. What are the orders now?

KRUPP. To keep the peace down here on the waterfront.

MCCARTHY. Keep it for who? (*To* JOE) Right?

JOE (*sorrowfully*). Right.

KRUPP. How do I know for who? The peace. Just keep it.

MCCARTHY. It's got to be kept for somebody. Who would you suspect it's kept for?

KRUPP. For citizens!

MCCARTHY. I'm a citizen!

KRUPP. All right, I'm keeping it for you.

MCCARTHY. By hitting me over the head with a club? (*To* JOE) Right?

JOE (*melancholy, with remembrance*). I don't know.

KRUPP. Mac, you know I never hit you over the head with a club.

MCCARTHY. But you will if you're on duty at the time and happen to stand on the opposite side of myself, on duty.

KRUPP. We went to Mission High together. We were always good friends. The only time we ever fought was that time over Alma Haggerty. Did *you* marry Alma Haggerty? (*To* JOE) Right?

JOE. Everything's right.

MCCARTHY. No. Did you? (*To* JOE) Joe, are you with me or against me?

JOE. I'm with everybody. One at a time.

KRUPP. No. And that's just what I mean.

MCCARTHY. You mean neither one of us is going to marry the thing we're fighting for?

KRUPP. *I don't even know what it is.*

MCCARTHY. You don't read enough, I tell you.

KRUPP. Mac, you don't know what you're fighting for, either.

MCCARTHY. It's so simple, it's fantastic.

KRUPP. All right, what are you fighting for?

MCCARTHY. For the rights of the inferior. Right?

JOE. Something like that.

KRUPP. The who?

MCCARTHY. The inferior. The world full of Mahoneys who haven't got what it takes to make monkeys out of everybody else, near by. The men who were created equal. Remember?

KRUPP. Mac, you're not inferior.

MC CARTHY. I'm a longshoreman. And an idealist. I'm a man with too much brawn to be an intellectual, exclusively. I married a small, sensitive, cultured woman so that my kids would be sissies instead of suckers. A strong man with any sensibility has no choice in this world but to be a heel, or a *worker*. I haven't the heart to be a heel, so I'm a worker. I've got a son in high school who's already thinking of being a writer.

KRUPP. I wanted to be a writer once.

JOE. Wonderful. (*He puts down the paper, looks at* KRUPP *and* MC CARTHY.)

MC CARTHY. They *all* wanted to be writers. Every maniac in the world that ever brought about the murder of people through war started out in an attic or a basement writing poetry. It stank. So they got even by becoming important heels. And it's still going on.

KRUPP. Is it really, Joe?

JOE. Look at today's paper.

MC CARTHY. Right now on Telegraph Hill is some punk who is trying to be Shakespeare. Ten years from now he'll be a senator. Or a communist.

KRUPP. Somebody ought to do something about it.

MC CARTHY (*mischievously, with laughter in his voice*). The thing to do is to have more magazines. Hundreds of them. *Thousands*. Print everything they write, so they'll believe they're immortal. That way keep them from going haywire.

KRUPP. Mac, you ought to be a writer yourself.

MC CARTHY. I hate the tribe. They're mischief-makers. Right?

JOE (*swiftly*). Everything's right. Right and wrong.

KRUPP. Then why do you read?

MC CARTHY (*laughing*). It's relaxing. It's soothing. (*Pause*) The lousiest people born into the world are writers. Language is all right. It's the people who use language that are lousy. (*The* ARAB *has moved a little closer, and is listening carefully. To the* ARAB) What do you think, Brother?

ARAB (*after making many faces, thinking very deeply*). No foundation. All the way down the line. What. What-not. Nothing. I go walk and look at sky. (*He goes.*)

KRUPP. What? What-not? (*To* JOE) What's that mean?

JOE (*slowly, thinking, remembering*). What? What-not? That

means this side, that side. Inhale, exhale. What: birth. What-not: death. The inevitable, the astounding, the magnificent seed of growth and decay in all things. Beginning, and end. That man, in his own way, is a prophet. He is one who, with the help of *beer*, is able to reach that state of deep understanding in which what and what-not, the reasonable and the unreasonable, are *one*.

MCCARTHY. Right.

KRUPP. If you can understand that kind of talk, how can you be a longshoreman?

MCCARTHY. I come from a long line of McCarthys who never married or slept with anything but the most powerful and quarrelsome flesh. (*He drinks beer.*)

KRUPP. I could listen to you two guys for hours, but I'll be damned if I know what the hell you're talking about.

MCCARTHY. The consequence is that all the McCarthys are too great and too strong to be heroes. Only the weak and unsure perform the heroic. They've *got* to. The more heroes you have, the worse the history of the world becomes. Right?

JOE. Go outside and look at it.

KRUPP. You sure can philos—philosoph— Boy, you can talk.

MCCARTHY. I wouldn't talk this way to anyone but a man in uniform, and a man who couldn't understand a word of what I was saying. The party I'm speaking of, my friend, is *YOU*.

The phone rings. HARRY *gets up from his table suddenly and begins a new dance.*

KRUPP (*noticing him, with great authority*). Here. Here. What do you think you're doing?

HARRY (*stopping*). I just got an idea for a new dance. I'm trying it out. Nick. Nick, the phone's ringing.

KRUPP (*to* MCCARTHY). Has he got a right to do that?

MCCARTHY. The living have danced from the beginning of time. I might even say, the dance and the life have moved along together, until now we have— (*To* HARRY) Go into your dance, son, and show us what we have.

HARRY. I haven't got it worked out *completely* yet, but it starts out like this. (*He dances.*)

NICK (*on phone*). Nick's Pacific Street Restaurant, Saloon, and Entertainment Palace. Good afternoon. Nick speaking. (*Listens*) Who? (*Turns around.*) Is there a Dudley Bostwick in the joint?

DUDLEY *jumps to his feet and goes to phone.*

DUDLEY (*on phone*). Hello. Elsie? (*Listens*) You're coming down? (*Elated. To the saloon*) She's coming down. (*Pause*) No. I won't drink. Aw, gosh, Elsie. (*He hangs up, looks about him strangely, as if he were just born, walks around touching things, putting chairs in place, and so on.*)

MCCARTHY (*to* HARRY). Splendid. Splendid.

HARRY. Then I go into this little routine. (*He demonstrates.*)

KRUPP. Is that good, Mac?

MCCARTHY. It's awful, but it's honest and ambitious, like everything else in this great country.

HARRY. Then I work along into this. (*He demonstrates.*) And *this* is where I *really* get going. (*He finishes the dance.*)

MCCARTHY. Excellent. A most satisfying demonstration of the present state of the American body and soul. Son, you're a genius.

HARRY (*delighted, shaking hands with* MCCARTHY). I go on in front of an audience for the first time in my life tonight.

MCCARTHY. They'll be delighted. Where'd you learn to dance?

HARRY. Never took a lesson in my life. I'm a natural-born dancer. And *comedian*, too.

MCCARTHY (*astounded*). You can make people *laugh*?

HARRY (*dumbly*). I can be funny, but they won't laugh.

MCCARTHY. That's odd. Why not?

HARRY. I don't know. They just won't laugh.

MCCARTHY. Would you care to be funny now?

HARRY. I'd like to try out a new monologue I've been thinking about.

MCCARTHY. Please do. I promise you if it's funny I shall *roar* with laughter.

HARRY. This is it. (*Goes into the act, with much energy.*) I'm up at Sharkey's on Turk Street. It's a quarter to nine, daylight saving. Wednesday, the eleventh. What I've got is a headache and a 1918 nickel. What I *want* is a cup of coffee. If I buy a cup of coffee with the nickel, I've got to walk home. I've got an eight-ball problem. George the Greek is shooting a game of snooker with Pedro the Filipino. *I'm in rags.* They're wearing thirty-five dollar suits, made to order. I haven't got a cigarette. They're smoking Bobby Burns panatelas. I'm thinking it over, like I always do. George the Greek is in a tough spot. If I buy a cup of coffee, I'll want another cup. What happens? My ear aches! My ear. George the Greek takes the cue. Chalks it. Studies the table. Touches the cue-ball delicately. Tick. What happens? He makes the three-ball! What do I do? I get confused. *I go out and buy a morning paper.* What the hell do I want with a morning paper? What I *want* is a cup of coffee, and a good used car. I go out and buy a morning paper. Thursday, the twelfth. Maybe the headline's about *me.* I take a quick look. *No. The headline is not about me.* It's about Hitler. Seven thousand miles away. I'm here. Who the hell is Hitler? Who's behind the eight-ball? I turn around. *Everybody's behind the eight-ball!*

Pause. KRUPP *moves toward* HARRY *as if to make an important arrest.* HARRY *moves to the swinging doors.* MCCARTHY *stops* KRUPP.

MCCARTHY (*to* HARRY). It's the funniest thing I've ever heard. Or *seen,* for that matter.

HARRY (*coming back to* MCCARTHY). Then, why don't you laugh?

MCCARTHY. I don't know, *yet.*

HARRY. I'm always getting funny ideas that nobody will laugh at.

MCCARTHY (*thoughtfully*). It may be that you've stumbled headlong into a new kind of comedy.

HARRY. Well, what good is it if it doesn't make anybody laugh?

MCCARTHY. There are *kinds* of laughter, son. I must say, in all truth, that I *am* laughing, although not *out loud.*

HARRY. I want to *hear* people laugh. *Out loud.* That's why I keep thinking of funny things to say.

MCCARTHY. Well. They may catch on in time. Let's go, Krupp. So long, Joe. (MCCARTHY *and* KRUPP *go.*)

JOE. So long. (*After a moment's pause.*) Hey, Nick.

NICK. Yeah.

JOE. Bet McCarthy in the last race.

NICK. You're crazy. That horse is a double-crossing, no-good—

JOE. Bet everything you've got on McCarthy.

NICK. I'm not betting a nickel on him. *You* bet everything you've got on McCarthy.

JOE. I don't need money.

NICK. What makes you think McCarthy's going to win?

JOE. McCarthy's name's McCarthy, isn't it?

NICK. Yeah. So what?

JOE. The *horse* named McCarthy is going to win, *that's all.* Today.

NICK. Why?

JOE. You do what I tell you, and everything will be all right.

NICK. McCarthy likes to talk, that's all. (*Pause*) Where's Tom?

JOE. He'll be around. He'll be miserable, but he'll be around. Five or ten minutes more.

NICK. You don't believe that Kitty, do you? About being in burlesque?

JOE (*very clearly*). I believe dreams sooner than statistics.

NICK (*remembering*). She sure is somebody. Called me a dentist.

TOM, *turning about, confused, troubled, comes in, and hurries to* JOE'*s table.*

JOE. What's the matter?

TOM. Here's your five, Joe. I'm in trouble again.

JOE. If it's not organic, it'll cure itself. If it is organic, science will cure it. What is it, organic or non-organic?

TOM. Joe, I don't know—(*He seems to be completely broken-down.*)

JOE. What's eating you? I want you to go on an errand for me.

TOM. It's Kitty.

JOE. What about her?

TOM. She's up in her room, crying.

JOE. Crying?

TOM. Yeah, she's been crying for over an hour. I been talking to her all this time, but she won't stop.

JOE. What's she crying about?

TOM. I don't know. I couldn't understand anything. She kept crying and telling me about a big house and collie dogs all around and flowers and one of her brothers dead and the other one lost somewhere. Joe, I can't stand Kitty crying.

JOE. You want to marry the girl?

TOM (*nodding*). Yeah.

JOE (*curious and sincere*). Why?

TOM. I don't know why, exactly, Joe. (*Pause*) Joe, I don't like to think of Kitty out in the streets. I guess I love her, that's all.

JOE. She's a nice girl.

TOM. She's like an angel. She's not like those other streetwalkers.

JOE (*swiftly*). Here. Take all this money and run next door to Frankie's and bet it on the nose of McCarthy.

TOM (*swiftly*). All this money, Joe? McCarthy?

JOE. Yeah. Hurry.

TOM (*going*). Ah, Joe. If McCarthy wins we'll be rich.

JOE. Get going, will you?

TOM *runs out and nearly knocks over the* ARAB *coming back in.* NICK *fills him a beer without a word.*

ARAB. No foundation, anywhere. Whole world. No foundation. All the way down the line.

NICK (*angry*). McCarthy! Just because you got a little lucky this morning, you have to go to work and throw away eighty bucks.

JOE. He wants to marry her.

NICK. Suppose she doesn't want to marry *him?*

JOE (*amazed*). Oh, yeah. (*Thinking*) Now, why wouldn't she want to marry a nice guy like Tom?

NICK. She's been in burlesque. She's had flowers sent to her by European royalty. She's dined with young men of quality and social position. She's above Tom.

TOM *comes running in.*

TOM (*disgusted*). They were running when I got there. Frankie wouldn't take the bet. McCarthy didn't get a call till the stretch. I thought we were going to save all this money. Then McCarthy won by *two* lengths.

JOE. What'd he pay, fifteen to one?

TOM. Better, but Frankie wouldn't take the bet.

NICK (*throwing a dish towel across the room*). Well, for the love of Mike.

JOE. Give me the money.

TOM (*giving back the money*). We would have had about a thousand five hundred dollars.

JOE (*bored, casually, inventing*). Go up to Schwabacher-Frey and get me the biggest Rand-McNally map of the nations of Europe they've got. On your way back stop at one of the pawn shops on Third Street, and buy me a good revolver and some cartridges.

TOM. She's up in her room crying, Joe.

JOE. Go get me those things.

NICK. What are you going to do, study the map, and then go out and shoot somebody?

JOE. I want to read the names of some European towns and rivers and valleys and mountains.

NICK. What do you want with the revolver?

JOE. I want to study it. I'm interested in things. Here's twenty dollars, Tom. Now go get them things.

TOM. A big map of Europe. And a revolver.

JOE. Get a good one. Tell the man you don't know anything about firearms and you're trusting him not to fool you. Don't pay more than ten dollars.

TOM. Joe, you got something on your mind. Don't go fool with a revolver.

JOE. Be sure it's a good one.

TOM. Joe.

JOE (*irritated*). What, Tom?

TOM. Joe, what do you send me out for crazy things for all the time?

JOE (*angry*). They're not crazy, Tom. Now, get going.

TOM. What about Kitty, Joe?

JOE. Let her cry. It'll do her good.

TOM. If she comes in here while I'm gone, talk to her, will you, Joe? Tell her about me.

JOE. O.K. Get going. Don't load that gun. Just buy it and bring it here.

TOM (*going*). You won't catch me loading any gun.

JOE. Wait a minute. Take these toys away.

TOM. Where'll I take them?

JOE. Give them to some kid. (*Pause*) No. Take them up to Kitty. Toys stopped me from crying once. That's the reason I had you buy them. I wanted to see if I could find out *why* they stopped me from crying. I remember they seemed awfully stupid at the time.

TOM. Shall I, Joe? Take them up to Kitty? Do you think they'd stop *her* from crying?

JOE. They might. You get curious about the way they work and you forget whatever it is you're remembering that's making you cry. That's what they're for.

TOM. Yeah. Sure. The girl at the store asked me what I wanted with toys. I'll take them up to Kitty. (*Tragically*) She's like a little girl. (*He goes.*)

WESLEY. Mr. Nick, can I play the piano again?

NICK. Sure. Practice all you like—until I tell you to stop.

WESLEY. You going to pay me for playing the piano?

NICK. Sure. I'll give you enough to get by on.

WESLEY (*amazed and delighted*). Get money for playing the piano? (*He goes to the piano and begins to play quietly.*)

HARRY *goes up on the little stage and listens to the music. After a while he begins a soft shoe dance.*

NICK. What were you crying about?

JOE. My mother.

NICK. What about her?

JOE. She was dead. I stopped crying when they gave me the toys.

NICK'*s* MOTHER, *a little old woman of sixty or so, dressed plainly in black, her face shining, comes in briskly, chattering loudly in Italian, gesturing.* NICK *is delighted to see her.*

NICK'S MOTHER (*in Italian*). Everything all right, Nickie?

NICK (*in Italian*). Sure, Mamma.

NICK'*s* MOTHER *leaves as gaily and as noisily as she came, after half a minute of loud Italian family talk.*

JOE. Who was that?

NICK (*to* JOE, *proudly and a little sadly*). My mother. (*Still looking at the swinging doors.*)

JOE. What'd she say?

NICK. Nothing. Just wanted to see me. (*Pause*) What do you want with that gun?

JOE. I study things, Nick.

An old man who looks as if he might have been Kit Carson at one time walks in importantly, moves about, and finally stands at JOE'*s table.*

KIT CARSON. Murphy's the name. Just an old trapper. Mind if I sit down?

JOE. Be delighted. What'll you drink?

KIT CARSON (*sitting down*). Beer. Same as I've been drinking. And thanks.

JOE (*to* NICK). Glass of beer, Nick.

NICK *brings the beer to the table,* KIT CARSON *swallows it in one swig, wipes his big white mustache with the back of his right hand.*

KIT CARSON (*moving in*). I don't suppose you ever fell in love with a midget weighing thirty-nine pounds?

JOE (*studying the man*). Can't say I have, but have another beer.

KIT CARSON (*intimately*). Thanks, thanks. Down in Gallup, twenty years ago. Fellow by the name of Rufus Jenkins came to town with six white horses and two black ones. Said he wanted a man to break the horses for him because his left leg was wood and he couldn't do it. Had a meeting at Parker's Mercantile Store and finally came to blows, me and Henry Walpal. Bashed his head with a brass cuspidor and ran away to Mexico, but he didn't die.

Couldn't speak a word. Took up with a cattle-breeder named Diego, educated in California. Spoke the language better than you and me. Said, Your job, Murph, is to feed them prize bulls. I said, Fine, what'll I feed them? He said, Hay, lettuce, salt, beer, and aspirin.

Came to blows two days later over an accordion he claimed I stole. I had *borrowed* it. During the fight I busted it over his head; ruined one of the finest accordions I ever saw. Grabbed a horse and rode back across the border. Texas.

Got to talking with a fellow who looked honest. Turned out to be a Ranger who was looking for me.

JOE. Yeah. You were saying, a thirty-nine-pound midget.

KIT CARSON. Will I ever forget that lady? Will I ever get over that amazon of small proportions?

JOE. Will you?

KIT CARSON. If I live to be sixty.

JOE. Sixty? You look more than sixty now.

KIT CARSON. That's trouble showing in my face. Trouble and complications. I was fifty-eight three months ago.

JOE. That accounts for it, then. Go ahead, tell me more.

KIT CARSON. Told the Texas Ranger my name was Rothstein, mining engineer from Pennsylvania, looking for something worth while. Mentioned two places in Houston. Nearly lost an eye early one morning, going down the stairs. Ran into a six-footer with an iron claw where his right hand was supposed to be. Said, You broke up my home. Told him I was a stranger in Houston. The girls gathered at the top of the stairs to see a fight. Seven of them. Six feet and an iron claw. That's bad on the nerves. Kicked him in the mouth when he swung for my head with the claw. Would have lost an eye except for quick thinking. He rolled into the gutter and pulled a gun. Fired seven times. I was back upstairs. Left the place an hour later, dressed in silk and feathers, with a hat swung around over my face. Saw him standing on the corner, waiting. Said, Care for a wiggle? Said he didn't. I went on down the street and left town. I don't suppose you ever had to put a dress on to save your skin, did you?

JOE. No, and I never fell in love with a midget weighing thirty-nine pounds. Have another beer?

KIT CARSON. Thanks. (*Swallows glass of beer.*) Ever try to herd cattle on a bicycle?

JOE. No. I never got around to that.

KIT CARSON. Left Houston with sixty cents in my pocket, gift of a girl named Lucinda. Walked fourteen miles in fourteen hours. Big house with barb-wire all around, and big dogs. One thing I never could get around. Walked past the gate, anyway, from hunger and thirst. Dogs jumped up and came for me. Walked right into them, growing older every second. Went up to the door and knocked. Big negress opened the door, closed it quick. Said, On your way, white trash.

Knocked again. Said, On your way. Again. On your way. Again. This time the old man himself opened the door, ninety, if he was a day. Sawed-off shotgun, too.

Said, I ain't looking for trouble, Father. I'm hungry and thirsty, name's Cavanaugh.

Took me in and made mint juleps for the two of us.

Said, Living here alone, Father?

Said, Drink and ask no questions. Maybe I am and maybe I ain't. You saw the lady. Draw your own conclusions.

I'd heard of that, but didn't wink out of tact. If I told you that old Southern gentleman was my grandfather, you wouldn't believe me, would you?

JOE. I might.

KIT CARSON. Well, it so happens he wasn't. Would have been romantic if he had been, though.

JOE. Where did you herd cattle on a bicycle?

KIT CARSON. Toledo, Ohio, 1918.

JOE. Toledo, Ohio? They don't herd cattle in Toledo.

KIT CARSON. They don't anymore. They did in 1918. One fellow did, leastaways. Bookkeeper named Sam Gold. Straight from the East Side, New York. Sombrero, lariats, Bull Durham, two head of cattle and two bicycles. Called his place The Gold Bar Ranch, two acres, just outside the city limits.

That was the year of the War, you'll remember.

JOE. Yeah, I remember, but how about herding them two cows on a bicycle? How'd you do it?

KIT CARSON. Easiest thing in the world. Rode no hands. Had to, otherwise couldn't lasso the cows. Worked for Sam Gold till the cows ran away. Bicycles scared them. They went into Toledo. Never saw hide nor hair of them again. Advertised in every paper, but never got them back. Broke his heart. Sold both bikes and returned to New York.

Took four aces from a deck of red cards and walked to town. Poker. Fellow in the game named Chuck Collins, liked to gamble. Told him with a smile I didn't suppose he'd care to bet a hundred dollars I wouldn't hold four aces the next hand. Called it. My cards were red on the blank side. The other cards were blue. Plumb forgot all about it. Showed him four aces. Ace of spades, ace of clubs, ace of diamonds, ace of hearts. I'll remember them four cards if I live to be sixty. Would have been killed on the spot except for the hurricane that year.

JOE. Hurricane?

KIT CARSON. You haven't forgotten the Toledo hurricane of 1918, have you?

JOE. No. There was no hurricane in Toledo in 1918, or any other year.

KIT CARSON. For the love of God, then what do you suppose that commotion was? And how come I came to in Chicago, dream-walking down State Street?

JOE. I guess they scared you.

KIT CARSON. No, that wasn't it. You go back to the papers of November 1918, and I think you'll find there was a hurricane in Toledo. I remember sitting on the roof of a two-story house, floating northwest.

JOE (*seriously*). Northwest?

KIT CARSON. Now, son, don't tell me *you* don't believe me, either?

JOE (*pause. Very seriously, energetically, and sharply*). Of course I believe you. Living is an art. It's not bookkeeping. It takes a lot of rehearsing for a man to get to be himself.

KIT CARSON (*thoughtfully, smiling, and amazed*). You're the first man I've ever met who believes me.

JOE (*seriously*). Have another beer.

TOM *comes in with the Rand-McNally book, the revolver, and the box of cartridges.* KIT *goes to bar.*

JOE (*to* TOM). Did you give her the toys?

TOM. Yeah, I gave them to her.

JOE. Did she stop crying?

TOM. No. She started crying harder than ever.

JOE. That's funny. I wonder why.

TOM. Joe, if I was a minute earlier, Frankie would have taken the bet and now we'd have about a thousand five hundred dollars. How much of it would you have given me, Joe?

JOE. If she'd marry you—*all* of it.

TOM. Would you, Joe?

JOE (*opening packages, examining book first, and revolver

next). Sure. In this realm there's only one subject, and you're it. It's my duty to see that my subject is happy.

TOM. Joe, do you think we'll ever have eighty dollars for a race sometime again when there's a fifteen-to-one shot that we like, weather good, track fast, they get off to a good start, our horse doesn't get a call till the stretch, we think we're going to lose all that money, and then it wins, by a nose?

JOE. I didn't quite get that.

TOM. You know what I mean.

JOE. You mean the impossible. No, Tom, we won't. We were just a little late, that's all.

TOM. We might, Joe.

JOE. It's not likely.

TOM. Then how am I ever going to make enough money to marry her?

JOE. I don't know, Tom. Maybe you aren't.

TOM. Joe, I got to marry Kitty. (*Shaking his head.*) You ought to see the crazy room she lives in.

JOE. What kind of a room is it?

TOM. It's little. It crowds you in. It's bad, Joe. Kitty don't belong in a place like that.

JOE. You want to take her away from there?

TOM. Yeah. I want her to live in a house where there's room enough to live. Kitty ought to have a garden, or something.

JOE. You want to take care of her?

TOM. Yeah, sure, Joe. I ought to take care of somebody good that makes me feel like *I'm* somebody.

JOE. That means you'll have to get a job. What can you do?

TOM. I finished high school, but I don't know what I can do.

JOE. Sometimes when you think about it, what do you think you'd like to do?

TOM. Just sit around like you, Joe, and have somebody run errands for me and drink champagne and take things easy and never be broke and never worry about money.

JOE. That's a noble ambition.

NICK (*to* JOE). How do you do it?

JOE. I really don't know, but I think you've got to have the full co-operation of the Good Lord.

NICK. I can't understand the way you talk.

TOM. Joe, shall I go back and see if I can get her to stop crying?

JOE. Give me a hand and I'll go with you.

TOM (*amazed*). What! You're going to get up already?

JOE. She's crying, isn't she?

TOM. She's crying. Worse than ever now.

JOE. I thought the toys would stop her.

TOM. I've seen you sit in one place from four in the morning till two the next morning.

JOE. At my best, Tom, I don't travel by foot. That's all. Come on. Give me a hand. I'll find some way to stop her from crying.

TOM (*helping* JOE). Joe, I never did tell you. You're a different kind of a guy.

JOE (*swiftly, a little angry*). Don't be silly. I don't understand things. I'm trying to understand them.

JOE *is a little drunk. They go out together. The lights go down slowly, while* WESLEY *plays the piano, and come up slowly on:*

ACT THREE

A cheap bed in Nick's to indicate room 21 of The New York Hotel, upstairs, around the corner from Nick's. The bed can be at the center of Nick's, or up on the little stage. Everything in Nick's is the same, except that all the people are silent, immobile and in darkness, except WESLEY *who is playing the piano softly and sadly.* KITTY DUVAL, *in a dress she has carried around with her from the early days in Ohio, is seated on the bed, tying a ribbon in her hair. She looks at herself in a hand mirror. She is deeply grieved at the change she sees in herself. She takes off the ribbon, angry and hurt. She lifts a book from the bed and tries to read. She begins to sob again. She picks up an old picture of herself and looks at it. Sobs harder than ever, falling on the bed and burying her face. There is a knock, as if at the door.*

KITTY (*sobbing*). Who is it?

TOM'S VOICE. Kitty, it's me. Tom. Me and Joe.

JOE, *followed by* TOM, *comes to the bed quietly.* JOE *is holding a rather large toy carousel.* JOE *studies* KITTY *a moment. He sets the toy carousel on the floor, at the foot of Kitty's bed.*

TOM (*standing over* KITTY *and bending down close to her*). Don't cry any more, Kitty.

KITTY (*not looking, sobbing*). I don't like this life.

JOE *starts the carousel which makes a strange, sorrowful, tinkling music. The music begins slowly, becomes swift, gradually slows down, and ends.* JOE *himself is interested in the toy, watches and listens to it carefully.*

TOM (*eagerly*). Kitty. Joe got up from his chair at Nick's just to get you a toy and come here. This one makes music. We rode all over town in a cab to get it. Listen.

KITTY *sits up slowly, listening, while* TOM *watches her. Everything happens slowly and somberly.* KITTY *notices the photograph of herself when she was a little girl. Lifts it, and looks at it again.*

TOM (*looking*). Who's that little girl, Kitty?

KITTY. That's me. When I was seven. (*She hands the photo to* TOM.)

TOM (*looking, smiling*). Gee, you're pretty, Kitty.

JOE *reaches up for the photograph, which* TOM *hands to him.* TOM *returns to* KITTY *whom he finds as pretty now as she was at seven.* JOE *studies the photograph.* KITTY *looks up at* TOM. *There is no doubt that they really love one another.* JOE *looks up at them.*

KITTY. Tom?

TOM (*eagerly*). Yeah, Kitty.

KITTY. Tom, when you were a little boy what did you want to be?

TOM (*a little bewildered, but eager to please her*). What, Kitty?

KITTY. Do you remember when you were a little boy?

TOM (*thoughtfully*). Yeah, I remember sometimes, Kitty.

KITTY. What did you want to be?

TOM (*looks at* JOE. JOE *holds* TOM's *eyes a moment. Then* TOM *is able to speak*). Sometimes I wanted to be a locomotive engineer. Sometimes I wanted to be a policeman.

KITTY. I wanted to be a great actress. (*She looks up into* TOM'*s face.*) Tom, didn't you ever want to be a doctor?

TOM (*looks at* JOE. JOE *holds* TOM'*s eyes again, encouraging* TOM *by his serious expression to go on talking*). Yeah, now I remember. Sure, Kitty. I wanted to be a doctor—*once.*

KITTY (*smiling sadly*). I'm so glad. Because I wanted to be an actress and have a young doctor come to the theater and see me and fall in love with me and send me flowers.

JOE *pantomimes to* TOM, *demanding that he go on talking.*

TOM. I would do that, Kitty.

KITTY. I wouldn't know who it was, and then one day I'd see him in the street and fall in love with him. I wouldn't know *he* was the one who was in love with me. I'd think about him all the time. I'd dream about him. I'd dream of being near him the rest of my life. I'd dream of having children that looked like him. I wouldn't be an actress all the time. Only until I found him and fell in love with him. After that we'd take a train and go to beautiful cities and see the wonderful people everywhere and give money to the poor and whenever people were sick he'd go to them and make them well again.

TOM *looks at* JOE, *bewildered, confused, and full of sorrow.* KITTY *is deep in memory, almost in a trance.*

JOE (*gently*). Talk to her, Tom. Be the wonderful young doctor she dreamed about and never found. Go ahead. Correct the errors of the world.

TOM. Joe. (*Pathetically*) I don't know what to say.

There is rowdy singing in the hall. A loud young VOICE *sings: "Sailing, sailing, over the bounding main."*

VOICE. Kitty. Oh, Kitty! (KITTY *stirs, shocked, coming out of the trance.*) Where the hell are you? Oh, Kitty.

TOM *jumps up, furiously.*

WOMAN'S VOICE (*in the hall*). Who you looking for, Sailor Boy?

VOICE. The most beautiful lay in the world.

WOMAN'S VOICE. Don't go any further.

VOICE (*with impersonal contempt*). You? No. Not you. Kitty. You stink.

WOMAN'S VOICE (*rasping, angry*). Don't you dare talk to me that way. You pickpocket.

VOICE (*still impersonal, but louder*). Oh, I see. Want to get tough, hey? Close the door. Go hide.

WOMAN'S VOICE. You pickpocket. All of you.

The door slams.

VOICE (*roaring with laughter which is very sad*). Oh—Kitty. Room 21. Where the hell is that room?

TOM (*to* JOE). Joe, I'll kill him.

KITTY (*fully herself again, terribly frightened*). Who is it? (*She looks long and steadily at* TOM *and* JOE. TOM *is standing, excited and angry.* JOE *is completely at ease, his expression full of pity.* KITTY *buries her face in the bed.*)

JOE (*gently*). Tom. Just take him away.

VOICE. Here it is. Number 21. Three naturals. Heaven. My blue heaven. The west, a nest, and you. Just Molly and me. (*Tragically*) Ah, to hell with everything.

A young SAILOR, *a good-looking boy of no more than twenty or so, who is only drunk and lonely, comes to the bed, singing sadly.*

SAILOR. Hi-ya, Kitty. (*Pause*) Oh. Visitors. Sorry. A thousand apologies. (*To* KITTY) I'll come back later.

TOM (*taking him by the shoulders, furiously*). If you do, I'll kill you.

JOE *holds* TOM. TOM *pushes the frightened boy away.*

JOE (*somberly*). Tom. You stay here with Kitty. I'm going down to Union Square to hire an automobile. I'll be back in a few minutes. We'll ride out to the ocean and watch the sun go down. Then we'll ride down the Great Highway to Half Moon Bay. We'll have supper down there, and you and Kitty can dance.

TOM (*stupefied, unable to express his amazement and gratitude*). Joe, you mean you're going to go on an errand for *me*? You mean you're not going to send me?

JOE. That's right. (*He gestures toward* KITTY, *indicating that*

TOM *shall talk to her, protect the innocence in her which is in so much danger when* TOM *isn't near, which* TOM *loves so deeply.* JOE *leaves.)*

TOM *studies* KITTY, *his face becoming child-like and somber. He sets the carousel into motion, listens, watching* KITTY, *who lifts herself slowly, looking only at* TOM. TOM *lifts the turning carousel and moves it slowly toward* KITTY, *as though the toy were his heart. The piano music comes up loudly and the lights go down, while* HARRY *is heard dancing swiftly.*

ACT FOUR

A little later.

WESLEY, *the colored boy, is at the piano.* HARRY *is on the little stage, dancing.* NICK *is behind the bar. The* ARAB *is in his place.* KIT CARSON *is asleep on his folded arms.*

The DRUNKARD *comes in. Goes to the telephone for the nickel that might be in the return-chute.* NICK *comes to take him out. He gestures for* NICK *to hold on a minute. Then produces a half dollar.* NICK *goes behind the bar to serve the* DRUNKARD *whiskey.*

THE DRUNKARD. To the old, God bless them. (*Another*) To the new, God love them. (*Another*) To—children and small animals, like little dogs that don't bite. (*Another. Loudly*) To reforestation. (*Searches for money. Finds some.*) To—President Taft. (*He goes out. The telephone rings.*)

KIT CARSON (*jumping up, fighting*). Come on, *all* of you, if you're looking for trouble. I never asked for quarter and I always gave it.

NICK (*reproachfully*). Hey, Kit Carson.

DUDLEY (*on the phone*). Hello. Who? Nick? Yes. He's here. (*To* NICK) It's for you. I think it's important.

NICK (*going to the phone*). Important! *What's* important?

DUDLEY. He sounded like big-shot.

NICK. Big *what?* (*To* WESLEY *and* HARRY) Hey, you. Quiet. I want to hear this important stuff.

WESLEY *stops playing the piano.* HARRY *stops dancing.* KIT CARSON *comes close to* NICK.

KIT CARSON. If there's anything I can do, name it. I'll do it for you. I'm fifty-eight years old; been through three wars; married four times; the father of countless children whose *names* I don't even know. I've got no money. I live from hand to mouth. But if there's anything I can do, name it. I'll do it.

NICK (*patiently*). Listen, Pop. For a moment, please sit down and go back to sleep—*for me.*

KIT CARSON. I can do that, too. (*He sits down, folds his arms, and puts his head into them. But not for long. As* NICK *begins to talk, he listens carefully, gets to his feet, and then begins to express in pantomime the moods of each of* NICK'*s remarks.*)

NICK (*on phone*). Yeah? (*Pause*) Who? Oh, I see. (*Listens*) Why don't you leave them alone? (*Listens*) The church-people? Well, to hell with the church-people. I'm a Catholic myself. (*Listens*) All right. I'll send them away. I'll tell them to lay low for a couple of days. Yeah, I know how it is. (NICK'*s daughter* ANNA *comes in shyly, looking at her father, and stands unnoticed by the piano.*) What? (*Very angry*) Listen. I don't like that Blick. He was here this morning, and I told him not to come back. I'll keep the girls out of here. You keep Blick out of here. (*Listens*) I know his brother-in-law is important, but I don't want him to come down here. He looks for trouble everywhere, and he always finds it. I don't break any laws. I've got a dive in the lousiest part of town. Five years nobody's been robbed, murdered, or gypped. I leave people alone. Your swanky joints uptown make trouble for you every night. (NICK *gestures to* WESLEY—*keeps listening on the phone—puts his hand over the mouthpiece. To* WESLEY *and* HARRY) Start playing again. My ears have got a headache. Go into your dance, son. (WESLEY *begins to play again.* HARRY *begins to dance.* NICK, *into mouthpiece*) Yeah. I'll keep them out. Just see that Blick doesn't come around and start something. (*Pause*) O.K. (*He hangs up.*)

KIT CARSON. Trouble coming?

NICK. That lousy Vice Squad again. It's that gorilla Blick.

KIT CARSON. Anybody at all. You can count on me. What kind of a gorilla is this gorilla Blick?

NICK. Very dignified. Toenails on his fingers.

ANNA (*to* KIT CARSON, *with great, warm, beautiful pride, pointing at* NICK). That's my father.

KIT CARSON (*leaping with amazement at the beautiful voice, the wondrous face, the magnificent event*). Well, bless your heart, child. Bless your lovely heart. I had a little daughter point me out in a crowd once.

NICK (*surprised*). Anna. What the hell are you doing here? Get back home where you belong and help Grandma cook me some supper. (ANNA *smiles at her father, understanding him, knowing that his words are words of love. She turns and goes, looking at him all the way out, as much as to say that she would cook for him the rest of her life.* NICK *stares at the swinging doors.* KIT CARSON *moves toward them, two or three steps.* ANNA *pushes open one of the doors and peeks in, to look at her father again. She waves to him. Turns and runs.* NICK *is very sad. He doesn't know what to do. He gets a glass and a bottle. Pours himself a drink. Swallows some. It isn't enough, so he pours more and swallows the whole drink. To himself*) My beautiful, beautiful baby. Anna, she is you again. (*He brings out a handkerchief, touches his eyes, and blows his nose.* KIT CARSON *moves close to* NICK, *watching* NICK'S *face.* NICK *looks at him. Loudly, almost making* KIT *jump*) You're broke, aren't you?

KIT CARSON. Always. Always.

NICK. All right. Go into the kitchen and give Sam a hand. Eat some food and when you come back you can have a couple of beers.

KIT CARSON (*studying* NICK). Anything at all. I know a good man when I see one. (*He goes.*)

ELSIE MANDELSPIEGEL *comes into Nick's. She is a beautiful, dark girl, with a sorrowful, wise, dreaming face, almost on the verge of tears, and full of pity. There is an aura of dream about her. She moves softly and gently, as if everything around her were unreal and pathetic.* DUDLEY *doesn't notice her for a moment or two. When he does finally see her, he is so amazed, he can barely move or speak. Her presence has the effect of changing him completely. He gets up from his chair, as if in a trance, and walks toward her, smiling sadly.*

ELSIE (*looking at him*). Hello, Dudley.

DUDLEY (*broken-hearted*). Elsie.

ELSIE. I'm sorry. (*Explaining*) So many people are sick. Last night a little boy died. I love you, but—(*She gestures, trying to indicate how hopeless love is. They sit down.*)

DUDLEY (*staring at her, stunned and quieted*). Elsie. You'll never know how glad I am to see you. Just to *see* you. (*Pathetically*) I was afraid I'd never see you again. It was driving me crazy. I didn't want to live. Honest. (*He shakes his head mournfully, with dumb and beautiful affection.* TWO STREETWALKERS *come in, and pause near* DUDLEY, *at the bar.*) I know. You told me before, but I can't help it, Elsie. I love you.

ELSIE (*quietly, somberly, gently, with great compassion*). I know you love me, and I love you, but don't you see love is impossible in this world?

DUDLEY. Maybe it isn't, Elsie.

ELSIE. Love is for birds. They have wings to fly away on when it's time for flying. For tigers in the jungle because they don't know their end. We know *our* end. Every night I watch over poor, dying men. I hear them breathing, crying, talking in their sleep. Crying for air and water and love, for mother and field and sunlight. We can never know love or greatness. We *should* know both.

DUDLEY (*deeply moved by her words*). Elsie, I love you.

ELSIE. You want to live. *I* want to live, too, but where? Where can we escape our poor world?

DUDLEY. Elsie, we'll find a place.

ELSIE (*smiling at him*). All right. We'll try again. We'll go together to a room in a cheap hotel, and dream that the world is beautiful, and that living is full of love and greatness. But in the morning, can we forget debts, and duties, and the cost of ridiculous things?

DUDLEY (*with blind faith*). Sure, we can, Elsie.

ELSIE. All right, Dudley. Of course. Come on. The time for the new pathetic war has come. Let's hurry, before they dress you, stand you in line, hand you a gun, and have you kill and be killed. (ELSIE *looks at him gently, and takes his hand.* DUDLEY *embraces her shyly, as if he might hurt her. They go, as if they were a couple of young animals. There is a moment of silence. One of the* STREETWALKERS *bursts out laughing.*)

KILLER. Nick, what the hell kind of a joint are you running?

NICK. Well, it's not out of the world. It's on a street in a city, and people come and go. They bring whatever they've got with them and they say what they must say.

THE OTHER STREETWALKER. It's floozies like her that raise hell with our racket.

NICK (*remembering*). Oh, yeah. Finnegan telephoned.

KILLER. That mouse in elephant's body?

THE OTHER STREETWALKER. What the hell does *he* want?

NICK. Spend your time at the movies for the next couple of days.

KILLER. They're all lousy. (*Mocking*) All about love.

NICK. Lousy or not lousy, for a couple of days the flat-foots are going to be romancing you, so stay out of here, and lay low.

KILLER. I always was a pushover for a man in uniform, with a badge, a club and a gun.

KRUPP *comes into the place. The* GIRLS *put down their drinks.*

NICK. O.K., get going.

The GIRLS *begin to leave and meet* KRUPP.

THE OTHER STREETWALKER. We was just going.

KILLER. We was formerly models at Magnin's. (*They go.*)

KRUPP (*at the bar*). The strike isn't enough, so they've got to put us on the tails of the girls, too. I don't know. I wish to God I was back in the Sunset holding the hands of kids going home from school, where I belong. I don't like trouble. Give me a beer. (NICK *gives him a beer. He drinks some.*) Right now, McCarthy, my best friend, is with sixty strikers who want to stop the finks who are going to try to unload the *Mary Luckenbach* tonight. Why the hell McCarthy ever became a longshoreman instead of a professor of some kind is something I'll never know.

NICK. Cowboys and Indians, cops and robbers, longshoremen and finks.

KRUPP. They're all guys who are trying to be happy; trying to make a living; support a family; bring up children; enjoy sleep. Go to a movie; take a drive on Sunday. They're all good guys, so out of nowhere, comes trouble. All they want is a chance to get out of debt and relax in front of a radio while Amos and Andy go through their act. What the hell do they always want to make trouble for? I been thinking everything over, Nick, and you know what I think?

NICK. No. What?

KRUPP. I think we're all crazy. It came to me while I was on my way to Pier 27. All of a sudden it hit me like a ton of bricks. A thing like that never happened to me before. Here we are in this wonderful world, full of all the wonderful things—here we are—all of us, and look at us. Just look at us. We're crazy. We're nuts. We've got everything, but we always feel lousy and dissatisfied just the same.

NICK. Of course we're crazy. Even so, we've got to go on living together. (*He waves at the people in his joint.*)

KRUPP. There's no hope. I don't suppose it's right for an officer of the law to feel the way I feel, but, by God, right or not right, that's how I feel. Why are we all so lousy? This is a good world. It's wonderful to get up in the morning and go out for a little walk and smell the trees and see the streets and the kids going to school and the clouds in the sky. It's wonderful just to be able to move around and whistle a song if you feel like it, or maybe try to sing one. This is a nice world. So why do they make all the trouble?

NICK. I don't know. Why?

KRUPP. We're crazy, that's why. We're no good any more. All the corruption everywhere. The poor kids selling themselves. A couple of years ago they were in grammar school. Everybody trying to get a lot of money in a hurry. Everybody betting the horses. Nobody going quietly for a little walk to the ocean. Nobody taking things easy and not wanting to make some kind of a killing. Nick, I'm going to quit being a cop. Let somebody else keep law and order. The stuff I hear about at headquarters. I'm thirty-seven years old, and I still can't get used to it. The only trouble is, the wife'll raise hell.

NICK. Ah, the wife.

KRUPP. She's a wonderful woman, Nick. We've got two of the swellest boys in the world. Twelve and seven years old.

The ARAB *gets up and moves closer to listen.*

NICK. I didn't know that.

KRUPP. Sure. But what'll I do? I've wanted to quit for seven years. I wanted to quit the day they began putting me through the school. I didn't quit. What'll I do if I quit? Where's money going to be coming in from?

NICK. That's one of the reasons we're all crazy. We don't know where it's going to be coming in from, except from wherever it happens to be coming in from at the time, which we don't usually like.

KRUPP. Every once in a while I catch myself being mean, hating people just because they're down and out, broke and hungry, sick or drunk. And then when I'm with the stuffed shirts at headquarters, all of a sudden I'm nice to them, trying to make an impression. On who? People I don't like. And I feel disgusted. (*With finality*) I'm going to quit. That's all. Quit. Out. I'm going to give them back the uniform and the gadgets that go with it. I don't want any part of it. This is a good world. What do they want to make all the trouble for all the time?

ARAB (*quietly, gently, with great understanding*). No foundation. All the way down the line.

KRUPP. What?

ARAB. No foundation. No foundation.

KRUPP. I'll say there's no foundation.

ARAB. All the way down the line.

KRUPP (*to* NICK). Is that all he ever says?

NICK. That's all he's been saying *this* week.

KRUPP. What is he, anyway?

NICK. He's an Arab, or something like that.

KRUPP. No, I mean what's he do for a living?

NICK. (*to* ARAB). What do you do for a living, Brother?

ARAB. Work. Work all my life. All my life, work. From small boy to old man, work. In old country, work. In new country, work. In New York. Pittsburgh. Detroit. Chicago. Imperial Valley. San Francisco. Work. No beg. Work. For what?

Nothing. Three boys in old country. Twenty years, not see. Lost. Dead. Who knows? What. What-not. No foundation. All the way down the line.

KRUPP. What'd he say last week?

NICK. Didn't say anything. Played the harmonica.

ARAB. Old country song, I play. (*He brings a harmonica from his back pocket.*)

KRUPP. Seems like a nice guy.

NICK. Nicest guy in the world.

KRUPP (*bitterly*). But crazy. Just like all the rest of us. Stark raving mad.

WESLEY *and* HARRY *long ago stopped playing and dancing. They sat at a table together and talked for a while; then began playing casino or rummy. When the* ARAB *begins his solo on the harmonica, they stop their game to listen.*

WESLEY. You hear that?

HARRY. That's *something.*

WESLEY. That's crying. That's crying.

HARRY. I want to make people laugh.

WESLEY. That's deep, deep crying. That's crying a long time ago. That's crying a thousand years ago. Some place five thousand miles away.

HARRY. Do you think you can play to that?

WESLEY. I want to *sing* to that, but I can't *sing.*

HARRY. You try and play to that. I'll try to dance.

WESLEY *goes to the piano, and after closer listening, he begins to accompany the harmonica solo.* HARRY *goes to the little stage and after a few efforts begins to dance to the song. This keeps up quietly for some time.* KRUPP *and* NICK *have been silent, and deeply moved.*

KRUPP (*softly*). Well, anyhow, Nick.

NICK. Hmmmmmmm?

KRUPP. What I said. Forget it.

NICK. Sure.

KRUPP. It gets me down once in a while.

NICK. No harm in talking.

KRUPP (*the* POLICEMAN *again, loudly*). Keep the girls out of here.

NICK (*loud and friendly*). Take it easy.

The music and dancing are now at their height.

ACT FIVE

That evening. Fog-horns are heard throughout the scene. A man in evening clothes and a top hat, and his woman, also in evening clothes, are entering.

WILLIE *is still at the marble game.* NICK *is behind the bar.* JOE *is at his table, looking at the book of maps of the countries of Europe. The box containing the revolver and the box containing the cartridges are on the table, beside his glass. He is at peace, his hat tilted back on his head, a calm expression on his face.* TOM *is leaning against the bar, dreaming of love and* KITTY. *The* ARAB *is gone.* WESLEY *and* HARRY *are gone.* KIT CARSON *is watching the boy at the marble game.*

LADY. Oh, come on, please. (*The gentleman follows miserably.*)

The SOCIETY MAN *and* WIFE *take a table.* NICK *gives them a menu.*

Outside, in the street, the Salvation Army people are playing a song. Big drum, tambourines, cornet, and singing. They are singing "The Blood of the Lamb." The music and words come into the place faintly and comically. This is followed by an old sinner testifying. It is the DRUNKARD. *His words are not intelligible, but his message is unmistakable. He is saved. He wants to sin no more. And so on.*

DRUNKARD (*testifying, unmistakably drunk*). Brothers and sisters. I was a sinner. I chewed tobacco and chased women. Oh, I sinned, brothers and sisters. And then I was saved. Saved by the Salvation Army, God forgive me.

JOE. Let's see now. Here's a city. Pribor. Czecho-slovakia. Little, lovely, lonely Czecho-slovakia. I wonder what kind of a place Pribor was? (*Calling*) Pribor! *Pribor!* (TOM *leaps.*)

LADY. What's the matter with him?

MAN (*crossing his legs, as if he ought to go to the men's room*). Drunk.

TOM. Who you calling, Joe?

JOE. Pribor.

TOM. Who's Pribor?

JOE. He's a Czech. And a Slav. A Czecho-slovakian.

LADY. How interesting.

MAN (*uncrosses legs*). He's drunk.

JOE. Tom, Pribor's a city in Czecho-slovakia.

TOM. Oh. (*Pause*) You sure were nice to her, Joe.

JOE. Kitty Duval? She's one of the finest people in the world.

TOM. It sure was nice of you to hire an automobile and take us for a drive along the ocean-front and down to Half Moon Bay.

JOE. Those three hours were the most delightful, the most somber, and the most beautiful I have ever known.

TOM. Why, Joe?

JOE. Why? I'm a student. (*Lifting his voice*) Tom. (*Quietly*) I'm a student. I study all things. All. All. And when my study reveals something of beauty in a place or in a person where by all rights only ugliness or death should be revealed, then I know how full of goodness this life is. And that's a good thing to know. That's a truth I shall always seek to verify.

LADY. Are you *sure* he's drunk?

MAN (*crossing his legs*). He's either drunk, or just naturally crazy.

TOM. Joe?

JOE. Yeah.

TOM. You won't get sore or anything?

JOE (*impatiently*). What is it, Tom?

TOM. Joe, where do you get all that money? You paid for the automobile. You paid for supper and the two bottles of champagne at the Half Moon Bay Restaurant. You moved Kitty out of the New York Hotel around the corner to the St. Francis Hotel on Powell Street. I saw you pay her rent.

I saw you give her money for new clothes. Where do you get all that money, Joe? Three years now and I've never asked.

JOE (*looking at* TOM *sorrowfully, a little irritated, not so much with* TOM *as with the world and himself, his own superiority. He speaks clearly, slowly and solemnly*). Now don't be a fool, Tom. Listen carefully. If anybody's got any money—to hoard or to throw away—you can be sure he stole it from other people. Not from rich people who can spare it, but from poor people who can't. From their lives and from their dreams. I'm no exception. I *earned* the money I throw away. I stole it like everybody else does. I hurt people to get it. Loafing around this way, I *still* earn money. The money itself earns *more.* I *still* hurt people. I don't know who they are, or where they are. If I did, I'd feel worse than I do. I've got a Christian conscience in a world that's got no conscience at all. The world's trying to get some sort of a *social* conscience, but it's having a devil of a time trying to do *that.* I've got money. I'll always have money, as long as this world stays the way it is. I don't work. I don't make anything. (*He sips.*) I drink. I worked when I was a kid. I worked *hard.* I mean hard, Tom. People are supposed to enjoy living. I got tired. (*He lifts the gun and looks at it while he talks.*) I decided to get even on the world. Well, you can't enjoy living unless you work. Unless you do something. I don't do anything. I don't *want* to do anything any more. There isn't anything I can do that won't make me feel embarrassed. Because I can't do simple, good things. I haven't the patience. And I'm too smart. Money is the guiltiest thing in the world. It stinks. Now, don't ever bother me about it again.

TOM. I didn't mean to make you feel bad, Joe.

JOE (*slowly*). Here. Take this gun out in the street and give it to some worthy hold-up man.

LADY. What's he saying?

MAN (*uncrosses legs*). You wanted to visit a honky-tonk. Well, *this* is a honky-tonk. (*To the world*) Married twenty-eight years and she's still looking for adventure.

TOM. How should I know who's a hold-up man?

JOE. Take it away. Give it to somebody.

TOM (*bewildered*). Do I *have* to *give* it to somebody?

JOE. Of course.

TOM. Can't I take it back and get some of our money?

JOE. Don't talk like a business man. Look around and find somebody who appears to be in need of a gun and give it to him. It's a good gun, isn't it?

TOM. The man said it was, but how can I tell who needs a gun?

JOE. Tom, you've seen good people who needed guns, haven't you?

TOM. I don't remember. Joe, I might give it to the wrong kind of guy. He might do something crazy.

JOE. All right. I'll find somebody myself. (TOM *rises.*) Here's some money. Go get me this week's *Life, Liberty, Time,* and six or seven packages of chewing gum.

TOM (*swiftly, in order to remember each item*). *Life, Liberty, Time,* and six or seven packages of chewing gum?

JOE. That's right.

TOM. All that chewing gum? What kind?

JOE. Any kind. Mix 'em up. All kinds.

TOM. Licorice, too?

JOE. Licorice, by all means.

TOM. Juicy Fruit?

JOE. Juicy Fruit.

TOM. Tutti-frutti?

JOE. Is there such a gum?

TOM. I think so.

JOE. All right. Tutti-frutti, too. Get *all* the kinds. Get as many kinds as they're selling.

TOM. *Life, Liberty, Time,* and all the different kinds of gum. (*He begins to go.*)

JOE (*calling after him loudly*). Get some jelly beans too. All the different colors.

TOM. All right, Joe.

JOE. And the longest panatela cigar you can find. Six of them.

TOM. Panatela. I got it.

JOE. Give a news-kid a dollar.

TOM. O.K., Joe.

JOE. Give some old man a dollar.

TOM. O.K., Joe.

JOE. Give them Salvation Army people in the street a couple of dollars and ask them to sing that song that goes—(*He sings loudly*)

> Let the lower lights be burning,
> Send a gleam across the wave.

TOM (*swiftly*).

> Let the lower lights be burning,
> Send a gleam across the wave.

JOE. That's it. (*He goes on with the song, very loudly and religiously.*)

> Some poor, dying, struggling seaman,
> You may rescue, you may save. (*Halts.*)

TOM. O.K., Joe. I got it. *Life, Liberty, Time,* all the kinds of gum they're selling, jelly beans, six panatela cigars, a dollar for a news-kid, a dollar for an old man, two dollars for the Salvation Army. (*Going*)

> Let the lower lights be burning,
> Send a gleam across the wave.

JOE. That's it.

LADY. He's absolutely insane.

MAN (*wearily crossing legs*). You asked me to take you to a honky-tonk, instead of to the Mark Hopkins. You're *here* in a honky-tonk. I can't help it if he's crazy. Do you want to go back to where people *aren't* crazy?

LADY. No, not just yet.

MAN. Well, all right then. Don't be telling me every minute that he's crazy.

LADY. You needn't be huffy about it. (MAN *refuses to answer, uncrosses legs.*)

When JOE *began to sing,* KIT CARSON *turned away from the marble game and listened. While the* MAN *and* WOMAN *are arguing he comes over to* JOE*'s table.*

KIT CARSON. Presbyterian?

JOE. I attended a Presbyterian Sunday School.

KIT CARSON. Fond of singing?

JOE. On occasion. Have a drink?

KIT CARSON. Thanks.

JOE. Get a glass and sit down. (KIT CARSON *gets a glass from* NICK, *returns to the table, sits down,* JOE *pours him a drink, they touch glasses just as the Salvation Army people begin to fulfill the request. They sip some champagne, and at the proper moment begin to sing the song together, sipping champagne, raising hell with the tune, swinging it, and so on. The* SOCIETY LADY *joins them, and is stopped by her* HUSBAND.) Always was fond of that song. Used to sing it at the top of my voice. Never saved a seaman in my life.

KIT CARSON (*flirting with the* SOCIETY LADY *who loves it*). I saved a seaman once. Well, he wasn't exactly a seaman. He was a darky named Wellington. Heavy-set sort of a fellow. Nice personality, but no friends to speak of. Not until I came along, at any rate. In New Orleans. In the summer of the year 1899. No. Ninety-eight. I was a lot younger of course, and had no mustache, but was regarded by many people as a man of means.

JOE. Know anything about guns?

KIT CARSON (*flirting*). All there is to know. Didn't fight the Ojibways for nothing. Up there in the Lake Takalooca Country, in Michigan. (*Remembering*) Along about in 1881 or two. Fought 'em right up to the shore of the Lake. Made 'em swim for Canada. One fellow in particular, an Indian named Harry Daisy.

JOE (*opening the box containing the revolver*). What sort of a gun would you say this is? Any good?

KIT CARSON (*at sight of gun, leaping*). Yep. That looks like a pretty nice hunk of shooting iron. That's a six-shooter. Shot a man with a six-shooter once. Got him through the palm of his right hand. Lifted his arm to wave to a friend. Thought it was a bird. Fellow named, I believe, Carroway. Larrimore Carroway.

JOE. Know how to work one of these things? (*He offers* KIT CARSON *the revolver, which is old and enormous.*)

KIT CARSON (*laughing at the absurd question*). Know how to work it? Hand me that little gun, son, and I'll show you all about it. (JOE *hands* KIT *the revolver. Importantly*) Let's see now. This is probably a new kind of six-shooter. After my time. Haven't nicked an Indian in years. I believe this here place is supposed to move out. (*He fools around and gets the barrel out for loading.*) That's it. There it is.

JOE. Look all right?

KIT CARSON. It's a good gun. You've got a good gun there, son. I'll explain it to you. You see these holes? Well, that's where you put the cartridges.

JOE (*taking some cartridges out of the box*). Here. Show me how it's done.

KIT CARSON (*a little impatiently*). Well, son, you take 'em one by one and put 'em in the holes, like this. There's one. Two. Three. Four. Five. Six. Then you get the barrel back in place. Then cock it. Then all you got to do is aim and fire. (*He points the gun at the* LADY *and* GENTLEMAN *who scream and stand up, scaring* KIT CARSON *into paralysis. The gun is loaded, but uncocked.*)

JOE. It's all set?

KIT CARSON. Ready to kill.

JOE. Let me hold it.

KIT *hands* JOE *the gun. The* LADY *and* GENTLEMAN *watch, in terror.*

KIT CARSON. Careful, now, son. Don't cock it. Many a man's lost an eye fooling with a loaded gun. Fellow I used to know named Danny Donovan lost a nose. Ruined his whole life. Hold it firm. Squeeze the trigger. Don't snap it. Spoils your aim.

JOE. Thanks. Let's see if I can unload it. (*He begins to unload it.*)

KIT CARSON. Of course you can.

JOE *unloads the revolver, looks at it very closely, puts the cartridges back into the box.*

JOE (*looking at gun*). I'm mighty grateful to you. Always wanted to see one of those things close up. Is it really a good one?

KIT CARSON. It's a beaut, son.

JOE (*aims the empty gun at a bottle on the bar*). Bang!

WILLIE (*at the marble game, as the machine groans*). *Oh, Boy!* (*Loudly, triumphantly*) There you are, Nick. Thought I couldn't do it, hey? *Now*, watch. (*The machine begins to make a special kind of noise. Lights go on and off. Some red, some green. A bell rings loudly six times.*) One. Two. Three. Four. Five. Six. (*An American flag jumps up.* WILLIE *comes to attention. Salutes.*) Oh, boy, what a beautiful country. (*A loud music-box version of the song* "America." JOE, KIT, *and the* LADY *get to their feet. Singing*)

My country, 'tis of thee,
Sweet land of liberty,
Of thee I sing.

(*Everything quiets down. The flag goes back into the machine.* WILLIE *is thrilled, amazed, delighted. Everybody has watched the performance of the defeated machine from wherever he happened to be when the performance began.* WILLIE, *looking around at everybody, as if they had all been on the side of the machine*) O.K. How's that? I knew I could do it. (*To* NICK) Six nickels. (NICK *hands him six nickels.* WILLIE *goes over to* JOE *and* KIT.) Took me a little while, but I finally did it. It's scientific, really. With a little skill a man can make a modest living beating the marble games. Not that that's what I want to do. I just don't like the idea of anything getting the best of me. A machine or anything else. Myself, I'm the kind of a guy who makes up his mind to do something, and then goes to work and does it. There's no other way a man can be a success at anything. (*Indicating the letter "F" on his sweater.*) See that letter? That don't stand for some little-bitty high school somewhere. That stands for *me.* Faroughli. Willie Faroughli. I'm an Assyrian. We've got a civilization six or seven centuries old, I think. Somewhere along in there. Ever hear of Osman? Harold Osman? He's an Assyrian, too. He's got an orchestra down in Fresno. (*He goes to the* LADY *and* GENTLEMAN.) I've never seen you before in my life, but I can tell from the clothes you wear and the company you keep (*graciously indicating the* LADY) that you're a man who looks every problem straight in the eye, and then goes to work and *solves* it. I'm that way myself. Well. (*He smiles beautifully, takes the* GENTLEMAN'*s hand furiously.*) It's been wonderful talking to a nicer type of people for a change. Well. I'll be seeing you. So long. (*He turns, takes two steps, returns to the table. Very politely and seriously*) Good-by, lady. You've got a good man there. Take good care of him. (WILLIE *goes, saluting* JOE *and the world.*)

KIT CARSON (*to* JOE). By God, for a while there I didn't think that young Assyrian was going to do it. That fellow's got something.

TOM *comes back with the magazines and other stuff.*

JOE. Get it all?
TOM. Yeah. I had a little trouble finding the jelly beans.
JOE. Let's take a look at them.
TOM. These are the jelly beans.

JOE *puts his hand into the cellophane bag and takes out a handful of the jelly beans, looks at them, smiles, and tosses a couple into his mouth.*

JOE. Same as ever. Have some. (*He offers the bag to* KIT.)
KIT CARSON (*flirting*). Thanks! I remember the first time I ever ate jelly beans. I was six, or at the most seven. Must have been in (*slowly*) eighteen—seventy-seven. Seven or eight. Baltimore.
JOE. Have some, Tom. (TOM *takes some.*)
TOM. Thanks, Joe.
JOE. Let's have some of that chewing gum. (*He dumps all the packages of gum out of the bag onto the table.*)
KIT CARSON (*flirting*). Me and a boy named Clark. Quinton Clark. Became a senator.
JOE. Yeah. Tutti-frutti, all right. (*He opens a package and folds all five pieces into his mouth.*) Always wanted to see how many I could chew at one time. Tell you what, Tom. I'll bet I can chew more at one time than you can.
TOM (*delighted*). All right. (*They both begin to fold gum into their mouths.*)
KIT CARSON. I'll referee. Now, one at a time. How many you got?
JOE. Six.
KIT CARSON. All right. Let Tom catch up with you.
JOE (*while* TOM'*s catching up*). Did you give a dollar to a news-kid?
TOM. Yeah, sure.
JOE. What'd he say?
TOM. Thanks.
JOE. What sort of a kid was he?
TOM. Little, dark kid. I guess he's Italian.

JOE. Did he seem pleased?

TOM. Yeah.

JOE. That's good. Did you give a dollar to an old man?

TOM. Yeah.

JOE. Was he pleased?

TOM. Yeah.

JOE. Good. How many you got in your mouth?

TOM. Six.

JOE. All right. I got six, too. (*Folds one more in his mouth.* TOM *folds one too.*)

KIT CARSON. Seven. Seven each. (*They each fold one more into their mouths, very solemnly, chewing them into the main hunk of gum.*) Eight. Nine. Ten.

JOE (*delighted*). Always wanted to do this. (*He picks up one of the magazines.*) Let's see what's going on in the world. (*He turns the pages and keeps folding gum into his mouth and chewing.*)

KIT CARSON. Eleven. Twelve. (KIT *continues to count while* JOE *and* TOM *continue the contest. In spite of what they are doing, each is very serious.*)

TOM. Joe, what'd you want to move Kitty into the St. Francis Hotel for?

JOE. She's a better woman than any of them tramp society dames that hang around that lobby.

TOM. Yeah, but do you think she'll feel at home up there?

JOE. Maybe not at first, but after a couple of days she'll be all right. A nice big room. A bed for sleeping in. Good clothes. Good food. She'll be all right, Tom.

TOM. I hope so. Don't you think she'll get lonely up there with nobody to talk to?

JOE (*looking at* TOM *sharply, almost with admiration, pleased but severe*). There's nobody *anywhere* for *her* to talk to—except *you.*

TOM (*amazed and delighted*). *Me,* Joe?

JOE (*while* TOM *and* KIT CARSON *listen carefully,* KIT *with great appreciation*). Yes, you. By the grace of God, you're the other half of that girl. Not the angry woman that swaggers into this waterfront dive and shouts because the world has kicked her around. *Anybody* can have *her.* You belong to the little kid in Ohio who once dreamed of living. Not with her carcass, for *money*, so she can have food and clothes, and pay rent. With *all* of her. I put her in that hotel, so she can have a chance to gather herself together again. She can't do that in the New York Hotel. You saw what happens there. There's nobody anywhere for her to talk to, except you. They all make her talk like a whore. After a while, she'll *believe* them. Then she won't be able to remember. She'll get lonely. Sure. People can get lonely for *misery*, even. I want her to go on being lonely for *you*, so she can come together again the way she was meant to be from the beginning. Loneliness is good for people. Right now it's the only thing for Kitty. Any more licorice?

TOM (*dazed*). What? Licorice? (*Looking around busily.*) I guess we've chewed all the licorice in. We still got Clove, Peppermint, Doublemint, Beechnut, Teaberry, and Juicy Fruit.

JOE. Licorice used to be my favorite. Don't worry about her, Tom, she'll be all right. You really want to marry her, don't you?

TOM (*nodding*). Honest to God, Joe. (*Pathetically*) Only, I haven't got any money.

JOE. Couldn't you be a prize-fighter or something like that?

TOM. Naaaah. I couldn't hit a man if I wasn't sore at him. He'd have to do something that made me hate him.

JOE. You've got to figure out something to do that you won't mind doing very much.

TOM. I wish I could, Joe.

JOE (*thinking deeply, suddenly*). Tom, would you be embarrassed driving a truck?

TOM (*hit by a thunderbolt*). Joe, I never thought of that. I'd like that. Travel. Highways. Little towns. Coffee and hot cakes. Beautiful valleys and mountains and streams and trees and daybreak and sunset.

JOE. There *is* poetry in it, at that.

TOM. Joe, that's just the kind of work I *should* do. Just sit there and travel, and look, and smile, and bust out laughing. Could Kitty go with me, sometimes?

JOE. I don't know. Get me the phone book. Can you drive a truck?

TOM. Joe, you know I can drive a truck, or any kind of thing with a motor and wheels. (TOM *takes* JOE *the phone book.* JOE *turns the pages.*)

JOE (*looking*). Here! Here it is. Tuxedo 7900. Here's a nickel. Get me that number. (TOM *goes to telephone, dials the number.*)

TOM. Hello.

JOE. Ask for Mr. Keith.

TOM (*mouth and language full of gum*). I'd like to talk to Mr. Keith. (*Pause*) Mr. Keith.

JOE. Take that gum out of your mouth for a minute. (TOM *removes the gum.*)

TOM. Mr. Keith? Yeah. That's right. Hello, Mr. Keith?

JOE. Tell him to hold the line.

TOM. Hold the line, please.

JOE. Give me a hand, Tom. (TOM *helps* JOE *to the telephone. At phone, wad of gum in fingers delicately*) Keith? Joe. Yeah. Fine. Forget it. (*Pause*) Have you got a place for a good driver? (*Pause*) I don't think so. (*To* TOM) You haven't got a driver's license, have you?

TOM (*worried*). No. But I can get one, Joe.

JOE (*at phone*). No, but he can get one easy enough. To hell with the union. He'll join later. All right, call him a Vice-President and say he drives for relaxation. Sure. What do you mean? Tonight? I don't know why not. San Diego? All right, let him start driving without a license. What the hell's the difference? Yeah. Sure. Look him over. Yeah. I'll send him right over. Right. (*He hangs up.*) Thanks. (*To telephone.*)

TOM. Am I going to get the job?

JOE. He wants to take a look at you.

TOM. Do I look all right, Joe?

JOE (*looking at him carefully*). Hold up your head. Stick out your chest. How do you feel? (TOM *does these things.*)

TOM. Fine.

JOE. You *look* fine, too. (JOE *takes his wad of gum out of his mouth and wraps* Liberty *magazine around it.*)

JOE. You win, Tom. Now, look. (*He bites off the tip of a very long panatela cigar, lights it, and hands one to* TOM, *and another to* KIT.) Have yourselves a pleasant smoke. Here. (*He hands two more to* TOM.) Give those slummers one each. (*He indicates the* SOCIETY LADY *and* GENTLEMAN.)

TOM *goes over and without a word gives a cigar each to the* MAN *and the* LADY. *The* MAN *is offended; he smells and tosses aside his cigar. The* WOMAN *looks at her cigar a moment, then puts the cigar in her mouth.*

MAN. What do you think you're doing?

LADY. Really, dear. I'd like to.

MAN. Oh, this is too much.

LADY. I'd *really,* really like to, dear. (*She laughs, puts the cigar in her mouth. Turns to* KIT. *He spits out tip. She does the same.*)

MAN (*loudly*). The mother of five grown men, and she's still looking for *romance.* (*Shouts as* KIT *lights her cigar*) No. I forbid it.

JOE (*shouting*). What's the matter with you? Why don't you leave her alone? What are you always pushing your women around for? (*Almost without a pause*) Now, look, Tom. (*The* LADY *puts the lighted cigar in her mouth, and begins to smoke, feeling wonderful.*) Here's ten bucks.

TOM. Ten bucks?

JOE. He may want you to get into a truck and begin driving to San Diego tonight.

TOM. Joe, I got to tell Kitty.

JOE. I'll tell her.

TOM. Joe, take care of her.

JOE. She'll be all right. Stop worrying about her. She's at the St. Francis Hotel. Now, look. Take a cab to Townsend and Fourth. You'll see the big sign. Keith Motor Transport Company. He'll be waiting for you.

TOM. O.K., Joe. (*Trying hard*) Thanks, Joe.

JOE. Don't be silly. Get going.

TOM *goes.* LADY *starts puffing on cigar. As* TOM *goes,* WESLEY *and* HARRY *come in together.*

NICK. Where the hell have you been? We've got to have some entertainment around here. Can't you see them fine people from uptown? (*He points at the* SOCIETY LADY *and* GENTLEMAN.)

WESLEY. You said to come back at ten for the second show.

NICK. Did I say that?

WESLEY. Yes, sir, Mr. Nick, that's exactly what you said.

HARRY. Was the first show all right?

NICK. That wasn't a show. There was no one here to see it. How can it be a show when no one sees it? People are afraid to come down to the waterfront.

HARRY. Yeah. We were just down to Pier 27. One of the longshoremen and a cop had a fight and the cop hit him over the head with a blackjack. We saw it happen, didn't we?

WESLEY. Yes, sir, we was standing there looking when it happened.

NICK (*a little worried*). Anything else happen?

WESLEY. They was all talking.

HARRY. A man in a big car came up and said there was going to be a meeting right away and they hoped to satisfy everybody and stop the strike.

WESLEY. Right away. *Tonight.*

NICK. Well, it's about time. Them poor cops are liable to get nervous and—shoot somebody. (*To* HARRY, *suddenly*) Come back here. I want you to tend bar for a while. I'm going to take a walk over to the pier.

HARRY. Yes, sir.

NICK (*to the* SOCIETY LADY *and* GENTLEMAN). You society people made up your minds yet?

LADY. Have you champagne?

NICK (*indicating* JOE). What do you think he's pouring out of that bottle, water or something?

LADY. Have you a chill bottle?

NICK. I've got a dozen of them chilled. He's been drinking champagne here all day and all night for a month now.

LADY. May we have a bottle?

NICK. It's six dollars.

LADY. I think we can manage.

MAN. I don't know. I *know* I don't know.

NICK takes off his coat and helps HARRY into it. HARRY takes a bottle of champagne and two glasses to the LADY and the GENTLEMAN, dancing, collects six dollars, and goes back behind the bar, dancing. NICK gets his coat and hat.

NICK (*to* WESLEY). Rattle the keys a little, son. Rattle the keys.

WESLEY. Yes, sir, Mr. Nick.

NICK *is on his way out. The* ARAB *enters.*

NICK. Hi-ya, *Mahmed.*
ARAB. No foundation.
NICK. All the way down the line. (*He goes.*)

WESLEY *is at the piano, playing quietly. The* ARAB *swallows a glass of beer, takes out his harmonica, and begins to play.* WESLEY *fits his playing to the* ARAB*'s.*

KITTY DUVAL, *strangely beautiful, in new clothes, comes in. She walks shyly, as if she were embarrassed by the fine clothes, as if she had no right to wear them. The* LADY *and* GENTLEMAN *are very impressed.* HARRY *looks at her with amazement.* JOE *is reading* Time *magazine.* KITTY *goes to his table.* JOE *looks up from the magazine, without the least amazement.*

JOE. Hello, Kitty.
KITTY. Hello, Joe.
JOE. It's nice seeing you again.
KITTY. I came in a cab.
JOE. You been crying again? (KITTY *can't answer.*)
JOE (*to* HARRY). Bring a glass. (HARRY *comes over with a glass.* JOE *pours* KITTY *a drink.*)
KITTY. I've got to talk to you.
JOE. Have a drink.
KITTY. I've never been in burlesque. We were just poor.
JOE. Sit down, Kitty.
KITTY (*sits down*). I tried other things.
JOE. Here's to you, Katerina Koranovsky. Here's to you. And Tom.
KITTY (*sorrowfully*). Where *is* Tom?
JOE. He's getting a job tonight driving a truck. He'll be back in a couple of days.
KITTY (*sadly*). I told him I'd marry him.
JOE. He wanted to see you and say good-by.
KITTY. He's too good for me. He's like a little boy. (*Wearily*) I'm— Too many things have happened to me.
JOE. Kitty Duval, you're one of the few truly innocent people I have ever known. He'll be back in a couple of days. Go back to the hotel and wait for him.

KITTY. That's what I mean. I can't stand being alone. I'm no good. I tried very hard. I don't know what it is. I miss—(*She gestures.*)

JOE (*gently*). Do you really want to come back here, Kitty?

KITTY. I don't know. I'm not sure. Everything *smells* different. I don't know how to feel, or what to think. (*Gesturing pathetically*) I know I don't belong there. It's what I've wanted all my life, but it's too *late.* I try to be happy about it, but all I can do is remember everything and cry.

JOE. I don't know what to tell you, Kitty. I didn't mean to hurt you.

KITTY. You haven't hurt me. You're the only person who's ever been good to me. I've never known anybody like you. I'm not sure about love any more, but I know I love you, and I know I love Tom.

JOE. I love you too, Kitty Duval.

KITTY. He'll want babies. I know he will. I know *I* will, too. Of course I will. I can't—(*She shakes her head.*)

JOE. Tom's a baby himself. You'll be very happy together. He wants you to ride with him in the truck. Tom's good for you. You're good for Tom.

KITTY (*like a child*). Do you want me to go back and wait for him?

JOE. I can't *tell* you what to do. I think it would be a good idea, though.

KITTY. I wish I could tell you how it makes me feel to be alone. It's almost worse.

JOE. It might take a whole week, Kitty. (*He looks at her sharply, at the arrival of an idea.*) Didn't you speak of reading a book? A book of poems?

KITTY. I didn't know what I was saying.

JOE (*trying to get up*). Of course you knew. I think you'll like poetry. Wait here a minute, Kitty. I'll go see if I can find some books.

KITTY. All right, Joe.

JOE *walks out of the place, trying very hard not to wobble. Fog-horn. Music. The* NEWSBOY *comes in. Looks for* JOE. *Is broken-hearted because* JOE *is gone.*

NEWSBOY (*to* SOCIETY GENTLEMAN). Paper?

MAN (*angry*). No.

The NEWSBOY *goes to the* ARAB.

NEWSBOY. Paper, Mister?
ARAB (*irritated*). No foundation.
NEWSBOY. What?
ARAB (*very angry*). No foundation.

The NEWSBOY *starts out, turns, looks at the* ARAB, *shakes head.*

NEWSBOY. No foundation?

BLICK *and two* COPS *enter.*

NEWSBOY (*to* BLICK). Paper, Mister? (BLICK *pushes him aside. The* NEWSBOY *goes.*)
BLICK (*walking authoritatively about the place, to* HARRY). Where's Nick?
HARRY. He went for a walk.
BLICK. Who are you?
HARRY. Harry.
BLICK (*to the* ARAB *and* WESLEY). Hey, you. Shut up. (*The* ARAB *stops playing the harmonica,* WESLEY *the piano.*)
BLICK (*studies* KITTY). What's your name, sister?
KITTY (*looking at him*). Kitty Duval. What's it to you? (KITTY'*s voice is now like it was at the beginning of the play: tough, independent, bitter and hard.*)
BLICK (*angry*). Don't give me any of your gutter lip. Just answer my questions.
KITTY. You go to hell, you.
BLICK (*coming over, enraged*). Where do you live?
KITTY. The New York Hotel. Room 21.
BLICK. Where do you work?
KITTY. I'm not working just now. I'm looking for work.
BLICK. What kind of work? (KITTY *can't answer.*) What kind of work? (KITTY *can't answer. Furiously*) WHAT KIND OF WORK? (KIT CARSON *comes over.*)
KIT CARSON. You can't talk to a lady that way in *my* presence.

BLICK *turns and stares at* KIT. *The* COPS *begin to move from the bar.*

BLICK (*to the* COPS). It's all right, boys. I'll take care of this. (*To* KIT) *What'd you say?*

KIT CARSON. You got no right to hurt people. Who are *you?*

BLICK, without a word, takes KIT to the street. Sounds of a blow and a groan. BLICK returns, breathing hard.

BLICK (*to the* COPS). O.K., boys. You can go now. Take care of him. Put him on his feet and tell him to behave himself from now on. (*To* KITTY *again*) Now answer my question. What kind of work?

KITTY (*quietly*). I'm a whore, you son of a bitch. You know what kind of work I do. And I know what kind you do.

MAN (*shocked and really hurt*). Excuse me, officer, but it seems to me that your attitude—

BLICK. Shut up.

MAN (*quietly*).—is making the poor child say things that are not true.

BLICK. Shut up, I said.

LADY. Well. (*To the* MAN) Are you going to stand for such insolence from such a coarse person?

BLICK (*to* MAN, *who is standing*). Are you?

MAN (*taking the* WOMAN*'s arm*). I'll get a divorce. I'll start life all over again. (*Pushing the* WOMAN) Come on. Get the hell out of here! (*The* MAN *hurries his* WOMAN *out of the place,* BLICK *watching them go.*)

BLICK (*to* KITTY). Now. Let's begin again, and see that you tell the truth. What's your name?

KITTY. Kitty Duval.

BLICK. Where do you live?

KITTY. Until this evening I lived at the New York Hotel. Room 21. This evening I moved to the St. Francis Hotel.

BLICK. Oh. To the St. Francis Hotel. Nice place. Where do you work?

KITTY. I'm looking for work.

BLICK. What kind of work do you do?

KITTY. I'm an actress.

BLICK. I see. What movies have I seen you in?

KITTY. I've worked in burlesque.

BLICK. You're a liar.

WESLEY *stands, worried and full of dumb resentment.*

KITTY (*pathetically, as at the beginning of the play*). It's the truth.

BLICK. What are you doing here?

KITTY. I came to see if I could get a job here.

BLICK. Doing what?

KITTY. Singing—and—dancing.

BLICK. You can't sing or dance. What are you lying for?

KITTY. I can. I sang and danced in burlesque all over the country.

BLICK. You're a liar.

KITTY. I said lines, too.

BLICK. So you danced in burlesque?

KITTY. Yes.

BLICK. All right. Let's see what you did.

KITTY. I can't. There's no music, and I haven't got the right clothes.

BLICK. There's music. (*To* WESLEY) Put a nickel in that phonograph. (WESLEY *can't move.*) Come on. Put a nickel in that phonograph. (WESLEY *does so. To* KITTY) All right. Get up on that stage and do a hot little burlesque number. (KITTY *stands. Walks slowly to the stage, but is unable to move.* JOE *comes in, holding three books.*) Get going, now. Let's see you dance the way you did in burlesque, all over the country. (KITTY *tries to do a burlesque dance. It is beautiful in a tragic way.*)

BLICK. All right, start taking them off!

KITTY *removes her hat and starts to remove her jacket.* JOE *moves closer to the stage, amazed.*

JOE (*hurrying to* KITTY). Get down from there. (*He takes* KITTY *into his arms. She is crying. To* BLICK) What the hell do you think you're doing!

WESLEY (*like a little boy, very angry*). It's that man, Blick. *He* made her take off her clothes. He beat up the old man, too.

BLICK *pushes* WESLEY *off, as* TOM *enters.* BLICK *begins beating up* WESLEY.

TOM. What's the matter, Joe. What's happened?

JOE. Is the truck out there?

TOM. Yeah, but what's happened? Kitty's crying again!

JOE. You driving to San Diego?

TOM. Yeah, Joe. But what's he doing to that poor colored boy?

JOE. Get going. Here's some money. Everything's O.K. (*To* KITTY) Dress in the truck. Take these books.

WESLEY'S VOICE. You can't hurt me. You'll get yours. You wait and see.

TOM. Joe, he's hurting that boy. I'll kill him!

JOE (*pushing* TOM). Get out of here! Get married in San Diego. I'll see you when you get back. (TOM *and* KITTY *go.* NICK *enters and stands at the lower end of bar.* JOE *takes the revolver out of his pocket. Looks at it.*) I've always wanted to kill somebody, but I never knew who it should be. (*He cocks the revolver, stands real straight, holds it in front of him firmly and walks to the door. He stands a moment watching* BLICK, *aims very carefully, and pulls trigger. There is no shot.*)

NICK *runs over and grabs the gun, and takes* JOE *aside.*

NICK. What the hell do you think you're doing?

JOE (*casually, but angry*). That dumb Tom. Buys a six-shooter that won't even shoot once. (JOE *sits down, dead to the world.*)

BLICK *comes out, panting for breath.* NICK *looks at him. He speaks slowly.*

NICK. Blick! I told you to stay out of here! Now get out of here. (*He takes* BLICK *by the collar, tightening his grip as he speaks, and pushing him out.*) If you come back again, I'm going to take you in that room where you've been beating up that colored boy, and I'm going to murder you—slowly—with my hands. Beat it! (*He pushes* BLICK *out. To* HARRY) Go take care of the colored boy.

HARRY *runs out.* WILLIE *returns and doesn't sense that anything is changed.* WILLIE *puts another nickel into the machine, but he does so very violently. The consequence of this violence is that the flag comes up again and the music-box version of* "America" *begins again.* WILLIE, *amazed, stands at attention and salutes. The flag goes down. He shakes his head.*

WILLIE (*thoughtfully*). As far as I'm concerned, this is the *only* country in the world. If you ask me, *nuts* to Europe! (*He is about to push the slide in again when the flag comes up again and the music begins again. Furiously, to* NICK, *while he salutes and stands at attention, pleadingly*) Hey, Nick. This machine is out of order.

NICK (*somberly*). Give it a whack on the side.

WILLIE *does so. A hell of a whack. The result is the whole business starts all over again, except that now the flag comes up and down, and* WILLIE *keeps saluting.*

WILLIE (*saluting*). Hey, Nick. Something's wrong.

The machine quiets down abruptly. WILLIE *very stealthily slides a new nickel in, and starts a new game. From a distance two pistol shots are heard, each carefully timed.* NICK *runs out. The* NEWSBOY *enters, crosses to* JOE*'s table, senses something is wrong.*

NEWSBOY (*softly*). Paper, Mister?

JOE *can't hear him. The* NEWSBOY *backs away, studies* JOE, *wishes he could cheer* JOE *up. Notices the phonograph, goes to it, and puts a coin in it, hoping music will make* JOE *happier. The* NEWSBOY *sits down. Watches* JOE. *The music begins. "The Missouri Waltz."*

The DRUNKARD *comes in and walks around. Then sits down.* NICK *comes back.*

NICK (*delighted*). Joe, Blick's dead! Somebody just shot him, and none of the cops are trying to find out who.

JOE *doesn't hear.* NICK *steps back, studying* JOE.

NICK (*shouting*). Joe.

JOE (*looking up*). What?

NICK. Blick's dead.

JOE. Blick? Dead? Good! That God damn gun wouldn't go off. I *told* Tom to get a good one.

NICK (*picking up gun and looking at it*). Joe, you wanted to kill that guy! (HARRY *returns.*) I'm going to buy you a bottle of champagne. (NICK *goes to bar.*)

JOE *rises, takes hat from rack, puts coat on. The* NEWSBOY *jumps up, helps* JOE *with coat.*

NICK. What's the matter, Joe?
JOE. Nothing. Nothing.
NICK. How about the champagne?
JOE. Thanks. (*Going.*)
NICK. It's not eleven yet. Where you going, Joe?
JOE. I don't know. Nowhere.
NICK. Will I see you tomorrow?
JOE. I don't know. I don't think so.

KIT CARSON *enters, walks to* JOE. JOE *and* KIT *look at one another knowingly.*

JOE. Somebody just shot a man. How are you feeling?
KIT. Never felt better in my life. (*Loudly, bragging, but somber*) I shot a man once. In San Francisco. Shot him two times. In 1939, I think it was. In October. Fellow named Blick or Glick or something like that. Couldn't stand the way he talked to ladies. Went up to my room and got my old pearl-handled revolver and waited for him on Pacific Street. Saw him walking, and let him have it, two times. Had to throw the beautiful revolver into the Bay. (HARRY, NICK, *the* ARAB *and the* DRUNKARD *close in around him.*)
JOE (*searches his pockets, brings out the revolver, puts it in* KIT'*s hand, looks at him with great admiration and affection, loudly*). Kit, did I ever tell you about the time I fell in love with a midget weighing thirty-nine pounds?
KIT (*amazed*). Now, son.

JOE *walks slowly to the stairs leading to the street, turns and waves.* KIT, *and then one by one everybody else, waves, and the marble game goes into its beautiful American routine again. The play ends.*

INTERPRETATION

1. *The Time of Your Life* contains a greater variety of characters than any of the plays you have yet read. From the way in which he presents his characters, what can you discover about Saroyan's feelings about people? What kind of people is he interested in? Are his characters believable? Do they talk the way you would expect such people to talk? Find evidence in the play to support one of the following statements: a) Saroyan's characters are drawn from his observation of real life. b) Saroyan's characters are stereotyped creations with no relation to real people.

2. Blick, the detective, is a variation of a type of character found in many comedies, the killjoy. The killjoy is usually a sour, rigid fellow bristling with scruples and pretending to superior strength and knowledge, who is mocked and humiliated in the course of the play. Blick's fate, however, goes beyond mockery. Is the harshness of the killing of Blick incompatible with the mood of comedy? Does Saroyan present Blick as a real character or as a symbol of some quality present in all human beings? The play was written at the time that Hitler was rising to power in Germany. In what way might Saroyan's depiction of Blick have been influenced by that circumstance?

3. Would this play be easy or difficult to produce? What aspects of the play do you think would especially hold an audience's interest? Can you think of ways to focus the audience's attention when many people are on the stage at once? Choose a moment in the play when most of the characters are present in Nick's Saloon and draw a floor plan, showing where you would place the various characters. Explain why or why not the clothing styles of 1938 would be important to a revival of this play. The script calls for the playing of "The Missouri Waltz." Is this a good theme song for this comedy? Why?

4. In Act Two McCarthy says: "The more heroes you have, the worse the history of the world becomes." What does he mean? Is this an adequate statement of the play's theme? What things does Saroyan value in life? Does he find life good or bad? Explain why you agree or disagree with Saroyan's values and his view of life.

The Madwoman of Chaillot

In the twentieth century many writers, like Jean Giraudoux, have posed the question, "Who among us are the truly mad?" We live, and have lived for decades, in a time of unsettled values, a time when the very future of humanity is sometimes questioned. What have those disturbing facts to do with comedy? How does the comic artist sustain his vision of reconciliation without ignoring the reality of his age?

The Madwoman of Chaillot is one of many such answers to this question. In the modern theater new meanings have been found in comedy, for the range of comedy is capable of vast extension, embracing as it does the grotesque, the irrational, the fanciful, the absurd. *The Madwoman of Chaillot* partakes of all these qualities and transforms them into a vision of modern man which is both gay and bitter, hopeful and pessimistic, fantastic and realistic.

Giraudoux' method is to ask questions of great seriousness and answer them with apparent frivolity. His heroine is mad and so are her followers. But Giraudoux implies that we, too, share their madness if we insist on preferring love, fresh air, music, invisible animals, and feather boas to oil, industry, profits, and press-agentry. We are mad if we prefer rag-pickers to presidents and lovers to prospectors. We are mad if we would rather spend our afternoons remembering the words to old songs than descend into the sewers looking for oily riches. And because the play is tinged with fantasy we can accept this kind of "madness" as a positive and beautiful approach to life. But only in make-believe is the good and bad in human life so distinctly etched as in *The Madwoman of Chaillot*. In everyday life the choices are not so simple. In a sense Giraudoux stacks the cards in favor of the things and people he likes. At the same time, however, his fantasy enables us to free ourselves from the complexities of daily living in order to glimpse what is perhaps a more truthful vision of the whole of things. As a celebration of the possibilities of madness, *The Madwoman of Chaillot* may even offer a new and refreshing definition of sanity.

The Madwoman of Chaillot

JEAN GIRAUDOUX

English adaptation by Maurice Valency

Characters

THE WAITER
THE LITTLE MAN
THE PROSPECTOR
THE PRESIDENT
THE BARON
THERESE
THE STREET SINGER
THE FLOWER GIRL
THE RAGPICKER
PAULETTE
THE DEAF-MUTE
IRMA
THE SHOELACE PEDDLER
THE BROKER
THE STREET JUGGLER
DR. JADIN
THE DOORMAN
THE POLICEMAN
PIERRE
THE SERGEANT
THE SEWER MAN
THE PRESIDENTS
THE PROSPECTORS
THE PRESS AGENTS
THE ADOLPHE BERTAUTS
THE LADIES

COUNTESS AURELIA, The Madwoman of Chaillot
MME. CONSTANCE, The Madwoman of Passy
MLLE. GABRIELLE, The Madwoman of St. Sulpice
MME. JOSEPHINE, The Madwoman of La Concorde

ACT ONE

SCENE: *The café terrace at* Chez Francis, *on the Place de l'Alma in Paris. The Alma is in the stately quarter of Paris known as Chaillot, between the Champs Élysées and the Seine, across the river from the Eiffel Tower.*

Chez Francis *has several rows of tables set out under its awning, and, as it is lunch time, a good many of them are occupied. At a table, downstage, a somewhat obvious* BLONDE *with ravishing legs is sipping a vermouth-cassis and trying hard to engage the attention of the* PROSPECTOR, *who sits at an adjacent table taking little sips of water and rolling them over his tongue with the air of a connoisseur. Downstage right, in front of the tables on the sidewalk, is the usual Paris bench, a stout and uncomfortable affair provided by the municipality for the benefit of those who prefer to sit without drinking. A* POLICEMAN *lounges about, keeping the peace without unnecessary exertion.*

TIME: *It is a little before noon in the Spring of next year.*

AT RISE: *The* PRESIDENT *and the* BARON *enter with importance, and are ushered to a front table by the* WAITER.

THE PRESIDENT. Baron, sit down. This is a historic occasion. It must be properly celebrated. The waiter is going to bring out my special port.

THE BARON. Splendid.

THE PRESIDENT (*offers his cigar case*). Cigar? My private brand.

THE BARON. Thank you. You know, this all gives me the feeling of one of those enchanted mornings in the *Arabian Nights* when thieves foregather in the market place. Thieves —pashas . . . (*He sniffs the cigar judiciously, and begins lighting it.*)

THE PRESIDENT (*chuckles*). Tell me about yourself.

THE BARON. Well, where shall I begin?

The STREET SINGER *enters. He takes off a battered*

black felt with a flourish and begins singing an ancient mazurka.[1]

STREET SINGER (*sings*).

Do you hear, Mademoiselle,
Those musicians of hell?

THE PRESIDENT. Waiter! Get rid of that man.

WAITER. He is singing *La Belle Polonaise*.

THE PRESIDENT. I didn't ask for the program. I asked you to get rid of him. (*The* WAITER *doesn't budge. The* SINGER *goes by himself.*) As you were saying, Baron . . . ?

THE BARON. Well, until I was fifty . . . (*The* FLOWER GIRL *enters through the café door, center.*) my life was relatively uncomplicated. It consisted of selling off one by one the various estates left me by my father. Three years ago, I parted with my last farm. Two years ago, I lost my last mistress. And now—all that is left me is . . .

THE FLOWER GIRL (*to the* BARON). Violets, sir?

THE PRESIDENT. Run along

The FLOWER GIRL *moves on.*

THE BARON (*staring after her*). So that, in short, all I have left now is my name.

THE PRESIDENT. Your name is precisely the name we need on our board of directors.

THE BARON (*with an inclination of his head*). Very flattering.

THE PRESIDENT. You will understand when I tell you that mine has been a very different experience. I came up from the bottom. My mother spent most of her life bent over a washtub in order to send me to school. I'm eternally grateful to her, of course, but I must confess that I no longer remember her face. It was no doubt beautiful—but when I try to recall it, I see only the part she invariably showed me—her rear.

THE BARON. Very touching.

THE PRESIDENT. When I was thrown out of school for the fifth and last time, I decided to find out for myself what makes

[1] **mazurka:** lively Polish country dance music.

the world go round. I ran errands for an editor, a movie star, a financier. . . . I began to understand a little what life is. Then, one day, in the subway, I saw a face. . . . My rise in life dates from that day.

THE BARON. Really?

THE PRESIDENT. One look at that face, and I knew. One look at mine, and he knew. And so I made my first thousand—passing a boxful of counterfeit notes. A year later, I saw another such face. It got me a nice berth in the narcotics business. Since then, all I do is to look out for such faces. And now here I am—president of eleven corporations, director of fifty-two companies, and, beginning today, chairman of the board of the international combine in which you have been so good as to accept a post. (*The* RAGPICKER *passes, sees something under the* PRESIDENT'*s table, and stoops to pick it up.*) Looking for something?

THE RAGPICKER. Did you drop this?

THE PRESIDENT. I never drop anything.

THE RAGPICKER. Then this hundred-franc note isn't yours?

THE PRESIDENT. Give it here.

The RAGPICKER *gives him the note, and goes out.*

THE BARON. Are you sure it's yours?

THE PRESIDENT. All hundred-franc notes, Baron, are mine.

THE BARON. Mr. President, there's something I've been wanting to ask you. What exactly is the purpose of our new company? Or is that an indiscreet question . . . ?

THE PRESIDENT. Indiscreet? Not a bit. Merely unusual. As far as I know, you're the first member of a board of directors ever to ask such a question.

THE BARON. Do we plan to exploit a commodity? A utility?

THE PRESIDENT. My dear sir, I haven't the faintest idea.

THE BARON. But if you don't know—who does?

THE PRESIDENT. Nobody. And at the moment, it's becoming just a trifle embarrassing. Yes, my dear Baron, since we are now close business associates, I must confess that for the time being we're in a little trouble.

THE BARON. I was afraid of that. The stock issue isn't going well?

THE PRESIDENT. No, no—on the contrary. The stock issue is

going beautifully. Yesterday morning at ten o'clock we offered 500,000 shares to the general public. By 10:05 they were all snapped up at par. By 10:20, when the police finally arrived, our offices were a shambles. . . . Windows smashed —doors torn off their hinges—you never saw anything so beautiful in your life! And this morning our stock is being quoted over the counter at 124 with no sellers, and the orders are still pouring in.

THE BARON. But in that case—what is the trouble?

THE PRESIDENT. The trouble is we have a tremendous capital, and not the slightest idea of what to do with it.

THE BARON. You mean all those people are fighting to buy stock in a company that has no object?

THE PRESIDENT. My dear Baron, do you imagine that when a subscriber buys a share of stock, he has any idea of getting behind a counter or digging a ditch? A stock certificate is not a tool, like a shovel, or a commodity, like a pound of cheese. What we sell a customer is not a share in a business, but a view of the Elysian Fields.[2] A financier is a creative artist. Our function is to stimulate the imagination. We are poets!

THE BARON. But in order to stimulate the imagination, don't you need some field of activity?

THE PRESIDENT. Not at all. What you need for that is a name. A name that will stir the pulse like a trumpet call, set the brain awhirl like a movie star, inspire reverence like a cathedral. *United General International Consolidated!* Of course that's been used. That's what a corporation needs.

THE BARON. And do we have such a name?

THE PRESIDENT. So far we have only a blank space. In that blank space a name must be printed. This name must be a masterpiece. And if I seem a little nervous today, it's because—somehow—I've racked my brains, but it hasn't come to me. Oho! Look at that! Just like the answer to a prayer . . . ! (*The* BARON *turns and stares in the direction of the* PROSPECTOR.) You see? There's one. And what a beauty!

THE BARON. You mean that girl?

[2] **Elysian Fields:** in Greek mythology, a place of blessedness reserved for the good after death.

THE PRESIDENT. No, no, not the girl. That face. You see . . . ? The one that's drinking water.

THE BARON. You call that a face? That's a tombstone.

THE PRESIDENT. It's a milestone. It's a signpost. But is it pointing the way to steel, or wheat, or phosphates? That's what we have to find out. Ah! He sees me. He understands. He will be over.

THE BARON. And when he comes . . . ?

THE PRESIDENT. He will tell me what to do.

THE BARON. You mean business is done this way? You mean, you would trust a stranger with a matter of this importance?

THE PRESIDENT. Baron, I trust neither my wife, nor my daughter, nor my closest friend. My confidential secretary has no idea where I live. But a face like that I would trust with my inmost secrets. Though we have never laid eyes on each other before, that man and I know each other to the depths of our souls. He's no stranger—he's my brother, he's myself. You'll see. He'll be over in a minute. (*The* DEAF-MUTE *enters and passes slowly among the tables, placing a small envelope before each customer. He comes to the* PRESIDENT*'s table.*) What is this anyway? A conspiracy? We don't want your envelopes. Take them away. (*The* DEAF-MUTE *makes a short but pointed speech in sign language.*) Waiter, what the devil's he saying?

WAITER. Only Irma understands him.

THE PRESIDENT. Irma? Who's Irma?

WAITER (*calls*). Irma! It's the waitress inside, sir. Irma!

IRMA *comes out. She is twenty. She has the face and figure of an angel.*

IRMA. Yes?

WAITER. These gentlemen would . . .

THE PRESIDENT. Tell this fellow to get out of here, for God's sake! (*The* DEAF-MUTE *makes another manual oration.*) What's he trying to say, anyway?

IRMA. He says it's an exceptionally beautiful morning, sir. . . .

THE PRESIDENT. Who asked him?

IRMA. But, he says, it was nicer before the gentleman stuck his face in it.

THE PRESIDENT. Call the manager!

IRMA shrugs. She goes back into the restaurant. The DEAF-MUTE walks off, Left. Meanwhile a SHOELACE PEDDLER has arrived.

PEDDLER. Shoelaces? Postcards?

THE BARON. I think I could use a shoelace.

THE PRESIDENT. No, no . . .

PEDDLER. Black? Tan?

THE BARON (*showing his shoes*). What would you recommend?

PEDDLER. Anybody's guess.

THE BARON. Well, give me one of each.

THE PRESIDENT (*putting a hand on the* BARON'*s arm*). Baron, although I am your chairman, I have no authority over your personal life—none, that is, except to fix the amount of your director's fees, and eventually to assign a motor car for your use. Therefore, I am asking you, as a personal favor to me, not to purchase anything from this fellow.

THE BARON. How can I resist so gracious a request? (*The* PEDDLER *shrugs, and passes on.*) But I really don't understand . . . What difference would it make?

THE PRESIDENT. Look here, Baron. Now that you're with us, you must understand that between this irresponsible riff-raff and us there is an impenetrable barrier. *We* have no dealings whatever with *them*.

THE BARON. But without us, the poor devil will starve.

THE PRESIDENT. No, he won't. He expects nothing from us. He has a clientele of his own. He sells shoelaces exclusively to those who have no shoes. Just as the necktie peddler sells only to those who wear no shirts. And that's why these street hawkers can afford to be insolent, disrespectful and independent. They don't need us. They have a world of their own. Ah! My broker. Splendid. He's beaming.

BROKER (*walking up and grasping the* PRESIDENT'*s hand with enthusiasm*). Mr. President! My heartiest congratulations! What a day! What a day!

The STREET JUGGLER *appears, Right. He removes his coat, folds it carefully, and puts it on the bench. Then he opens a suitcase, from which he extracts a number of colored clubs.*

THE PRESIDENT (*presenting the* BROKER). Baron Tommard, of our Board of Directors. My broker. (*The* BROKER *bows. So does the* JUGGLER. *The* BROKER *sits down and signals for a drink. The* JUGGLER *prepares to juggle.*) What's happened?

BROKER. Listen to this. Ten o'clock this morning. The market opens. (*As he speaks, the* JUGGLER *provides a visual counterpart to the* BROKER*'s lines, his clubs rising and falling in rhythm to the* BROKER*'s words.*) Half million shares issued at par, par value a hundred, quoted on the curb at 124 and we start buying at 126, 127, 129—and it's going up—up—up—(*The* JUGGLER*'s clubs rise higher and higher.*) 132—133—138—141—141—141—141 . . .

THE BARON. May I ask . . . ?

THE PRESIDENT. No, no—any explanation would only confuse you.

BROKER. Ten forty-five we start selling short on rumors of a Communist plot, market bearish. . . . 141—138—133—132—and it's down—down—down—102—and we start buying back at 93. Eleven o'clock, rumors denied—95—98—101—106—124—141—and by 11:30 we've got it all back—net profit three and a half million francs.

THE PRESIDENT. Classical. Pure. (*The* JUGGLER *bows again.* A LITTLE MAN *leans over from a near-by table, listening intently, and trembling with excitement.*) And how many shares do we reserve to each member of the board?

BROKER. Fifty, as agreed.

THE PRESIDENT. Bit stingy, don't you think?

BROKER. All right—three thousand.

THE PRESIDENT. That's a little better. (*To the* BARON) You get the idea?

THE BARON. I'm beginning to get it.

BROKER. And now we come to the exciting part . . . (*The* JUGGLER *prepares to juggle with balls of fire.*) Listen carefully: With 35 percent of our funded capital under Section 32 I buy 50,000 United at 36 which I immediately reconvert into 32,000 National Amalgamated two's preferred which I set up as collateral on 150,000 General Consols which I deposit against a credit of fifteen billion to buy Eastern Henequin which I immediately turn into Argentine wheat realizing 136 percent of the original investment which naturally accrues as capital gain and not as corporate income thus saving twelve millions in taxes, and at once convert the 25 percent cotton reserve into lignite, and as our people swing into action in London and New York, I beat up the price on greige[3] goods from 26 to 92—114—203—306—(*The* JUGGLER *by now is juggling his fireballs in the sky. The balls no longer return to his hands.*) 404. . . .

The LITTLE MAN *can stand no more. He rushes over and dumps a sackful of money on the table.*

LITTLE MAN. Here—take it—please, take it!

BROKER (*frigidly*). Who is this man? What is this money?

LITTLE MAN. It's my life's savings. Every cent. I put it all in your hands.

BROKER. Can't you see we're busy?

LITTLE MAN. But I beg you . . . It's my only chance . . . Please don't turn me away.

BROKER. Oh, all right. (*He sweeps the money into his pocket.*) Well?

LITTLE MAN. I thought—perhaps you'd give me a little receipt. . . .

THE PRESIDENT. My dear man, people like us don't give receipts for money. We take them.

LITTLE MAN. Oh, pardon. Of course. I was confused. Here it is. (*Scribbles a receipt.*) Thank you—thank you—thank you. (*He rushes off joyfully.*)

The STREET SINGER *reappears.*

STREET SINGER (*sings*).

Do you hear, Mademoiselle,
Those musicians of hell?

THE PRESIDENT. What, again? Why does he keep repeating those two lines like a parrot?

WAITER. What else can he do? He doesn't know any more and the song's been out of print for years.

THE BARON. Couldn't he sing a song he knows?

WAITER. He likes this one. He hopes if he keeps singing the beginning someone will turn up to teach him the end.

THE PRESIDENT. Tell him to move on. We don't know the song.

[3] **greige:** unprocessed woven fabric.

The PROFESSOR *strolls by, swinging his cane. He overhears.*

PROFESSOR (*stops and addresses the* PRESIDENT *politely*). Nor do I, my dear sir. Nor do I. And yet, I'm in exactly the same predicament. I remember just two lines of my favorite song, as a child. A mazurka also, in case you're interested. . . .

THE PRESIDENT. I'm not.

PROFESSOR. Why is it, I wonder, that one always forgets the words of a mazurka? I suppose they just get lost in that damnable rhythm. All I remember is: (*He sings*)

From England to Spain
I have drunk, it was bliss . . .

STREET SINGER (*walks over, and picks up the tune*).

Red wine and champagne
And many a kiss.

PROFESSOR. Oh, God! It all comes back to me . . . ! (*He sings*)

Red lips and white hands I have known
Where the nightingales dwell. . . .

THE PRESIDENT (*holding his hands to his ears*). Please—please . . .

STREET SINGER.

And to each one I've whispered, "My own,"
And to each one, I've murmured: "Farewell."

THE PRESIDENT. Farewell. Farewell.

STREET SINGER, PROFESSOR (*duo*).

But there's one I shall never forget. . . .

THE PRESIDENT. This isn't a café. It's a circus!

The two go off, still singing: "There is one that's engraved in my heart." The PROSPECTOR *gets up slowly and walks toward the* PRESIDENT'*s table. He looks down without a word. There is a tense silence.*

PROSPECTOR. Well?

THE PRESIDENT. I need a name.

PROSPECTOR (*nods, with complete comprehension*). I need fifty thousand.

THE PRESIDENT. For a corporation.

PROSPECTOR. For a woman.

THE PRESIDENT. Immediately.

PROSPECTOR. Before evening.

THE PRESIDENT. Something . . .

PROSPECTOR. Unusual?

THE PRESIDENT. Something . . .

PROSPECTOR. Provocative?

THE PRESIDENT. Something . . .

PROSPECTOR. Practical.

THE PRESIDENT. Yes.

PROSPECTOR. Fifty thousand. Cash.

THE PRESIDENT. I'm listening.

PROSPECTOR. *International Substrate of Paris, Inc.*

THE PRESIDENT (*snaps his fingers*). That's it! (*To the* BROKER) Pay him off. (*The* BROKER *pays with the* LITTLE MAN'*s money.*) Now—what does it mean?

PROSPECTOR. It means what it says. I'm a prospector.

THE PRESIDENT (*rises*). A prospector! Allow me to shake your hand. Baron. You are in the presence of one of nature's noblemen. Shake his hand. This is Baron Tommard. (*They shake hands.*) It is this man, my dear Baron, who smells out in the bowels of the earth those deposits of metal or liquid on which can be founded the only social unit of which our age is capable—the corporation. Sit down, please. (*They all sit.*) And now that we have a name . . .

PROSPECTOR. You need a property.

THE PRESIDENT. Precisely.

PROSPECTOR. I have one.

THE PRESIDENT. A claim?

PROSPECTOR. Terrific.

THE PRESIDENT. Foreign?

PROSPECTOR. French.

THE BARON. In Indo-China?

BROKER. Morocco?

THE PRESIDENT. In France?

PROSPECTOR (*matter of fact*). In Paris.

THE PRESIDENT. In Paris? You've been prospecting in Paris?

THE BARON. For women, no doubt.

THE PRESIDENT. For art?

BROKER. For gold?

PROSPECTOR. Oil.

BROKER. He's crazy.

THE PRESIDENT. Sh! He's inspired.

PROSPECTOR. You think I'm crazy. Well, they thought Columbus was crazy.

THE BARON. Oil in Paris?

BROKER. But how is it possible?

PROSPECTOR. It's not only possible. It's certain.

THE PRESIDENT. Tell us.

PROSPECTOR. You don't know, my dear sir, what treasures Paris conceals. Paris is the least prospected place in the world. We've gone over the rest of the planet with a fine-tooth comb. But has anyone ever thought of looking for oil in Paris? Nobody. Before me, that is.

THE PRESIDENT. Genius!

PROSPECTOR. No. Just a practical man. I use my head.

THE BARON. But why has nobody ever thought of this before?

PROSPECTOR. The treasures of the earth, my dear sir, are not easy to find nor to get at. They are invariably guarded by dragons. Doubtless there is some reason for this. For once we've dug out and consumed the internal ballast of the planet, the chances are it will shoot off on some irresponsible tangent and smash itself up in the sky. Well, that's the risk we take. Anyway, that's not my business. A prospector has enough to worry about.

THE BARON. I know—snakes—tarantulas—fleas . . .

PROSPECTOR. Worse than that, sir. Civilization.

THE PRESIDENT. Does that annoy you?

PROSPECTOR. Civilization gets in our way all the time. In the first place, it covers the earth with cities and towns which are damned awkward to dig up when you want to see what's underneath. It's not only the real-estate people—you can always do business with them—it's human sentimentality. How do you do business with that?

THE PRESIDENT. I see what you mean.

PROSPECTOR. They say that where we pass, nothing ever grows again. What of it? Is a park any better than a coal mine? What's a mountain got that a slag pile hasn't? What would you rather have in your garden—an almond tree or an oil well?

THE PRESIDENT. Well . . .

PROSPECTOR. Exactly. But what's the use of arguing with

these fools? Imagine the choicest place you ever saw for an excavation, and what do they put there? A playground for children! Civilization!

THE PRESIDENT. Just show us the point where you want to start digging. We'll do the rest. Even if it's in the middle of the Louvre. Where's the oil?

PROSPECTOR. Perhaps you think it's easy to make an accurate fix in an area like Paris where everything conspires to put you off the scent? Women—perfume—flowers—history. You can talk all you like about geology, but an oil deposit, gentlemen, has to be smelled out. I have a good nose. I go further. I have a phenomenal nose. But the minute I get the right whiff—the minute I'm on the scent—a fragrance rises from what I take to be the spiritual deposits of the past—and I'm completely at sea. Now take this very point, for example, this very spot.

THE BARON. You mean—right here in Chaillot?

PROSPECTOR. Right under here.

THE PRESIDENT. Good heavens! (*He looks under his chair.*)

PROSPECTOR. It's taken me months to locate this spot.

THE BARON. But what in the world makes you think . . . ?

PROSPECTOR. Do you know this place, Baron?

THE BARON. Well, I've been sitting here for thirty years.

PROSPECTOR. Did you ever taste the water?

THE BARON. The water? Good God, no!

PROSPECTOR. It's plain to see that you are no prospector! A prospector, Baron, is addicted to water as a drunkard to wine. Water, gentlemen, is the one substance from which the earth can conceal nothing. It sucks out its innermost secrets and brings them to our very lips. Well—beginning at Notre Dame, where I first caught the scent of oil three months ago, I worked my way across Paris, glassful by glassful, sampling the water, until at last I came to this café. And here—just two days ago—I took a sip. My heart began to thump. Was it possible that I was deceived? I took another, a third, a fourth, a fifth. I was trembling like a leaf. But there was no mistake. Each time that I drank, my taste-buds thrilled to the most exquisite flavor known to a prospector—the flavor of— (*with utmost lyricism*) Petroleum!

THE PRESIDENT. Waiter! Some water and four glasses. Hurry.

This round, gentlemen, is on me. And as a toast—I shall propose International Substrate of Paris, Incorporated. (*The* WAITER *brings a decanter and the glasses. The* PRESIDENT *pours out the water amid profound silence. They taste it with the air of connoisseurs savoring something that has never before passed human lips. Then they look at each other doubtfully. The* PROSPECTOR *pours himself a second glass and drinks it off.*) Well . . .

BROKER. Ye-es . . .

THE BARON. Mm . . .

PROSPECTOR. Get it?

THE BARON. Tastes queer.

PROSPECTOR. That's it. To the unpracticed palate it tastes queer. But to the taste-buds of the expert—ah!

THE BARON. Still, there's one thing I don't quite understand . . .

PROSPECTOR. Yes?

THE BARON. This café doesn't have its own well, does it?

PROSPECTOR. Of course not. This is Paris water.

BROKER. Then why should it taste different here than anywhere else?

PROSPECTOR. Because, my dear sir, the pipes that carry this water pass deep through the earth, and the earth just here is soaked with oil, and this oil permeates the pores of the iron and flavors the water it carries. Ever so little, yes—but quite enough to betray its presence to the sensitive tongue of the specialist.

THE BARON. I see.

PROSPECTOR. I don't say everyone is capable of tasting it. No. But I—I can detect the presence of oil in water that has passed within fifteen miles of a deposit. Under special circumstances, twenty.

THE PRESIDENT. Phenomenal!

PROSPECTOR. And so here I am with the greatest discovery of the age on my hands—but the blasted authorities won't let me drill a single well unless I show them the oil! Now how can I show them the oil unless they let me dig? Completely stymied! Eh?

THE PRESIDENT. What? A man like you?

PROSPECTOR. That's what they think. That's what they want.

Have you noticed the strange glamor of the women this morning? And the quality of the sunshine? And this extraordinary convocation of vagabonds buzzing about protectively like bees around a hive? Do you know why it is? Because they know. It's a plot to distract us, to turn us from our purpose. Well, let them try. I know there's oil here. And I'm going to dig it up, even if I . . . (*He smiles.*) Shall I tell you my little plan?

THE PRESIDENT. By all means.

PROSPECTOR. Well . . . For heaven's sake, what's that?

At this point, the MADWOMAN *enters. She is dressed in the grand fashion of 1885, a taffeta skirt with an immense train—which she has gathered up by means of a clothespin—ancient button shoes, and a hat in the style of Marie Antoinette. She wears a lorgnette on a chain, and an enormous cameo pin at her throat. In her hand she carries a small basket. She walks in with great dignity, extracts a dinner bell from the bosom of her dress, and rings it sharply.* IRMA *appears.*

COUNTESS. Are my bones ready, Irma?

IRMA. There won't be much today, Countess. We had broilers. Can you wait? While the gentleman inside finishes eating?

COUNTESS. And my gizzard?

IRMA. I'll try to get it away from him.

COUNTESS. If he eats my gizzard, save me the giblets. They will do for the tomcat that lives under the bridge. He likes a few giblets now and again.

IRMA. Yes, Countess.

IRMA *goes back into the café. The* COUNTESS *takes a few steps and stops in front of the* PRESIDENT'*s table. She examines him with undisguised disapproval.*

THE PRESIDENT. Waiter. Ask that woman to move on.

WAITER. Sorry, sir. This is her café.

THE PRESIDENT. Is she the manager of the café?

WAITER. She's the Madwoman of Chaillot.

THE PRESIDENT. A Madwoman? She's mad?

WAITER. Who says she's mad?

THE PRESIDENT. You just said so yourself.

WAITER. Look, sir. You asked me who she was. And I told you. What's mad about her? She's the Madwoman of Chaillot.

THE PRESIDENT. Call a policeman.

The COUNTESS *whistles through her fingers. At once, the* DOORMAN *runs out of the café. He has three scarves in his hands.*

COUNTESS. Have you found it? My feather boa?

DOORMAN. Not yet, Countess. Three scarves. But no boa.

COUNTESS. It's five years since I lost it. Surely you've had time to find it.

DOORMAN. Take one of these, Countess. Nobody's claimed them.

COUNTESS. A boa like that doesn't vanish, you know. A feather boa nine feet long!

DOORMAN. How about this blue one?

COUNTESS. With my pink ruffle and my green veil? You're joking! Let me see the yellow. (*She tries it on.*) How does it look?

DOORMAN. Terrific.

With a magnificent gesture, she flings the scarf about her, upsetting the PRESIDENT'*s glass and drenching his trousers with water. She stalks off without a glance at him.*

THE PRESIDENT. Waiter! I'm making a complaint.

WAITER. Against whom?

THE PRESIDENT. Against her! Against you! The whole gang of you! That singer! That shoelace peddler! That female lunatic! Or whatever you call her!

THE BARON. Calm yourself, Mr. President. . . .

THE PRESIDENT. I'll do nothing of the sort! Baron, the first thing we have to do is to get rid of these people! Good heavens, look at them! Every size, shape, color and period of history imaginable. It's utter anarchy! I tell you, sir, the only safeguard of order and discipline in the modern world is a standardized worker with interchangeable parts. That would solve the entire problem of management. Here, the manager . . . And there—one composite drudge grunting and sweating all over the world. Just we two. Ah, how beautiful! How easy on the eyes! How restful for the conscience!

THE BARON. Yes, yes—of course.

THE PRESIDENT. Order. Symmetry. Balance. But instead of that, what? Here in Chaillot, the very citadel of management, these insolent phantoms of the past come to beard us with their raffish individualism—with the right of the voiceless to sing, of the dumb to make speeches, of trousers to have no seats and bosoms to have dinner bells!

THE BARON. But, after all, do these people matter?

THE PRESIDENT. My dear sir, wherever the poor are happy, and the servants are proud, and the mad are respected, our power is at an end. Look at that! That waiter! That madwoman! That flower girl! Do I get that sort of service? And suppose that I—president of twelve corporations and ten times a millionaire—were to stick a gladiolus in my buttonhole and start yelling— (*He tinkles his spoon in a glass violently, yelling*) Are my bones ready, Irma?

THE BARON (*reprovingly*). Mr. President . . .

People at the adjoining tables turn and stare with raised eyebrows. The WAITER *starts to come over.*

THE PRESIDENT. You see? Now.

PROSPECTOR. We were discussing my plan.

THE PRESIDENT. Ah yes, your plan. (*He glances in the direction of the* MADWOMAN'*s table.*) Careful—she's looking at us.

PROSPECTOR. Do you know what a bomb is?

THE PRESIDENT. I'm told they explode.

PROSPECTOR. Exactly. You see that white building across the river. Do you happen to know what that is?

THE PRESIDENT. I do not.

PROSPECTOR. That's the office of the City Architect. That man has stubbornly refused to give me a permit to drill for oil anywhere within the limits of the city of Paris. I've tried everything with him—influence, bribes, threats. He says I'm crazy. And now . . .

THE PRESIDENT. Oh, my God! What is this one trying to sell us?

A little OLD MAN *enters left, and doffs his hat politely. He is somewhat ostentatiously respectable—gloved, pomaded, and carefully dressed, with a white handkerchief peeping out of his breast pocket.*

DR. JADIN. Nothing but health, sir. Or rather the health of the feet. But remember—as the foot goes, so goes the man. May I present myself . . . ? Dr. Gaspard Jadin, French Navy, retired. Former specialist in the extraction of ticks and chiggers. At present specializing in the extraction of bunions and corns. In case of sudden emergency, Martial the waiter will furnish my home address. My office is here, second row, third table, week days, twelve to five. Thank you very much. (*He sits at his table.*)

WAITER. Your vermouth, Doctor?

DR. JADIN. My vermouth. My vermouths. How are your gallstones today, Martial?

WAITER. Fine. Fine. They rattle like anything.

DR. JADIN. Splendid. (*He spies the* COUNTESS.) Good morning, Countess. How's the floating kidney? Still afloat? (*She nods graciously.*) Splendid. Splendid. So long as it floats, it can't sink.

THE PRESIDENT. This is impossible! Let's go somewhere else.

PROSPECTOR. No. It's nearly noon.

THE PRESIDENT. Yes. It is. Five to twelve.

PROSPECTOR. In five minutes' time you're going to see that City Architect blown up, building and all—boom!

BROKER. Are you serious?

PROSPECTOR. That imbecile has no one to blame but himself. Yesterday noon, he got my ultimatum—he's had twenty-four hours to think it over. No permit? All right. Within two minutes my agent is going to drop a little package in his coal bin. And three minutes after that, precisely at noon . . .

THE BARON. You prospectors certainly use modern methods.

PROSPECTOR. The method may be modern. But the idea is old. To get at the treasure, it has always been necessary to slay the dragon. I guarantee that after this, the City Architect will be more reasonable. The new one, I mean.

THE PRESIDENT. Don't you think we're sitting a little close for comfort?

PROSPECTOR. Oh no, no. Don't worry. And, above all, don't stare. We may be watched. (*A clock strikes.*) Why, that's noon. Something's wrong! Good God! What's this? (*A* POLICEMAN *staggers in bearing a lifeless body on his shoulders in the manner prescribed as "The Fireman's Lift."*) It's Pierre! My agent! (*He walks over with affected nonchalance.*) I say, Officer, what's that you've got?

POLICEMAN. Drowned man. (*He puts him down on the bench.*)

WAITER. He's not drowned. His clothes are dry. He's been slugged.

POLICEMAN. Slugged is also correct. He was just jumping off the bridge when I came along and pulled him back. I slugged him, naturally, so he wouldn't drag me under. Life Saving Manual, Rule 5: "In cases where there is danger of being dragged under, it is necessary to render the subject unconscious by means of a sharp blow." He's had that. (*He loosens the clothes and begins applying artificial respiration.*)

PROSPECTOR. The stupid idiot! What the devil did he do with the bomb? That's what comes of employing amateurs!

THE PRESIDENT. You don't think he'll give you away?

PROSPECTOR. Don't worry. (*He walks over to the policeman.*) Say, what do you think you're doing?

POLICEMAN. Lifesaving. Artificial respiration. First aid to the drowning.

PROSPECTOR. But he's not drowning.

POLICEMAN. But he thinks he is.

PROSPECTOR. You'll never bring him round that way, my friend. That's meant for people who drown in water. It's no good at all for those who drown without water.

POLICEMAN. What am I supposed to do? I've just been sworn in. It's my first day on the beat. I can't afford to get in trouble. I've got to go by the book.

PROSPECTOR. Perfectly simple. Take him back to the bridge where you found him and throw him in. Then you can save his life and you'll get a medal. This way, you'll only get fined for slugging an innocent man.

POLICEMAN. What do you mean, innocent? He was just going to jump when I grabbed him.

PROSPECTOR. Have you any proof of that?

POLICEMAN. Well, I saw him.

PROSPECTOR. Written proof? Witnesses?

POLICEMAN. No, but . . .

PROSPECTOR. Then don't waste time arguing. You're in trouble. Quick—before anybody notices—throw him in and dive after him. It's the only way out.

POLICEMAN. But I don't swim.

THE PRESIDENT. You'll learn how on the way down. Before you were born, did you know how to breathe?

POLICEMAN (*convinced*). All right. Here we go. (*He starts lifting the body.*)

DR. JADIN. One moment, please. I don't like to interfere, but it's my professional duty to point out that medical science has definitely established the fact of intra-uterine respiration. Consequently, this policeman, even before he was born, knew not only how to breathe but also how to cough, hiccup and belch.

THE PRESIDENT. Suppose he did—how does it concern you?

DR. JADIN. On the other hand, medical science has never established the fact of intra-uterine swimming or diving. Under the circumstances, we are forced to the opinion, Officer, that if you dive in you will probably drown.

POLICEMAN. You think so?

PROSPECTOR. Who asked you for an opinion?

THE PRESIDENT. Pay no attention to that quack, Officer.

DR. JADIN. Quack, sir?

PROSPECTOR. This is not a medical matter. It's a legal problem. The officer has made a grave error. He's new. We're trying to help him.

BROKER. He's probably afraid of the water.

POLICEMAN. Nothing of the sort. Officially, I'm afraid of nothing. But I always follow doctor's orders.

DR. JADIN. You see, Officer, when a child is born . . .

PROSPECTOR. Now, what does he care about when a child is born? He's got a dying man on his hands. . . . Officer, if you want my advice . . .

POLICEMAN. It so happens, I care a lot about when a child is born. It's part of my duty to aid and assist any woman in childbirth or labor.

THE PRESIDENT. Can you imagine!

POLICEMAN. Is it true, Doctor, what they say, that when you have twins, the first born is considered to be the youngest?

DR. JADIN. Quite correct. And what's more, if the twins happen to be born at midnight on December 31st, the older is a whole year younger. He does his military service a year later. That's why you have to keep your eyes open. And that's the reason why a queen always gives birth before witnesses. . . .

POLICEMAN. God! The things a policeman is supposed to know! Doctor, what does it mean if, when I get up in the morning sometimes . . .

PROSPECTOR (*nudging the* PRESIDENT *meaningfully*). The old woman . . .

BROKER. Come on, Baron.

THE PRESIDENT. I think we'd better all run along.

PROSPECTOR. Leave him to me.

THE PRESIDENT. I'll see you later. (*The* PRESIDENT *steals off with the* BROKER *and the* BARON.)

POLICEMAN (*still in conference with* DR. JADIN). But what's really worrying me, Doctor, is this—don't you think it's a bit risky for a man to marry after forty-five?

The BROKER *runs in breathlessly.*

BROKER. Officer! Officer!

POLICEMAN. What's the trouble?

BROKER. Quick! Two women are calling for help—on the sidewalk—Avenue Wilson!

POLICEMAN. Two women at once? Standing up or lying down?

BROKER. You'd better go and see. Quick!

PROSPECTOR. You'd better take the Doctor with you.

POLICEMAN. Come along, Doctor, come along. . . . (*Pointing to* PIERRE) Tell him to wait till I get back. Come along, Doctor.

He runs out, the DOCTOR *following. The* PROSPECTOR *moves over toward* PIERRE, *but* IRMA *crosses in front of him and takes the boy's hand.*

IRMA. How beautiful he is! Is he dead, Martial?

WAITER (*handing her a pocket mirror*). Hold this mirror to his mouth. If it clouds over . . .

IRMA. It clouds over.

WAITER. He's alive. (*He holds out his hand for the mirror.*)

IRMA. Just a sec— (*She rubs it clean and looks at herself intently. Before handing it back, she fixes her hair and applies her lipstick. Meanwhile the* PROSPECTOR *tries to get around the other side, but the* COUNTESS' *eagle eye drives him off. He shrugs his shoulders and exits with the* BARON.) Oh, look—he's opened his eyes!

PIERRE *opens his eyes, stares intently at* IRMA, *and closes them again with the expression of a man who is among the angels.*

PIERRE (*murmurs*). Oh! How beautiful!

VOICE (*from within the café*). Irma!

IRMA. Coming. Coming.

She goes in, not without a certain reluctance. The COUNTESS *at once takes her place on the bench, and also the young man's hand.* PIERRE *sits up suddenly, and finds himself staring, not at* IRMA, *but into the very peculiar face of the* COUNTESS. *His expression changes.*

COUNTESS. You're looking at my iris? Isn't it beautiful?

PIERRE. Very. (*He drops back, exhausted.*)

COUNTESS. The Sergeant was good enough to say it becomes me. But I no longer trust his taste. Yesterday, the flower girl gave me a lily, and he said it didn't suit me.

PIERRE (*weakly*). It's beautiful.

COUNTESS. He'll be very happy to know that you agree with him. He's really quite sensitive. (*She calls*) Sergeant!

PIERRE. No, please—don't call the police.

COUNTESS. But I must. I think I hurt his feelings.

PIERRE. Let me go, Madame.

COUNTESS. No, no. Stay where you are. Sergeant!

PIERRE (*struggling weakly to get up*). Please let me go.

COUNTESS. I'll do nothing of the sort. When you let someone go, you never see him again. I let Charlotte Mazumet go. I never saw her again.

PIERRE. Oh, my head.

COUNTESS. I let Adolphe Bertaut go. And I was holding him. And I never saw him again.

PIERRE. Oh, God!

COUNTESS. Except once. Thirty years later. In the market. He had changed a great deal—he didn't know me. He sneaked a melon from right under my nose, the only good one of the year. Ah, here we are. Sergeant!

The POLICE SERGEANT *comes in with importance.*

SERGEANT. I'm in a hurry, Countess.

COUNTESS. With regard to the iris. This young man agrees with you. He says it suits me.

SERGEANT (*going*). There's a man drowning in the Seine.

COUNTESS. He's not drowning in the Seine. He's drowning here. Because I'm holding him tight—as I should have held Adolphe Bertaut. But if I let him go, I'm sure he will go and drown in the Seine. He's a lot better looking than Adolphe Bertaut, wouldn't you say? (PIERRE *sighs deeply.*)

SERGEANT. How would I know?

COUNTESS. I've shown you his photograph. The one with the bicycle.

SERGEANT. Oh, yes. The one with the harelip.

COUNTESS. I've told you a hundred times! Adolphe Bertaut had no harelip. That was a scratch in the negative. (*The* SERGEANT *takes out his notebook and pencil.*) What are you doing?

SERGEANT. I am taking down the drowned man's name, given name and date of birth.

COUNTESS. You think that's going to stop him from jumping in the river? Don't be silly, Sergeant. Put that book away and try to console him.

SERGEANT. I should try and console him?

COUNTESS. When people want to die, it is your job as a guardian of the state to speak out in praise of life. Not mine.

SERGEANT. I should speak out in praise of life?

COUNTESS. I assume you have some motive for interfering with people's attempts to kill each other, and rob each other, and run each other over? If you believe that life has some value, tell him what it is. Go on.

SERGEANT. Well, all right. Now look, young man . . .

COUNTESS. His name is Roderick.

PIERRE. My name is not Roderick.

COUNTESS. Yes, it is. It's noon. At noon all men become Roderick.

SERGEANT. Except Adolphe Bertaut.

COUNTESS. In the days of Adolphe Bertaut, we were forced to change the men when we got tired of their names. Nowadays, we're more practical—each hour on the hour all names are automatically changed. The men remain the same. But you're not here to discuss Adolphe Bertaut, Sergeant. You're here to convince the young man that life is worth living.

PIERRE. It isn't.

SERGEANT. Quiet. Now then—what was the idea of jumping off the bridge, anyway?

COUNTESS. The idea was to land in the river. Roderick doesn't seem to be at all confused about that.

SERGEANT. Now how can I convince anybody that life is worth living if you keep interrupting all the time?

COUNTESS. I'll be quiet.

SERGEANT. First of all, Mr. Roderick, you have to realize that suicide is a crime against the state. And why is it a crime against the state? Because every time anybody commits suicide, that means one soldier less for the army, one taxpayer less for the . . .

COUNTESS. Sergeant, isn't there something about life that you really enjoy?

SERGEANT. That I enjoy?

COUNTESS. Well, surely, in all these years, you must have found something worth living for. Some secret pleasure, or passion. Don't blush. Tell him about it.

SERGEANT. Who's blushing? Well, naturally, yes—I have my passions—like everybody else. The fact is, since you ask me—I love—to play—casino. And if the gentleman would like to join me, by and by when I go off duty, we can sit down to a nice little game in the back room with a nice cold glass of beer. If he wants to kill an hour, that is.

COUNTESS. He doesn't want to kill an hour. He wants to kill himself. Well? Is that all the police force has to offer by way of earthly bliss?

SERGEANT. Huh? You mean— (*he jerks a thumb in the direction of the pretty* BLONDE, *who has just been joined by a*

BRUNETTE *of the same stamp*) Paulette? (*The young man groans.*)

COUNTESS. You're not earning your salary, Sergeant. I defy anybody to stop dying on your account.

SERGEANT. Go ahead, if you can do any better. But you won't find it easy.

COUNTESS. Oh, this is not a desperate case at all. A young man who has just fallen in love with someone who has fallen in love with him!

PIERRE. She hasn't. How could she?

COUNTESS. Oh, yes, she has. She was holding your hand, just as I'm holding it, when all of a sudden . . . Did you ever know Marshal Canrobert's niece?

SERGEANT. How could he know Marshal Canrobert's niece?

COUNTESS. Lots of people knew her—when she was alive. (PIERRE *begins to struggle energetically.*) No, no, Roderick —stop—stop!

SERGEANT. You see? You won't do any better than I did.

COUNTESS. No? Let's bet. I'll bet my iris against one of your gold buttons. Right?—Roderick, I know very well why you tried to drown yourself in the river.

PIERRE. You don't at all.

COUNTESS. It's because that Prospector wanted you to commit a horrible crime.

PIERRE. How did you know that?

COUNTESS. He stole my boa, and now he wants you to kill me.

PIERRE. Not exactly.

COUNTESS. It wouldn't be the first time they've tried it. But I'm not so easy to get rid of, my boy, oh, no . . . Because . . .

The DOORMAN *rides in on his bicycle. He winks at the* SERGEANT, *who has now seated himself while the* WAITER *serves him a beer.*

DOORMAN. Take it easy, Sergeant.

SERGEANT. I'm busy saving a drowning man.

COUNTESS. They can't kill me because—I have no desire to die.

PIERRE. You're fortunate.

COUNTESS. To be alive is to be fortunate, Roderick. Of course, in the morning, when you first awake, it does not always seem so very gay. When you take your hair out of the drawer, and your teeth out of the glass, you are apt to feel a little out of place in this world. Especially if you've just been dreaming that you're a little girl on a pony looking for strawberries in the woods. But all you need to feel the call of life once more is a letter in your mail giving you your schedule for the day—your mending, your shopping, that letter to your grandmother that you never seem to get around to. And so, when you've washed your face in rosewater, and powdered it—not with this awful rice-powder they sell nowadays, which does nothing for the skin, but with a cake of pure white starch—and put on your pins, your rings, your brooches, bracelets, earrings and pearls—in short, when you are dressed for your morning coffee—and have had a good look at yourself—not in the glass, naturally—it lies—but in the side of the brass gong that once belonged to Admiral Courbet—then, Roderick, then you're armed, you're strong, you're ready—you can begin again. (PIERRE *is listening now intently. There are tears in his eyes.*)

PIERRE. Oh, Madame . . . ! Oh, Madame . . . !

COUNTESS. After that, everything is pure delight. First the morning paper. Not, of course, these current sheets full of lies and vulgarity. I always read the *Gaulois,* the issue of March 22, 1903. It's by far the best. It has some delightful scandal, some excellent fashion notes, and, of course, the last-minute bulletin on the death of Leonide Leblanc. She used to live next door, poor woman, and when I learn of her death every morning, it gives me quite a shock. I'd gladly lend you my copy, but it's in tatters.

SERGEANT. Couldn't we find him a copy in some library?

COUNTESS. I doubt it. And so, when you've taken your fruit salts—not in water, naturally—no matter what they say, it's water that gives you gas—but with a bit of spiced cake—then in sunlight or rain, Chaillot calls. It is time to dress for your morning walk. This takes much longer, of course—without a maid, impossible to do it under an hour, what with your corset, corset-cover and drawers all of which lace or button in the back. I asked Madame Lanvin, a while ago, to fit the drawers with zippers. She was quite charming, but she declined. She thought it would spoil the style.

The DEAF-MUTE *comes in.*

WAITER. I know a place where they put zippers on anything.

The RAGPICKER *enters.*

COUNTESS. I think Lanvin knows best. But I really manage very well, Martial. What I do now is, I lace them up in front, then twist them around to the back. It's quite simple, really. Then you choose a lorgnette, and then the usual fruitless search for the feather boa that the Prospector stole—I know it was he: he didn't dare look me in the eye—and then all you need is a rubber band to slip around your parasol—I lost the catch the day I struck the cat that was stalking the pigeon—it was worth it—ah, that day I earned my wages!

THE RAGPICKER. Countess, if you can use it, I found a nice umbrella catch the other day with a cat's eye in it.

COUNTESS. Thank you, Ragpicker. They say these eyes sometimes come to life and fill with tears. I'd be afraid . . .

PIERRE. Go on, Madame, go on . . .

COUNTESS. Ah! So life is beginning to interest you, is it? You see how beautiful it is?

PIERRE. What a fool I've been!

COUNTESS. Then, Roderick, I begin my rounds. I have my cats to feed, my dogs to pet, my plants to water. I have to see what the evil ones are up to in the district—those who hate people, those who hate plants, those who hate animals. I watch them sneaking off in the morning to put on their disguises—to the baths, to the beauty parlors, to the barbers. But they can't deceive me. And when they come out again with blonde hair and false whiskers, to pull up my flowers and poison my dogs, I'm there, and I'm ready. All you have to do to break their power is to cut across their path from the left. That isn't always easy. Vice moves swiftly. But I have a good long stride and I generally manage. . . . Right, my friends? (*The* WAITER *and the* RAGPICKER *nod their heads with evident approval.*) Yes, the flowers have been marvelous this year. And the butcher's dog on the Rue Bizet, in spite of that wretch that tried to poison him, is friskier than ever . . .

SERGEANT. That dog had better look out. He has no license.

COUNTESS. He doesn't seem to feel the need for one.

THE RAGPICKER. The Duchess de la Rochefoucauld's whippet is getting awfully thin. . . .

COUNTESS. What can I do? She bought that dog full grown from a kennel where they didn't know his right name. A dog without his right name is bound to get thin.

THE RAGPICKER. I've got a friend who knows a lot about dogs —an Arab . . .

COUNTESS. Ask him to call on the Duchess. She receives Thursdays, five to seven. You see, then, Roderick. That's life. Does it appeal to you now?

PIERRE. It seems marvelous.

COUNTESS. Ah! Sergeant. My button. (*The* SERGEANT *gives her his button and goes off. At this point the* PROSPECTOR *enters.*) That's only the morning. Wait till I tell you about the afternoon!

PROSPECTOR. All right, Pierre. Come along now.

PIERRE. I'm perfectly all right here.

PROSPECTOR. I said, come along now.

PIERRE (*to the* COUNTESS). I'd better go, Madame.

COUNTESS. No.

PIERRE. It's no use. Please let go my hand.

PROSPECTOR. Madame, will you oblige me by letting my friend go?

COUNTESS. I will not oblige you in any way.

PROSPECTOR. All right. Then I'll oblige you . . . ! (*He tries to push her away. She catches up a soda water siphon and squirts it in his face.*)

PIERRE. Countess . . .

COUNTESS. Stay where you are. This man isn't going to take you away. In the first place, I shall need you in a few minutes to take me home. I'm all alone here and I'm very easily frightened.

The PROSPECTOR *makes a second attempt to drag* PIERRE *away. The* COUNTESS *cracks him over the skull with the siphon. They join battle. The* COUNTESS *whistles. The* DOORMAN *comes, then the other* VAGABONDS, *and lastly the* POLICE SERGEANT.

PROSPECTOR. Officer! Arrest this woman!

SERGEANT. What's the trouble here?

PROSPECTOR. She refuses to let this man go.

SERGEANT. Why should she?

PROSPECTOR. It's against the law for a woman to detain a man on the street.

IRMA. Suppose it's her son whom she's found again after twenty years?

THE RAGPICKER (*gallantly*). Or her long-lost brother? The Countess is not so old.

PROSPECTOR. Officer, this is a clear case of disorderly conduct. (*The* DEAF-MUTE *interrupts with frantic signals.*)

COUNTESS. Irma, what is the Deaf-Mute saying?

IRMA (*interpreting*). The young man is in danger of his life. He mustn't go with him.

PROSPECTOR. What does he know?

IRMA. He knows everything.

PROSPECTOR. Officer, I'll have to take your number.

COUNTESS. Take his number. It's 2133. It adds up to nine. It will bring you luck.

SERGEANT. Countess, between ourselves, what are you holding him for, anyway?

COUNTESS. I'm holding him because it's very pleasant to hold him. I've never really held anybody before, and I'm making the most of it. And because so long as *I* hold him, he's free.

PROSPECTOR. Pierre, I'm giving you fair warning. . . .

COUNTESS. And I'm holding him because Irma wants me to hold him. Because if I let him go, it will break her heart.

IRMA. Oh, Countess!

SERGEANT (*to the* PROSPECTOR). All right, you—move on. Nobody's holding you. You're blocking traffic. Move on.

PROSPECTOR (*menacingly*). I have your number. (*And murderously, to* PIERRE) You'll regret this, Pierre. (*Exits.*)

PIERRE. Thank you, Countess.

COUNTESS. They're blackmailing you, are they? (PIERRE *nods.*) What have you done? Murdered somebody?

PIERRE. No.

COUNTESS. Stolen something?

PIERRE. No.

COUNTESS. What then?

PIERRE. I forged a signature.

COUNTESS. Whose signature?

PIERRE. My father's. To a note.

COUNTESS. And this man has the paper, I suppose?

PIERRE. He promised to tear it up, if I did what he wanted. But I couldn't do it.

COUNTESS. But the man is mad! Does he really want to destroy the whole neighborhood?

PIERRE. He wants to destroy the whole city.

COUNTESS (*laughs*). Fantastic.

PIERRE. It's not funny, Countess. He can do it. He's mad, but he's powerful, and he has friends. Their machines are already drawn up and waiting. In three months' time you may see the city covered by a forest of derricks and drills.

COUNTESS. But what are they looking for? Have they lost something?

PIERRE. They're looking for oil. They're convinced that Paris is sitting on a lake of oil.

COUNTESS. Suppose it is. What harm does it do?

PIERRE. They want to bring the oil to the surface, Countess.

COUNTESS (*laughs*). How silly! Is that a reason to destroy a city? What do they want with this oil?

PIERRE. They want to make war, Countess.

COUNTESS. Oh, dear, let's forget about these horrible men. The world is beautiful. It's happy. That's how God made it. No man can change it.

WAITER. Ah, Countess, if you only knew . . .

COUNTESS. If I only knew what?

WAITER. Shall we tell her now? Shall we tell her?

COUNTESS. What is it you are hiding from me?

THE RAGPICKER. Nothing, Countess. It's you who are hiding.

WAITER. You tell her. You've been a pitchman. You can talk.

ALL. Tell her. Tell her. Tell her.

COUNTESS. You're frightening me, my friends. Go on. I'm listening.

THE RAGPICKER. Countess, there was a time when old clothes were as good as new—in fact, they were better. Because when people wore clothes, they gave something to them. You may not believe it, but right this minute, the highest-priced shops in Paris are selling clothes that were thrown away thirty years ago. They're selling them for new. That's how good they were.

COUNTESS. Well?

THE RAGPICKER. Countess, there was a time when garbage was a pleasure. A garbage can was not what it is now. If it smelled a little strange, it was because it was a little confused—there was everything there—sardines, cologne, iodine, roses. An amateur might jump to a wrong conclusion. But to a professional—it was the smell of God's plenty.

COUNTESS. Well?

THE RAGPICKER. Countess, the world has changed.

COUNTESS. Nonsense. How could it change? People are the same, I hope.

THE RAGPICKER. No, Countess. The people are not the same. The people are different. There's been an invasion. An infiltration. From another planet. The world is not beautiful any more. It's not happy.

COUNTESS. Not happy? Is that true? Why didn't you tell me this before?

THE RAGPICKER. Because you live in a dream, Countess. And we don't like to disturb you.

COUNTESS. But how could it have happened?

THE RAGPICKER. Countess, there was a time when you could walk around Paris, and all the people you met were just like yourself. A little cleaner, maybe, or dirtier, perhaps, or angry, or smiling—but you knew them. They were you. Well, Countess, twenty years ago, one day, on the street, I saw a face in the crowd. A face, you might say, without a face. The eyes—empty. The expression—not human. Not a human face. It saw me staring, and when it looked back at me with its gelatine eyes, I shuddered. Because I knew that to make room for this one, one of us must have left the earth. A while after, I saw another. And another. And since then, I've seen hundreds come in—yes—thousands.

COUNTESS. Describe them to me.

THE RAGPICKER. You've seen them yourself, Countess. Their clothes don't wrinkle. Their hats don't come off. When they talk, they don't look at you. They don't perspire.

COUNTESS. Have they wives? Have they children?

THE RAGPICKER. They buy the models out of shop windows,

furs and all. They animate them by a secret process. Then they marry them. Naturally, they don't have children.

COUNTESS. What work do they do?

THE RAGPICKER. They don't do any work. Whenever they meet, they whisper, and then they pass each other thousand-franc notes. You see them standing on the corner by the Stock Exchange. You see them at auctions—in the back. They never raise a finger—they just stand there. In theater lobbies, by the box office—they never go inside. They don't do anything, but wherever you see them, things are not the same. I remember well the time when a cabbage could sell itself just by being a cabbage. Nowadays it's no good being a cabbage—unless you have an agent and pay him a commission. Nothing is free any more to sell itself or give itself away. These days, Countess, every cabbage has its pimp.

COUNTESS. I can't believe that.

THE RAGPICKER. Countess, little by little, the pimps have taken over the world. They don't do anything, they don't make anything—they just stand there and take their cut. It makes a difference. Look at the shopkeepers. Do you ever see one smiling at a customer any more? Certainly not. Their smiles are strictly for the pimps. The butcher has to smile at the meat-pimp, the florist at the rose-pimp, the grocer at the fresh-fruit-and-vegetable-pimp. It's all organized down to the slightest detail. A pimp for bird-seed. A pimp for fishfood. That's why the cost of living keeps going up all the time. You buy a glass of beer—it costs twice as much as it used to. Why? 10 percent for the glass-pimp, 10 percent for the beer-pimp, 20 percent for the glass-of-beer-pimp—that's where our money goes. Personally, I prefer the old-fashioned type. Some of those men at least were loved by the women they sold. But what feelings can a pimp arouse in a leg of lamb? Pardon my language, Irma.

COUNTESS. It's all right. She doesn't understand it.

THE RAGPICKER. So now you know, Countess, why the world is no longer happy. We are the last of the free people of the earth. You saw them looking us over today. Tomorrow, the street singer will start paying the song-pimp, and the garbage-pimp will be after me. I tell you, Countess, we're finished. It's the end of free enterprise in this world!

COUNTESS. Is this true, Roderick?

PIERRE. I'm afraid it's true.

COUNTESS. Did you know about this, Irma?

IRMA. All I know is the doorman says that faith is dead.

DOORMAN. I've stopped taking bets over the phone.

JUGGLER. The very air is different, Countess. You can't trust it any more. If I throw my torches up too high, they go out.

THE RAGPICKER. The sky-pimp puts them out.

FLOWER GIRL. My flowers don't last over night now. They wilt.

JUGGLER. Have you noticed, the pigeons don't fly any more?

THE RAGPICKER. They can't afford to. They walk.

COUNTESS. They're a lot of fools and so are you! You should have told me at once! How can you bear to live in a world where there is unhappiness? Where a man is not his own master? Are you cowards? All we have to do is to get rid of these men.

PIERRE. How can we get rid of them? They're too strong.

The SERGEANT *walks up again.*

COUNTESS (*smiling*). The Sergeant will help us.

SERGEANT. Who? Me?

IRMA. There are a great many of them, Countess. The Deaf-Mute knows them all. They employed him once, years ago, because he was deaf. (*The* DEAF-MUTE *wigwags a short speech.*) They fired him because he wasn't blind. (*Another flash of sign language.*) They're all connected like the parts of a machine.

COUNTESS. So much the better. We shall drive the whole machine into a ditch.

SERGEANT. It's not that easy, Countess. You never catch these birds napping. They change before your very eyes. I remember when I was in the detectives . . . You catch a president, pfft! He turns into a trustee. You catch him as trustee, and pfft! he's not a trustee—he's an honorary vice-chairman. You catch a Senator dead to rights: he becomes Minister of Justice. You get after the Minister of Justice—he is Chief of Police. And there you are—no longer in the detectives.

PIERRE. He's right, Countess. They have all the power. And all the money. And they're greedy for more.

COUNTESS. They're greedy? Ah, then, my friends, they're lost.

If they're greedy, they're stupid. If they're greedy—don't worry, I know exactly what to do. Roderick, by tonight you will be an honest man. And, Juggler, your torches will stay lit. And your beer will flow freely again, Martial. And the world will be saved. Let's get to work.

THE RAGPICKER. What are you going to do?

COUNTESS. Have you any kerosene in the house, Irma?

IRMA. Yes. Would you like some?

COUNTESS. I want just a little. In a dirty bottle. With a little mud. And some mange-cure,[4] if you have it. (*To the* DEAF-MUTE) Deaf-Mute! Take a letter. (IRMA *interprets in sign language. To the* SINGER) Singer, go and find Madame Constance. (IRMA *and the* WAITER *go into the café.*)

SINGER. Yes, Countess.

COUNTESS. Ask her to be at my house by two o'clock. I'll be waiting for her in the cellar. You may tell her we have to discuss the future of humanity. That's sure to bring her.

SINGER. Yes, Countess.

COUNTESS. And ask her to bring Mademoiselle Gabrielle and Madame Josephine with her. Do you know how to get in to speak to Madame Constance? You ring twice, and then meow three times like a cat. Do you know how to meow?

SINGER. I'm better at barking.

COUNTESS. Better practise meowing on the way. Incidentally, I think Madame Constance knows all the verses of your mazurka. Remind me to ask her.

SINGER. Yes, Countess. (*Exits.*)

IRMA *comes in. She is shaking the oily concoction in a little perfume vial, which she now hands the* COUNTESS.

IRMA. Here you are, Countess.

COUNTESS. Thanks, Irma. (*She assumes a presidential manner.*) Deaf-Mute! Ready?

IRMA *interprets in sign language. The* WAITER *has brought out a portfolio of letter paper and placed it on a table. The* DEAF-MUTE *sits down before it, and prepares to write.*

[4] **mange-cure:** skin disease medicine.

IRMA (*speaking for the* DEAF-MUTE). I'm ready.

COUNTESS. My dear Mr.—What's his name?

IRMA *wigwags the question to the* DEAF-MUTE, *who answers in the same manner. It is all done so deftly that it is as if the* DEAF-MUTE *were actually speaking.*

IRMA. They are all called Mr. President.

COUNTESS. My dear Mr. President: I have personally verified the existence of a spontaneous outcrop of oil in the cellar of Number 21 Rue de Chaillot, which is at present occupied by a dignified person of unstable mentality. (*The* COUNTESS *grins knowingly.*) This explains why, fortunately for us, the discovery has so long been kept secret. If you should wish to verify the existence of this outcrop for yourself, you may call at the above address at three P.M. today. I am herewith enclosing a sample so that you may judge the quality and consistency of the crude.[5] Yours very truly. Roderick, can you sign the Prospector's name?

PIERRE. You wish me to?

COUNTESS. One forgery wipes out the other.

PIERRE *signs the letter. The* DEAF-MUTE *types the address on an envelope.*

IRMA. Who is to deliver this?

COUNTESS. The Doorman, of course. On his bicycle. And as soon as you have delivered it, run over to the Prospector's office. Leave word that the President expects to see him at my house at three.

DOORMAN. Yes, Countess.

COUNTESS. I shall leave you now. I have many pressing things to do. Among others, I must press my red gown.

THE RAGPICKER. But this only takes care of two of them, Countess.

COUNTESS. Didn't the Deaf-Mute say they are all connected like the works of a machine?

IRMA. Yes.

COUNTESS. Then, if one comes, the rest will follow. And we shall have them all. My boa, please.

[5] **crude:** unrefined oil.

DOORMAN. The one that's stolen, Countess?

COUNTESS. Naturally. The one the Prospector stole.

DOORMAN. It hasn't turned up yet, Countess. But someone has left an ermine collar.

COUNTESS. Real ermine?

DOORMAN. Looks like it.

COUNTESS. Ermine and iris were made for each other. Let me see it.

DOORMAN. Yes, Countess.

Exit DOORMAN.

COUNTESS. Roderick, you shall escort me. You still look pale. I have some old Chartreuse at home. I always take a glass each year. Last year I forgot. You shall have it.

PIERRE. If there is anything I can do, Countess . . . ?

COUNTESS. There is a great deal you can do. There are all the things that need to be done in a room that no man has been in for twenty years. You can untwist the cord on the blind and let in a little sunshine for a change. You can take the mirror off the wardrobe door, and deliver me once and for all from the old harpy that lives in the mirror. You can let the mouse out of the trap. I'm tired of feeding it. (*To her friends*) Each man to his post. See you later, my friends. (*The* DOORMAN *puts the ermine collar around her shoulders.*) Thank you, my boy. It's rabbit. (*One o'clock strikes.*) Your arm, Valentine.

PIERRE. Valentine?

COUNTESS. It's just struck one. At one, all men become Valentine.

PIERRE (*he offers his arm*). Permit me.

COUNTESS. Or Valentino. It's obviously far from the same, isn't it, Irma? But they have that much choice. (*She sweeps out majestically with* PIERRE. *The others disperse. All but* IRMA.)

IRMA (*clearing off the table*). I hate ugliness. I love beauty. I hate meanness. I adore kindness. It may not seem so grand to some to be a waitress in Paris. I love it. A waitress meets all sorts of people. She observes life. I hate to be alone. I love people. But I have never said I love you to a man. Men try to make me say it. They put their arms around me—I pretend I don't see it. They pinch me—I pretend I don't feel it. They kiss me—I pretend I don't know it. They take me out in the evening and make me drink—but I'm careful, I never say it. If they don't like it, they can leave me alone. Because when I say I love you to Him, He will know just by looking in my eyes that many have held me and pinched me and kissed me, but I have never said I love you to anyone in the world before. Never. No. (*Looking off in the direction in which* PIERRE *has gone, she whispers softly*) I love you.

VOICE (*from within the café*). Irma!

IRMA. Coming. (*Exits.*)

ACT TWO

SCENE: *The cellar of the* COUNTESS' *house. An ancient vault set deep in the ground, with walls of solid masonry, part brick and part great ashlars, mossy and sweating. A staircase of medieval pattern is built into the thickness of the wall, and leads up to the street level from a landing halfway down. In the corners of the cellar are piled casks, packing cases, birdcages, and other odds and ends—the accumulation of centuries—the whole effect utterly fantastic.*

In the center of the vast underground room, some furniture has been arranged to give an impression of a sitting-room of the 1890's. There is a venerable chaise-longue piled with cushions that once were gay, three armchairs, a table with an oil lamp and a bowl of flowers, a shaggy rug. It is two P.M., *the same day.*

AT RISE: *The* COUNTESS *is sitting over a bit of mending, in one of the armchairs.* IRMA *appears on the landing and calls down.*

IRMA. Countess! The Sewer Man is here.

COUNTESS. Thank goodness, Irma. Send him down. (*The* SEWER MAN *enters. He carries his hip-boots in his hand.*) How do you do, Mr. Sewer Man? (*The* SEWER MAN *bows.*) But why do you have your boots in your hand instead of on your feet?

SEWER MAN. Etiquette, Countess. Etiquette.

COUNTESS. How very American! I'm told that Americans nowadays apologize for their gloves if they happen to take one's hand. As if the skin of a human were nicer to touch than the skin of a sheep! And particularly if they have sweaty hands . . . !

SEWER MAN. My feet never sweat, Countess.

COUNTESS. How very nice! But please don't stand on ceremony here. Put your boots on. Put them on.

SEWER MAN (*complying*). Thanks very much, Countess.

COUNTESS (*while he draws on his boots*). I'm sure you must have a very poor opinion of the upper world, from what you see of it. The way people throw their filth into your territory is absolutely scandalous! I burn all my refuse, and I scatter the ashes. All I ever throw in the drain is flowers. Did you happen to see a lily float by this morning? Mine. But perhaps you didn't notice?

SEWER MAN. We notice a lot more down there, Countess, than you might think. You'd be surprised the things we notice. There's lots of things come along that were obviously intended for us—little gifts, you might call them—sometimes a brand-new shaving brush—sometimes, *The Brothers Karamazov* . . . Thanks for the lily, Countess. A very sweet thought.

COUNTESS. Tomorrow you shall have this iris. But now, let's come to the point. I have two questions to ask you.

SEWER MAN. Yes, Countess?

COUNTESS. First—and this has nothing to do with our problem—it's just something that has been troubling me. . . . Tell me, is it true that the sewer men of Paris have a king?

SEWER MAN. Oh, now, Countess, that's another of those fairy tales out of the Sunday supplements. It just seems those writers can't keep their minds off the sewers! It fascinates them. They keep thinking of us moving around in our underground canals like gondoliers in Venice, and it sends them into a fever of romance! The things they say about us! They say we have a race of girls down there who never see the light of day! It's completely fantastic! The girls naturally come out—every Christmas and Easter. And orgies by torchlight with gondolas and guitars! With troops of rats that dance as they follow the piper! What nonsense! The rats are not allowed to dance. No, no, no. Of course we have no king. Down in the sewers, you'll find nothing but good Republicans.

COUNTESS. And no queen?

SEWER MAN. No. We may run a beauty contest down there once in a while. Or crown a mermaid Queen of the May. But no queen what you'd call a queen. And, as for these swimming races they talk so much about . . . possibly once in a while—in the summer—in the dog days . . .

COUNTESS. I believe you. I believe you. And now tell me. Do you remember that night I found you here in my cellar—looking very pale and strange—you were half-dead as a matter of fact—and I gave you some brandy . . .

SEWER MAN. Yes, Countess.

COUNTESS. That night you promised if ever I should need it—you would tell me the secret of this room.

SEWER MAN. The secret of the moving stone?

COUNTESS. I need it now.

SEWER MAN. Only the King of the Sewer Men knows this secret.

COUNTESS. I'm sure of it. I know most secrets, of course. As a matter of fact, I have three magic words that will open any door that words can open. I have tried them all—in various tones of voice. They don't seem to work. And this is a matter of life and death.

SEWER MAN. Look, Countess.

He locates a brick in the masonry, and pushes it. A huge block of stone slowly pivots and uncovers a trap from which a circular staircase winds into the bowels of the earth.

COUNTESS. Good heavens! Where do those stairs lead?

SEWER MAN. Nowhere.

COUNTESS. But they must go somewhere.

SEWER MAN. They just go down.

COUNTESS. Let's go and see.

SEWER MAN. No, Countess. Never again. That time you found me, I had a pretty close shave. I kept going down and around, and down and around for an hour, a year—I don't know. There's no end to it, Countess. Once you start you can't stop. . . . Your head begins to turn—you're lost. No—once you start down, there's no coming up.

COUNTESS. You came up.

SEWER MAN. I—I am a special case. Besides, I had my tools, my ropes. And I stopped in time.

COUNTESS. You could have screamed—shouted.

SEWER MAN. You could fire off a cannon.

COUNTESS. Who could have built a thing like this?

SEWER MAN. Paris is old, you know. Paris is very old.

COUNTESS. You don't suppose, by any chance, there is oil down there?

SEWER MAN. There's only death down there.

COUNTESS. I should have preferred a little oil too—or a vein of gold—or emeralds. You're quite sure there is nothing?

SEWER MAN. Not even rats.

COUNTESS. How does one lower this stone?

SEWER MAN. Simple. To open, you press here. And to close it, you push there. (*He presses the brick. The stone descends.*) Now there's two of us in the world that knows it.

COUNTESS. I won't remember long. Is it all right if I repeat my magic words while I press it?

SEWER MAN. It's bound to help.

IRMA *enters.*

IRMA. Countess, Madame Constance and Mademoiselle Gabrielle are here.

COUNTESS. Show them down, Irma. Thank you very much, Mr. Sewer Man.

SEWER MAN. Like that story about the steam laundry that's supposed to be running day and night in my sewer . . . I can assure you . . .

COUNTESS (*edging him toward the door*). Thank you very much.

SEWER MAN. Pure imagination! They never work nights. (*He goes off, bowing graciously.*)

CONSTANCE, *the Madwoman of Passy, and* GABRIELLE, *the Madwoman of St. Sulpice,*[6] *come down daintily.*

[6] ***Passy . . . St. Sulpice:*** fashionable sections of Paris.

CONSTANCE *is all in white. She wears an enormous hat graced with ostrich plumes, and a lavender veil.* GABRIELLE *is costumed with the affected simplicity of the 1880's. She is atrociously made up in a remorseless parody of blushing innocence, and she minces down the stairs with macabre coyness.*

CONSTANCE. Aurelia! Don't tell us they've found your feather boa?

GABRIELLE. You don't mean Adolphe Bertaut has proposed at last! I knew he would.

COUNTESS. How are you, Constance? (*She shouts.*) How are you, Gabrielle?

GABRIELLE. You needn't shout today, my dear. It's Wednesday. Wednesdays, I hear perfectly.

CONSTANCE. It's Thursday.

GABRIELLE. Oh, dear. Well, never mind. I'm going to make an exception just this once.

CONSTANCE (*to an imaginary dog who has stopped on the landing*). Come along, Dickie. Come along. And stop barking. What a racket you're making! Come on, darling—we've come to see the longest boa and the handsomest man in Paris. Come on.

COUNTESS. Constance, it's not a question of my boa today. Nor of poor Adolphe. It's a question of the future of the human race.

CONSTANCE. You think it has a future?

COUNTESS. Please don't make silly jokes. Sit down and listen to me. Today we must make a decision which may alter the fate of the world.

CONSTANCE. Couldn't we do it tomorrow? I want to wash my slippers. Now, Dickie—please!

COUNTESS. We haven't a moment to waste. Where is Josephine? Well, we'd best have our tea, and the moment Josephine comes . . .

GABRIELLE. Josephine is sitting on her bench in front of the palace waiting for President Wilson to come out. She says she's sorry, but she positively must see him today.

CONSTANCE. Dickie!

COUNTESS. What a pity! (*She gets the tea things from the side table, pours tea, and serves cake and honey.*) I wish she were here to help us. She has a first-class brain.

CONSTANCE. Go ahead, dear. We're listening. (*To* DICKIE) What is it, Dickie? You want to sit in Aunt Aurelia's lap. All right, darling. Go on. Jump, Dickie.

COUNTESS. Constance, we love you, as you know. And we love Dickie. But this is a serious matter. So let's stop being childish for once.

CONSTANCE. And what does that mean, if you please?

COUNTESS. It means Dickie. You know perfectly well that we love him and fuss over him just as if he were still alive. He's a sacred memory and we wouldn't hurt his feelings for the world. But please don't plump him in my lap when I'm settling the future of mankind. His basket is in the corner—he knows where it is, and he can just go and sit in it.

CONSTANCE. So you're against Dickie too! You too!

COUNTESS. Constance! I'm not in the least against Dickie! I adore Dickie. But you know as well as I that Dickie is only a convention with us. It's a beautiful convention—but it doesn't have to bark all the time. Besides, it's you that spoil him. The time you went to visit your niece and left him with me, we got on marvelously together. He didn't bark, he didn't tear things, he didn't even eat. But when you're with him, one can pay attention to nothing else. I'm not going to take Dickie in my lap at a solemn moment like this, no, not for anything in the world. And that's that!

GABRIELLE (*very sweetly*). Constance, dear, I don't mind taking him in my lap. He loves to sit in my lap, don't you, darling?

CONSTANCE. Kindly stop putting on angelic airs, Gabrielle. I know you very well. You're much too sweet to be sincere. There's plenty of times that I make believe that Dickie is here, when really I've left him home, and you cuddle and pet him just the same.

GABRIELLE. I adore animals.

CONSTANCE. If you adore animals, you shouldn't pet them when they're not there. It's a form of hypocrisy.

COUNTESS. Now, Constance, Gabrielle has as much right as you . . .

CONSTANCE. Gabrielle has no right to do what she does. Do

you know what she does? She invites *people* to come to tea with us. *People* whom we know nothing about. *People* who exist only in her imagination.

COUNTESS. You think that's not an existence?

GABRIELLE. I don't invite them at all. They come by themselves. What can I do?

CONSTANCE. You might introduce us.

COUNTESS. If you think they're only imaginary, there's no point in your meeting them, is there?

CONSTANCE. Of course they're imaginary. But who likes to have imaginary people staring at one? Especially strangers.

GABRIELLE. Oh, they're really very nice. . . .

CONSTANCE. Tell me just one thing, Gabrielle—are they here now?

COUNTESS. Am I to be allowed to speak? Or is this going to be the same as the argument about inoculating Josephine's cat, when we didn't get to the subject at all?

CONSTANCE. Never! Never! Never! I'll never give my consent to that. (*To* DICKIE) I'd never do a thing like that to you, Dickie sweet. . . . Oh, no! Oh, no! (*She begins to weep softly.*)

COUNTESS. Good heavens! Now we have her in tears. What an impossible creature! With the fate of humanity hanging in the balance! All right, all right, stop crying. I'll take him in my lap. Come, Dickie, Dickie.

CONSTANCE. No. He won't go now. Oh, how can you be so cruel? Don't you suppose I know about Dickie? Don't you think I'd rather have him here alive and woolly and frisking around the way he used to? You have your Adolphe. Gabrielle has her birds. But I have only Dickie. Do you think I'd be so silly about him if it wasn't that it's only by pretending that he's here all the time that I get him to come sometimes, really? Next time I won't bring him!

COUNTESS. Now let's not get ourselves worked up over nothing. Come here, Dickie. . . . Irma is going to take you for a nice walk. (*She rings her bell.*) Irma!

IRMA *appears on the landing.*

CONSTANCE. No. He doesn't want to go. Besides, I didn't bring him today. So there!

COUNTESS. Very well, then. Irma, make sure the door is locked.

IRMA. Yes, Countess. (*Exits.*)

CONSTANCE. What do you mean? Why locked? Who's coming?

COUNTESS. If you'd let me get a word in, you'd know by now. A terrible thing has happened. This morning, this very morning, exactly at noon . . .

CONSTANCE (*thrilled*). Oh, how exciting!

COUNTESS. Be quiet. This morning, exactly at noon, thanks to a young man who drowned himself in the Seine . . . Oh, yes, while I think of it—do you know a mazurka called *La Belle Polonaise?*

CONSTANCE. Yes, Aurelia.

COUNTESS. Could you sing it now? This very minute?

CONSTANCE. Yes, Aurelia.

COUNTESS. All of it?

CONSTANCE. Yes, Aurelia. But who's interrupting now, Aurelia?

COUNTESS. You're right. Well, this morning, exactly at noon, I discovered a horrible plot. There is a group of men who intend to tear down the whole city!

CONSTANCE. Is that all?

GABRIELLE. But I don't understand, Aurelia. Why should men want to tear down the city? It was they themselves who put it up.

COUNTESS. You are so innocent, my poor Gabrielle. There are people in the world who want to destroy everything. They have the fever of destruction. Even when they pretend that they're building, it is only in order to destroy. When they put up a new building, they quietly knock down two old ones. They build cities so that they can destroy the countryside. They destroy space with telephones and time with airplanes. Humanity is now dedicated to the task of universal destruction. I am speaking, of course, primarily of the male sex.

GABRIELLE (*shocked*). Oh . . . !

CONSTANCE. Aurelia! Must you talk sex in front of Gabrielle?

COUNTESS. There *are* two sexes.

CONSTANCE. Gabrielle is a virgin, Aurelia!

COUNTESS. Oh, she can't be as innocent as all that. She keeps canaries.

GABRIELLE. I think you're being very cruel about men, Aurelia. Men are big and beautiful, and as loyal as dogs. I preferred not to marry, it's true. But I hear excellent reports from friends who have had an opportunity to observe them closely.

COUNTESS. My poor darling! You are still living in a dream. But one day, you will wake up as I have, and then you will see what is happening in the world. The tide has turned, my dear. Men are changing back into beasts. They know it. They no longer try to hide it. There was once such a thing as manners. I remember a time when the hungriest was the one who took the longest to pick up his fork. The one with the broadest grin was the one who needed most to go to the . . . It was such fun to keep them grinning like that for hours. But now they no longer pretend. Just look at them—snuffling their soup like pigs, tearing their meat like tigers, crunching their lettuce like crocodiles! A man doesn't take your hand nowadays. He gives you his paw.

CONSTANCE. Would that trouble you so much if they turned into animals? Personally, I think it's a good idea.

GABRIELLE. Oh, I'd love to see them like that. They'd be sweet.

CONSTANCE. It might be the salvation of the human race.

COUNTESS (*to* CONSTANCE). You'd make a fine rabbit, wouldn't you?

CONSTANCE. I?

COUNTESS. Naturally. You don't think it's only the men who are changing? You change along with them. Husbands and wives together. We're all one race, you know.

CONSTANCE. You think so? And why would my poor husband have to be a rabbit if he were alive?

COUNTESS. Remember his front teeth? When he nibbled his celery?

CONSTANCE. I'm happy to say, I remember absolutely nothing about him. All I remember on that subject is the time that Father Lacordaire tried to kiss me in the park.

COUNTESS. Yes, yes, of course.

CONSTANCE. And what does that mean, if you please, "Yes, yes, of course"?

COUNTESS. Constance, just this once, look us in the eye and tell us truly—did that really happen or did you read about it in a book?

CONSTANCE. Now I'm being insulted!

COUNTESS. We promise you faithfully that we'll believe it all over again afterwards, won't we, Gabrielle? But tell us the truth this once.

CONSTANCE. How dare you question my memories? Suppose I said your pearls were false!

COUNTESS. They were.

CONSTANCE. I'm not asking what they were. I'm asking what they are. Are they false or are they real?

COUNTESS. Everyone knows that little by little, as one wears pearls, they become real.

CONSTANCE. And isn't it exactly the same with memories?

COUNTESS. Now do not let us waste time. I must go on.

CONSTANCE. I think Gabrielle is perfectly right about men. There are still plenty who haven't changed a bit. There's an old Senator who bows to Gabrielle every day when he passes her in front of the palace. And he takes off his hat each time.

GABRIELLE. That's perfectly true, Aurelia. He's always pushing an empty baby carriage, and he always stops and bows.

COUNTESS. Don't be taken in, Gabrielle. It's all make-believe. And all we can expect from these make-believe men is itself make-believe. They give us facepowder made of stones, sausages made of sawdust, shirts made of glass, stockings made of milk. It's all a vulgar pretence. And if that is the case, imagine what passes, these days, for virtue, sincerity, generosity and love! I warn you, Gabrielle, don't let this Senator with the empty baby carriage pull the wool over your eyes.

GABRIELLE. He's really the soul of courtesy. He seems very correct.

COUNTESS. Those are the worst. Gabrielle, beware! He'll make you put on black riding boots, while he dances the can-can around you, singing God knows what filth at the top of his voice. The very thought makes one's blood run cold!

GABRIELLE. You think that's what he has in mind?

COUNTESS. Of course. Men have lost all sense of decency. They are all equally disgusting. Just look at them in the evening, sitting at their tables in the café, working away in unison with their toothpicks, hour after hour, digging up roast beef, veal, onion . . .

CONSTANCE. They don't harm anyone that way.

COUNTESS. Then why do you barricade your door, and make your friends meow before you let them come up? Incidentally, we must make an interesting sight, Gabrielle and I, yowling together on your doorstep like a couple of tomcats!

CONSTANCE. There's no need at all for you to yowl together. One would be quite enough. And you know perfectly well why I have to do it. It's because there are murderers.

COUNTESS. I don't quite see what prevents murderers from meowing like anybody else. But why are there murderers?

CONSTANCE. Why? Because there are thieves.

COUNTESS. And why are there thieves? Why is there almost nothing but thieves?

CONSTANCE. Because they worship money. Because money is king.

COUNTESS. Ah—now we've come to it. Because we live in the reign of the Golden Calf. Did you realize that, Gabrielle? Men now publicly worship the Golden Calf!

GABRIELLE. How awful! Have the authorities been notified?

COUNTESS. The authorities do it themselves, Gabrielle.

GABRIELLE. Oh! Has anyone talked to the bishop?

COUNTESS. Nowadays only money talks to the bishop. And so you see why I asked you to come here today. The world has gone out of its mind. Unless we do something, humanity is doomed! Constance, have you any suggestions?

CONSTANCE. I know what I always do in a case like this. . . .

COUNTESS. You write to the Prime Minister.

CONSTANCE. He always does what I tell him.

COUNTESS. Does he ever answer your letters?

CONSTANCE. He knows I prefer him not to. It might excite gossip. Besides, I don't always write. Sometimes I wire. The time I told him about the Archbishop's frigidaire, it was by wire. And they sent a new one the very next day.

COUNTESS. There was probably a commission in it for someone. And what do you suggest, Gabrielle?

CONSTANCE. Now, how can she tell you until she's consulted her voices?

GABRIELLE. I could go right home and consult them, and we could meet again after dinner.

COUNTESS. There's no time for that. Besides, your voices are not real voices.

GABRIELLE (*furious*). How dare you say a thing like that?

COUNTESS. Where do your voices come from? Still from your sewing-machine?

GABRIELLE. Not at all. They've passed into my hot-water bottle. And it's much nicer that way. They don't chatter any more. They gurgle. But they haven't been a bit nice to me lately. Last night they kept telling me to let my canaries out. "Let them out. Let them out. Let them out."

CONSTANCE. Did you?

GABRIELLE. I opened the cage. They wouldn't go.

COUNTESS. I don't call that *voices*. Objects talk—everyone knows that. It's the principle of the phonograph. But to ask a hot-water bottle for advice is silly. What does a hot-water bottle know? No, all we have to consult here is our own judgment.

CONSTANCE. Very well then, tell us what you have decided. Since you're asking our opinion, you've doubtless made up your mind.

COUNTESS. Yes, I've thought the whole thing out. All I really needed to discover was the source of the infection. Today I found it.

CONSTANCE. Where?

COUNTESS. You'll see soon enough. I've baited a trap. In just a few minutes, the rats will be here.

GABRIELLE (*in alarm*). Rats!

COUNTESS. Don't be alarmed. They're still in human form.

GABRIELLE. Heavens! What are you going to do with them?

COUNTESS. That's just the question. Suppose I get these wicked men all here at once—in my cellar—have I the right to exterminate them?

GABRIELLE. To kill them? (COUNTESS *nods.*)

CONSTANCE. That's not a question for us. You'll have to ask Father Bridet.

COUNTESS. I have asked him. Yes. One day, in confession, I told him frankly that I had a secret desire to destroy all wicked people. He said: "By all means, my child. And when you're ready to go into action, I'll lend you the jawbone of an ass."

CONSTANCE. That's just talk. You get him to put that in writing.

GABRIELLE. What's your scheme, Aurelia?

COUNTESS. That's a secret.

CONSTANCE. It's not so easy to kill them. Let's say you had a tank full of vitriol all ready for them. You could never get them to walk into it. There's nothing so stubborn as a man when you want him to do something.

COUNTESS. Leave that to me.

CONSTANCE. But if they're killed, they're bound to be missed, and then we'll be fined. They fine you for every little thing these days.

COUNTESS. They won't be missed.

GABRIELLE. I wish Josephine were here. Her sister's husband was a lawyer. She knows all about these things.

COUNTESS. Do you miss a cold when it's gone? Or the germs that caused it? When the world feels well again, do you think it will regret its illness? No, it will stretch itself joyfully, and it will smile—that's all.

CONSTANCE. Just a moment! Gabrielle, are they here now? Yes or no?

COUNTESS. What's the matter with you now?

CONSTANCE. I'm simply asking Gabrielle if her friends are in the room or not. I have a right to know.

GABRIELLE. I'm not allowed to say.

CONSTANCE. I know very well they are. I'm sure of it. Otherwise you wouldn't be making faces.

COUNTESS. May I ask what difference it makes to you if her friends are in the room?

CONSTANCE. Just this: If they're here, I'm not going to say another word! I'm certainly not going to commit myself in a matter involving the death sentence in the presence of third parties, whether they exist or not.

GABRIELLE. That's not being very nice to my guests, is it?

COUNTESS. Constance, you must be mad! Or are you so stupid as to think that just because we're alone, there's nobody with us? Do you consider us so boring or repulsive that of all the millions of beings, imaginary or otherwise, who are prowling about in space, there's not one who might possibly enjoy spending a little time with us? On the contrary, my dear—my house is full of guests always. They know that here they have a place in the universe where they can come when they're lonely and be sure of a welcome. For my part, I'm delighted to have them.

GABRIELLE. Thank you, Aurelia.

CONSTANCE. You know perfectly well, Aurelia . . .

COUNTESS. I know perfectly well that at this moment the whole universe is listening to us—and that every word we say echoes to the remotest star. To pretend otherwise is the sheerest hypocrisy.

CONSTANCE. Then why do you insult me in front of everybody? I'm not mean. I'm shy. I feel timid about giving an opinion in front of such a crowd. Furthermore, if you think I'm so bad and so stupid, why did you invite me, in the first place?

COUNTESS. I'll tell you. And I'll tell you why, disagreeable as you are, I always give you the biggest piece of cake and my best honey. It's because when you come there's always someone with you—and I don't mean Dickie—I mean someone who resembles you like a sister, only she's young and lovely, and she sits modestly to one side and smiles at me tenderly all the time you're bickering and quarreling, and never says a word. That's the Constance to whom I give the cake that you gobble, and it's because of her that you're here today, and it's her vote that I'm asking you to cast in this crucial moment. And not yours, which is of no importance whatever.

CONSTANCE. I'm leaving.

COUNTESS. Be so good as to sit down. I can't let her go yet.

CONSTANCE (*crossing toward the stairs*). No. This is too much. I'm taking her with me.

IRMA *enters.*

IRMA. Madame Josephine.
COUNTESS. Thank heaven!
GABRIELLE. We're saved.

JOSEPHINE, *the Madwoman of La Concorde,*[7] *sweeps in majestically in a get-up somewhere between the regal and the priestly.*

JOSEPHINE. My dear friends, today once again, I waited for President Wilson—but he didn't come out.
COUNTESS. You'll have to wait quite a while longer before he does. He's been dead since 1924.
JOSEPHINE. I have plenty of time.
COUNTESS. In anyone else, Josephine, these extravagances might seem a little childish. But a person of your judgment doubtless has her reasons for wanting to talk to a man to whom no one would listen when he was alive. We have a legal problem for you. Suppose you had all the world's criminals here in this room. And suppose you had a way of getting rid of them forever. Would you have the right to do it?
JOSEPHINE. Why not?
COUNTESS. Exactly my point.
GABRIELLE. But, Josephine, so many people!
JOSEPHINE. *De minimis non curat lex!*[8] The more there are, the more legal it is. It's impersonal. It's even military. It's the cardinal principle of battle—you get all your enemies in one place, and you kill them all together at one time. Because if you had to track them down one by one in their houses and offices, you'd get tired, and sooner or later you'd stop. I believe your idea is very practical, Aurelia. I can't imagine why we never thought of it before.
GABRIELLE. Well, if you think it's all right to do it. . . .
JOSEPHINE. By all means. Your criminals have had a fair trial, I suppose?
COUNTESS. Trial?
JOSEPHINE. Certainly. You can't kill anybody without a trial.

[7] ***La Concorde:*** the central square of Paris.
[8] ***De minimis non curat lex:*** The law takes no account of trifles.

That's elementary. "No man shall be deprived of his life, liberty and property without due process of law."

COUNTESS. They deprive us of ours.

JOSEPHINE. That's not the point. You're not accused of anything. Every accused—man, woman or child—has the right to defend himself at the bar of justice. Even animals. Before the Deluge, you will recall, the Lord permitted Noah to speak in defense of his fellow mortals. He evidently stuttered. You know the result. On the other hand, Captain Dreyfus[9] was not only innocent—he was defended by a marvelous orator. The result was precisely the same. So you see, in having a trial, you run no risk whatever.

COUNTESS. But if I give them the slightest cause for suspicion —I'll lose them.

JOSEPHINE. There's a simple procedure prescribed in such cases. You can summon the defendants by calling them three times—mentally, if you like. If they don't appear, the court may designate an attorney who will represent them. This attorney can then argue their case to the court, *in absentia*,[10] and a judgment can then be rendered, *in contumacio*.[11]

COUNTESS. But I don't know any attorneys. And we have only ten minutes.

GABRIELLE. Hurry, Josephine, hurry!

JOSEPHINE. In case of emergency, it is permissible for the court to order the first passer-by to act as attorney for the defense. A defense is like a baptism. Absolutely indispensable, but you don't have to know anything to do it. Ask Irma to get you somebody. Anybody.

COUNTESS. The Deaf-Mute?

JOSEPHINE. Well—that's getting it down a bit fine. That might be questionable on appeal.

COUNTESS (*calls*). Irma! What about the Police Sergeant?

JOSEPHINE. He won't do. He's under oath to the state.

IRMA *appears.*

[9] **Captain Dreyfus:** French officer whose unjust trial for treason stirred French political, social, and intellectual life in the 1890's.

[10] ***in absentia:*** in the absence (of the person concerned).

[11] ***in contumacio:*** *in contumaciam;* in contempt (of court).

IRMA. Yes, Countess?

COUNTESS. Who's out there, Irma?

IRMA. All our friends, Countess. There's the Ragpicker and . . .

COUNTESS. Send down the Ragpicker.

CONSTANCE. Do you think it's wise to have all those millionaires represented by a ragpicker?

JOSEPHINE. It's a first-rate choice. Criminals are always represented by their opposites. Murderers, by someone who obviously wouldn't hurt a fly. Rapists, by a member of the League for Decency. Experience shows it's the only way to get an acquittal.

COUNTESS. But we must not have an acquittal. That would mean the end of the world!

JOSEPHINE. Justice is justice, my dear.

The RAGPICKER *comes down, with a stately air. Behind him, on the landing, appear the other* VAGABONDS.

THE RAGPICKER. Greetings, Countess. Greetings, ladies. My most sincere compliments.

COUNTESS. Has Irma told you . . . ?

THE RAGPICKER. She said something about a trial.

COUNTESS. You have been appointed attorney for the defense.

THE RAGPICKER. Terribly flattered, I'm sure.

COUNTESS. You realize, don't you, how much depends on the outcome of this trial?

JOSEPHINE. Do you know the defendants well enough to undertake the case?

THE RAGPICKER. I know them to the bottom of their souls. I go through their garbage every day.

CONSTANCE. And what do you find there?

THE RAGPICKER. Mostly flowers.

GABRIELLE. It's true, you know, the rich are always surrounded with flowers.

CONSTANCE. How beautiful!

COUNTESS. Are you trying to prejudice the court?

THE RAGPICKER. Oh no, Countess, no.

COUNTESS. We want a completely impartial defense.

THE RAGPICKER. Of course, Countess, of course. Permit me to make a suggestion.

COUNTESS. Will you preside, Josephine?

THE RAGPICKER. Instead of speaking as attorney, suppose you let me speak directly as defendant. It will be more convincing, and I can get into it more.

JOSEPHINE. Excellent idea. Motion granted.

COUNTESS. We don't want you to be too convincing, remember.

THE RAGPICKER. Impartial, Countess, impartial.

JOSEPHINE. Well? Have you prepared your case?

THE RAGPICKER. How rich am I?

JOSEPHINE. Millions. Billions.

THE RAGPICKER. How did I get them? Theft? Murder? Embezzlement?

COUNTESS. Most likely.

THE RAGPICKER. Do I have a wife? A mistress?

COUNTESS. Everything.

THE RAGPICKER. All right. I'm ready.

GABRIELLE. Will you have some tea?

THE RAGPICKER. Is that good?

CONSTANCE. Very good for the voice. The Russians drink nothing but tea. And they talk like anything.

THE RAGPICKER. All right. Tea.

JOSEPHINE (*to the* VAGABONDS). Come in. Come in. All of you. You may take places. The trial is public. (*The* VAGABONDS *dispose themselves on the steps and elsewhere.*) Your bell, if you please, Aurelia.

COUNTESS. But what if I should need to ring for Irma?

JOSEPHINE. Irma will sit here, next to me. If you need her, she can ring for herself. (*To the* POLICE SERGEANT *and the* POLICEMAN) Conduct the accused to the bar. (*The officers conduct the* RAGPICKER *to a bar improvised with a rocking chair and a packing case marked FRAGILE. The* RAGPICKER *mounts the box. She rings the bell.*) The court is now in session. (*All sit.*) Counsel for the defense, you may take the oath.

THE RAGPICKER. I swear to tell the truth, the whole truth, and nothing but the truth, so help me God.

JOSEPHINE. Nonsense! You're not a witness. You're an attorney. It's your duty to lie, conceal and distort everything, and slander everybody.

THE RAGPICKER. All right. I swear to lie, conceal and distort everything, and slander everybody.

JOSEPHINE (*rings stridently*). Quiet! Begin.

THE RAGPICKER. May it please the honorable, august and elegant Court . . .

JOSEPHINE. Flattery will get you nowhere. That will do. The defense has been heard. Cross-examination.

COUNTESS. Mr. President . . .

THE RAGPICKER (*bowing with dignity*). Madame.

COUNTESS. Do you know what you are charged with?

THE RAGPICKER. I can't for the life of me imagine. My life is an open book. My ways are known to all. I am a pillar of the church and the sole support of the Opera. My hands are spotless.

COUNTESS. What an atrocious lie! Just look at them!

CONSTANCE. You don't have to insult the man. He's only lying to please you.

COUNTESS. Be quiet, Constance! You don't get the idea at all. (*To the* RAGPICKER) You are charged with the crime of worshipping money.

THE RAGPICKER. Worshipping money? Me?

JOSEPHINE. Do you plead guilty or not guilty? Which is it?

THE RAGPICKER. Why, Your Honor . . .

JOSEPHINE. Yes or no?

THE RAGPICKER. Yes or no? No! I don't worship money, Countess. Heavens, no! Money worships me. It adores me. It won't let me alone. It's damned embarrassing, I can tell you.

JOSEPHINE. Kindly watch your language.

COUNTESS. Defendant, tell the Court how you came by your money.

THE RAGPICKER. The first time money came to me, I was a mere boy, a little golden-haired child in the bosom of my dear family. It came to me suddenly in the guise of a gold brick which, in my innocence, I picked out of a garbage can one day while playing. I was horrified, as you can imagine. I immediately tried to get rid of it by swapping it for a little rundown one-track railroad which, to my consternation, at once sold itself for a hundred times its value. In a desperate effort to get rid of this money, I began to buy things. I bought the Northern Refineries, the Galeries Lafayette,[12] and the Schneider-Creusot Munition Works. And now I'm stuck

[12] **Galeries Lafayette:** one of the largest department stores in Paris.

with them. It's a horrible fate—but I'm resigned to it. I don't ask for your sympathy, I don't ask for your pity—all I ask for is a little common human understanding. . . . (*He begins to cry.*)

COUNTESS. I object. This wretch is trying to play on the emotions of the Court.

JOSEPHINE. The Court has no emotions.

THE RAGPICKER. Everyone knows that the poor have no one but themselves to blame for their poverty. It's only just that they should suffer the consequences. But how is it the fault of the rich if they're rich?

COUNTESS. Dry your tears. You're deceiving nobody. If, as you say, you're ashamed of your money, why is it you hold onto it with such a death-grip?

THE RAGPICKER. Me?

STREET PEDDLER. You never part with a franc!

JUGGLER. You wouldn't even give the poor Dear-Mute a sou!

THE RAGPICKER. Me, hold onto money? What slander! What injustice! What a thing to say to me in the presence of this honorable, august and elegant Court! I spend all my time trying to spend my money. If I have tan shoes, I buy black ones. If I have a bicycle, I buy a motor car. If I have a wife, I buy . . .

JOSEPHINE (*rings*). Order!

THE RAGPICKER. I dispatch a plane to Java for a bouquet of flowers. I send a steamer to Egypt for a basket of figs. I send a special representative to New York to fetch me an ice-cream cone. And if it's not just exactly right, back it goes. But no matter what I do, I can't get rid of my money! If I play a hundred to one shot, the horse comes in by twenty lengths. If I throw a diamond in the Seine, it turns up in the trout they serve me for lunch. Ten diamonds—ten trout. Well, now, do you suppose I can get rid of forty millions by giving a sou to a deaf-mute? Is it even worth the effort?

CONSTANCE. He's right.

THE RAGPICKER. Ah! You see, my dear? At last, there is somebody who understands me! Somebody who is not only beautiful, but extraordinarily sensitive and intelligent.

COUNTESS. I object!

JOSEPHINE. Overruled!

THE RAGPICKER. I should be delighted to send you some flowers, Miss—directly I'm acquitted. What flowers do you prefer?

CONSTANCE. Roses.

THE RAGPICKER. You shall have a bale every morning for the next five years. Money means nothing to me.

CONSTANCE. And amaryllis.

THE RAGPICKER. I'll make a note of the name. (*In his best lyrical style*) The lady understands, ladies and gentlemen. The lady is no fool. She's been around and she knows what's what. If I gave the Deaf-Mute a franc, twenty francs, twenty million francs—I still wouldn't make a dent in the forty times a thousand million francs that I'm afflicted with! Right, little lady?

CONSTANCE. Right.

JOSEPHINE. Proceed.

THE RAGPICKER. Like on the Stock Exchange. If *you* buy a stock, it sinks at once like a plummet. But if *I* buy a stock, it turns around and soars like an eagle. If I buy it at 33 . . .

PEDDLER. It goes up to a thousand.

THE RAGPICKER. It goes to twenty thousand! That's how I bought my twelve chateaux, my twenty villas, my 234 farms. That's how I endow the Opera and keep my twelve ballerinas.

FLOWER GIRL. I hope every one of them deceives you every moment of the day!

THE RAGPICKER. How can they deceive me? Suppose they try to deceive me with the male chorus, the general director, the assistant electrician or the English horn—I own them all, body and soul. It would be like deceiving me with my big toe.

CONSTANCE. Don't listen, Gabrielle.

GABRIELLE. Listen to what?

THE RAGPICKER. No. I am incapable of jealousy. I have all the women—or I can have them, which is the same thing. I get the thin ones with caviar—the fat ones with pearls . . .

COUNTESS. So you think there are no women with morals?

THE RAGPICKER. I mix morals with mink—delicious combination. I drip pearls into protests. I adorn resistance with rubies. My touch is jeweled; my smile, a motor car. What woman can withstand me? I lift my little finger—and do they fall?—Like leaves in autumn—like tin cans from a second-story window.

CONSTANCE. That's going a little too far!

COUNTESS. You see where money leads.

THE RAGPICKER. Of course. When you have no money, nobody trusts you, nobody believes you, nobody likes you. Because to have money is to be virtuous, honest, beautiful and witty. And to be without is to be ugly and boring and stupid and useless.

COUNTESS. One last question. Suppose you find this oil you're looking for. What do you propose to do with it?

THE RAGPICKER. I propose to make war! I propose to conquer the world!

COUNTESS. You have heard the defense, such as it is. I demand a verdict of guilty.

THE RAGPICKER. What are you talking about? Guilty? I? I am never guilty!

JOSEPHINE. I order you to keep quiet.

THE RAGPICKER. I am never quiet!

JOSEPHINE. Quiet, in the name of the law!

THE RAGPICKER. I am the law. When I speak, that is the law. When I present my backside, it is etiquette to smile and to apply the lips respectfully. It is more than etiquette—it is a cherished national privilege, guaranteed by the Constitution.

JOSEPHINE. That's contempt of court. The trial is over.

COUNTESS. And the verdict?

ALL. Guilty!

JOSEPHINE. Guilty as charged.

COUNTESS. Then I have full authority to carry out the sentence?

ALL. Yes!

COUNTESS. I can do what I like with them?

ALL. Yes!

COUNTESS. I have the right to exterminate them?

ALL. Yes!

JOSEPHINE. Court adjourned!

COUNTESS (*to the* RAGPICKER). Congratulations, Ragpicker. A marvelous defense. Absolutely impartial.

THE RAGPICKER. Had I known a little before, I could have

done better. I could have prepared a little speech, like the time I used to sell the Miracle Spot Remover. . . .

JOSEPHINE. No need for that. You did very well, extempore. The likeness was striking and the style reminiscent of Clemenceau.[13] I predict a brilliant future for you. Good-bye, Aurelia. I'll take our little Gabrielle home.

CONSTANCE. I'm going to walk along the river. (*To* DICKIE) Oh! So here you are. And your ear all bloody! Dickie! Have you been fighting again? Oh, dear . . . !

COUNTESS (*to the* RAGPICKER). See that she gets home all right, won't you? She loses everything on the way. And in the queerest places. Her prayer book in the butcher shop. And her corset in church.

THE RAGPICKER (*bowing and offering his arm*). Permit me, Madame.

STREET SINGER. Oh, Countess—my mazurka. Remember?

COUNTESS. Oh, yes. Constance, wait a moment. (*To the* SINGER) Well? Begin.

SINGER (*sings*).

Do you hear, Mademoiselle,
Those musicians of hell?

CONSTANCE. Why, of course, it's *La Belle Polonaise. . . .* (*She sings*)

From Poland to France
Comes this marvelous dance,
So gracious,
Audacious,
Will you foot it, perchance?

SINGER. I'm saved!

JOSEPHINE (*reappearing at the head of the stairs*).

Now my arm I entwine
Round these contours divine,
So pure, so impassioned,
Which Cupid has fashioned. . . .

GABRIELLE (*reappearing also, she sings a quartet with the others*).

[13] **Clemenceau:** statesman and politician of the Third French Republic, noted for his publications in defense of Dreyfus and for his leadership in World War I.

Come, let's dance the mazurka, that devilish measure,
'Tis a joy that's reserved to the gods for their pleasure—
Let's gallop, let's hop,
With never a stop,
My blonde Polish miss,
Let our heads spin and turn
As the dance-floor we spurn—
There was never such pleasure as this! (*They all exit, dancing.*)

IRMA. It's time for your afternoon nap.

COUNTESS. But suppose they come, Irma!

IRMA. I'll watch out for them.

COUNTESS. Thank you, Irma. I *am* tired. (*She smiles.*) Did you ever see a trial end more happily in your life?

IRMA. Lie down and close your eyes a moment.

The COUNTESS *stretches out on the chaise-longue and shuts her eyes.* IRMA *tiptoes out. In a moment,* PIERRE *comes down softly, the feather boa in his hands. He stands over the chaise-longue, looking tenderly down at the sleeping woman, then kneels beside her and takes her hand.*

COUNTESS (*without opening her eyes*). Is it you, Adolphe Bertaut?

PIERRE. It's only Pierre.

COUNTESS. Don't lie to me, Adolphe Bertaut. These are your hands. Why do you complicate things always? Say that it's you.

PIERRE. Yes. It is I.

COUNTESS. Would it cost you so much to call me Aurelia?

PIERRE. It's I, Aurelia.

COUNTESS. Why did you leave me, Adolphe Bertaut? Was she so very lovely, this Georgette of yours?

PIERRE. No. You are a thousand times lovelier.

COUNTESS. But she was clever.

PIERRE. She was stupid.

COUNTESS. It was her soul, then, that drew you? When you looked into her eyes, you saw a vision of heaven, perhaps?

PIERRE. I saw nothing.

COUNTESS. That's how it is with men. They love you because

you are beautiful and clever and soulful—and at the first opportunity they leave you for someone who is plain and dull and soulless. But why does it have to be like that, Adolphe Bertaut? Why?

PIERRE. Why, Aurelia?

COUNTESS. I know very well she wasn't rich. Because when I saw you that time at the grocer's, and you snatched the only good melon from right under my nose, your cuffs, my poor friend, were badly frayed. . . .

PIERRE. Yes. She was poor.

COUNTESS. "Was" poor? Is she dead then? If it's because she's dead that you've come back to me—then no. Go away. I will not take their leavings from the dead. I refuse to inherit you. . . .

PIERRE. She's quite well.

COUNTESS. Your hands are still the same, Adolphe Bertaut. Your touch is young and firm. Because it's the only part of you that has stayed with me. The rest of you is pretty far gone, I'm afraid. I can see why you'd rather not come near me when my eyes are open. It's thoughtful of you.

PIERRE. Yes. I've aged.

COUNTESS. Not I. I am young because I haven't had to live down my youth, like you. I have it with me still, as fresh and beautiful as ever. But when you walk now in the park at Colombes with Georgette, I'm sure . . .

PIERRE. There is no longer a park at Colombes.

COUNTESS. Is there a park still at St. Cloud? Is there a park at Versailles? I've never gone back to see. But I think, if they could move, those trees would have walked away in disgust the day you went there with Georgette. . . .

PIERRE. They did. Not many are left.

COUNTESS. You take her also, I suppose, to hear *Denise?*[14]

PIERRE. No one hears *Denise* any more.

COUNTESS. It was on the way home from *Denise*, Adolphe Bertaut, that I first took your arm. Because it was windy and it was late. I have never set foot in that street again. I go the other way round. It's not easy, in the winter, when there's ice. One is quite apt to fall. I often do.

[14] ***Denise:*** a vaudeville show.

PIERRE. Oh, my darling—forgive me.

COUNTESS. No, never. I will never forgive you. It was very bad taste to take her to the very places where we'd been together.

PIERRE. All the same, I swear, Aurelia . . .

COUNTESS. Don't swear. I know what you did. You gave her the same flowers. You bought her the same chocolates. But has she any left? No. I have all your flowers still. I have twelve chocolates. No, I will never forgive you as long as I live.

PIERRE. I always loved you, Aurelia.

COUNTESS. You "loved" me? Then you too are dead, Adolphe Bertaut?

PIERRE. No. I love you. I shall always love you, Aurelia.

COUNTESS. Yes. I know. That much I've always known. I knew it the moment you went away, Adolphe, and I knew that nothing could ever change it. Georgette is in his arms now—yes. But he loves me. Tonight he's taken Georgette to hear *Denise*—yes. But he loves me. . . . I know it. You never loved her. Do you think I believed for one moment that absurd story about her running off with the osteopath? Of course not. Since you didn't love her, obviously she stayed with you. And, after that, when she came back, and I heard about her going off with the surveyor—I knew that couldn't be true, either. You'll never get rid of her, Adolphe Bertaut —never. Because you don't love her.

PIERRE. I need your pity, Aurelia. I need your love. Don't forget me. . . .

COUNTESS. Farewell, Adolphe Bertaut. Farewell. Let go my hand, and give it to little Pierre. (PIERRE *lets go her hand, and after a moment takes it again. The* COUNTESS *opens her eyes.*) Pierre? Ah, it's you. Has he gone?

PIERRE. Yes, Countess.

COUNTESS. I didn't hear him go. Oh, he knows how to make a quick exit, that one. (*She sees the boa.*) Good heavens! Wherever did you find it?

PIERRE. In the wardrobe, Countess. When I took off the mirror.

COUNTESS. Was there a purple felt shopping bag with it?

PIERRE. Yes, Countess.

COUNTESS. And a little child's sewing box?

PIERRE. No, Countess.

COUNTESS. Oh, they're frightened now. They're trembling for their lives. You see what they're up to? They're quietly putting back all the things they have stolen. I never open that wardrobe, of course, on account of the old woman in the mirror. But I have sharp eyes. I don't need to open it to see what's in it. Up to this morning, that wardrobe was empty. And now—you see? But, dear me, how stupid they are! The one thing I really miss is my little sewing box. It's something they stole from me when I was a child. They haven't put it back? You're quite sure?

PIERRE. What was it like?

COUNTESS. Green cardboard with paper lace and gold stamping. I got it for Christmas when I was seven. They stole it the very next day. I cried my eyes out every time I thought of it—until I was eight.

PIERRE. It's not there, Countess.

COUNTESS. The thimble was gilt. I swore I'd never use any other. Look at my poor fingers. . . .

PIERRE. They've kept the thimble too.

COUNTESS. Splendid! Then I'm under no obligation to be merciful. Put the boa around my neck, Pierre. I want them to see me wearing it. They'll think it's a real boa.

IRMA *runs in excitedly.*

IRMA. Here they come, Countess! You were right—it's a procession. The street is full of limousines and taxis!

COUNTESS. I will receive them. (*As* PIERRE *hesitates to leave her.*) Don't worry. There's nothing to be frightened of. (PIERRE *goes out.*) Irma, did you remember to stir the kerosene into the water?

IRMA. Yes, Countess. Here it is.

COUNTESS (*looking critically at the bottle*). You might as well pour in what's left of the tea. (IRMA *shakes up the liquid.*) Don't forget, I'm supposed to be deaf. I want to hear what they're thinking.

IRMA. Yes, Countess.

COUNTESS (*putting the finishing touches to her make-up*). I don't have to be merciful—but, after all, I do want to be just. . . .

IRMA goes up to the landing and exits. As soon as she is alone, the COUNTESS presses the brick, and the trap door opens. There is a confused sound of auto horns in the street above, and the noise of an approaching crowd.

IRMA (*offstage*). Yes, Mr. President. Come in, Mr. President. You're expected, Mr. President. This way, Mr. President. (*The* PRESIDENTS *come down, led by the* PRESIDENT. *They all look alike, are dressed alike, and all have long cigars.*) The Countess is quite deaf, gentlemen. You'll have to shout. (*She announces.*) The presidents of the boards of directors!

THE PRESIDENT. I had a premonition, Madame, when I saw you this morning, that we should meet again. (*The* COUNTESS *smiles vaguely. He continues, a tone louder.*) I want to thank you for your trust. You may place yourself in our hands with complete confidence.

SECOND PRESIDENT. Louder. The old trot[15] can't hear you.

THE PRESIDENT. I have a letter here, Madame, in which . . .

SECOND PRESIDENT. Louder. Louder.

THIRD PRESIDENT (*shouting*). Is it true that you've located . . . ? (*The* COUNTESS *stares at him blankly. He shouts at the top of his voice.*) Oil? (*The* COUNTESS *nods with a smile, and points down. The* PRESIDENT *produces a legal paper and a fountain pen.*) Sign here.

COUNTESS. What is it? I haven't my glasses.

THE PRESIDENT. Your contract. (*He offers the pen.*)

COUNTESS. Thank you.

SECOND PRESIDENT (*normal voice*). What is it?

THIRD PRESIDENT. Waiver of all rights. (*He takes it back signed.*) Thank you. (*He hands it to the* SECOND PRESIDENT.) Witness. (*The* SECOND PRESIDENT *witnesses it. The* PRESIDENT *passes it on to the* THIRD PRESIDENT.) Notarize. (*The paper is notarized. The* PRESIDENT *turns to the* COUNTESS *and shouts*) My congratulations. And now, Madame— (*He produces a gold brick wrapped in tissue paper.*) If you'll show us the well, this package is yours.

COUNTESS. What is it?

THE PRESIDENT. Pure gold. Twenty-four karat. For you.

COUNTESS. Thank you very much (*She takes it.*) It's heavy.

[15] **trot:** crone; withered old woman.

SECOND PRESIDENT. Are you going to give her that?

THE PRESIDENT. Don't worry. We'll pick it up again on the way out. (*He shouts at the* COUNTESS, *pointing at the trap door.*) Is this the way?

COUNTESS. That's the way.

The SECOND PRESIDENT *tries to slip in first. The* PRESIDENT *pulls him back.*

THE PRESIDENT. Just a minute, Mr. President. After me, if you don't mind. And watch those cigars. It's oil, you know.

But as he is about to descend, the COUNTESS *steps forward.*

COUNTESS. Just one moment . . .

THE PRESIDENT. Yes?

COUNTESS. Did any of you happen to bring along a little sewing box?

THE PRESIDENT. Sewing box? (*He pulls back another impatient* PRESIDENT.) Take it easy.

COUNTESS. Or a little gold thimble?

THE PRESIDENT. Not me.

THE PRESIDENTS. Not us.

COUNTESS. What a pity!

THE PRESIDENT. Can we go down now?

COUNTESS. Yes. You may go down now. Watch your step!

They hurry down eagerly. When they have quite disappeared, IRMA *appears on the landing and announces the next echelon.*

IRMA. Countess, the Prospectors.

COUNTESS. Heavens! Are there more than one?

IRMA. There's a whole delegation.

COUNTESS. Send them down.

The PROSPECTOR *comes in, following his nose.*

IRMA. Come in, please.

THE PROSPECTOR (*sniffing the air like a bloodhound*). I smell something. . . . Who's that?

IRMA. The Countess. She is very deaf.

THE PROSPECTOR. Good.

The PROSPECTORS *also look alike. Sharp clothes, Western hats, and long noses. They crowd down the stairs after the* PROSPECTOR, *sniffing in unison. The* PROSPECTOR *is especially talented. He casts about on the scent until it leads him to the decanter on the table. He pours himself a glass, drinks it off, and belches with much satisfaction. The others join him at once, and follow his example. They all belch in unison.*

THE PROSPECTORS. Oil?

THE PROSPECTOR. Oil!

COUNTESS. Oil.

THE PROSPECTOR. Traces? Puddles?

COUNTESS. Pools. Gushers.

SECOND PROSPECTOR. Characteristic odor? (*He sniffs.*)

THE PROSPECTOR. Chanel Number 5. Nectar! Undoubtedly—the finest—rarest! (*He drinks.*) Sixty gravity crude: straight gasoline! (*To the* COUNTESS) How found? By blast? Drill?

COUNTESS. By finger.

THE PROSPECTOR (*whipping out a document*). Sign here, please.

COUNTESS. What is it?

THE PROSPECTOR. Agreement for dividing the profits . . . (*The* COUNTESS *signs.*)

SECOND PROSPECTOR (*to* FIRST PROSPECTOR). What is it?

THE PROSPECTOR (*pocketing the paper*). Application to enter a lunatic asylum. Down there?

COUNTESS. Down there.

The PROSPECTORS *go down, sniffing.* IRMA *enters.*

IRMA. The gentlemen of the press are here.

COUNTESS. The rest of the machine! Show them in.

IRMA. The Public Relations Counsellors! (*They enter, all shapes and sizes, all in blue pin-striped suits and black homburg hats.*) The Countess is very deaf, gentlemen. You'll have to shout!

FIRST PRESS AGENT. You don't say— Delighted to make the acquaintance of so charming and beautiful a lady . . .

SECOND PRESS AGENT. Louder. She can't hear you.

FIRST PRESS AGENT. What a face! (*Shouts*) Madame, we are the press. You know our power. We fix all values. We set all standards. Your entire future depends on us.

COUNTESS. How do you do?

FIRST PRESS AGENT. What will we charge the old trull?[16] The usual thirty?

SECOND PRESS AGENT. Forty.

THIRD PRESS AGENT. Sixty.

FIRST PRESS AGENT. All right—seventy-five. (*He fills in a form and offers it to the* COUNTESS.) Sign here, Countess. This contract really gives you a break.

COUNTESS. That is the entrance.

FIRST PRESS AGENT. Entrance to what?

COUNTESS. The oil well.

FIRST PRESS AGENT. Oh, we don't need to see that, Madame.

COUNTESS. Don't need to see it?

FIRST PRESS AGENT. No, no—we don't have to see it to write about it. We can imagine it. An oil well is an oil well. "That's oil we know on earth, and oil we need to know." (*He bows.*)

COUNTESS. But if you don't see it, how can you be sure the oil is there?

FIRST PRESS AGENT. If it's there, well and good. If it's not, by the time we get through, it will be. You underestimate the creative aspect of our profession, Madame. (*The* COUNTESS *shakes her head, handing back the papers.*) I warn you, if you insist on rubbing our noses in this oil, it will cost you 10 percent extra.

COUNTESS. It's worth it. (*She signs. They cross toward the trap door.*)

SECOND PRESS AGENT (*descending*). You see, Madame, we of the press can refuse a lady nothing.

THIRD PRESS AGENT. Especially, such a lady. (*He starts down.*)

SECOND PRESS AGENT (*going down. Gallantly*). It's plain to see, Madame, that even fountains of oil have their nymphs. . . . I can use that somewhere. That's copy!

The PRESS AGENTS *go down. As he disappears, the* FIRST PRESS AGENT *steals the gold brick and blows a kiss gallantly to the* COUNTESS, *who blows one back.*

[16] **trull:** morally loose woman.

There is a high-pitched chatter offstage, and IRMA *comes in, trying hard to hold back* THREE WOMEN *who pay no attention to her whatever. These* WOMEN *are tall, slender, and as soulless as if they were molded of wax. They march down the steps, erect and abstracted like animated window models, but chattering incessantly.*

IRMA. But, ladies, please—you have no business here—you are not expected. (*To the* COUNTESS) There are some strange ladies coming. . . .

COUNTESS. Show them in, Irma. (*The* WOMEN *come down, without taking the slightest interest in their surroundings.*) Who are you?

FIRST WOMAN. Madame, we are the most powerful pressure group in the world.

SECOND WOMAN. We are the ultimate dynamic.

THIRD WOMAN. The mainspring of all combinations.

FIRST WOMAN. Nothing succeeds without our assistance. Is that the well, Madame?

COUNTESS. That is the well.

FIRST WOMAN. Put out your cigarettes, girls. We don't want any explosions. Not with my brand-new eyelashes.

They go down, still chattering. The COUNTESS *crosses to the wall to close the trap. As she does so, there is a commotion on the landing.*

IRMA. Countess . . . (*A* MAN *rushes in breathlessly.*)

MAN. Just a minute! Just a minute! (*He rushes for the trap door.*)

COUNTESS. Wait! Who are you?

MAN. I'm in a hurry. Excuse me. It's my only chance! (*He rushes down.*)

COUNTESS. But . . . (*But he is gone. She shrugs her shoulders, and presses the brick. The trap closes. She rings the bell for* IRMA.) My gold brick! Why, they've stolen my gold brick! (*She moves toward the trap. It is now closed.*) Well, let them take their god with them.

IRMA *enters and sees with astonishment that the stage is empty of all but the* COUNTESS. *Little by little, the scene is suffused with light, faint at first, but increasing as if the very walls were glowing with the quiet radiance of universal joy. Only around the closed trap a shadow lingers.*

IRMA. But what's happened? They've gone! They've vanished!

COUNTESS. They've evaporated, Irma. They were wicked. Wickedness evaporates.

PIERRE *enters. He is followed by the* VAGABONDS, *all of them. The new radiance of the world is now very perceptible. It glows from their faces.*

PIERRE. Oh, Countess . . . !

WAITER. Countess, everything's changed. Now you can breathe again. Now you can see.

PIERRE. The air is pure! The sky is clear!

IRMA. Life is beautiful again.

THE RAGPICKER (*rushes in*). Countess—the pigeons! The pigeons are flying!

FLOWER GIRL. They don't have to walk any more.

THE RAGPICKER. They're flying. . . . The air is like crystal. And young grass is sprouting on the pavements.

COUNTESS. Is it possible?

IRMA (*interpreting for the* DEAF-MUTE). Now, Juggler, you can throw your fireballs up as high as you please—they won't go out.

SERGEANT. On the street, utter strangers are shaking hands, they don't know why, and offering each other almond bars!

COUNTESS. Oh, my friends . . .

WAITER. Countess, we thank you. . . .

They go on talking with happy and animated gestures, but we no longer hear them, for their words blend into a strain of unearthly music which seems to thrill from the uttermost confines of the universe. And out of this music comes a voice.

FIRST VOICE. Countess . . . (*Only the* COUNTESS *hears it. She turns from the group of* VAGABONDS *in wonder.*)

SECOND VOICE. Countess . . .

THIRD VOICE. Countess . . . (*As she looks up in rapture, the* FIRST VOICE *speaks again.*)

FIRST VOICE. Countess, we thank you. We are the friends of animals.

SECOND VOICE. We are the friends of people.

THIRD VOICE. We are the friends of friendship.

FIRST VOICE. You have freed us!

SECOND VOICE. From now on, there will be no hungry cats. . . .

THIRD VOICE. And we shall tell the Duchess her dog's right name!

The VOICES *fade off. And now another group of voices is heard.*

FIRST VOICE. Countess, we thank you. We are the friends of flowers.

SECOND VOICE. From now on, every plant in Paris will be watered. . . .

THIRD VOICE. And the sewers will be fragrant with jasmine!

These voices, too, are silent. For an instant, the stage is vibrant with music. Then the DEAF-MUTE *speaks, and his voice is the most beautiful of all.*

DEAF-MUTE. Sadness flies on the wings of the morning, and out of the heart of darkness comes the light.

Suddenly a group of figures detaches itself from the shadows. These are exactly similar in face and figure and in dress. They are shabby in the fashion of 1900 and their cuffs are badly frayed. Each bears in his hand a ripe melon.

FIRST ADOLPHE BERTAUT. Countess, we thank you. We, too, are freed at last. We are the Adolphe Bertauts of the world.

COUNTESS. Good. (*She puts the bones into her basket and starts for the stairs.*) Well, let's get on to more important things. Four o'clock. My poor cats must be starved. What a bore for them if humanity had to be saved every afternoon. They don't think much of it, as it is.

INTERPRETATION

1. Unlike *The Rivals* and *Arms and the Man,* in which the problems of young love occupied the foreground of the action, *The Madwoman of Chaillot* focuses on the activities of a member of the older generation, the Madwoman herself. In what way is the main plot served by the love story of Pierre and Irma? Aside from the fact that a comedy usually has a pair of lovers in it, is there another reason for the inclusion of Pierre and Irma?

2. There are two basic groups of characters, those who are with the Madwoman and those who are against her. What are the contrasting characteristics of each group? In what way does the cast of characters reflect the real world? What is Giraudoux' method of endowing them with an aura of fantasy? How many different human types are represented? With whom do you most strongly identify?

3. What colors do you imagine when you think of seeing this play in a theater? In what way do the moods of the two settings contrast with each other? What details of decor would be suitable to the Madwoman's cellar?

Describe the range of styles possible in the costumes of the play. Although the play is set in the post-World War II era, the Madwoman is described as "dressed in the grand fashion of 1885." Why did the author choose to dress her in the clothes of 1885? What quality would this kind of costume bring to the play?

4. Do any of the circumstances or events of the play remind you of the world of today? Does the play confront any of the permanent problems of human nature? In what spirit are we intended to understand the Madwoman's solution to the problem of evil? Are there people in the news today who share any of the ideas and attitudes expressed in the play?

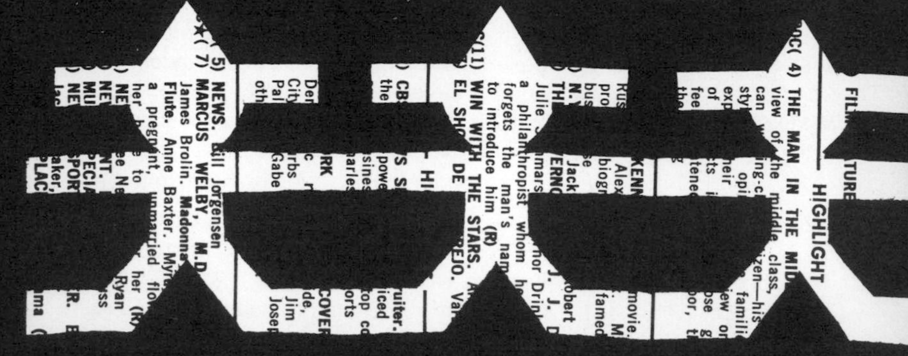

Captain Fantastic Meets the Ectomorph

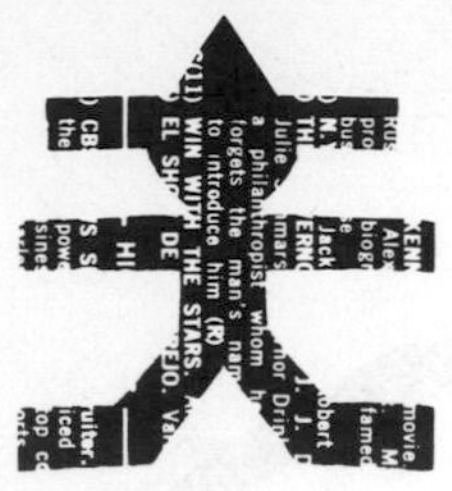

The term "dark comedy" usually describes a play in which comic characters or situations are used to achieve complex effects which are only partly comic. Although writers of the past, including Euripides and Shakespeare, have written dark comedies, a number of modern authors have made this style their specialty. Such playwrights as Samuel Beckett, Eugene Ionesco, Harold Pinter, and Edward Albee rely heavily on comedy in creating dramatic works which emphasize the loneliness and futility of human life. In the theater, dark comedies can be excruciatingly funny, but they rarely leave an audience in that mood of reconciliation and harmony which characterizes traditional comedy. The writer of dark comedy uses laughter as a two-edged sword, both to ridicule the vanity of human striving and to celebrate the mere fact, meaningless or not, of being alive. Christopher Fry, the English playwright, once wrote that laughter is "the surest touch of genius in the creation." The laughter of dark comedy seems ironically to affirm that genius in the very act of mockery.

In *Captain Fantastic Meets the Ectomorph* the author, Barry Pritchard, demonstrates the absurdity of the human struggle for dignity. The play contains elements of pop farce and social satire in depicting a cruel contest of oneupmanship which brings out the worst of both characters in this two-character play. As we laugh at the ridiculousness of Fredrick Regent and Rex Crain we also slowly learn of the despair to which they have been driven by the hollowness of their lives. Both men have lost all sense of their value as individual human beings and appear to see the meaning of life in the clichés of the mass media and the advertising business. Is this all that modern life has to offer? Can a sense of accomplishment only be had by destroying another human being, as Rex Crain finally does? Pritchard raises these disturbing questions at the same time that he delights us with the absurd behavior of two bizarre characters on a Los Angeles rooftop.

Captain Fantastic Meets the Ectomorph

BARRY PRITCHARD

Characters

FREDRICK REGENT, in his early 40's
REX CRAIN, in his early 30's

SCENE: *A summer night. The roof of an apartment building in Los Angeles. The outlines of other buildings and the city can be seen in the background.*

TIME: *The present.*

A hatch, off to one side, opens slowly and FREDRICK REGENT *comes up through it and out onto the roof. He is a big man, handsome and powerfully built, dressed in a neat fashionable summer suit, a summer hat and wearing thick-rimmed glasses. He looks uncertainly about, then walks to the edge of the roof and peers cautiously over the side down to the street. He draws back sharply at what he sees and moves hastily inland and paces nervously. He stops suddenly as he seems to reach a decision. He removes his glasses and puts them in his breast pocket. He removes his hat and places it at his feet. Then piece by piece he removes all the rest of his outer clothing, arranging it in a neat pile and revealing underneath a costume not unlike that of the comic-strip character Superman. There is an emblem on the front of the costume that encloses the initials "C.F.," which stand for Captain Fantastic. He stands sadly for a moment then turns and goes again to the edge of the roof. He avoids looking over the side and seems about to jump. Suddenly, he remembers something, comes down off the ledge, goes to his suit, gets a pad of paper and a ball-point pen and returns to the ledge where he sits and begins to write. He only writes a few words when the pen runs out of ink. He looks at it, shakes it and tries again without success.*

FREDRICK (*wearily*). Goddamn it.

He goes back to his clothing and begins looking through it for a pen or pencil but can't find anything to write with. He sighs, crumples the piece of paper and tosses it away. He hears someone else coming through the hatch and goes quickly to the edge of the roof and mounts the ledge. He seems about to plunge over and makes several false starts, but like a swimmer hesitating before diving into an icy stream, cannot quite bring himself to do it.

During this, REX CRAIN, *a thin young man with a severe case of acne emerges from the hatch, pulling a partially filled duffle bag after him. He sees* FREDRICK *poised on the ledge and becomes immediately alarmed.*

REX (*going quickly to edge of roof*). Hey! Hey, what're ya' doin'? Hey, hold it for cryin' out loud!

FRED (*desperately*). Get out of here! (*Still can't make himself jump.*)

REX. Listen, don't be stupid. (*Recognition*) Hey, I know you. You're Captain Fantastic on television . . . Fredrick, uh, whatzizname . . . Fredrick Regent. . . .

FRED. Leave me alone!

REX. I'll be darned, Mr. Regent, what're you doing up here?

FRED (*sobbing*). Goddamn it. . . .

REX. Gee, imagine that, me and Captain Fantastic on the same roof! (*Shakes his head in wonder.* FREDRICK *strains.*) What is it, some kind of publicity stunt or somethin', huh? Hey listen, do me a favor, would'ja and hold it for just a sec so I can get a picture of this. (*Goes to duffle bag, takes out a flash camera and quickly begins adjusting it.*) This'll just take a sec. (*Coming in close and focusing on* FRED.) O.K., we're just about all set here . . . Could ya' look a little more, you know, determined or heroic or somethin'? Ya' look a little down in the dumps . . . Okie doakie, any time you're ready . . . go 'head . . . O.K. . . .

FRED (*breaking, he slumps to his knees in despair*). I . . . can't. . . .

REX. O.K., all set. . . .

FRED (*sobbing*). I can't do it . . . I can't do it. . . .

REX (*disappointed*). Aw, heck, (*Resigned*) Oh well, somethin's better than nothin', I guess.

Snaps picture of FRED *kneeling on the ledge. The sudden explosion of the flashbulb so startles* FRED *that he falls over the side and is saved from plummeting to the street below only by desperately clinging to the rim of the ledge.*

FRED (*dangling*). Help . . . oh God, please help me . . . please . . . I don't want to die. . . .

REX (*focusing camera*). Just hold it a sec. . . .

FRED (*desperately*). Please . . . help me . . . I want to live . . . please, I'll do anything . . . PLEASE!

REX. Aw for. . . . (*Puts down camera and helps* FRED.)

FRED (*near collapse*). Thank you . . . thank you. . . .

REX. Jeez, it's lucky I was here. (FRED *makes it over the ledge and collapses inside on the roof. He sits in a heap, panting and sobbing.*) Think of the picture I missed. Do you know the *Daily News* pays ten bucks for dramatic pictures like that?

FRED. I'll . . . pay . . . you. . . .

REX. Aw, it isn't only the money in a thing like this. Shoot, they'd probably put my picture in the paper, too. (*He goes to his duffle bag, removes a portable watercooler and paper cup, pours a cup of water and takes it to* FRED.) Here—ya' want a drink of water?

FRED (*taking it gratefully*). Thanks. . . .

REX (*moves about looking at* FRED *from different angles—regarding him as something of a curiosity*). Boy, you sure are different in real life than you are on TV, Mr. Regent. (*No answer*) Would you mind if I call ya' Fredrick? I mean, considering I just saved your life and all? (FRED *indifferently waves consent.*) Gee, thanks a lot Fredrick; I'll really get a boot out of this. I've never talked to any movie or TV stars before, so as you can imagine, this is really a pretty big thrill for me. Don't worry, I won't ask ya' any embarrassin' questions or anything like that. I just want to be able to say that we were up here talkin' together . . . (*Tentatively, not wanting to overextend himself*) Maybe even that we're acquaintances . . . (*No reaction—he tries it one further.*) Even . . . friends, sorta. . . . (*He takes silence for acceptance of this definition and relaxes a little, smiling.*) As a normal, average human being I take a great deal of interest in you stars. You know, I just like to try to figure out what it is that makes you people tick. So . . . (*There doesn't seem to be any more to say but the silence makes him uncomfortable and he feels he must say something.*) Once I followed Jayne Mansfield's laundry truck all the way across town. I didn't get to see anything though. Everything was all bundled up. Still. . . . (*He sighs and becomes uncomfortably silent.*)

FRED (*weakly*). I couldn't do it . . . I just couldn't go through with it. . . .

REX (*awed*). Were you really going to . . . ?

FRED. I thought I'd made up my mind . . . but I couldn't do it. . . .

REX. It's lucky for you I just happened to come along.

FRED. Thanks.

REX. How come ya' got all dressed up in your Captain Fantastic outfit? (FRED *shakes his head.*) Say, just in case this gets in the newspapers and they want to know who I am, my name's Rex Crain. C-R-A-I-N. (*Pause*) My friends call me something else which I'm not gonna tell ya' what it is because it makes me so mad. (*No reaction*) I mean, it's *interesting*, ya' understand, it's just that it's cruel and ended up by givin' me an inferiority complex. (*No response*) I don't know when it started, but this nickname I'm tellin' ya' about is based on an unfortunate skin condition that I happen to have. You probably noticed. (*No response*) Well, since it's really not fair to get your curiosity up and then not tell ya', I'm gonna tell ya' what this nickname is that I was tellin' ya' about. (*No response*) What they call me is Pimples. Can ya' imagine the insensitivity of some people? (FRED *continues lost in his own thoughts.*) See, it's based on this acne condition I got all over my face. Boy, talk about jumpin' off of roofs, that's *nothin'* compared to what I've thought of doin' to myself because of the emotional problems this thing has caused me. Boy, have I got emotional problems!

So if ya' don't want to get me upset, just don't call me Pimples.

FRED. Can I have some more water? (*Holds out cup.*)

REX. Sure, as much as ya' want. (*Fills cup, hands it back to* FRED.)

FRED. Thanks. (*Drinks.*)

REX. What the heck, it's nothin'. To tell the truth, it's my pleasure. Like I said, I never talked to any movie star before.

FRED. Some movie star.

REX. As a matter of fact, ya' might say I'm sorta in show biz myself. (*He waits in vain for a reaction. Receiving none, he suppresses a slight irritation.*) You sure don't talk much, do ya'?

FRED. Leave me alone.

REX. Sure I get it: "I vahnt to be alone." (*Shakes his head—walks aimlessly about the roof.*) Anyway, my line of work, it's not actually show biz but it *does* come under the entertainment category so in a way it's related—What I do is, I'm a yo-yo demonstrator. (*Pause*) Yeah, an honest-to-God professional. You might even have caught my act.

FRED. Afraid not.

REX. Oh, I don't mean in a theater or anything like that—on street corners, near schools. See, I go to these different grammar schools, say about three, three-thirty in the afternoon, just when the kids are gettin' out for the day, and stand on a corner there and very casually, I start fooling around with my yo-yo . . . (*He takes a yo-yo from his pocket and begins to work it.*) So I do a few tricks. (*He performs a few tricks with the yo-yo.*)

FRED (*becoming reluctantly interested—momentarily forgetting about himself*). That's pretty good.

REX. Aw, well, it comes with practice. I been working on it a long time now. (*Continues doing tricks.*) So, in no time at all I got fifty or a hundred kids standin' around watchin' me. I get a little fancy. (*He does some tricks that are more elaborate.*) They're eating it up. By God, ya' can't get a better audience than kids—or more honest. If you're lousy, they let ya' know it. But if you got it, they love ya'. As you can probably tell, I got it. Pretty soon I say to one of 'em—you try it. Then another one tries it, then another one. Pretty soon, all of 'em want to try it. So I show 'em how to do a few simple tricks—you know—"Walk the doggie," "rock-a-by-baby"—old standards. Then I say, okay, you practice these tricks and I'll come back one week from today and we'll have a contest. And the winner gets the golden yo-yo. Ah, they love me. So a week later I come back, we hold the contest, and the winner gets the golden yo-yo. (*Takes a golden yo-yo from his pocket, works it once and puts it away.*)

FRED (*guardedly*). This is how you make a living!

REX. Sure. See, it's the yo-yo manufacturers that hire me. They know just what day I go to each school and they stock all the stores in the area. They sell 'em like hot cakes. I mean it figures, if the kids are gonna practice up for the big contest, they got to have a yo-yo to practice with.

FRED. Yeah, I guess so.

REX. Sure, it's a million dollar business. Then when the yo-yos get stale, we come back with somethin' else—hula-hoops, frisbees—there's always somethin' new.

FRED. That's very . . . interesting.

REX (*shrugs*). Well, it's creative, that's what I like about it. Then there's always the kids.

FRED (*sadly appreciative*). Yeah, the kids.

REX (*warmly*). Boy, you said it. There's nothing like 'em. The energy, the enthusiasm, the imagination, that open quality —ya' know what I mean? Ask an honest question, ya' get an honest answer. None of this fakey business.

FRED. Yeah.

REX (*pause*). The stinking part about it is they have to grow up. Boy, that's what frosts me.

FRED. Oh well, everybody's got to grow up.

REX. Yeah? Well, it's a pretty goddamn stupid setup if ya' ask me.

FRED. I don't think there's much that can be done about it. That's just the way. . . .

REX. Well *somebody* oughta do *somethin'* about it.

FRED. Like what?

REX. I don't know what . . . just . . . *somethin'*.

FRED. Well I don't see. . . .

REX. Ah, don't tell me. I see it happen all the time—right

before my eyes practically. Eight, nine, ten years old—beautiful kids, innocent, lovely, clean. Then in the next year or so something starts to happen to them already—they start to get smart, think they know somethin'. Practically overnight, they get shifty-eyed, can't look atcha when they're talkin'. Filthy thoughts on their minds—I can tell by the way they look. Acch, it's terrible! Don't tell me there's any God when he invents a system like this—a bunch of monsters.

FRED. (*dropping it*). Yeah, well. . . .

REX (*gesturing over the side to the people below*). Sure, look at 'em. A bunch of finks. *Dirty* finks. Dirty *old* finks!

FRED (*to himself*). That's the kind of fan I attract.

REX (*with a firmness of purpose he sets his watercooler on the ledge, takes some paper sacks from his duffle bag and begins filling one of them with water from the cooler. He glances appreciatively up at the sky*). Ah, a bomber's moon—an honest-to-God bomber's moon! (*He bunches together the sack at the top, holds it over the side of the building, takes aim on a target below and releases it.*) Die you bastards! (*He makes the whistling sound of a falling bomb.*) Ahhh, stupid bloody wind—missed a mile. (*He begins filling another sack.*)

FRED. What're you doing?

REX. Come on—help yourself. (*Drops another sack over the side.*) The phantom strikes again!

FRED. Hey, quit that!

REX *excitedly fills another sack. He is about to drop it but* FRED *comes quickly up to him and strikes him on the arm, knocking him backwards.* REX *stumbles against the watercooler, knocking it over the side.*

REX. Ow!

FRED (*making a desperate lunge to save the watercooler*). Hey!

REX. My watercooler! What'a ya' think you're doin'!

FRED (*looking over the side*). My God, you almost hit somebody!

REX. It was you did it, not me.

FRED. You could've killed somebody.

REX (*pulling back from ledge*). Get back, get back—somebody'll see us.

FRED (*beginning to panic*). God, you ruined everything—now they'll all be up here.

REX. Naw, don't worry, nobody saw us. It coulda fallen out of a hundred different windows. They won't know where it came from.

FRED. Do you think so?

REX. Sure, it happens all the time. Los Angeles is full of nuts.

FRED (*calming down*). Yeah, I guess you're right.

REX. Jeez, my watercooler.

FRED. A lot your watercooler matters if somebody got killed.

REX (*rubbing his arm*). You really hit hard. (*Impressed*) Boy, you sure are strong.

FRED (*depressed by this*). Yeah, that's me all right, big and strong. No brains, but plenty of muscle.

REX. That's the way to be all right, then nobody pushes ya' around. When you're a skinny little runt like me everybody tries to take advantage of ya'.

FRED. That's all I ever had, looks and muscle, and now they're going.

REX. God, I tried everything to build myself up. I ate 'til I was ready to explode, I squeezed those little rubber balls to get muscles in my arms, I even drank beer, which I hate. God, I drank gallons of it.

FRED (*pinches a roll of fat around his middle*). Look at that. That's middle age. If I go off my diet or stop exercising for so much as a couple of days I start to sag all over.

REX. Beer, ugh! It makes me sick to think how much of it I drank.

FRED. A couple more years I'll just be a blob anyway, so what's the difference?

REX. I even tried one of those muscle-building courses ya' send away for advertised on the back of comic books.

FRED. The human blob.

REX. You know, where the bully on the beach comes up and kicks sand in your face and steals your girl. That's me, the 97-pound weakling.

FRED. No career, no self-respect, nothin'.

REX. Only I never had no girl to steal. Where's a guy like me gonna get a girl?

FRED. Finally I figured, there's nothing left for me; I might as well get it over with. (*He sinks his head into his hands.*)

REX. So I said to myself, by golly, I'll do it—I'll gamble a five-cent stamp and see if dynamic tension doesn't change my life. Five-cent stamp, huh! You should see what that set me back by the time I was through. Oh, I went the whole route. But d'ya think it did any good? Just take a look at me, there's your answer. (*Pause—they both brood.*) And then there's my acne. That's a whole other chapter. (*Shakes his head*) Naw, I guess there's nothing can be done about it—I'm stuck with what I am. (*Pause*) But just once I'd like to get one of those finks and pay him back. Pow! (*He strikes an imaginary adversary.*) Crunch! (*He begins to shadowbox now and this turns into a complete annihilation of his imaginary foe by beating him to death in pantomime. When he finishes he is breathing hard, a look of bitter satisfaction on his face. He sits on the ledge near* FRED.) No sir, don't feel bad about bein' strong. That's what counts in this world.

FRED (*shakes his head*). I'm not strong. I'm not anything. I can't even look anybody in the eye anymore.

REX. Ah, what're ya' talkin' about? You got nothin' to feel bad over. You're rich, famous, and ya' got a career—what more could ya' want?

FRED. Money doesn't mean anything. When I had money I wasn't happy anyway. And my career—that's done for.

REX. Whata ya' mean, done for?

FRED (*sighs, and then slowly*). About two months ago the head of the studio calls me in. "Freddy," he says, "I've got good news for you—we've decided to stop making the Captain Fantastic series."

REX. Where do they get off? They can't do that.

FRED (*shrugs*). Well, they've got over a thousand segments in the can and. . . .

REX. In the can?

FRED. On film.

REX. Oh I get it—show biz talk.

FRED. With a backlog like that they can re-run 'em forever.

REX. Well what about when those are done? They'll need new ones.

FRED. By the time they get through with all those there'll be a whole new audience of kids old enough so they can start all over again. There's no end to it.

REX. We'll just see about that. The fans won't stand for it.

FRED. Where does that leave me, I said to him. I've been playing Captain Fantastic for over fifteen years now—where do I go from here? "Why Freddy," he says, "that's the best part of it. This sets you free so you can go on to better things. You don't want to play Captain Fantastic all your life. You're getting a little older now—find yourself some parts that aren't quite so strenuous."

REX. That ungrateful rat!

FRED. Well, fat chance of finding anything else after playing Captain Fantastic for more than fifteen years. You're hopelessly typed. Nobody'll touch ya' with a ten foot pole for other roles.

REX. Sure, that's show biz.

FRED. Oh, I tried; don't think I didn't try. I called everybody I ever met in the last ten years to see if they might have something for me. But it was the same old story: you can't change the image after all this time.

REX. A fine bunch of fair-weather friends.

FRED. It isn't their fault, that's just the way things are. But still, that doesn't make it any easier on me. I mean, where do I go from here?

REX. Listen Fredrick, don't you worry about that. All we need to do is sound the call and your fans will raise an overwhelming cry of protest that'll warm the cockles of your heart.

FRED. I don't even care about that anymore—that was only the beginning. (*Pause*) About a week ago, just when things were at their worst, I get an invitation to this party. I don't mean just any old party—I mean this is from the king of Hollywood himself. You know who I mean.

REX (*impressed*). No kiddin'!

FRED. I mean, after all these years of being totally ignored by these guys, here comes a special invitation from the chief himself. What the hell, I figure they might even want me for a part in some movie, now I wasn't doing the Captain Fantastic bit anymore. They run the whole shebang, y'know; they call their own shots.

REX. Makes perfectly good sense. I mean, they write their own ticket.

FRED. But no, I got delusions of grandeur. They don't want me for a part in any movie. I'm not even invited to the party really.

REX. So then what's the invitation all about?

FRED. See, it's not exactly a regular party, it's a . . . stag party. (*Swallows*) The reason they ask me there is . . . well see, everybody knows I play Captain Fantastic and . . . what they want me to do is . . . during the entertainment . . . to pop out of this cake . . . Oh God. . . .

REX (*nods, not understanding*). You mean, dressed up like Captain Fantastic?

FRED. Yeah. Well, not exactly. They wanted me . . . they wanted me to dress . . . like a go-go girl.

REX. Oh, I see. (*Pause*) You mean with. . . . (*He gestures, indicating a female figure.*)

FRED. Yeah, you got the idea. It was just sort of . . . a joke.

REX. Captain Fantastic dressed like a go-go girl! What kind of a joke is that? It's disgusting!

FRED. And then . . . I get up on this pedestal . . . and perform. . . .

REX. You mean . . . right in front of all those people?

FRED (*nods slowly*). Accompanied by a rock 'n roll band. (*Slumps.*)

REX. Oh God! That's disgusting!

FRED. It sure is.

REX. Of all the perverted, immoral . . . ! Acch! It makes me sick! To think that these people dictate the trends and tastes in our entertainment! Of all the filthy, animal . . . Well, I hope you told 'em to go to hell, Fredrick. (*He looks at* FRED, *but* FRED *will not meet his eyes.*) You *did* tell 'em where to head, didn't you Fredrick? (FRED *shakes his head, no.*) Oh Fredrick. . . .

FRED. At first I said no—I was so surprised when they told me what they wanted me to do, I didn't know what to say . . . I just wanted to leave. But then they started to talk me into it. I don't know . . . they seemed like a bunch of regular guys, just wanted to have a lot of fun . . . made me feel right at home. I told 'em to get somebody else. They said I was the only one that would do, being Captain Fantastic and all—that was the whole point of the joke. They started giving me drinks—we were all laughing—it got so I was feeling like one of them. They were so funny and treated me so regular, it didn't seem like anything they could do would be so bad. After a while it started to seem like a pretty funny idea to me too, so . . . (*Slumps*) When it was over they gave me a thousand dollars.

REX. Christ!

FRED. But it wasn't the money really. It was just . . . they made it seem so . . . *funny* . . . like it was the thing to do if I ever wanted to be on the inside. Christ, don't ya' understand? For fifteen years I've been jumpin' around in this monkey suit while everybody else in the business laughed at me. For fifteen years I've been eating my heart out to be one of them while they wouldn't even acknowledge I was alive. Well, in some cock-eyed way I thought this was their way of accepting me. I thought, this is the way it happens. I don't know, maybe I was drunk or something, but I thought at last I'd arrived and that if I went along with the gag, they'd be . . . impressed.

REX (*a little self-consciously*). Are you pretty . . . impressive in a go-go costume, Fredrick?

FRED. Yeah, I must be. The next day I got three phone calls asking if I was available for other parties. On top of that, I got a movie offer. (*Pause*) You can imagine what kind of movie.

REX. Boy, news like that really travels fast. I know 'cause practically the same thing happened to me. Once, when I'm a kid in grammar school, there's this teacher, name of Mrs. Wooley—she's really got it in for me. Always keepin' me after school for no reason. She just doesn't like me. So one time after she's kept me after school, I'm so mad, I figure I'll get back at her. So I get this can of red paint, see, and on the side of the school I paint in big letters, "Mrs. Wooley sleeps in her underwear." Heh heh. You know, boys will be boys. Well, I figured nobody saw me and they wouldn't know who did it. But wow, the next day, I no sooner walk in the classroom—Mrs. Wooley's screamin' at me, I have to go down to the principal's office, I get expelled, my mother has to come to school . . . I don't know what all. (*Shakes his head.*) Boy, don't tell me.

FRED. If I was a big joke before, you can imagine what I am now. "Captain Fantastic: available for private parties and other informal gatherings." I'm just a bad joke.

REX. Yeah, I see what ya' mean. It really sounds like the end of the old road as far as you're concerned.

FRED. That's why I came up here. I'm as good as dead. I figured I might as well add the finishing touches. I wore the Captain Fantastic costume so they'd know why I did it.

REX. Under ordinary circumstances I'd do everything humanly possible to talk ya' out of it, but in your case, I dunno. . . . (*Goes to camera, begins adjusting it.*)

FRED. Christ, I can't even do that—I don't have the guts. Too stupid to live and too gutless to die. I'm nothing—just a vegetable.

REX. Well, as the man says, that's better than bein' a fruit. Heh, heh. (*Silence, as he adjusts camera.*) It's none of my business or anything like that. I mean, everybody knows you Hollywood stars got problems we normal folks don't have any idea about. But if you're gonna do something like this—you know, do yourself in—I'd just like to suggest that you try to pull it off with a little . . . dignity. Am I out of line? I mean, if ya' don't mind me sayin' so, a little while back, you just reduced yourself to a quivering blob. Now for a fan, that's a shattering experience. I mean, I was practically raised on Captain Fantastic. Since I was this high—on the radio, the Saturday matinee movie serial, on the TV . . . So you know, maybe a little dignity. Am I off limits? (FRED *stares at him blankly.*) Just once a single ounce of human dignity?

FRED (*pause—slowly shakes his head*). I can't do it. There's no other way, but I just can't do it.

REX (*unsuccessfully attempting to take the edge off of what he says by smiling*). You're really a Roman of the old school, aren't ya' Fredrick?

FRED (*vaguely*). What?

REX. Oh . . . you know, like Pliny,[1] when he heard Nero was sending soldiers to rub 'im out, he sat in his pool and opened all his veins and slowly let all the blood run out while he made jokes with his servants and wrote funny notes to his friends.

FRED. Oh God . . . Don't . . . please. . . .

REX. Gee, you're really in bad shape, aren't ya' Fredrick?

FRED. I'm so . . . fragile . . . any little thing lately . . . it's like somebody throwing darts.

REX (*tasting power*). Huh . . . imagine that . . . a guy like me with acne and all able to bugger somebody like you.

FRED. It's like a nightmare . . . nothing seems real. . . .

REX (*shakes his head—smiles a little*). Ah, you can say what you want about the bright lights; it's probably a big thrill and all that, but boy, ya' really pay the price.

FRED (*shaking his head sadly*). It's not what you think.

REX. No sir, me for the simple life. No sour grapes, ya' understand, I never even tried to make it in the big-time. (*Shrugs*) Probably couldn't've. I dunno. . . .

FRED. If you don't mind, talk about something else.

REX. Oh sure, nothin' personal. (FRED *slumps.* REX *moves away and moves about, agitated, as if not knowing what to do next. He seems to be controlling a certain excitement as he moves closer to* FRED *again.*) Sure, it all sounds good from the outside—people askin' ya' for your autograph wherever ya' go; loose women beggin' ya' to fool around with 'em; posin' for photographers when ya' get off the airplane. But I suppose ya' get so much of that sort of thing, that after a while it wears sort of thin—ya' gotta find some other way to get your kicks. Maybe you try your vice-versa, as the saying goes. You know, (*affecting an effeminate lisp*) "Path the Theven-up, Brucie." Or a . . . "tea parties"? (*Lifts his eyebrows insinuatingly*) Or maybe just popping out of cakes dressed like a go-go girl.

[1] **Pliny**: Pliny the Elder and Pliny the Younger were men of letters and Roman public servants. However, it was Seneca, a Roman Stoic, writer, and lawyer, who committed suicide on Nero's orders and dictated a dissertation in his final moments.

FRED (*painfully*). Goddamn it!

REX (*momentarily frightened he moves quickly out of reach but realizes immediately that* FRED *is not about to retaliate. Changing his tone*). Gee, I didn't mean you in particular, Fredrick. I mean, that's just the general pattern, isn't it? That's what ya' read in the magazines.

FRED. Go away, would ya'?

REX (*hesitates*). Sure. (*He goes through the motions of gathering his things, watching* FRED.)

FRED. No . . . don't go . . . stay here. . . .

REX (*shrugs*). All right. (*Puts his things down and comes back towards* FRED. *He regards him silently for a moment.*) How'd ya' get into this business anyhow, Fredrick?

FRED. Well . . . (*Sighs*) I was just a young guy, fresh out of the service going to trade school on the G.I. Bill. (*Longingly*) I wanted to learn to be a TV repairman. . . . (REX *bursts out laughing hilariously.*) What's so funny?

REX. Oh Christ . . . there's your irony . . . you a TV repairman. . . !

FRED (*frowns*). What?

REX. From repairman to Captain Fantastic . . . at least you ended up in the same business. . . .

FRED (*smiling slightly*). Yeah, I just got promoted.

REX. An American success story! (*He continues laughing uproariously.*)

FRED (*still smiling*). Yeah, I never thought of it that way before.

REX (*gradually subsiding and wiping the tears from his eyes*). Jeez, I'm sorry . . . it just struck me as funny.

FRED. Yeah, I guess it's pretty funny.

REX. Please, go ahead.

FRED. I was working part-time as a car hop in a drive-in restaurant. We used to get quite a few of the movie crowd come in just to grab a quick bite. After they come in for a while you sort of get to know each other; you know, "How are ya'?" "How's it goin'?"

REX. "What'll ya' have to eat?" "What looks good today?"

FRED. Sure, like that.

REX. I know how those things go.

FRED. Well, I'm getting particularly friendly with one of

these guys—name of Sidney Adler. He took a liking to me, I guess he felt sorry for me because he knew I was busting my ass trying to go to school and working. So right out of a clear blue sky he asks me if I want to play a small part in one of these movies he's producing. That's what he did, produced those low-budget Bible spectaculars. It paid $500, which was more than I made in a couple months. I never acted or anything like that before but this didn't take any talent—all they needed was some big strong guy to wrestle with this lion and I was just as good as anybody else. . . .

REX (*frowns*). Hey, what was the name of that picture?

FRED. "The Children of Sodom and Gomorrah."

REX. "The Children of Sodom and Gomorrah"! Hey, I saw that!

FRED. Yeah?

REX. Hey, was that *you* fighting that goddamn lion?

FRED. Yeah, that was me.

REX. Hey, that was *good!*

FRED. Well, it wasn't as dangerous as it looked. Actually, it wasn't dangerous at all. I mean, the lion was so old he could hardly walk.

REX. But still—a lion and all.

FRED. He didn't even have any teeth and his claws were filed.

REX. Boy, you sure took that old lion apart.

FRED. Yeah, well . . . So, that was the start of it.

REX. Gee, I didn't know that was you.

FRED. I must have done all right, I guess, because Sidney gave me parts all the time after that. You know, just the kind of parts that called for a big strong guy that looked good in a loin cloth.

REX. God, what a small world.

FRED. So, when he started to produce this Captain Fantastic series, I just walked right into it.

REX. It's just a matter of being at the right place at the right time.

FRED. Poor old Sidney—he had a heart as big as the whole outdoors. He never wanted anything except to help people out. (*Pause*) He was the only real friend I ever had and two years ago he dropped dead.

REX. We need more men like that.

FRED. Ahhh . . . (*Gets up, moves restlessly about.*) So where do I go from here?

REX (*shaking his head*). Pretty grim, all right. (*Pause*) If ya' don't mind a guy like me makin' a suggestion, I think I've figured out just what your problem is. (FRED *doesn't reply, so he continues.*) The problem with you is that you can't accept yourself for what you are.

FRED. What am I? Nothin'.

REX (*encouraging*). That's the idea. Get a clear picture of just what you are. Not what you were yesterday or what you're gonna be tomorrow, but what you are right this very instant.

FRED. That's me O.K., I can never really enjoy what I'm doing because all I can think about is how great things were in the good old days, or how much better they're going to be in the future. (*Snorts*) Some future!

REX. But see, that's just it—we're changing all the time. You're not the same as you were five years ago or even yesterday, and you're gonna change a lot more as time goes on. So what ya' gotta do if ya' want to be well-adjusted is, as you change, the image you got of yourself gotta change right along with it.

FRED (*listlessly*). I guess so.

REX. There ya' are—that's the secret to the whole thing. Look at me: perfectly well-adjusted, and why? Because I got no delusions of grandeur. I know that I'm a skinny, ugly, pimply little weasel with a terrible personality, but I accept it and so I'm happy.

FRED. Yeah, but you've *always* been that way. Me, I've been up there—I know what it tastes like. I can't forget that.

REX (*close now—masking contempt*). Man, you better *learn* to forget it, because you only got one other alternative. (*Indicates over the side of the building, then backs away apologetically.*) If ya' don't mind me sayin' so, that is.

FRED (*sinking in*). Yeah . . . (*He rises and moves about aimlessly, becoming discouraged.*) Ahhh . . . where do ya' start this late in the game?

REX. Well, in the first place, take a good look at yourself. I mean physically. Like you said, the spare tire around the middle, the old jaw line begins to sag. . . .

FRED. I'm over the hill.

REX. Well, let's face it, you're a little too bulgy for this kind of get-up. (*Referring to costume.*)

FRED. God, it used to be all solid muscle. And I never even worked to get it—I was just born that way.

REX. Yeah, that's the trouble with you muscular types—you all have tendencies toward the endomorphic when you get a little older.

FRED. The what?

REX. Endomorphic, endomorphic. You know, the pear-shaped type—all stomach. Blobby.

FRED (*discouraged*). Yeah.

REX. So don't let it get you down. I mean that's what we're talkin' about: your changing image. All your life you been the mesomorphic type—muscular, well-built, athletic. Well, now you're slowin' down, the muscle turns to flab—you become an endomorph.

FRED. Yeah, I guess so. (*Sighs.*)

REX. So don't fight it—accept it. Grow endomorphic gracefully. It has its advantages.

FRED. Like what?

REX. Well . . . people don't push ya' around so much. Now with your mesomorph, a lot of people are envious. But nobody resents an endomorph. They're known for their ability to get along with people.

FRED (*reluctantly*). Sounds like something out of a guide for buying dogs.

REX. Now me, I'm your ectomorph. Wiry. Quick reflexes. Sinewy. Clever. Tidy. Intelligent. Durable. Seldom prone to heart attacks. Of course, there are advantages and disadvantages to each type.

FRED. Yeah, I can see where there would be.

REX. But the idea is to live with what you've got.

FRED (*sighs*). Well, if nature intended me to be a . . . what?

REX. Endomorph.

FRED. If nature intended me to be an endomorph, I guess I'm stuck with it.

REX. Hey, that's the idea, Fredrick!

FRED. Except after I've accepted, what do I do with it? I mean, where do I go from here? I can't see where there'd be much call for fat ex-actors, 43 years old, who don't know how to do anything except flex their . . . flab.

REX. Well, what about character parts? I mean like Orson Welles, Burl Ives, that sort of thing?

FRED (*resenting this categorization, but trying to suppress it*). Naw. (*Paces, agitated*) Besides, like I already explained, I'm washed up in that field since my little . . . performance at that party. When they see me on the street, they all point their fingers and laugh.

REX. Oh yeah, that's right. (*Smiles slightly.*) Yeah, this is gonna call for some thought.

FRED. I've tried everything I can think of but I can't come up with anything. There isn't anybody in the industry who'd take a chance on me now.

REX. Well, maybe you should forget show biz—get into something else.

FRED. What else can I do? I've never had any training in anything else except in that TV repair course, and I quit that before I finished.

REX. Hmmm. (*Pauses, thinking*) Have ya' ever thought of goin' into somethin' like youth work?

FRED. Naw, what do I know about any youth work?

REX. Sure, you're a natural. With your background ya' can't miss.

FRED. I don't know anything about it.

REX. What's to know? You're their hero—all they want to do is hang around ya'. When they ask ya' questions you give 'em advice.

FRED. Oh, I'm a great one to be giving advice, all right. Look at me—ready to jump off a roof because I'm nothing but an old whore.

REX. There's nothing to it. There are standard answers for every question. All you need to know is what they are. It's practically a matter of yes and no.

FRED. Ah, I wouldn't know what to say.

REX. Believe me, there's nothin' to it. Look . . . some eight-year-old kid comes up to ya' with a problem: uh . . . he's got a little brother and he hates his little brother and wants to kill him because his little brother keeps stealing his marbles. So, you tell him, don't kill your little brother . . . it's against the law and they'll send you to the electric chair. He only steals your marbles because he likes you. *Give* him your marbles, then he won't want them anymore.

FRED. Yeah, that makes sense.

REX. Or, a 13-year-old girl wants to know should she "go all the way" with her boyfriend. He says if she really loves him she'll prove it. What should she do? The answer is, don't give in to temptation—keep yourself pure until you are married. Any boy who makes you prove your love in this way is not worth having anyway.

FRED. Kids that age shouldn't be thinking about such things.

REX. That's the idea, Fredrick—you're gonna do just fine. (FRED *smiles a little, becoming interested.*) O.K., here's another—see if you can answer this one. A kid about ten years old, every week he's been taking the money his folks give him for the collection plate at Sunday school and using it to buy cigarettes. Recently he has developed a hacking cough and is worried that God is punishing him for his dishonesty by giving him a case of TB. This has led him to see the light and he is now truly sorry for what he has done. What can he do to make things right? Answer that one.

FRED (*feeling his way*). Well . . . in the first place . . . pray to God for forgiveness—He is very understanding about things like this. Secondly . . . quit smoking . . . it is a dangerous habit and can result in lung cancer, tuberculosis, pleurisy, heart trouble . . . uh . . . makes you short of breath, stunts your growth, leads to other vices, makes you smell bad, burns holes in your clothes, is expensive, stains your fingers, makes people regard you as a shady character, and can generally kill you. . . .

REX. Good, good!

FRED (*encouraged*). Confess what you have done to your parents. Offer to repay what you have wrongfully taken, out of your allowance. Chances are they will be so impressed by your honesty that they will increase your allowance and forget all about any repayment.

REX. The old reverse psychology!

FRED. And last—if cough persists, see your doctor.

REX. What did I tell ya'—a regular Ann Landers![2]

FRED. Was I any good?

REX. Good? Christ, you were great! They'll love ya'.

[2] **Ann Landers:** American writer whose popular newspaper column provides advice to the troubled.

FRED (*a little astounded*). Huh!

REX. I'm tellin' ya', ain't I? Ya' can't miss.

FRED. God, I'd really like that, working with kids.

REX. If I ever saw a natural, you're a natural.

FRED. I wonder. . . .

REX. You're a cinch.

FRED. Wouldn't that be something?

REX. Every cloud has a silver lining.

FRED. I might find a whole new way of life.

REX. Sure, this is what you should'a been doing all along.

FRED (*quiet resolve*). By God, I'm going to try it!

REX. That's the ticket.

FRED (*truly grateful—a little amazed*). If it wasn't for you I'd be lying down there right now, splattered all over the sidewalk.

REX. Naw, forget it.

FRED. No. You saved my life and I'll never forget it.

REX (*shrugs modestly*). Aw. . . .

FRED. Yes you did, and I'll find some way to repay you if it's the last thing I do.

REX (*moving thoughtfully about the roof*). Y'know Fred, I'm just thinkin' . . . maybe this is the kind of deal where we could work together . . . help each other out.

FRED. How do ya' mean?

REX. Well I'm thinkin', with the background the two of us could bring to a deal like this, we'd be a pretty unbeatable combination.

FRED. You think so?

REX. Individually, we're not so much: you don't have my know-how and I don't have your . . . star appeal. But between the two of us we got just about everything you need to really make it big in this field.

FRED. Yeah, I really don't know the ropes.

REX. I mean, this could really be something fantastic. With a drawing card like you, we could probably get to every kid in town . . . in the country!

FRED. Don't forget, the serial was broadcast in 57 foreign countries.

REX. In the world! Hey, how about this for a name: Fantastic Kids, Incorporated!

FRED. Hey, that's good!

REX. Good? It's terrific! "Be a Fantastic Kid." That's an enrollment gimmick.

FRED. But what're we gonna do?

REX. First we draw up a plan, see? Then we show it around to people and sell stock in it and ask people to make contributions—tax deductible. Then we set up a couple chapters see . . . plan out youth programs: ball games, dances, picnics, hikes, boxing matches, music lessons, arts and crafts, swimming, poetry reading, public hygiene classes, movies. We train other instructors, we get some publicity, more contributions come in, we expand. Pretty soon we got offices all over the country, then all over the world!

FRED. Us?

REX. Sure us—who do ya' think?

FRED. Well . . . it sounds so . . . huge. I sort of had in mind just somethin' like workin' for the park department, or the police athletic league, or somethin'.

REX. Naw, why hide our light under a bushel basket? Get out of the habit of thinking in such small terms. If you're gonna be big, ya' gotta think big!

FRED (*really smiles for the first time*). Hey, you've got quite a mind for this sort of thing.

REX. Oh well. . . . (*Shrugs modestly.*)

FRED. C'mon, don't be so modest. (*Pokes him playfully on the shoulder.*) You old . . . endomorph, you.

REX (*suddenly cold, he moves away. When he speaks it is with a controlled voice*). I am not an endomorph. I am an ectomorph. The endomorph is characteristically fat, sloppy, and slow. I am lean, neat, and quick.

FRED. All right, all right, so you're an ectomorph.

REX. If there's anybody with endomorphic tendencies around here, it's you!

FRED. What are ya' gettin' so upset about? I didn't mean anything.

REX. I am *not* upset. I just think it's important that we keep our identities straight, that's all.

FRED. All right, you're an ectomorph. I'm the endomorph.

REX (*sighs impatiently*). You are *not* an endomorph. You are a mesomorph with endomorphic tendencies.

FRED. All right, I'm an ectomorph . . . I mean an endomorph with ectomorphic tendencies.

REX. You are a *mesomorph* with *endomorphic* tendencies!

FRED (*rattled*). All right, for Chris'sakes! I'm a . . . (*confused*) I don't know what I am!

REX. Well, figure it out.

FRED. Yeah, well . . . (*Stops—then slowly*) I'm a mesomorph with endomorphic tendencies. (*Pause*) Does that meet with your approval?

REX. And don't talk to me in that patronizing tone of voice.

FRED. What the hell do you want?

REX. I want a little ordinary respect. Don't you talk down to me just because you used to be on some two-bit TV serial. That doesn't cut any ice with me.

FRED. I am not talking down to you.

REX. What's worse, you don't even know you're doing it. And while we're at it, let's get a couple of other things straight.

FRED. Like what?

REX. Like your cute little Hollywood tricks. Any of that stuff and you're finished.

FRED. *What* cute little Hollywood tricks?

REX. You know goddamn well *what* cute little Hollywood tricks. Like renting yourself out for parties and jumping out of cakes dressed like a go-go girl.

FRED (*hit hard*). I . . . how can you. . . .

REX. And like getting up on a pedestal and doing a couple numbers for the enlightenment and edification of the other guests at the party.

FRED (*reeling*). You . . . son of a bitch . . . !

REX. Oh come on now, Freddy, you're not going to tell me that was all a big story, are you?

FRED. I told you how that happened.

REX. Yeah, you told me how it happened. I just want to make sure it doesn't happen again, is all.

FRED. Are you gonna hold that over my head?

REX. I'm not holding anything over your head. But like I said before, we've got to be realistic, and realistically speaking, it appears that you've got a weakness for a certain kind of unsavory behavior.

FRED (*sinking*). Please . . . don't say that. . . .

REX. I mean, we've all got our faults, haven't we? But how's it gonna look is what I'm saying, if word leaks out about some of these indiscretions of yours?

FRED. But there's nothing wrong with me. It's just that I'm all screwed up.

REX. Now that's a bit of a contradiction right there, isn't it? How's it gonna look if it gets out that a fellow with your past is working with kids. Supposing somebody like *Confidential* magazine gets hold of something like that? There goes your Fantastic Kids, Incorporated, shot right in the ass.

FRED. But it's got nothing to do with it!

REX. Oh now, I don't know about that. I mean, we've got to think this out, haven't we?

FRED. Think *what* out?

REX. Well, whether or not you're going to be able to resist all that temptation.

FRED. All *what* temptation?

REX. Oh come off it, Fred—the temptation of being around all those impressionable young kids all day long.

FRED. Just what do you think I'm gonna do?

REX. That's just what we're tryin' to find out. I mean after we get this thing all set up with all these people investing and believing in it, I'll be damned if we're gonna blow it all because you get caught molesting some kid.

FRED (*enraged*). I'll kill you!

REX (*moving cautiously away*). I'm just being realistic, is all . . . I'm not condemning you for it.

FRED. Shut your goddamn mouth! (*Slowly begins stalking* REX *who manages to stay just out of reach.*)

REX. Come on Fred, you want to know the truth, don't ya'?

FRED. You lousy. . . .

REX. It's better to face it now before ya' get into any more trouble.

FRED. Shut up! Shut up!

REX. It's there, Fred . . . this funny degenerate streak in ya' . . .

FRED *lunges at* REX, *knocks him down, and begins strangling him.* REX *fights and protests fiercely, but he is no match for* FRED*'s great strength. He starts to weaken and could be finished now in a matter of seconds. But suddenly,* FRED *stops and sits back, sobbing and exhausted.* REX *gasps for breath.*

FRED (*holding his hands out—looking at them*). What am I? What am I? What the hell kind of an animal am I?

FRED *breaks down completely, sobbing.* REX *rises to a sitting position, catching his breath and looking at* FRED *—a strange look of satisfaction on his face.*

REX. You pervert . . . you stinking pervert . . . Some rapo-strangler like ya' read about in the paper, that's all that's left for you.

FRED. Where did I get so screwed up? . . .

REX. There's nothin' left for you . . . except to kill . . . and to corrupt!

FRED (*gets to his feet, staggers to the ledge*). What the hell's the use? . . . What the hell's the use?

REX (*sees what* FRED *is doing—becomes alarmed*). Hey. what're ya' doing? Hey, don't do that—stay here with me (FRED *mounts the ledge.*) . . . It's better than nothin'.

FRED (*wearily*). Like hell it is. (*As he stands on the ledge,* REX *goes quickly to his camera and focuses it on* FRED. *Spreading his arms,* FRED *shouts into the night—the dying animal*) Ahhhhhhh!

FRED *leaps over the side of the building head-first. A flashbulb goes off as* REX *takes a picture of* FRED *in full flight. There is the sound of* FRED *screaming as he falls, a dull thud, then silence.*

REX (*amazed—dumbly*). Jesus, the silly bastard did it. (*Becoming frightened, he moves about anxiously.*) Jesus, Jesus, Jesus, Jesus, Jesus . . . He did it . . . There was no talkin' him out of it . . . (*He notices the clothing* FRED *has left in a pile and goes over to it. Cautiously, he picks up* FRED'*s hat and puts it on. It is too big for him, but he leaves it on anyway. He finds* FRED'*s glasses and puts them on. He stands and seems exultant, as if with some new power.*) Jesus!

A siren sounds in the distance. REX *quickly gathers his belongings and exits through the hatch. The set is empty for a moment, then the curtain falls.*

INTERPRETATION

1. Although apparently casual and colloquial, *Captain Fantastic Meets the Ectomorph* contains very carefully written dialogue. Of special importance in the composition of this play is the use of clichés of many kinds. How do these clichés reflect the quality of mind of the characters? What do they tell us about the characters' backgrounds and aspirations? What do they tell us about the society in which the characters live?

2. The play is set on a rooftop in Los Angeles. What kind of atmosphere does this setting provide? Why is it an appropriate place for the happenings of the play? How might a theater audience react when Fredrick removes his clothes and reveals his Captain Fantastic costume? In what way is this costume both realistic and farcical?

3. Unlike most, but not all, comedies, this play does not have a happy ending. The proposed partnership of Fredrick and Rex in the creation of Fantastic Kids, Inc., points the way to a reconciliation of their differences with society, but this partnership soon becomes unworkable. What are the obstacles to reconciliation? Is society at fault or are Rex and Fredrick? Can you imagine a play in which Rex and Fredrick find a way to belong to society? Is the ending of the play the right one?

4. Show how elements of absurdity and pathos are blended in the character of Fredrick Regent: Why is he laughable? Why is he pitiable? Does the playwright keep these qualities in balance? What are Rex Crain's main drives and goals? What does he seek in life? Contrast the physical rhythms of the two characters. How do they stand, walk, talk? Can you think of any two-man comedy teams who might physically resemble Rex and Fredrick?

5. As a comedy, this play directs our attention to the amusing obsessions and pretensions of the characters, but it does not show us a way in which those anti-social "humors" can be reconciled to society. What values in our society are implicitly criticized in the play? What positive values are shown or implied?

Elements of Drama

The questions following each play examine five elements of drama: *plot, character, theme, language,* and *spectacle.* It is well to remember that such critical categories, while tidy and convenient, are essentially artificial, since these aspects of a play are really as interdependent as the root, branch, leaf, and blossom of a tree. And as trees are dependent on sunlight, water, temperature, and adjacent forms of life, so whether a play will wither or flourish depends on how hospitable an environment is provided by audience or reader—that is, how open, understanding, and responsive they are. As reader, you are an integral part of the ecology of comedy.

Plot·The basis of plot is *conflict.* Someone (usually called the *protagonist,* or hero) wants something, but someone or something else stands in his (or her) way. This obstacle to the protagonist's desires may be another person (sometimes called the *antagonist*), a set of circumstances, the protagonist's own shortcomings or confusions, or a combination of these. The basic conflict of a play can be identified by filling in the blanks in the following formula sentence: ________ wants to ________, but ________. The way in which this basic conflict is set forth, developed (often in various sub-conflicts), and resolved is the plot. The audience's interest is held as it awaits the answer to the questions asked by the conflict. In comedy, the resolution usually brings together all of the characters in a play in a newer, freer association in which illusions are exchanged for realities and anti-social forces are converted or expelled.

Character· A play shows human beings in action; the playwright's selection of the number and kinds of human beings and the way in which he portrays them come under the heading of character. The essence of characterization in comedy is the development of carefully observed human *types.* The playwright makes each of his characters distinct and vivid by investing them with what one critic has called "a permanent potential of human nature." The playwright selects those aspects of human nature which he feels are true, lively, and of interest to an audience and excludes what is irrelevant and incidental. Unlike the novelist, the playwright does not accumulate a wealth of character detail. He cannot, because theater must be immediate; there is no time for the lengthy descriptions which are possible in a novel. The good playwright seizes upon some luminous central truth about the character he is creating and develops the character from that truth. The less skillful playwright, on the other hand, is likely to make use of stereotypes, that is, characters who are drawn, not from life, but from literature or the theater. The central problem in characterization is the creation of living types based in human reality.

Theme · Because a playwright must select only a few aspects of human experience and because he constantly makes *choices* about what to put in his play and what to leave out, he can never claim to be totally objective about the meaning of life. Every play in some way takes a stand on the basic questions of existence. The way in which these questions are asked and/or answered constitutes a play's theme.

Because a play is a work of art, however, there is not always a fixed and certain answer to the question: What is the theme? The playwright sends his play into the world as a parent sends his child—he knows what he is but not what he may become. Your perception of a play's theme depends upon your interpretation of the experience of the play in terms of your own experience. In order to make such interpretations valid, however, you must discover the playwright's wavelength and tune in to his particular view of reality.

Language · Just as the painter's basic material is paint, so the playwright's basic material is language. The interesting thing about plays, however, is that, except in stage directions (which the audience doesn't hear), the author never speaks in his own voice. Only the people in the play speak and they speak not as writers telling a story to an audience but as they are compelled to by their needs and circumstances. Of course the playwright has great freedom in choosing the style of his characters' language and these choices help to create the tone and texture of the play. But the good playwright never sacrifices the credibility of a character through the use of language which is not motivated by the character's personality or situation. On the other hand, it is clear that there is no such thing as completely realistic dialogue. If you have ever tried to write a realistic play, you have probably discovered that trying to write exactly the way people talk poses as many challenges, although of a different kind, as the composition of a Shakespearean sonnet.

Spectacle · The spoken text of a play is only one of the means by which a story is told in the theater. The contributions of actors, directors, and designers is an essential one and, in writing a play, the playwright anticipates these contributions. Each of the five comedies in this book has another dimension which can only be implied and suggested on the printed page—the dimension of spectacle. Spectacle is not simply the application of theatrical cosmetics to the text of a play. It is, rather, the final realization of the playwright's intentions. The selection of a costume, the casting of a particular actor, the placement of a door or a table on the stage, even the style of a poster advertising the performance—all these elements of spectacle serve to fulfill the blueprint laid out in the text. It is important, then, to be alert, when reading these comedies, to those details of spectacle which help to fully realize a character or a situation. While dogged attempts to imagine every detail of staging can make play-reading a frustrating experience (especially if you are not trained in the theater) the reader can enhance his enjoyment of a play by answering for himself some general questions, such as: How many people are in the scene? What do they do when they are not talking? What are they wearing? What kind of surroundings are they in? What kinds of colors, shapes, and textures do you think would fulfill the spirit of the play?

ABCDEFGHIJ-CO-7987654321